COLUMBIA LEGAL STUDIES

EDITED UNDER THE AUSPICES OF THE

FACULTY OF LAW OF COLUMBIA UNIVERSITY

EDWIN W. PATTERSON, *Editor*

II

LEGAL ASPECTS OF COMMERCIAL LETTERS OF CREDIT

LEGAL ASPECTS
OF
COMMERCIAL LETTERS OF CREDIT

BY

HERMAN N. FINKELSTEIN, J. D.

MEMBER OF THE NEW YORK BAR

WITH AN INTRODUCTION BY

KARL N. LLEWELLYN

PROFESSOR OF LAW IN COLUMBIA UNIVERSITY

New York

COLUMBIA UNIVERSITY PRESS

1930

Published March, 1930

Printed in the United States of America
By Ad Press, Ltd., New York, N. Y.

TO THE MEMORY

OF

MY MOTHER

PREFACE

The letter of credit has been in use for centuries. Its present form, however, was not evolved until the expansion of commerce during the nineteenth century made necessary a more highly specialized instrument. Most of the decisions which have fixed its legal status were rendered within the last two decades. During this period the commercial letter of credit has assumed such importance that a study of its legal aspects needs no further justification.

Justice Holmes has pointed out that writers of the common law are apt to ignore jurisdictional limitations and to criticise all cases "as right or wrong according to the writer's notion of a single theory." The temptation thus to err is, of course, ever present in a study of this kind, where cases from nearly all of the common law jurisdictions have been assembled and discussed. In dealing with commercial law, however, the gravity of the offense is perhaps not so great. Essentially, the law merchant is a reflection and crystallization of the customs of tradesmen and must continuously readapt itself to their practices. Commerce knows no jurisdictional limitations and ebbs and flows without regard to the theories of the makers or expounders of the law. Hence, instruments used in interstate or international commerce in various jurisdictions must, to a large extent, be similar and should ideally be subject to similar rules of law, save where purely local customs require different results. Indeed, a diversity of legal rules with regard to instruments in common use would be highly artificial and would lead to endless inconvenience. The jurisdictional boundaries of a treatise on a commercial instrument are identical with the limits of its actual use.

Throughout this work I have viewed the commercial letter of credit in the light of its actual operation. Only with regard to virtual and extrinsic acceptances has the historical treatment seemed essential to an understanding of the problems involved. In fact, the courts themselves have been unusually successful in their efforts to make the law governing the letter of credit reflect commercial customs. While technical and theoretical difficulties still persist, partisans of the common law can find satisfaction in recognizing the readiness and facility with which the law in this field has taken cognizance of these factors.

I have endeavored also to resist the temptation, which was continually present, to follow the trails of the discussion into cognate fields. The task of defining the limits of a study such as this has not been without its difficulties. The importance, however, of presenting the subject as concisely as possible has been apparent, and accordingly several types of problems arising in connection with the use of commercial credits are mentioned only to be dismissed. Since the law on these subjects is not peculiar to letters of credit, adequate consideration would have taken us too far afield.

For the practitioner's benefit, all pertinent cases of every common law jurisdiction available to date have been cited. It was with some hesitation that I have ventured to prognosticate the future development in divers phases of the law governing commercial letters of credit. The genius of Justice Story, whose sensitiveness to changing commercial customs enabled him, against the opinion of the best authorities of the English bar of his day, to foretell a reversal by the English courts of their rules governing commercial credits, is not readily duplicated. Yet I have felt it part of my task, in so new a branch of the law, to attempt to prophesy the course of future decisions as well as to describe the results of the decisions already made. On occasion, I have even dared to argue for a change in the rules laid down in some of the cases.

This work could not have appeared in its present form without the generous assistance that has come to me from my contacts in the School of Law of Columbia University and from a number of associates and friends. Professor Karl N. Llewellyn, who has read the manuscript several times, was from the outset a most encouraging and friendly critic, giving me freely the benefit of his far-reaching knowledge of the subject of commercial credits. Professor Edwin W. Patterson, the editor of this series, Columbia Legal Studies, has contributed many useful and important suggestions both as to the form and as to the substance of this work. He has spared himself neither time nor effort in aiding me to see this volume through the press. The manuscript has been read, in part, by Professor Hessel E. Yntema of the John Hopkins Institute for the Study of Law, and to him I owe a number of important recommendations. Professor Underhill Moore, formerly of the School of Law of Columbia University, first suggested the possibilities of this subject, and was of great assistance in outlining the field and suggesting points of departure. To Mr. Louis S. Posner of the New York Bar, I am indebted for many helpful comments and for the immeasurable benefits which I have derived from his matured experience.

On the business aspects of the problems here discussed, the suggestions of Dr. H. Parker Willis, Professor of Banking in Columbia University, and of Mr. Wilbert Ward, of the National City Bank of New York, have been invaluable. I am indebted to Mr. Ward and to his publisher, the Ronald Press, for permission to reprint material contained in Mr. Ward's volume on American

Commercial Credits; and to the Yale University Press for permission to reprint from Dean Pound's "An Introduction to the Philosophy of Law." Professor William O. Douglass of the Yale School of Law has read the chapter on damages and has made a number of valuable comments. My thanks are also due to Mr. Thomas Epstein, of the New York Bar, for his careful study of the manuscript and for the many suggestions which he has made. The American Acceptance Council and others have kindly granted permission to reprint forms and to quote from various publications. Finally, the assistance of my wife in the dreary task of proof reading and her patience and encouragement throughout the long period that has elapsed during the preparation of this volume have been invaluable.

HERMAN N. FINKELSTEIN

New York,
January 1, 1930.

CONTENTS

Chapter IV

LEGAL RELATIONS BETWEEN RESPECTIVE PARTIES TO COMMERCIAL LETTER OF CREDIT TRANSACTIONS

Chapter V

CONDITIONS IN THE LETTER OF CREDIT

Chapter VI

THE RELATION BETWEEN THE LETTER OF CREDIT AND THE SALES CONTRACT

Chapter VII

THE MEASURE OF DAMAGES

Chapter VIII

THE LEGAL THEORY

Appendix A

MODERN FORMS OF COMMERCIAL LETTERS OF CREDIT

I. Issuing Bank Forms

II. Correspondent Bank Forms

III. Buyer's Forms

IV. Provisions for Interpretation of Credits

Appendix B

INTRODUCTION

We have been in need of Dr. Finkelstein's book. How much one does not fully comprehend until one has been through it. Here is the legal material, full, accurate, accessible. Here is a stimulus in checking and deepening one's own knowledge and experience by resort to his, which one hopes for in legal literature and seldom finds. I do not agree with every one of his conclusions; I do not share the faith he sometimes seems to have in the discoverability of the true principle. But I have learned more from his than from any other study in the field, and in attempting an introduction I shall not undertake to add to his presentation of the law. It will be less embarrassing to open a non-competitive line of discussion; it ought also to be more useful. Nor does it seem necessary to attempt any introduction for those who are already concerned with the law of foreign trade; they have only to pick the book up to see its value. But it may be worth while to sketch something of the business and economic background of the institution Dr. Finkelstein has chosen for his study. Its bearings are many; indeed many more than are currently suspected. Its importance is already great, and grows daily greater. Its huge and still unexploited latent possibilities offer a new world to the explorer.

Certainly no modern development in commercial law is more striking than that of the letter of credit. True, it is hardly accurate to call the commercial letter of credit (or, as the student of finance views it, the "banker's credit") modern. One finds traces of it in the books through at least a hundred years. On the other hand, its real importance in law (as contrasted with its importance merely as a commercial and financial device) dates from the war. And *a fortiori* its interest to American lawyers. For the commercial credit takes its origin in foreign trade, and the financing of foreign trade by American bankers was hardly a factor of importance before 1914; indeed, only since the Federal Reserve Act have accommodation acceptances become legally available to our bankers.

But the meaning of the commercial credit in the life of the mercantile community and in the world of short-term finance cannot be valued on the basis simply of the cases which in express terms deal with letters of credit. Those cases have indeed been striking. Since 1914, especially since the price decline of 1920, they have ripened like wheat to the harvest, and to a proud harvest. Their results are a signal monument to the adjustability of common law institutions to new demands, to the essential common sense of courts, both in this country and in England. Within that short span of years the courts were confronted over and over again, from ever novel angles, with a device with which even the bankers were still struggling to become familiar. The courts rose to the challenge. They shaped new law with surprising rapidity and consistency. They shaped it with even more surprising sensitivity to the needs of the situation. Not in isolated instances, but repeatedly, they showed a group wisdom often exceeding that of the business community whose institutions they were called on to sanction or reject. The extent to which the emerging problems branched and varied may be followed in Dr. Finkelstein's book. Their novelty is attested first of all by the time which elapsed between Hershey's pioneering article[1] and McCurdy's incisive analysis of the problem of irrevocability;[2] second, by the fact that all three papers of the latter author confined themselves substantially to that single problem; third, by the fact that bankers and courts alike in the early litigation of 1920 and 1921 had no thought for any problem but that of establishing the absolute independence of the banker's contract from that between buyer and seller. The extent to which commercial and financial practice was still groping in the matter comes out in the results of Dr. Edward's inquiries among bankers[3] and in Ward's masterly discussion of the movement toward unified practice and its background.[4] And yet none of these writers, nor even Furniss,[5] in his brilliant exposition of the functions of the letter of credit, seems to me to have set forth the bearing of that institution in its full perspective. And indeed, this was inevitable. It takes the accumulated thought of the successive writers, it takes the accumulated experience which the hitherto unceasing procession of cases has revealed, to suggest even the outline of that perspective. Our understanding of the whole is yet far ahead. But already we can begin to see that we are dealing with one of the most significant phenomena of modern commerce.

The Place of the Letter of Credit in the Relations Between Buyer and Seller

During the sweeping movement from the cash-and-carry market of the horse trade, of Cheapside or the early Bowery, to the nation-wide and international market of modern trade, our institutions developed with singular consistency in one direction: that of shifting an increasing number of burdens off the buyer's

[1] Cited *infra* p. 212.
[2] Cited *infra* p. 280.
[3] Cited *infra* pp. 4, 153.
[4] Cited *infra* p. 4.
[5] Cited *infra* p. 4.

shoulders and on to the seller's. Factual burdens and legal burdens moved together. *Caveat emptor* as a formula is with us still, but with us as a hollow echo of another age.[6] What follows suggests that there is in many places room still for the policy that echo calls to mind. But room not in general, only in particular; it is a problem of correcting, here and there, the exaggerations which always occur when an outworn policy goes down before its opposite.

The shift grew, of necessity, from dealings that extended over space and time. Once the seller undertook to ship to a distant market, he found on his shoulders first of all the risk of unknown glut at destination, and consequent price decline. He carried the risks of factorage, including the possible insolvency or bad faith of his factor; including, too, the trend of the law under factors' acts, under the modern law of negotiable bills of lading and warehouse receipts, under section 20 (4) of the Sales Act, all driving in the direction of increasing these, the seller's risks. Meanwhile, the practice of manufacturing for an expected market left with the seller all the risks of failure to find a buyer, all those of the turn of the business cycle. The development of credit terms, long or short, and especially the use of credit extension as a tool of competition, threw on the seller the credit strain during the period of resale by his buyer; the risk of the buyer's bad faith in contesting bills, or in making away with the goods without payment; the risk of the buyer's honest or even fraudulent insolvency.

More recently various devices have been developed either to shift these risks or to reduce them. The practice of manufacturing only against existing contracts is one obvious example. Nation-wide development of credit information as evidenced by Dun's and Bradstreet's services; the growth, in the larger concerns, of credit departments which can put some check upon the enthusiasm of salesmen; indeed, in more modern times, the practice of local or trade credit exchanges, are further instances. The law, in part, has followed suit; *vide* the bulk sales acts; even more that part of the law which offers men freedom to shape their bargains as they will. But the sweep of the credit market has carried with it the extension of the seller's obligations as to quality from the rule of *Chandelor v. Lopus*[7] and *Parkinson* v. *Lee*[8] to the comprehensive obligations imposed by the Sales Act.

In part this has been met by the introduction of form contracts, with limited warranties, and by vigorous attempts to limit the salesmen's powers to give warranties which go beyond the form. The practice of buying on specification shows definite

---

[6] Despite Heilbut, Symons & Company v. Buckleton, [1913] A. C. 30; or Cudahy Packing Co. v. Narzisenfeld, 3 F. (2d) 567 (C. C. A. 2d, 1924).

[7] Cro. Jac. 4 (Ex. Ch. 1603). [8] 2 East 314 (K. B. 1802).

signs under Sales Act, sec. 15 (4) and the corresponding common law rule, of going far to scythe down the seller's lush obligation to provide goods fit for known purposes. Meanwhile, the risk subsequent to delivery, that the buyer will take the goods and fail to pay, has, at least in the case of retailers, been distinctly limited by the widespread Bulk Sales Act. More, it has, in some quarters, been partially eliminated by the introduction of shipment C.O.D. or cash against order bill of lading, permitting inspection on arrival. The additional risk that the buyer, on inspection, will improperly reject, leaving the goods open to his attachment in an action for seller's breach, brought and tried before a local and prejudiced forum, has been met first by the practice of discounting the draft so that the seller's bank becomes the owner both of the goods and proceeds; and further, by insistence on cash against documents before inspection—the situation notably in c.i.f. contracts. But here, as in the early development of the credit market, as in the earlier development of order bills of lading, courts operate under the influence of the older point of view, and often fail to give the seller's protective device the effects which he had hoped: so notably those cases which regard the bank's power to charge the item back as evidencing a mere agency for collection, not as a protective purchase or pledge of the documents. Nor should it be lost sight of that cash against bill of lading (with or without prior inspection) is a type of transaction found chiefly in the case of agricultural produce moving to a central market, and almost not at all in the case of manufactured commodities moving from a central distributing point toward the consumer. Automobiles are an exception notable for its uniqueness. And documentary practices of the c.i.f. sort are still limited largely to overseas trade. So that in our domestic trade, while we find numerous signs of a reaction against that constant expansion of seller's risks and burdens which was the work of the nineteenth century, those signs remain spasmodic and leave sales between dealers, and especially between dealers in manufactured commodities, but little touched.

All these risks and more can, it is true, be met by putting the buyer wholly into the seller's hands, as by demanding cash with order. But the difficulties of this are twofold. In the first place, it amounts not at all to a *reduction* of risks, but only to *shifting* of the entire set from seller to buyer. In the second place, it throws upon the buyer a burden of raising cash which is out of line with our present credit structure (an objection not to be overlooked in judging the prospect for extension of the banker's credit in domestic trade). Cash with order, moreover, produces a situation which affords a banker who might be willing to finance the buyer no guaranties or security whatever, either against the seller's bad faith or against the buyer's insolvency. The commercial letter of credit is not open to the second of these criticisms; it is much less open to the first—compare the (growing?) practice of the seller demanding "a banker's guaranty" that his buyer will perform. The commercial credit, when it takes the form of a promise to accept, offers postponement of payment until the expected period of resale has elapsed; it offers distinctly worth-while security to the banker who does the financing; and at the same time it assures the buyer at least that shipment will be made before his definitive obligation is incurred. Flexible, many-sided, efficient, cheap, it lies between the absurdities of the *caveat emptor* fetish in the modern market and the exaggerations of the fetish-breakers. To the seller it offers protection not otherwise available; but when used with care it offers that protection at no undue burden to the buyer. Its net effect is to reduce risks as well as shift them. And to the public, as appears later, it offers for that reason the benefits of sounder (and therefore cheaper) mercantile credit and—a point often overlooked—insurance against one of the most vicious aspects of hard times under the prevailing system: the roll-up of credit stringency from ultimate buyer back through the whole chain of selling institutions.

The peculiar services of the commercial letter of credit to the seller come out most clearly in the case of foreign trade. There the need was greater; there the device quite naturally took its origin. A discussion of that extreme case may therefore be illuminating. But it must not be forgotten that everything said in such a discussion applies with considerable force to domestic transactions, to any intercity transaction at home. Not, to be sure, with equal force. Yet with force enough. With force enough—as the cases show, and as inquiry among bankers shows more clearly—to bring the letter of credit into use in domestic trade from time to time. This one must welcome; one must hope for its extension. I should be slow to argue that, in the present state of American institutions, the mere cheapening of credit would be a boon. But to make credit first, sounder, and second and only therefore cheaper, is an advantage too obvious to need discussion.

There is yet no adequate machinery of credit information available in the foreign field. This condition is on the wane, but it still holds. The risks, therefore, of dealing with a buyer who is not established, or who is not a known old customer, are peculiarly great. In the first place, he may cancel an order during or immediately after the process of manufacture, or (in the case of a seller who is not a manufacturer) after purchase to fill the order. In the second place, he may reject the goods on arrival, irrespective of whether or not the bill of lading is withheld until inspection, and may then use the seller's necessity as a means of bargaining for a downward adjustment of the price. For it is clear that the seller then is under heavy pressure to get the goods off his hands. He has already incurred shipping expenses; his goods are in a foreign market, to him largely unknown; and his only remedy is in a distant, foreign, and perhaps prejudiced court, and under unfamiliar law, and must be sought through attorneys whom he neither knows nor trusts. Moreover, credit terms in foreign trade are typically long, and the absence of credit information referred to before makes the buyer's acceptance, even when obtained, no safe assurance of ultimate payment. Finally, the period of transit is long, as well as expensive. And those unforeseen changes in the market from which commercial disputes flower, and which are also a potent source both of fraud and of buyer's insolvency, are likely to occur without notice during the period of transit; when found, their fruit is trouble, even where a buyer was originally acting in good faith. Meantime, the seller is waiting for his money. His credit is strained during the process of manufacture, is strained again during the period of shipment, is given the final fillip while waiting for payment of a four month's acceptance.

Other devices there are to meet some of these risks. The telegraph has given stoppage in transit a new importance in overseas trade. The order bill of lading in most countries is effective at least to assure a promise of payment in documentary form before the goods are surrendered; and it offers the seller's bank collateral (at least pending acceptance) with which to reduce, not the *credit* strain upon the seller, but the *cash* needs of current financing. Such a discount also typically overcomes any risk of attachment of the goods in an action by the buyer. But there is here no protection against initial cancellation, no protection against improper repudiation on arrival, and no protection, after the goods have been put into the buyer's hands, against his insolvency. The attempt to withhold control of the goods until the acceptance matures has, in the main, except in England, been found commercially impracticable, since the buyer requires their use and sale in order to meet his payment—quite apart from the competitive difficulty of insisting on this device where it is not usual. (And, it is worth remembering, a buyer's banker may insist on security with impunity, where a seller asking the same thing would give offense.)

In contrast, the letter of credit gives a banker's responsibility both that there will be no repudiation and that the price will be met when due. I speak of the irrevocable type of banker's credit. That type of credit also gives an immediate financing possibility and gives it as early as the period of preliminary manufacture. And it is to be noted that whereas formally the use of that possibility entails credit strain upon the seller, yet in fact that credit strain is immensely reduced; for the chief reliance of any banker who makes advances against pledge of a letter of credit is, and will remain, the responsibility of the bank which stands behind the letter. It is not only from that bank that payment is expected in the first instance—as is true of any buyer's acceptance discounted for a seller; but payment is expected from that bank with something approaching certainty—as is distinctly *not* true of the buyer's acceptance. The credit problem as to the seller becomes one largely as to whether he has taken on more than his manufacturing or selling facilities can carry in terms of output, a problem of production technique, not one of how far he is financially extended, a problem of financial organization. It is the latter, not the former, which is the true aspect of credit strain.

At the other end, the credit strain does of course devolve upon the buyer. But here two things are to be noted. The first, that by the use of the trust receipt a reasonable modicum of security may be retained by the buyer's banker even after the goods are in the buyer's hands, and *a fortiori,* under the English practice of holding the raws in warehouse subject to the banker's order and permitting withdrawals only in such quantities as are represented by present payments (anticipations) from the buyer. And the second point is that the buyer's ultimate payment of his obligations to his banker is subject to fewer contingencies than is the seller's payment of obligations to *his* banker. For the buyer is much closer to the ultimate purchaser for use, on whom normal liquidation ultimately will depend. Moreover, the buyer's circumstances have been subjected to examination by a local banker on the basis of the closely familiar local conditions of the buyer's business; whereas the seller's banker, irrespective of how much he knows of the seller, must of necessity gamble (in the absence of a letter of credit) on the possibility that the seller may fail to realize his outstanding accounts due from distant and unknown buyers operating in distant and unknown circumstances. It is this type of factor which gives point to the argument that the letter of credit serves the public by *reducing* risks as well as shifting them.

But the picture of the corresponding burdens on the buyer entailed by the protection of the seller must be faced in more detail. It is not only the shift of credit strain. It is the seller now who is able to cancel in bad faith before shipment and leave the buyer high and dry. But observe that this is not a risk attributable to the letter of credit *per se;* it would exist equally without the letter. Still, by the letter the buyer has been barred from such anticipatory repudiation; the seller, not; the buyer's promise has been given factual, well-nigh certain sanction; the seller's has behind it nothing but his business honor and the pressure of the law—weighty enough, in untroubled times, but both so dubious in the pinch that we contrast them with "security." More, and worse: the seller may ship doubtful goods; they may be less than contract quality; they may be bad or worthless; they may be sand for sugar, salt water for salt cod—as has occurred. The buyer's bank will pay against the documents if fair on their face;[9] once the bank has innocently paid, the buyer will be forced to reimburse, whatever the seller's fraud. Hardship. Apart from bad faith, there is the lesser risk of negligent mistake in the nature of the goods; this time it is the buyer who must seek recourse in a foreign tribunal, carrying the risks and expense of proof at a distance, through unknown counsel, and under local prejudice on the part of triers of fact and law. There is, moreover, the risk that the seller may go insolvent or conceal his assets before the buyer can get a judgment or levy execution under it. The seller has the money; the buyer has a remedy at law. Finally, the risk of the dropping market rests on the buyer. But this last, while an intensification of the situation, is again hardly a trouble attributable to the letter of credit itself. It rests upon the buyer, not by virtue of the letter, but by force of contracting to take goods at a price. The letter, however, forces him to settle up. In a mercantile sense, therefore, as mentioned previously, it puts on him an added risk. He must perform his contract irrespective of business conditions; he cannot use the seller's troubles as a means of forcing a commercial adjustment of an unprofitable deal.

But to stop here would be to set one extreme against the other, with no eye to intermediate gradations. There are devices aplenty which offer any buyer with intelligence to use them a means to meet, to a very considerable extent, one or more of the risks above set forth. He can require the seller to post a cash guaranty that shipment will be made. That will cover the risk of breach by cancellation. In the second place, he can, in the case of many commodities, especially such raw materials as are capable of grading and inspection, require as a condition of payment under the credit that the seller present certificates of weighers or graders as to the quantity and quality of the commodity. There is no protection to be had here against the more objectionable forms of fraud, and little in the case of unstandardized commodities such as typewriters or automobiles; but there is always something, and for many commodities a great deal of protection. Finally, the buyer can demand that the letter of credit be limited to some fixed percentage of the price, say 75 per cent or 50 per cent; which, as to the balance, leaves him both with a reasonable margin to allow for ordinary defects in goods, and even with a certain bargaining power *re* price adjustment in the event of price decline. To sum up, then, the letter of credit offers a means hitherto unsurpassed, for distributing equitably, instead of lopsidedly, the risks of buying and selling in a credit market. Not only this, but its machinery is sufficiently flexible to permit the

[9] Assuming, of course, no notice of fraud or forgery. The effect of fraud or forgery, discovered before acceptance, is one point on which I find myself unable wholly to agree with Dr. Finkelstein. See p. 243.

allocation of those risks in any desired fashion. For instance, the revocable credit (or authority to pay) covers the sellers against risks of shipment and all risks arising thereafter, but gives him no coverage as to cancellation before shipment. Cash against documents, whether the credit be irrevocable or no, covers the seller against all risks of shipment, but leaves out of account the financing of the buyer during the period of expected resale. The irrevocable acceptance credit covers all three phases of the matter, and yet is open, as indicated, to a number of modifications which keep the buyer from putting himself wholly in the seller's hands.

But this relation to the market for goods covers only the one part of the function of the device. There remains the question of its services to mercantile finance.

Some Financial Aspects of the Letter of Credit[10]

This aspect of the banker's credit has been the center of most economic discussion of the subject hitherto, and has been so ably treated by Furniss and by Ward as to leave me little to add; that little, moreover, is indicated in what has gone before. But it is perhaps worth while for the sake of completeness to call to mind the salient points.

There is no need to rehearse the advantages which the trade acceptance as an instrument of sales finance might have—at least in theory—over either assignment of book accounts, assignment of and advances against specific invoices, or single name paper of the seller. But it is vital to observe that the objections which have been raised to the trade acceptance fail, one and all, to touch the letter of credit. I shall mention only one, and that the most vital: that the trade acceptance tends (by virtue of its two-name character) to lull the seller's banker into false reliance on an acceptor whom he does not and cannot know. If that acceptor, however, is a known banker, any notion that the acceptor's name does not strengthen the paper blows gently down the wind; and one has the added factual security afforded by the legal limitations

[10] S. P. Meech, in the Jour. Bus. U. Chi. for April, 1929, has made it clear that the title of this section as it originally appeared ("The Place of the Letter of Credit in Short-Term Finance," *ibid.* Jan., 1-16) was too broad. I am discussing the financing of shipments, not short-term finance in general. Meech's discussion of the short-term finance situation in general seems to me therefore, despite its value in itself, to leave untouched all the essential points here made; especially the points of the general superiority of banker's credit judgment over seller's, and of the roll-up of stringency. I have taken advantage of his criticisms, however, to reword some passages to avoid both error and misconstruction. Meech's most vital criticism of my hopes herein expressed is rather implicit than explicit. The very satisfaction with which he views the present domestic credit structure evidences cogently the inertia of practices and of ideas which stand in the way of any substantial widening of letter of credit practice in domestic trade.

on the amount of a banker's acceptance, both *in toto,* and for any single customer.

One is more concerned with the outstanding difference which the letter of credit shows against every current method of shipping finance save one. In common with borrowing by the buyer from his banker, and the buyer's then using the loan to take his cash discount, the letter of credit involves financing primarily from the buyer's end.[11] On the other hand, trade acceptance, ordinary open account (the seller meanwhile borrowing on his single name paper), assignment of accounts, assignment of invoice on shipment, and advance against or discount of documentary draft (sight, in most domestic trade; time, in most foreign trade) are all alike in financing from the seller's end. On the seller rests the primary credit strain. His credit standing is the primary measure of the banker's loans. The paper received is only collateral. Its liquidation relieves the seller's credit, retires his debt. He and his circumstances are the center of the banker's attention.

From which flow consequences. The paper commands a rate of discount which reflects mercantile, not banking, risks; it is, relatively, an expensive form of credit.[12] And for a reason. Its payment is subject to all the contingencies of unknown, distant buyers. Let the market break, and the buyers' failure to resell means their failure to pay; their failure to pay means that the seller fails to meet his obligations—and so on back. Retailers' troubles bring on jobbers'; jobbers', wholesalers'; wholesalers', manufacturers'. The credit stringency rolls up; each insolvency threatens to bring on others—and since each seller's financing is dependent for liquidation on his buyers, there is neither halt nor help.

Contrast the situation under the letter of credit. Let the market break: the only parties involved will normally be the buyer and the buyer's bank. All sellers back of the transaction out of which the banker's credit originates will get the benefit of liquidation; the stringency does not roll up; indeed, there is a needed and welcome period of easing off which makes contraction of current finance a possibility. And between the seller (and those who sold to him) and the possibility of trouble stand the financial resources, not of a buyer who is dependent on the

[11] Automobile finance, as respects the manufacturer, is substantially on a letter of credit-trust receipt basis. It is the outstanding domestic example. But it has not progressed to the final phase of using a finance company's acceptances instead of cash payments against the bills of lading. It would be illuminating to discover how far this is accident and how far due to assignable needs of the situation.

[12] Certainly, to the consuming public, who do not profit by such ability as the seller may have to pass his credit losses on. And I suspect that the same would hold of the individual selling concern, at once; certainly, if the practice of using the letter of credit became more common.

market in a single field, but of a banker whose interests are more varied, and who may be hoped, by temperament and training, to have allowed himself less extravagance of extension than a mercantile entrepreneur.

Nor is one wholly dependent for this difference in credit[18] soundness on the hypothetical (though normal) make-up of the banker. The nature of the credit extension affords additional guaranty. The question goes here to that extension of credit to the buyer on which the initial possibility of roll-up turns. And the distinction is between seller and banker as credit-givers. A given seller may conceivably be as good a judge of credit standing and credit soundness as a banker. But it is not his business; his business is the creation and satisfaction of demand—for profit. The profit lies in the merchandising, not in the credit-giving. Indeed, the latter is more than likely to figure as a source of losses. It has been mentioned before that the seller is in no position, normally, to judge the buyer's circumstances with the keenness of the buyer's banker. It needs to be said here, further, that the seller has no interest to make him use that judgment as care-

[18] This is not a discussion of the theory of credit; hence it is unnecessary here to take nice distinctions in terms. But it may be noted in passing that most writing in the field suffers some confusion and considerable conflict over unreal issues because of failure to keep such distinctions in mind. It is obvious, for instance, that the fundamental fact of credit is *credit giving* —by someone giving up or foregoing some present advantage in reliance on some other person's promise of equivalent future performance. Back of this fundamental fact lies credit *motivation*: what induces the credit giver to give credit? This is often spoken of as the "basis" of credit. But in this aspect the motivation is obviously in terms of *appearances*, and of the credit giver's *expectations*—which *may* have nothing to do with the *facts*. Whether (and why) the credit giving proves to have been *sound*, looks ahead from the crucial point of credit giving, and raises *ex post facto* a purely historical question: did the credit-taker perform, and what resources did he in fact call on for his performance? Until the time for liquidation has come, true soundness and the true basis of ultimate liquidation are undeterminable; they are matters of judgment and of probabilities; and a wise and well-buttressed judgment may prove wrong. In this aspect too, much is written about the "basis" of credit. A relation to the other question of why credit-givers extend credit is obvious; but that the problems are not the same needs no argument, for the latter problems (of credit extension) involve the additional distortion of the facts by way of the credit-giver's ignorance, optimism, etc.

Beyond all these questions is the further one of credit as a medium of exchange. In dealing with this the terminological approach is commonly reversed, and the *promise* is spoken of as credit; a natural enough outcome of study via the traditional approach of "money and banking," but one which threatens with dire confusion the whole problem of basis of credit, whether in regard to credit extension, to credit standing, or to ultimate liquidation.

Finally, "credit" is used to denote credit instruments, and the present discussion has been led or misled into making letter of credit, commercial credit, and banker's credit more or less interchangeable terms. They are of course not interchangeable; Dr. Finkelstein provides abundant instances where discrimination is necessary, though it is not, for the purposes here in hand.

fully, when he has it to use. He wants to sell. He can take a chance on credit. His margin of profit is wide enough to absorb some errors of credit judgment. Not so with the banker. His margin of profit is low; he cannot risk losses. He extends credit with an eye as nearly single to safety as human institutions will allow. He is trained and spurred to that one item: safety. Often ill-trained, and often stubbornly unheedful of the spur, but to no such measure as a seller of goods.

Hence the argument that the letter of credit makes for sounder credit extension *to the buyer,* in addition to placing the incidence of the credit risk much further down the line, seems hard to escape. The argument means in brutal result less business, to the precise extent to which use of the letter of credit may spread.[14] But the business which is eliminated is precisely that which has no business being.

Remains the third vital matter. Not merely is the buyer's promise sounder, but the seller is not driven to rely upon the buyer's promise at all. He—and, if the drafts under the letter be time drafts, the purchaser from him—relies upon a banker, not a buyer. The point is trite, but important. For Dun's rating is substituted a banker's solvency; by application of one bank to another, a metropolitan banker's solvency; where necessary, by confirmation, the cumulative solvency of two bankers. A further, obvious, specialization in institutional structure. A cheapening of credit, a widening of the credit market, by virtue of reducing risks. A toughening of the whole credit structure. It is not for nothing that bankers speak of "discounting" a buyer's note or acceptance, but of "purchasing" bankers' acceptances.

It seems strange that this device should be so little used at home, that it should be found chiefly in the dealings of shoe-string cattle buyers, or of twenty Italians clubbing together to get a carload of wine grapes from California, and that it should be found encumbered with the phraseology and occasionally with the uncommercial technicality of the law of guaranty. The acceptance feature can of course develop only with an acceptance market; and one name paper, along with its greater risks, continues to produce a greater immediate return to bankers. Sooner or later, however, business pressure must force movement toward the line of lesser risks. When that time comes, the letter of credit is at hand, no longer an experiment, no longer a legal uncertainty. Its possibilities in risk and dispute *elimination,* moreover, have only been tapped. I will mention but one more. At any shipping point where important quantities of a single commodity are shipped, and where the letter of credit is in use, commercial pressure develops toward the employment of an inspector to represent either buyers or banks, or both, and to produce certificates

[14] Meech, *op. cit. supra* note 10, at 194, 197, 198, tellingly plays up my earlier phrasing: "if the letter of credit becomes the credit system."

of quality and packing as conditions to payment. What this means in obviating that most vexatious and uncertain of litigation—whether bad condition of goods on arrival was due to seller or to transit—speaks for itself.

The Place of the Letter of Credit in the Law

On the legal-technical phase of the subject, to which Dr. Finkelstein's attention is mainly directed, a word needs to be said. As is likely to be the case with any emerging institution, the letter of credit is backed, bounded, overlapped, by other institutions new and old. In one aspect it flows into the law of contracts, especially the doctrine of consideration, and more particularly those special phases of consideration which mark the law of bills and notes.[15] Here lay that paper of Hershey's which plays the same part in the law of letters of credit as does the Brandeis article in the law of privacy; here McCurdy exhausted the possibilities of existing legal theory in support of irrevocability. For the moment there seems in that aspect little more to say. I personally am persuaded that no existing theory will suffice unmodified to explain irrevocability in all its aspects; that the courts will from time to time take whatever theory suits the need of the moment; and that in another twenty years we shall have a special doctrine of consideration in letters of credit, as firmly fixed and as peculiar as that now found in some phases of negotiable paper. But that is guesswork.

In another aspect the law of letters of credit plays into the doctrines of virtual and extrinsic acceptances. And here Dr. Finkelstein—at a peculiarly happy time, in view of the pending modification of the Negotiable Instruments Law—has contributed as fine a study as one will readily find.

In still another aspect lie the perplexing interrelations of the letter of credit and the law of sales, evident peculiarly in the phases of conditions and of damages under the letter of credit. It is a happy thing that the studies of Goitein,[16] and especially of Kennedy,[17] in the hitherto neglected matter of c.i.f. contracts appeared in time to be drawn into comparison with Dr. Finkelstein's discussion of conditions.[18] Mutual illumination results. Needed illumination, for c.i.f. contracts are still as far from being understood in their full bearings as is the many-sided subject matter

[15] It is striking that it was in a case closely related to letters of credit that Mansfield launched his famous departure from the requirement of consideration. Pillans v. Van Mierop, 3 Burr. 1663 (K. B. 1765). The argument there is to the case in hand; the language about "commercial cases" in general is at most incidental. And the modern law seems to be re-establishing Mansfield's decision.

[16] Cited *infra* p. 182.

[17] Cited *infra* p. 182.

[18] *Cf.* also 1 Williston, Sales (2d ed. 1924) §§ 280 ff.; 2 *ibid.* §§ 599 f., and the writer's note in (1923) 32 Yale L. J., 711.

of the present work; yet every step toward that understanding is full of light for the law and practice of the bankers' credit. Dr. Finkelstein has begun the study of the interrelation, and begun it well, so well as to call forth the hope that at a later time he will develop it at length. Meantime, in the question of damages, he has broken new and fertile ground; and in his treatment of conditions under the letter he stands without a rival.

There is yet another field of law, of which we know as yet almost nothing, and yet on whose development some phases of the law of letters of credit may yet come to depend; hardly, to be sure, the law of formal letters of credit, but very possibly several phases of those informal credits opened by telegraph and informally advised which serve substantially the same purposes as the most formal letter, and should be similar in their results. The undeveloped field to which I refer is the law of third (and fourth) party deposits: "Herewith $5,000, which place to the credit of A," with all its variations. Here the courts in the few cases before them have shown little of that sensitivity to commercial needs which has marked their action in the more developed field. One hopes that if that continues the law of letters of credit will maintain itself in its present independence—whatever a critical study of foreign banking might offer to the contrary. And if it does, no small portion of the merit will belong to Dr. Finkelstein's cogent presentation and analysis of the law of the subject and its rationale.

KARL N. LLEWELLYN

CHAPTER I

HISTORY AND ANALYSIS

A. DEVELOPMENT OF COMMERCIAL LETTER OF CREDIT

"THE law of merchants," said Lord Mansfield, "and the law of the land is the same."[1] There can be no doubt that in his day and under his influence this was largely true. But Lord Mansfield's success in this effort toward the fusion of mercantile custom and law failed to maintain itself in subsequent legal history. Later courts were not equally ready to treat usages among merchants as part of the common law. This difficulty was partially met by the rule of law which permitted pleading and proof of a special custom with reference to which a particular contract had been made. This remedy, however, has been obviously insufficient to meet the needs of an ever-increasing and ever more complex mercantile world.

A striking instance of the failure of the common law adequately to meet changing mercantile conditions can be found in the history of the rules concerning negotiable instruments.[2] Negotiability as

---

[1] Pillans v. Van Mierop, 3 Burr. 1663, 1669, 97 Eng. R. 1035, 1038 (1765).

[2] The effect that the codification of the law merchant will have on the recognition of commercial letters of credit as a new type of mercantile specialty is not certain. While the British Bills of Exchange Act apparently does not prevent the recognition of new types of negotiable instruments, the effect of the Uniform Negotiable Instruments Law in this regard is more doubtful. See Aigler, *Recognition of New Types of Negotiable Instruments* (1924) 24 COL. L. REV. 563; also 24 *ibid.* 757; 25 *ibid.* 71; 25 *ibid.* 209. Briefly, the sounder opinion seems to be that the Negotiable Instruments Law does not prevent the recognition of new types of negotiable instruments. Certainly this is, commercially, the desirable view. Any other would lead to the stultification of the law and compel amendments of various kinds. At this point, it need only be indicated that even the adoption of the narrower view does not *ipso facto* mean that a letter of credit cannot be recognized as a new type of mercantile specialty. No claim is made that a letter of credit is negotiable. As will be seen, it would not be desirable that it be negotiable.

an element of a contractual obligation should not be confined to the few instruments known in the eighteenth century. Nevertheless, the courts have resisted the tendency of trade to develop new forms of mercantile specialties and have made every effort to settle the problems that have arisen around these new forms in terms of the general contract law requiring offer, acceptance, and consideration.[8]

The commercial letter of credit is a mercantile specialty of an entirely new type to which the Uniform Negotiable Instruments Law could not have been intended to apply. "Negotiable instruments may fall within one or other of two classes. They may represent interests in property, in which event they will give rise to rights *in rem*, or they may be promissory and executory, creating rights *in personam*. Negotiability was once determined by rules of the law merchant. In this state, a statute, the Negotiable Instruments Law, has codified those rules either wholly or in part. We assume, though there is no occasion to determine, that negotiable instruments of the first class, *i. e.*, those representing interests in property—are not within the purview of the statute, however broad its title. Other acts, more restricted in scope, deal with bills of lading, warehouse receipts, and certificates of stock, instruments quasi-negotiable, if not negotiable altogether. Our concern at the moment is with instruments of the second class, where the words, in effect at least, are those of promise merely. We do not now decide that even as to instruments of this order, the creative force of the law merchant has been extinguished altogether. Opportunities for growth, may exist along lines and in directions which can hardly be charted in advance. We are satisfied, however, that the law merchant is without capacity to make instruments negotiable against the express prohibition of a statute which says that they are not negotiable. . . . We do not mean to cast doubt through anything here written upon the capacity of merchants to create new forms of negotiability by contract or estoppel." Bank of Manhattan Co. v. Morgan, 242 N. Y. 38, 47, 50, 150 N. E. 594, 597, 598 (1926); see also State Bank v. Central Mercantile Bank, 248 N. Y. 428, 432, 162 N. E. 475, 476 (1928); (1926) 36 YALE L. J. 245, 249.

[8] "Letters of credit afford a striking illustration of the ill-adaptation of our American common law of contract to the needs of modern business in an urban society of highly complex economic organization. Well known abroad and worked out consistently on general theories in the commercial law of Continental Europe, these instruments came into use in this country on a large scale suddenly during the war. There was no settled theory with respect to them in our books and the decisions warranted four or five views leading to divergent results in matters of vital moment to the business man who acted on them. Characteristically the business world set out to make of them formal contracts of the law merchant by the use of certain distinctive words which gave the instruments character and made their nature clear to those who inspected them anywhere in the world. But for a season our category of mercantile specialties had ceased to admit of growth and the doctrine of consideration with its uncertain lines stood in the way of many things which the exigencies of business called for and business men found themselves doing in reliance on each other's business honor and the banker's jealousy of his business credit, with or without assistance from the law. Certainly no one

Much of the language used by the courts in discussing the requirements for a successful action by various parties under a letter of credit would be unintelligible if one did not realize that the courts were trying to find a consideration where none existed or an acceptance of an offer, not only where there was no offer to accept, but no acceptance intended.

Occasionally, the courts will also attempt to subsume under the definitions of the older forms of mercantile specialties such new instruments as may from time to time make their appearance in the commercial world. This effort, while it serves the immediate need, has a cramping effect on the possibilities for development of the newer forms of mercantile specialties. We shall see later how the entire doctrine of virtual and extrinsic acceptances, representing the tendency of the courts to enforce as an acceptance a promise to accept or to pay not written on the face of the draft, owes its continued existence to the failure of the courts adequately to solve the problems created by the use of instruments containing promises to accept drafts not yet drawn.

In connection with letters of credit, we shall find that the law has developed around both the tendency of some courts to limit the scope of letters of credit within the narrow confines of the law of contract and, on the other hand, the tendency of other courts to subsume letters of credit under the general category of older negotiable instruments. It is only within the last few years that courts have begun to recognize commercial letters of credit as distinct and new types of commercial instruments and have treated them as such. This recognition has been largely the result less of legal forces than of commercial forces, which have brought about the extended use of these instruments.[4]

---

would say that such a situation bears witness to wise social engineering in an economically organized society resting on credit." POUND, INTRODUCTION TO THE PHILOSOPHY OF LAW (1922) 277. See also Wright, *Opposition of the Law to Business Usages* (1926) 26 COL. L. REV. 917, 922, quoted *infra*, Ch. VIII, note 39.

[4] For further discussion of the economic and commercial considerations suggested here and elsewhere, as well as for a more detailed description of the actual workings and different types of commercial letters of credit,

Before the World War, the London banks were preëminent in the field of commercial credits, and in one way or another most of the financing of international trade was done by these institutions. As a result, it was not until the new era of commerce which set in after 1914 that American courts were called upon to discuss the problems involved in the use of letters of credit.[5]

Earlier American decisions which are said to have dealt with letters of credit involve, as a rule, buyers' letters of credit,[6] a type of instrument which, as we shall have occasion later to point out, is totally distinct from the modern commercial letter of credit with which we are here primarily concerned.

The rapid increase, during the last ten years, in the number and amount of letters of credit issued by American banks and the

---

see: WARD, AMERICAN COMMERCIAL CREDITS (1922); EDWARDS, FOREIGN COMMERCIAL CREDITS (1922); SPALDING, BANKERS' CREDITS (1921); WHITAKER, FOREIGN EXCHANGE (1922) ch. 7; FURNISS, FOREIGN EXCHANGE (1922) ch. 8; CROSS, DOMESTIC AND FOREIGN EXCHANGE (1923) ch. 9; YORK, INTERNATIONAL EXCHANGE (1923) ch. 19, 20, 21; SPALDING, FOREIGN EXCHANGE AND FOREIGN BILLS, (3d ed. 1919) ch. 15, 16; ESCHER, FOREIGN EXCHANGE EXPLAINED (1924) ch. 14, 15; WALTER, MODERN FOREIGN EXCHANGE (1923), ch. 6; BROOKS, FOREIGN EXCHANGE TEXT BOOK (2d ed. 1908) 173; 2 KNIFFIN, COMMERCIAL BANKING (1923) 780; MARGRAFF, INTERNATIONAL EXCHANGE (2d ed. 1904) 88.

[5] Even in England where the letter of credit was in constant use, litigation involving letters of credit was also most infrequent. Another reason for lack of litigation was, as will be seen, *infra* p. 26, the punctiliousness with which bankers honored their letters of credit. One result of the paucity of decisions involving letters of credit is that legal historians have failed to treat such documents with the same thoroughness which drafts and promissory notes have been accorded. Little has been written, therefore, from a common law point of view, of their early economic use and development. That they have been used for centuries is certain; see MALYNES, LEX MERCATORIA (ed. 1685) Pt. I, ch. XIV, for a description of the workings of early letters of credit. The differences in usage between early and modern letters of credit are so marked as to make them almost two distinct instruments, e. g., the modern letter of credit is almost always documentary, while the early one was generally "clean," and more in the nature of the modern traveler's letter of credit. See also MARIUS, ADVICE CONCERNING BILLS OF EXCHANGE (4th ed. 1684) 36; *cf.* STORY, BILLS OF EXCHANGE (1843) ch. XIII.

[6] The distinction between the buyer's letter of credit and the bank letter of credit, *i. e.*, the modern commercial letter of credit, is fundamental in any discussion of the law on this subject. The implications of this distinction are considered later, see *infra* p. 18. Unless otherwise indicated, the terms commercial letter of credit, commercial credit, and letter of credit are used to refer to the modern commercial letter of credit as the term is at present understood, see *infra* p. 146.

similar growth of participation by these institutions in the financing of foreign trade generally can, in the first instance, be traced to the Federal Reserve Act of 1914 which, in effect, permitted member banks to issue letters of credit.[7]

---

[7] It is the generally accepted opinion that, prior to the enactment of the Federal Reserve Act, national banks did not have the power to accept time drafts or to issue letters of credit. WHITAKER, FOREIGN EXCHANGE (1922) 134, n. 1; YORK, INTERNATIONAL EXCHANGE (1923) 298 *et seq.;* WARD, AMERICAN COMMERCIAL CREDITS (1922) c. I. However, since 1839 a few national banks had made use of foreign credits to finance our importations. Although the question was never directly passed upon in the Federal courts, that national banks did not have such authority is implied in several decisions. Bowen v. Needles Nat. Bank, 87 Fed. 430, 443 (C. C. S. D. Cal., 1898), *aff'd,* 94 Fed. 925 (C. C. A. 9th, 1899), *cert. den.,* 176 U. S. 682, 20 Sup. Ct. 1024 (1900); Merchants' Bank v. Baird, 160 Fed. 642, 17 L. R. A. (N. S.) 526 (C. C. A. 8th, 1908); see Thilmany v. Iowa Paper Bag Co., 108 Iowa 333, 79 N. W. 68 (1899), a decision by a state court to the effect that national banks could not issue letters of credit. See also Commercial Nat. Bank v. Pirie, 82 Fed. 799 (C. C. A. 8th, 1897). The general basis for this prohibition was the rule that banks could not lend their credit, 1 MORSE, BANKS AND BANKING (6th ed. 1928) § 65. Accordingly, as is indicated in several of the cases cited, a bank could probably issue letters of credit against cash or its equivalent, or undertake to honor drafts when put in funds by its depositor, see First Nat. Bank v. Merchants' Nat. Bank, 7 W. Va. 544 (1874). Decatur Bank v. St. Louis Bank is not in point, as the court expressly refused to consider the problem, 21 Wall. 294, 302, 22 L. Ed. 560, 562 (1874).

In support of the view that banks, in the absence of express authorization, do not have the power to issue letters of credit, much has been made of the fact that banks act under charters which bestow designated powers and that the power to issue letters of credit cannot be implied from those granted. See, however, Russell Grader Mfg. Co. v. Farmers' Exch. State Bank, 49 N. D. 999, 194 N. W. 387, decided in 1923, when power to issue letters of credit was being generally granted to banks, and where the court finds authority to engage in this type of transaction implied in the general powers granted to banks, N. D. COMP. LAWS ANN. (1913) § 5150 (7). Significantly, the court cites Border Nat. Bank v. American Nat. Bank, 282 Fed. 73 (C. C. A. 5th, 1922) *cert. den.,* 260 U. S. 701, 43 Sup. Ct. 96 (1922), a case decided after the adoption of the Federal Reserve Act and which considered the powers of a national bank. The Federal Reserve Act, adopted in 1913, merely authorizes member banks to accept time bills of exchange, 12 U. S. CODE, §§ 372, 373 (1926). Nevertheless, these sections have been relied upon as authorizing the issuance of letters of credit. That national banks have power today to issue letters of credit is no longer an open question, Border Nat. Bank v. American Nat. Bank, *ibid.* One need only compare this decision with Bowen v. Needles Nat. Bank, *ibid.,* to realize that the power granted banks at present is less a question of statutory authorization than a reflection of the needs of the times and of the changing attitude toward banks. Though most state enactments authorizing the issuance of letters of credit are subsequent to the adoption of the Federal Reserve Act, such authority had been granted in some states previously; see e. g. MD. STAT. (1910), c. 219, § 23, p. 12. And even where there was no such specific authority, courts might have decided that banks had such power, had the question

The position of American sellers during and just after the World War made it especially easy for them to exact their own terms in connection with foreign sales. Consequently, they were able to reject foreign credits and insist upon commercial credits, issued or confirmed by American banking institutions. These factors largely account for the tremendous increase in the use of commercial letters of credit in this country.

---

arisen. See the discussion of Russell Grader Mfg. Co. v. Farmers' Exch. State Bank, *ibid.* Compare, however, Ingersoll v. Kansas State Bank, 109 Kan. 534, 110 Kan. 122, 202 Pac. 837 (1921), where in the absence of specific legislative authority to issue letters of credit or to accept time drafts, the court held that state banks of Kansas had no power to accept time drafts. See also Swenson Bros. Co. v. Commercial State Bank, 98 Neb. 702, 154 N. W. 233, L. R. A. 1917F, 1096 (1915). But see Saylors v. State Bank of Allen, 99 Kan. 515, 163 Pac. 454 (1917); Ballard v. Home Nat. Bank, 91 Kan. 91, 97, 136 Pac. 935, 937, L. R. A. 1916 C, 161, 164 (1913).

The following states today expressly authorize the issuance of letters of credit and the acceptance of time drafts: ARK. DIG. STAT. (Crawford & Moses, 1921), c. 15, § 741; CAL. CODES & GENERAL LAWS (Supp. 1927), act 652, § 80, p. 885 *et seq.;* DEL. LAWS 1921, c. 103, § 12; 2 IND. ANN. STAT. (Burns, 1926), § 3950 (9); KY. STAT. (Carroll, 1922), § 579; 1 LA. CONST. & STAT. (Wolff, 1920), p. 130; MAINE L. 1923, c. 144, § 61; MD. ANN. CODE (Bagby, 1924), Art. 11, § 23 (6); 2 MASS. GEN. LAWS (1921), c. 172, §§ 36, 37; MO. REV. STAT. (1919), c. 108, § 11737 (2); 2 MONT. REV. CODES (Choate, 1921), pt. III, c. 13, § 6087; 1 N. J. COMP. STAT. (Cum. Supp., 1925), § 17-6a; N. Y. BANKING LAW (1914), §§ 106 (2), 185 (10); 1 OHIO GEN. CODE (Page, 1926), tit. III, div. II, c. 3, § 710-137; OKLA. COMP. STAT. ANN. (Supp. 1926), c. 24, art. IV, § 4194-1; 2 OREG. LAWS (Supp. 1927), tit. XXXV, c. I-IX, §§ 39 (6), 128; PA. STAT. (West, 1920), § 6348; R. I. GEN. LAWS (1923), c. 271, § 2; TENN. ANN. CODE (Supp. 1926), § 2097-a 1; VA. CODE ANN. (1924), tit. 37, c. 162, § 4112; W. VA. CODE ANN. (Barnes, 1923), c. 54, § 78. The following states expressly authorize the acceptance of time drafts without any provision for the issuance of letters of credit: ALA. CIV. CODE (1923), § 6377; 2 CONN. GEN. STAT. (1918), tit. 34, c. 200, § 3922; 8 GA. ANN. CODE (Park, Supp. 1922), tit. 2, c. 2, art. 1, sec. 19, § 2280 (t); IOWA CODE (1927), c. 415, § 9272; MICH. COMP. LAWS (Cahill, Supp. 1922), c. 152, § 7970; 2 MISS. ANN. CODE (Hem. 1927) § 3888; 1 N. C. CONS. STAT. ANN. (1919) c. 5, § 222; S. C. CODE OF LAWS (1922) tit. 12, c. 46, § 25. A few states expressly provide for the issuance of letters of credit without any express authority to accept time drafts: 2 S. D. REV. CODE (1919), pt. 18, c. 1, art. 2, § 8952 (6); VT. GEN. LAWS (1917) tit. 28, c. 225, § 5347 (VI); WIS. STAT. (1919) c. 94, § 2024-9, omitted in subsequent revision, see WIS. STAT. (1927) § 8221.04. It is doubtful whether Texas authorizes even the acceptance of time drafts. TEX. REV. CIV. STAT. (Vernon 1925) c. 17, art. 1513, authorizes any trust company "to accept bills or drafts drawn on it." As is indicated in (1924) 24 COL. L. REV. 633, 639, n. 28, by legislation permitting savings banks to purchase acceptances of state banks, several states impliedly authorize time acceptances. WASH. COMP. STAT. (Remington, 1922) §§ 3323, 3339; 2 MINN. STAT. (Mason, 1927) § 7714 (8); Vt. Acts 1919, no. 135. Statutes authorizing time acceptances should be

The convenience and security of this method of financing trade were quickly recognized.[8] Its use increased enormously, extended itself to import as well as to export trade, and is now gradually and increasingly being adopted in domestic trade. Letters of credit, instead of being issued by only a few English banking houses, are now issued by any number of banks in this country. This rapid increase, both in the number of letters of credit issued and in the number of banks issuing them, led to a bewildering diversity in the types of forms used. Each bank created its own forms which varied from formal printed blanks to informal typewritten letters.

With rising prices in the general prosperity during the War, the dangers involved in this confusion of forms were not noticed, since buyers desired to take the goods even though the requirements of the sales contract had not been complied with in all respects. In the general depression which continued from the middle of 1920 to about the middle of 1922, prices were falling, and buyers resorted to all sorts of pretexts to avoid the obligations under their contracts. The most usual basis for these repudiations was that the documents did not conform to the requirements of the letter of credit. Many problems thus raised found their way into court for adjudication, and some of the principles underlying the use of letters of credit were settled at this time.

One of the results of these developments was the realization

construed to include letters of credit, particularly if the same limitations on the extent of the bank's commitments are observed. Similarly, statutes authorizing letters of credit should be deemed to include time acceptances, as otherwise all letters of credit would require sight drafts, thus compelling the buyer to re-finance before he has had an opportunity to sell the goods delivered to him under a trust receipt or similar instrument. See, however, American Express Co. v. Citizens State Bank, 181 Wis. 172, 194 N. W. 427 (1923), where at the time of the decision the statute authorized the issuance of letters of credit and the court refused to permit the acceptance of time drafts. The statutes discussed here all deal with the authority of banks to issue letters of credit and to accept time drafts and are to be distinguished from the earlier enactments, considered *infra* note 41, which relate to rights under letters of credit.

[8] For other practical advantages in the use of letters of credit, see *infra* note 25; see also (1925) 34 Yale L. J. 775.

that the general adoption of standard forms for various types of letters of credit would go far toward stabilizing business practices, and the law in relation to them, and would aid in the recognition by the courts of the letter of credit as a mercantile specialty. Conferences directed toward this end were held by the most prominent banks in the country,[9] and a series of standard forms was drawn up. For a time, it seemed probable that these would be adopted generally. The movement has died down, however, and the banks have continued to prefer their individual forms. Nevertheless, forms today are more nearly standardized than ever before, and probably this tendency toward uniformity will continue.

B. Types of Bank Credit and Credit Instruments

The issuance of a commercial letter of credit is essentially a "credit" transaction and hence it bears a certain fundamental relation to other forms of bank credit. For the purposes of this discussion, credit may be viewed as involving the giving up of goods or money in the present in anticipation of the fulfillment of a present promise to deliver goods or to pay money in the future.[10] If the credit standing of the promisor is satisfactory to the promisee, this promise will be relied on by the latter, thus resulting in a giving of credit, or an extension of credit, to the promisor. The promise may be contained in a formal document, e. g., a promissory note or a letter of credit; or it may be expressed more informally as by word of mouth, or even implied from the acts of the promisor.

---

[9] See Ward, *op. cit. supra* note 4 for the details of these conferences.

[10] See Moulton, The Financial Organization of Society (2d ed. 1925) ch. VII. It has also been defined as "the ability to borrow on the opinion conceived by the lender that he will be repaid." 1 Bouvier, Law Dictionary (8th ed. 1914) 725. This latter view defines the term from the point of view of the borrower and recognizes the promise by the borrower only by implication. Since we are considering at this point various types of extensions of credit by lenders, the point of view of the latter is of more consequence for our purposes. The promise, therefore, becomes a most significant element in the definition of credit.

Promises may be divided into several classes, of which only two are important in this connection: those which have goods as their subject matter, and those which relate to money.

Promises relating to money may properly be grouped according to the nature of the business in which the promisor is engaged, e. g., those made by a banker and those made by a tradesman. An intermediate group may also be found which, to some extent, partakes of the character of both types, namely, promises made by commission merchants and factors whose business includes the acceptance of bills drawn by many principals. No matter what the exact nature of the promise is, it represents, when relied upon by the promisee, an extension of credit in one form or another. In the normal case, the tradesman's credit and the bank's credit differ to such a degree in usefulness, in acceptability, and in operation that, for the most part, different considerations must apply to each.[11]

A bank may be involved in the creation of credit in several ways:[12] by the promise implied in receiving deposits; by certifications and bank acceptances; and by the issuance of bank notes, bank or cashier's checks, travelers' letters of credit, commercial

---

[11] Government credit, as evidenced by government bonds, paper currency, and silver coins, is another type of credit that should be mentioned. This is even more desirable than bank credit and passes more freely. It need not concern us further, however, as in normal times it is treated as money or its equivalent.

[12] These illustrations deal only with one aspect of the activities of banks. In each of these situations, the bank assumes obligations and makes promises which are relied upon by others. While it creates credit, credit is extended to it by the holders of the bank checks, bank acceptances etc., because the credit standing of the bank is satisfactory to such holders. The other aspect of the functions of a banking institution is concerned with the lending of funds. In this type of situation, it is the bank that extends credit because the credit standing of the borrower is satisfactory to it. This aspect of the activities of the bank is of slight consequence at this point inasmuch as the issuance of a letter of credit involves primarily the assumption of obligations by the bank, which are relied on by the seller. It should also be noticed that the bank before issuing its letter of credit requires the buyer to make arrangements with the bank to reimburse it for payments made under the credit or to put it in funds before such payments become due under the terms of the credit. In issuing the credit, the bank is therefore extending credit to the buyer either directly or indirectly by permitting the buyer to borrow sufficient money from the bank to pay it for the issuance of the credit.

letters of credit, and other promises to pay money or accept drafts not contained in formal letters of credit.[13]

These various methods of indicating that credit has been created may be grouped in several ways according to their different characteristics and the varied functions which they perform. The most obvious classification is the distinction between a promise to pay any sums up to a certain amount, and a promise to pay only a specific amount. The promise implied in receiving deposits is clearly of the former type.[14] Bank notes, certifications, bank acceptances, and bank or cashier's checks are of the latter type.[15] Letters of credit and similar informal promises to honor or to pay drafts[16] may be of either type according to the kind of prom-

[13] There is also the bank guaranty which performs a function often similar to that of the commercial letter of credit. Indeed, the two types of instruments are at times indistinguishable, see *infra.* p. 32 to p. 42. In this country, the bank guaranty has not assumed much importance since banks are not generally authorized to incur that type of obligation, *infra* p. 35. The various instruments issued by the bank are usually termed credit instruments. The obligation is not always contained in an instrument, however, e. g., the promise implied in receiving deposits.

[14] The promise implied in receiving a deposit is a promise to pay on demand to the party to whose account the deposit is made, or to such persons as he may indicate, any sum he may desire up to the amount deposited. This indication is typically made by drawing a check. "A check is an order or request to pay another from one's deposit." Baker-Evans Grain Co. v. Ricord, 267 Pac. 14, 15 (Kan. 1928); see also: UNIFORM NEGOTIABLE INSTRUMENTS LAW, § 185; 1 MORSE, BANKS AND BANKING (6th ed. 1928) § 363; 2 DANIEL, NEGOTIABLE INSTRUMENTS (6th ed. 1913) ch. XLIX, § 1.

[15] A bank note is, in effect, a promissory note issued by a bank, payable to bearer, promising to pay any holder on demand the amount indicated in the note and under present federal rules passes as freely as government currency. AGGER, ORGANIZED BANKING (1918) 33, 37 *et seq.* A certification amounts to a promise to pay the sum represented by a particular check, stated on the check itself. A bank acceptance is a promise stamped on a draft by the bank on which it is drawn promising, in effect, to honor the draft. The bank or cashier's check is a distinct instrument which creates a relationship similar to that resulting from the certification of a check and by many banks is used as a substitute for certification. These instruments usually pass freely and in particular transactions among certain individuals, as in the sale of realty in localities where the bank is well known, are accepted as the equivalent of money.

[16] For example, promises made by telegram, cable, or oral statement. As will be seen, the usual commercial letter of credit is, under modern usage, a formal printed instrument though no particular form is required. Lamborn v. Nat. Park Bank, 240 N. Y. 520, 148 N. E. 664 (1925); Moss v. Old Colony Trust Co., 246 Mass. 139, 140 N. E. 803 (1923). The

ise that is made. In respect to the beneficiary, letters of credit proper, however, are generally of the former type. Another basis of classification can be found in the number of persons included as promisees. The obligation may be limited to one person or may be extended to all holders of the instrument evidencing such obligation. Promises involved in the receipt of deposits are clearly of the first type[17] and bank notes, cashier's checks,[18] and bank acceptances, of the second. A letter of credit is here again something of a hybrid. It is certainly not the intention of the bank that the promise shall be extended in favor of any one to whom the promisee may deliver the letter of credit. On the other hand, it is equally clear, and usually expressly stated, that the promise shall extend in favor of any one who takes a draft on the faith of the letter of credit. This instrument thus partakes of the nature of both groups. In relation to the beneficiary, it may be viewed as a promise to pay any amount up to a certain sum, but to all others as only a promise to pay the specific sum or sums

nature of the promise is, however, the same in all cases; therefore no distinction between the two need be made. See *infra* p. 25, note 42.

[17] From a commercial and factual point of view, this implied promise by the bank is directed only to the depositor and is only for his benefit. It is clearly not a promise to the payee of the check, and it has been uniformly held not to constitute legally a promise for the benefit of the payee. See (1926) 26 COL. L. REV. 459.

[18] A bank or cashier's check, being an order of a bank on itself, is in effect a promissory note and as such is irrevocable when in the hands of a bona fide purchaser. UNIFORM NEGOTIABLE INSTRUMENTS LAW § 130; see also: Causey v. Eiland, 175 Ark. 929, 934, 1 S. W. (2d) 1008, 1010, 56 A. L. R. 529, 532 (1928); Montana-Wyoming Ass'n. of Credit Men v. Commercial Nat. Bank, 80 Mont. 174, 177, 259 Pac. 1060, 1061 (1927); Anderson v. Bank of Tupelo, 135 Miss. 351, 100 So. 179 (1924). But *cf.* State v. Tyler County State Bank, 277 S. W. 625, 627, 42 A. L. R. 1347, 1350 (Tex. Com. App. 1925). A bank check may also be a check drawn by one bank as drawer on another as drawee. See 2 MICHIE, BANKS AND BANKING (1913) § 189. When the drawer does this at the request of a customer, the transaction closely resembles the issuance of a letter of credit authorizing the beneficiary to draw one draft for a fixed amount on a correspondent bank. See Bobrick v. Second Nat. Bank, 175 App. Div. 550, 162 N. Y. Supp. 147 (1916), *aff'd* without opinion, 224 N. Y. 637, 121 N. E. 856 (1918). A tradesman's check, certified at the request of the holder, relieves the drawer of all liability and also, in effect, becomes a promissory note. UNIFORM NEGOTIABLE INSTRUMENTS LAW, § 188. This clearly is similarly irrevocable. When certified at the request of the drawer, the latter still remains liable. In this type, therefore, the transaction more nearly approaches a draft drawn under a letter of credit.

indicated by the beneficiary in a specified manner, usually by drawing a draft.[19]

From the foregoing discussion, it becomes apparent that the peculiar characteristics of the commercial letter of credit are such as to render that instrument particularly useful in international trade. A check, for instance, has a limited use. It is acceptable only to those who know and have faith in the drawer's responsibility, since the bank assumes no obligations to the payee. When the depositor is about to travel or to deal with strangers and will need varying sums of money at different times, it is obvious that a check will not serve his purpose, since strangers will be loath to cash it. It is equally obvious that an accepted draft or a certified check is similarly unserviceable. Such types of instruments are too inelastic. They call for a particular amount which the holder must take on discounting the draft, whether or not he needs it all. In order to meet this situation and adequately provide for the needs of its depositors, the bank therefore issues a document called a traveler's letter of credit. This certifies that the bearer thereof has a credit with the bank up to a certain sum, and that the bank promises to pay all drafts drawn by such bearer up to that amount. This promise is intended for the benefit both of the bearer of the letter of credit and of all purchasers of drafts from him. The commercial letter of credit is in essence an adaptation of the traveler's letter of credit to transactions involving the sale of merchandise. Its functions are varied. Viewing it as a bank credit, however, it evidences that a certain named person, usually termed the beneficiary or seller, has a stated credit with the issuing bank, which was made available at the instance of the buyer.

---

[19] For a description of the various parties to a commercial letter of credit transaction, see *infra* ch. IV, p. 145, note 1. The operation of letters of credit is considered *infra* pp. 14-18. For discussion of the non-legal aspects of letters of credit, see the volumes cited *supra* note 4.

C. Types of Commercial Credit and Credit Instruments

Commercial credit, as distinguished from bank credit, may be similarly analyzed. First, every sale in which payment is not made immediately involves a giving of credit and therefore a promise to pay. This promise to pay may be implied as in an open account. It may be expressed, as when the contract calls for an acceptance of drafts by the buyer. In either case, it is similar to a deposit in a bank.[20] It is a promise to pay made to the seller and does not include any third party. Secondly, an acceptance of a draft by a merchant, like the bank acceptance, is a promise to pay money expressed in appropriate words in writing, on the bill itself, and signed by the acceptor. This promise, from the nature of commercial transactions, is directed not only to the person to whom it is made, but to all holders of the draft. Finally, there is an intermediate type of instrument. This is a letter given by the writer, usually a buyer of goods, to a seller, agent, or factor, promising to pay money on certain terms. The promise, in this instance, is made not only to the addressee but, in the absence of limitations and by commercial usage, extends to all those who bring themselves within its terms. This type of instrument, to distinguish it, may well be denominated a buyer's letter of credit.

There are thus three types of credit in use by tradesmen: a general credit for the benefit of a particular person, a specific credit to all who bring themselves within certain specified limitations, and a form of credit which partakes of the characteristics of both. The last type involves a general credit, for the benefit of one person, and for a stated sum determined in a specified manner, to all who bring themselves within certain stated limitations.

[20] The analogy is closer in the case of a factor with whom a principal has a running account and upon whom drafts are drawn at varying intervals for various amounts. In the case of the open account between a wholesale and a retail merchant, the amounts due are generally settled in lump sums. To this extent, therefore, the latter situation would be unlike a checking account in a bank.

It will be seen that this last type is closely analogous to the commercial letter of credit. As far as third parties are concerned, it performs a similar function in assuring them that a credit has been extended and that the promise is intended to cover all purchasers of drafts. In the unusual case where the credit standing of a buyer is equal to that of a bank, it is equally acceptable.[21]

These, then, are the various institutional forms which credit may take. It is clear that there is a great similarity in function among all of them. A corresponding similarity of legal rules may well be expected. In considering the commercial letter of credit, we must recognize that it is analogous to all the other types of credit instruments. In so far as it evidences a general credit in favor of one person, the letter of credit is comparable to the general credit in favor of the depositor and the holder of a traveler's letter of credit. As an indication of the creation of a specific credit to all holders of drafts, the analogy to accepted drafts, certified checks, and bank notes is clear and compelling. On the other hand, since it is issued in connection with a sales contract, conditions relating to the sale of goods are inserted within it. These are often the very conditions of the sales contract itself. Finally, the form we have called the buyer's letter of credit is obviously similar in appearance and use and, of necessity, must be treated in connection with commercial letters of credit.

D. Operation of Commercial Letter of Credit

The chief function of the irrevocable commercial letter of credit may be shown by the following illustration. *S* in Boston is selling goods under a c.i.f. contract[22] to *B* in Liverpool. As one of the terms of the contract, *B* agrees to procure an irrevocable letter

[21] First Nat. Bank v. Bowers, 141 Cal. 253, 74 Pac. 856 (1903). Another illustration can be found where a corporation dominates a certain trade in a definite locality and its credit, therefore, is relied on in the same manner as is a bank's credit, see Grays Harbor Commercial Co. v. Yakima Valley Producers' Ass'n, 130 Wash. 567, 228 Pac. 600 (1924).

[22] See *infra* ch. V, p. 178, for a discussion of the term c.i.f. contract.

of credit from a New York bank. *B* does so, requesting the bank to insert in the credit certain conditions of payment, usually those which conform in a general way to his contract with the seller. That is the essence of the transaction. All else affects merely the manner in which the transaction is carried out and the form given to the bank's obligation.

The bank has performed a very simple act in this instance. It has merely added to the buyer's undertaking its promise that the price will be paid upon the performance of certain conditions.[23] The reason underlying the seller's desire for this promise—the whole point of the transaction—lies obviously in the fact that the seller considers it undesirable to rely upon the promise of the buyer.[24] The former, therefore, insists on the binding obligation of another party, today almost always a bank, of whose financial responsibility he is more certain.[25] An irrevocable com-

---

[23] Occasionally, the parties to the contract may arrange for the bank to substitute its promise for that of the buyer. This, however, is unusual. See *infra* ch. IV, p. 156. It is highly important to note that the bank has not in this case *guaranteed* or acted as surety for the performance of any act by the buyer. The bank has merely undertaken to perform a certain act, e.g., accept a draft upon the performance of certain conditions by the seller or beneficiary. This distinction is legally of the utmost significance, see ch. II, pp. 32-39. While, commmercially, no such clear-cut distinction is recognized by merchants, it is submitted that the legal approach to these types of obligations is not wholly without foundation, as tradesmen generally tend to distinguish between the obligation of the bank when it stands behind, *i.e.*, guarantees, the undertaking of another, and when it makes a distinct, independent, and primary promise of its own. For an illustration of statutory confusion on the subject, see *infra* note 41, e.g., CAL. CIV. CODE (Deering 1923) § 2860, providing that the issuer is liable only upon default of the buyer.

[24] Arrangements substantially similar to the one described above may be made by a party not a bank, as the promisor or extender of credit. This is more likely to happen in a small domestic transaction, where the seller desires additional security, not necessarily that of a bank. For this type of case, see Mendelson v. Wechsler, 203 N. Y. Supp. 197, 198 (1924). "Defendants' obligation was analogous to that of a bank, which issues an irrevocable letter of credit." See also Scribner v. Schenkel, 128 Cal. 250, 60 Pac. 860 (1900). To what extent the rules relating to the modern commercial letter of credit apply also to this type of instrument must, in the absence of express adjudication, be doubtful. The solution must be deferred until the law on the subject has been considered in detail. See *infra* ch. III, pp. 114, 115, and ch. VIII, p. 293.

[25] This does not explain the use of a revocable letter of credit, which can only be understood in the light of the fact that the letter of credit performs other functions as well. It is also a method of obtaining capital

mercial letter of credit, therefore, is essentially a promise to pay for goods, usually represented by documents, made to a seller by a party whose primary interest in the transaction is to afford the seller greater security by adding the credit of the promisor to that of the buyer.[26]

This is the true function of the letter of credit.[27] The forms it may take, as has been said, vary widely. The simplest form,

---

and credit, and of throwing the financing of commercial transactions upon those whose function it is to bear this and who are also best able to do so, *i.e.*, the banks and the discount market. This and other functions can be performed equally well by a revocable letter of credit. For a discussion of these aspects of commercial credits, see WARD, *op. cit. supra* note 4, at 35, 192, 193; FURNISS, *op. cit. supra* note 4, at 230; WHITAKER, *op. cit. supra*, note 4, at 167; MARGRAFF, *op. cit. supra* note 4, at 88; YORK, *op. cit. supra* note 4, at 260.

[26] For definitions of a commercial letter of credit see Bridge v. Welda State Bank, 292 S. W. 1079, 1083 (Mo. App. 1927); Second Nat. Bank v. M. Samuel & Sons, 12 F. (2d) 963, 966, 53 A. L. R. 49, 54 (C. C. A. 2d, 1926), *cert. den.*, 273 U. S. 720, 47 Sup. Ct. 110 (1926); Second Nat. Bank v. Columbia Trust Co., 288 Fed. 17, 20, 30 A. L. R. 1299, 1303 (C. C. A. 3d, 1923); and cases cited in the note beginning p. 1310; American Steel Co. v. Irving Nat. Bank, 266 Fed. 41, 43 (C. C. A. 2d, 1920), 277 Fed. 1016 (C. C. A. 2d, 1921), *cert. den.*, 258 U. S. 617, 42 Sup. Ct. 271 (1922); Liggett v. Levy and Union Nat. Bank, 233 Mo. 590, 598, 136 S. W. 299, 301 (1911); Lafargue v. Harrison, 70 Cal. 380, 384, 9 Pac. 259, 261, 11 Pac. 636 (1886); Birckhead v. Brown, 5 Hill 634, 642 (N. Y. 1843), *aff'd*, 2 Denio 375 (N. Y. 1845); McCurdy, *Commercial Letters of Credit* (1922) 35 HARV. L. REV. 539, 542 and references there cited. Compare the statutory definitions adopted by several states, *infra* notes 27 and 41, and those given by non-legal writers *supra* note 4. The arrangement described above must be carefully distinguished from the situation in which the promisor, whether a bank or an individual, extends credit because of his interest in the transaction as such, e.g., where he does so in order to keep a business going and thus hopes eventually to obtain payment of a debt due him. See Guth v. First Nat. Bank, 137 Wash. 280, 242 Pac. 42 (1926).

[27] Accordingly, courts have been careful not to misinterpret the real function of the commercial letter of credit and have not allowed instruments of essentially different economic functions to be drawn into this category. It has been held, for example, that a telegram by a bank, "Am remitting $3000.00 for credit C," does not give rise to a cause of action, Carpenter v. Sparta Savings Bank, 182 N. Y. Supp. 172 (1920); that a deposit slip in a bank does not imply a promise to pay, First Nat. Bank v. Clark, 134 N. Y. 368, 32 N. E. 38, 17 L. R. A. 580 (1892); and that a stock certificate is not an instrument in the nature of a general letter of credit, Mechanics' Bank v. N. Y. N. H. & H. R. R. Co., 13 N. Y. 599, 630 (1856). See also: Liggett v. Levy and Union Nat. Bank, *supra* note 26; Parlin v. Hall, 2 N. D. 473, 52 N. W. 405 (1892); Bank of Commerce v. Shaw Blank Book Co., 22 J. & S. 83 (N. Y. 1886); Sherwin & Co. v. Brigham, 39 Ohio St. 137 (1883); Atlanta Nat. Bank v. Northwestern Fert. Co.. 83 Ga. 356, 9 S. E. 671 (1889); Scribner, Burroughs & Co. v. Rutherford, 65 Iowa 551 (1885). But see State Nat. Bank v. Young, 14 Fed. 889 (C. C. D. Neb. 1883). Here a letter promising to pay drafts was held to lack "the usual formalities, and the indispensable

though perhaps not the most usual one, is a letter addressed to the seller, promising to accept drafts drawn by the seller or beneficiary on the issuer of the credit. The letter, however, may be addressed to the buyer or to a correspondent of the issuing bank or it may have no addressee. The promise may be to honor sight drafts; to pay money without the presentation of any draft; to buy a draft drawn on the buyer or some other party;[28] that another bank, a correspondent of the issuing bank, will perform one of these acts; or it may be a subsidiary credit.[29] The letter may be conditional, or clean, *i. e.*, unconditional. It may be limited in time or amount; it may be unlimited; or it may be a revolving credit.[30] It may take the form of a letter, a cable, a telegram, or, in some jurisdictions, even of an oral statement. While many of these variations are, to some extent, merely of historical importance, others have some practical bearing on the rights of the par-

---

requisites of an ordinary letter of credit." (At 890.) The court was confusing the requirements in Coolidge v. Payson, which it cites, in regard to virtual acceptances, as requirements for letters of credit generally. It is a lone decision against the weight of authority; *cf.* Parrish v. Taggart-Delph Lumber Co., 11 Ga. App. 772, 76 S. E. 153 (1912); *infra* ch. III, p. 137, note 104. See Waterston v. Edinburgh & Glasgow Bank, 20 Sess. Cas. (2d Ser.) 642 (1858), where the following was held to be a letter of credit within the meaning of St. 16 and 17 Vict. c. 59: "Be so good as to pay the orders of Mr. M'Gregor on me, which will be paid on presentation here." The statute read: "All documents or writings usually termed letters of credit, or whereby any person to whom any such document or writing is or is intended to be delivered or sent, shall be entitled or be intended to be entitled to have credit with, or in account with, or to draw upon any other person for, or to receive from such other person any sum of money therein mentioned." Within this definition, many instruments would be included that are not at present deemed commercial letters of credit, e.g., buyer's letters of credit, see *infra* p. 18.

[28] This type is usually termed an authority to purchase or an authority to draw. CROSS, *op. cit. supra* note 4, at 293; WARD, *op. cit. supra* note 4, at 43; WHITAKER, *op. cit. supra* note 4, at 171. These are usually considered revocable credits except in the Far Eastern trade, where the irrevocable type of this credit is used. See Bank of East Asia v. Pang, 140 Wash. 603, 249 Pac. 1060 (1926); *infra* ch. IV, p. 164.

[29] *I.e.*, a credit issued by a bank collateral to, or supplementary to, or ancillary to, a previous credit. See DeBary, Jr., Inc., v. Agar-Bernson Corp., 208 App. Div. 645, 204 N. Y. Supp. 18 (1924); EDWARDS, *op. cit. supra* note 4, at 32.

[30] *I.e.*, a credit that automatically renews itself. See WARD, *op. cit. supra* note 4, at 42, for a further explanation. For statutory recognition of this type of credit, see *infra* note 41.

ties concerned. All of them, however, have in common the fundamental characteristics already described.[31] Despite these possible variations, a letter of credit is easily distinguishable by its essential characteristics.[32] It is a bank credit, *i. e.*, a promise made by a bank, usually to accept a draft. As such, it must be distinguished from a promise made by the buyer.

E. Distinction between the Modern Commercial Letter of Credit and the Buyer's Letter of Credit

The commercial letter of credit is used in connection with contracts for the sale of goods for the purpose of furnishing the seller additional security. To determine its essential function that relationship must be carefully considered. It can legitimately be considered a letter of credit only when the seller is induced to consent to a delay in payment because the credit of the issuer has been added to that of the buyer.[33] Where the promise is made to the seller by the buyer, the instrument evidencing the promise cannot therefore fairly be considered a commercial let-

[31] *Supra* p. 16. For various forms of commercial letters of credit now in use, see Appendix A, for earlier forms Appendix B. See also *supra* note 4.

[32] Ernesto Foglino & Co. v. Webster, 217 App. Div. 282, 216 N. Y. Supp. 225 (1926), *modified,* 244 N. Y. 516, 155 N. E. 878 (1926). See also cases cited *infra* ch. II, notes 26 and 27.

[33] Under this analysis, a letter promising to accept or to pay, issued by a bank for goods which it had purchased, would not be a letter of credit. Such a transaction would be analogous to the case where a tradesman's credit standing was so strong that his own promise was as readily acceptable as that of a bank. The implications of this distinction may be of some significance. See Atterbury v. Bank of Washington Heights, 241 N. Y. 231, 149 N. E. 841 (1925). In that case, the statute limiting bank acceptances to time drafts payable within one year, was held not to be applicable to an acceptance by a bank of a draft drawn upon it in payment for goods sold to it. The court said in part, at 239, 149 N. E. at 844: "Without deciding whether section 106 prohibits defendant from accepting a draft payable at a future date exceeding one year, we reach the conclusion that its provisions are not applicable where the bank is the purchaser of the goods sold. The transaction at its face value is a purchase on time evidenced by an instrument for the payment of money and is not the establishment of a credit by the acceptance of a draft drawn on the bank by its customers."

ter of credit.[34] If the seller should sell the draft to a bona fide purchaser who, in turn, should sue the buyer on his promise, the transaction, as the case would arise in court, would seem to be a case of a letter of credit. Yet it is not. The additional contingent liability of the seller should not deceive us. Every accepted draft has a drawer, as well as an acceptor, liable upon it. The important fact to be considered is that the promise was not fulfilling the normal economic function of a commercial letter of credit.

An even more deceptive case is that in which a letter is written by a buyer containing a promise to accept, directed to his agent, and an authorization to the latter, or to the seller, to draw on the buyer. The criterion lies in whether the seller draws or takes the draft on the responsibility of the agent, as well as on that of the buyer, or whether he draws on the responsibility of the buyer alone. If he draws on the responsibility of the buyer alone, it is not a case of a letter of credit, any more than if the authority given the agent were to draw promissory notes in the buyer's name. If the authority to the agent is merely to draw in favor of certain sellers of goods, this generally remains fairly clear.[35] If it is to draw in favor of any person who will discount the

---

[34] This distinction is admirably illustrated in the case of Armour & Co. v. Belton Nat. Bank, 22 F. (2d) 727 (C. C. A. 5th, 1927), *cert. den.*, 276 U. S. 636, 48 Sup. Ct. 420 (1928), where the defendant had sent a letter and a telegram promising to honor a draft drawn on it for goods which it had purchased. In an action based on the promise, the defendant pleaded that it had no corporate authority to issue letters of credit or to enter contracts of guaranty. The court found for the plaintiff, a purchaser of the draft in reliance on the promise, and stated in part, at 728: "It is conceded that the buying of turkeys was within the charter powers of the defendant; and it obviously follows from this that as a means to an end it could make a valid agreement to honor drafts as a method of making payment." The distinction becomes obvious when the promise is made by the buyer, not in a letter, but as one of the terms of a contract; clearly, it is not a letter of credit transaction; see e.g., American Water-Works Co. v. Venner, 18 N. Y. Supp. 379 (1892); see also Wauchula Dev. Co. v. Peoples Stock Yards State Bank, 86 Fla. 298, 98 So. 220 (1923), discussed *infra* ch. III, note 52.

[35] See, however, Watson v. Gray, 4 Keyes 385 (N. Y. 1868); *cf.* Murdock v. Mills, 11 Metc. 5 (Mass. 1846).

draft, it is occasionally a puzzling question to decide whether or not it is a letter of credit transaction.

The agent usually discounts the draft with a bank in order to raise money to buy goods for cash. If the agent is unknown and of no particular financial responsibility and is clearly acting as an agent, the transaction is obviously not a letter of credit transaction. He is looked on merely as drawing for his principal, the buyer. If the agent is a large factor or other well known person of good standing, then the instrument containing the promise may perform the function of a letter of credit, but only if the bank discounts the draft on the strength of the financial responsibility of both drawer and drawee.[36] The nature of the transaction can be tested to a large extent by determining whether the buyer can be held as drawer of the draft as well as acceptor, on the ground that the draft had been drawn by the agent of the buyer pursuant to the authority granted by the latter. If he is not liable as drawer, then any rights that may accrue against him must be based on the promise to accept. The drawer of the draft would then be subject to his usual contingent liability, and the resulting legal relations would be very similar to those arising from the use of the modern commercial letter of credit. If the promisor, the buyer as issuer of the letter, is also liable as drawer of the draft, his liabilities are not based on the promise to accept but on the authority given the agent, and the instrument evidencing such authority is clearly not a letter of credit.[37]

---

[36] This is particularly true when the letter of credit is issued by the writer for the accommodation of the addressee. This case approaches modern usage more closely and is very like a modern letter of credit. This type of transaction, however, was not usual. Even when the agent or factor was given power to draw in favor of anyone who would buy the draft, the authority was in connection with the sale of goods of which the issuer was the buyer, as mentioned above.

[37] Alex Woldert Co. v. Citizens' Bank, 234 S. W. 124, 126 (Tex. Civ. App. 1921); Bank of Michigan v. Ely. 17 Wend. 508, 513 (N. Y. 1837); Kohn v. First Nat. Bank, 15 Kan. 428 (1875); Exchange Bank v. Hubbard, 62 Fed. 112, 116 (C. C. A. 2d, 1894), 58 Fed. 530 (C. C. S. D. N. Y. 1892); see also Bank of Morganton v. Hay, 143 N. C. 326, 55 S. E. 811 (1906). Even without a promise, the drawee may be held as drawer if the draft was drawn by his agent, see Mayhew v. Prince, 11 Mass. 54, 56

In this country, during most of the nineteenth century, instruments containing promises to pay or to accept drafts were usually given by the buyer of goods to an agent, factor, or seller in a larger city. They were not commercial letters of credit in the modern sense, even when the purchaser of the draft discounted it in reliance on both principal and agent. It was not until banking houses in this country began to issue letters of credit to the seller that the modern instrument was evolved.

As a result of this rather definite line of demarcation between the early and later types of instruments, care must be taken to distinguish between the two. It is almost impossible to use the same terms in relation to both. In the modern letter of credit, the issuer is a third party and not a party to the contract for the sale of the goods. In the early type, the issuer is the buyer.

The law relating to modern letters of credit draws a clear distinction between the beneficiary of a letter of credit and the bona fide purchaser of a draft from him.[38] This distinction is of some consequence. In the buyer's letter of credit there is no real beneficiary, in the modern sense of the word, because the instrument is not in fact a commercial letter of credit. An attempt to analyze

(1814); Dougal v. Cowles, 5 Day 511, 515 (Conn. 1813); or the instrument may be treated as a promissory note, UNIFORM NEGOTIABLE INSTRUMENTS LAW § 130. This section applies also to drafts drawn by an agent on his principal, see Alex Woldert Co. v. Citizens' Bank, *ibid.;* First Nat. Bank v. Home Ins. Co., 16 N. M. 66, 113 Pac. 815 (1911); Clemens v. E. H. Stanton Co., 61 Wash. 419, 112 Pac. 494 (1911); Watauga County Bank v. McQueen, 130 Tenn. 382, 170 S. W. 1025 (1914); C. M. Keys Commission Co. v. Miller, 59 Okla. 42, 157 Pac. 1029 (1916); Kramer v. Mid-City Trust and Savings Bank, 225 Ill. App. 575, 578 (1922); Julian Petroleum Corp. v. Egger, 15 S. W. (2d) 36 (TEX. CIV. APP. 1929). The action in all these cases is on the theory that the defendant became, through the act of his agent, the drawer of the draft. It is not upon any promise that may have been made by the defendant in the written authorization given to the agent. The cases cannot therefore be considered as involving a commercial letter of credit transaction.

[38] Courteen Seed Co. v. Hong Kong & Shanghai Banking Corp., 245 N. Y. 377, 157 N. E. 272, 56 A. L. R. 1186 (1927), *aff'g*, 216 App. Div. 495, 215 N. Y. Supp. 525 (1926); Second Nat. Bank v. M. Samuel & Sons, *supra* note 26; Banco Nacional Ultramarino v. First Nat. Bank, 289 Fed. 169, 173 (D. Mass. 1923); Maurice O'Meara Co. v. Nat. Park Bank, 239 N. Y. 386, 401, 146 N. E. 636, 641, 39 A. L. R. 747, 755 (1925) (in dissent by Judge Cardozo).

the cases along these lines would be futile. The beneficiary of the modern letter of credit is the seller of goods under the sales contract in connection with which the letter of credit is issued. He is usually, though not necessarily, the drawer of the draft. The bona fide purchaser is the party buying the draft from him either as payee or indorsee. This distinction between the beneficiary and the bona fide purchaser is clear and definite and of use in discussing the rights of the parties.

In applying this classification to early letters of credit, the result is most perplexing. We have seen that the usual early letter of credit was given by a buyer to his agent who was authorized to draw in favor of the seller. We are tempted to say that the beneficiary is the agent. That is absurd, however, as it would make the buyer his own beneficiary. Therefore, the seller would have to be considered as the beneficiary—a meaningless conclusion for the purpose of comparison with the modern instrument. From this point of view, the seller under every sales contract is equally a beneficiary of the promise of the buyer. To widen the scope of the term in this manner would be to destroy its significance.

In addition, if we vary the terms of the letter of credit so that the agent is authorized to draw on his principal in favor of any banker and pay the seller in cash, an attempt at classification approaches the impossible. In this case, the seller is still the beneficiary. Legally, he has no relation to the letter of credit in any way. It is the banker who must be considered the beneficiary from the legal point of view. As we have been defining the term, however, it is clear that the banker is a bona fide purchaser, *i. e.*, he is buying a draft for the profit that there is in the transaction as such, without any relation to the sale of goods that called it forth.[39] It thus becomes evident that the classification is of no

[39] For a typical transaction of this sort, see Exchange Bank v. Hubbard, *supra* note 37. Compare the cases cited in ch. III, note 25. A similar problem arises in connection with the modern commercial letter of credit when the letter authorizes the drawing of drafts by an agent of the buyer and not the seller, see Royal Card & Paper Co. v. Dresdner Bank, 27 F. (2d) 791, (C. C. A. 2d, 1928); Duncan v. Edgerton, 6 Bosw. 36 (N. Y.

value when applied to the buyer's letter of credit, now under discussion. This distinction between the beneficiary and the bona fide purchaser must therefore be borne in mind only in relation to commercial letters of credit in the modern sense, *i. e.,* those issued at the request of the buyer by a bank or other party who has no interest in the contract of sale that called forth the credit, apart from his connection with the letter of credit itself.

The truth of the matter is that these two instruments, the commercial letter of credit and the buyer's letter of credit, are, from a business point of view, totally different and perform totally different functions. Those of the commercial credit have been mentioned. The functions of the buyer's letter of credit were evidently merely to indicate the fact that the agent had authority to draw drafts on his principal and to delimit the extent of that authority. The credit given to the buyer depended on his own financial standing as if it were a sale in the usual form. The fact that he wrote this letter did not enhance his credit standing in any way. This indicates clearly the essential difference between the two, since the function of the modern type is to enable the buyer to achieve a credit standing he otherwise would not have.

The implications of this distinction are obvious. The buyer's letter of credit is not a bank credit. It is little more than an express recognition in advance of an obligation that results from every purchase of goods.[40] Logically, where this promise is not a promise to accept or where, being a promise to accept, it is held

---

1860). In such a situation, to speak of a beneficiary would likewise be highly artificial. The transaction is more in the nature of the issuance of a traveler's letter of credit, except that the terms of the credit may not obligate the bank to pay drafts unless documents are attached. Certainly the purchasing bank must be deemed a purchaser of the draft and not a beneficiary under the credit.

[40] It is well settled that where the seller sends the documents attached to a draft, the buyer must accept and pay the draft if he desires to retain them. See UNIFORM SALES ACT, § 20 (4); 1 WILLISTON ON SALES (2d ed. 1924) 662. This is the rule whether or not there has been an express promise to accept. The letter of credit issued by the buyer does little more than create an express obligation where otherwise merely an implied condition or an implied duty would arise.

not to amount to an acceptance, the usual rules of offer and acceptance and of principal and agent should be applied. Actually, this has not been done. Because of commercial necessity and usage, the rules have been more or less relaxed, so that the action on the buyer's letter of credit has become virtually an action *sui generis*. With the development of the modern commercial letter of credit, this semi-chaotic state of the law proved very unsatisfactory, and it became necessary to evolve a new theory in order adequately to hold the promisor to his undertaking under the new type of credit instrument.[41]

---

[41] Some states have adopted a few fragmentary provisions purporting to govern the nature of the rights arising upon the issuance of letters of credit. Those of California are typical. CAL. CIV. CODE (Deering, 1923):

"§ 2858. LETTER OF CREDIT, WHAT. A letter of credit is a written instrument, addressed by one person to another, requesting the latter to give credit to the person in whose favor it is drawn.

"§ 2859. HOW ADDRESSED. A letter of credit may be addressed to several persons in succession.

"§ 2860. LIABILITY OF THE WRITER. The writer of a letter of credit is, upon the default of the debtor, liable to those who gave credit in compliance with its terms.

"§ 2861. LETTERS OF CREDIT EITHER GENERAL OR SPECIAL. A letter of credit is either general or special. When the request for credit in a letter is addressed to specified persons by name or description, the letter is special. All other letters of credit are general.

"§ 2862. NATURE OF GENERAL LETTER OF CREDIT. A general letter of credit gives any person to whom it may be shown authority to comply with its request, and by his so doing it becomes, as to him, of the same effect as if addressed to him by name.

"§ 2863. EXTENT OF GENERAL LETTER OF CREDIT. Several persons may successively give credit upon a general letter.

"§ 2864. A LETTER OF CREDIT MAY BE A CONTINUING GUARANTY. If the parties to a letter of credit appear, by its terms, to contemplate a course of future dealing between the parties, it is not exhausted by giving a credit, even to the amount limited by the letter, which is subsequently reduced or satisfied by payments made by the debtor, but is to be deemed a continuing guaranty.

"§ 2865. WHEN NOTICE TO THE WRITER IS NECESSARY. The writer of a letter of credit is liable for credit given upon it without notice to him, unless its terms express or imply the necessity of giving notice.

"§ 2866. THE CREDIT GIVEN MUST AGREE WITH THE TERMS OF THE LETTER. If a letter of credit prescribes the persons by whom, or the mode in which, the credit is to be given, or the term of credit, or limits the amount thereof, the writer is not bound except for transactions which, in these respects, conform strictly to the terms of the letter."

See also 2 MONT. REV. CODES (Choate, 1921) c. 82, §§ 8210-8218; 2 Okla. Comp. Stat. (Bunn, 1921) c. 32, art. IX, §§ 5162-5170; S. D. REV. CODE (1919) §§ 1513-1521. These provisions are based on the Draft of

F. Subject Matter and Problems to be Treated

From the foregoing it is clear that the modern commercial letter of credit must be discussed from two points of view, *i. e.,* as a bank credit and as a credit instrument involved in the sale of goods. In its former aspect, it is impossible to distinguish the formal letter of credit from the more informal promises by bankers to pay or accept drafts. The discussion to follow, therefore, must include as part of its subject matter not only formal letters of credit but also all types of informal bank promises to pay or accept drafts.[42] On the other hand, viewed as an instrument involved in the sale of goods, the modern commercial letter of credit is closely analogous in function to what has been denominated as the buyer's letter of credit. This latter type must also, therefore, also be considered.

New York Civil Code proposed by David Dudley Field in 1865 (see §§ 1573-1581 of the Report of 1865, §§ 2480-2488 of the Bill before the New York Legislature in 1886) long before the modern commercial letter of credit had emerged as a distinct type. In California, these provisions were adopted as early as 1872. From the nature of the enactments, it is clear that problems arising under modern letters of credit are inadequately treated. Performance of conditions is merely mentioned, section 2866, while the general problem of the relation between the letter of credit and the sales contract was evidently not in the contemplation of the draftsman. The problems considered are those typical of the early forms of letters of credit, e. g., special and general letters of credit and the necessity for notice to the issuer that the credit has been acted upon. Indeed, in a certain sense, it is questionable whether these sections can be deemed to apply to the modern commercial letter at all, in view of section 2860, providing that the issuer is not liable until the principal debtor defaults. Certainly, this is at variance with the fundamental concept of modern commercial credits, *supra* note 23, and is clearly not the present state of the law. Because of the nature of their provisions and because commercially important states have not as a rule adopted them, these enactments have largely become obsolete. Even in California, their influence is negligible. But see Lafargue v. Harrison, 70 Cal. 380, 384, 9 Pac. 259, 261, 11 Pac. 636 (1886); Parlin v. Hall, 2 N. D. 473, 475, 52 N. W. 405, 406 (1892). These provisions must be distinguished from the more recent enactments authorizing banks to issue letters of credit, *supra* note 7.

[42] In the discussion of cases generally, no distinction will be drawn between the formal commercial letter of credit and the more informal promises to pay, to accept, or to purchase, in view of the absence of a clear differentiation between them. In addition, this information would add nothing to the necessary comprehension of the problems discussed, since the same legal principles apply generally to both types. In one or two instances, the distinction is of some significance and will be indicated.

Letters of credit have been used for centuries.[43] There has been, until recently, slight litigation involved in their use. To a great extent, this has been due to the fact that the letters, until recently, were issued by comparatively few banking houses with a world-wide reputation for reliability.[44] These financial institutions were meticulously careful to honor the promise contained in each letter of credit, unless demands based upon such promise were obviously fraudulent. Moreover, since these promises were, to a great extent, freely actionable as virtual acceptances, the other type of action on the letter of credit, the action on the promise, developed much later. The first important step in the evolution of this type of action occurred in England soon after the abolition of the older form of action.[45]

In this country, as late as 1886, the California court, in passing on a letter of credit transaction, said:

> There is no case which we have had cited to us, or which we have been enabled to find, which in all respects is similar to the one under consideration.[46]

Since, as we have seen, most of the instruments issued in this country during the nineteenth century and described as letters of credit were issued by buyers and not by banks, and can, therefore, not be regarded as commercial letters of credit in the modern sense, we must be cautious in using as precedents cases dealing with this early type. While the legal problems are, in some as-

---

[43] 3 HALLAM, MIDDLE AGES (Eng. ed. 1878) 339 n. (b).

[44] "In fact, it is a matter of surprise that there has been until recently so little litigation about instruments which have been known and used for centuries. It is a tribute to the keen desire of bankers to honor their obligations without quibble." WARD, *op. cit. supra* note 4, at 10; see also (1926) 36 YALE L. J. 245.

[45] Virtual and extrinsic acceptances of inland bills were abolished in England in 1821 (St. 1 & 2 G. 4, c. 78 § 2) and of all bills in 1856 (St. 19 & 20 Vict. c. 97, § 6). The first case allowing a holder of a bill not a direct promisee to sue was decided in 1867; *In re* Agra and Masterman's Bank, *Ex parte* Asiatic Banking Corporation L. R. 2 Ch. App. 391 (1867). This aspect of the problem will be considered later in detail, *infra* ch. II, p. 44 *et seq.*

[46] Lafargue v. Harrison *supra* note 26, at 386, 9 Pac. at 262.

pects, similar, the economic and commercial considerations, practices, and functions often vary widely. A similar legal result may not be due to similar causes. The distinction, therefore, must be borne in mind throughout the following discussion.

In considering the modern commercial letter of credit, the chief problems that arise are: (1) the rights created by the various types of instruments in general use; (2) the performance of conditions contained in a letter of credit; (3) the relation between the letter of credit and the sales contract in connection with which the credit is issued; (4) the measure of damages upon a breach of duty by any one of the several parties related to the credit transaction; and (5) the theoretical basis of the right of the beneficiary or purchaser of the draft against the issuing bank. These problems will presently be treated in turn. Before doing so, however, attention must be given to the nature of the action which may be brought by the beneficiary, or by the purchaser of the draft, against the issuing bank when the latter has dishonored its credit It will be necessary in this connection to consider the historical development of this type of action and its relation to similar types, as well as certain additional factors, such as the distinction between a letter of credit and a commercial guaranty.

CHAPTER II

FORMS OF ACTION ON LETTERS OF CREDIT

From the foregoing discussion, it is clear that an action on a letter of credit is essentially an action on a promise. Actions to enforce promises may be brought in one of several of the common law forms of action. Each of these forms originally had its own requirements and, to a great extent, still retains them. It is, therefore, necessary to consider the requirements of each relevant form of action by which the promise contained in a letter of credit may be, or might have been, enforced. Before discussing these forms of action in detail, two factors may be considered—the words used as indicating a promise and the intention to become primarily bound.

A. THE PROMISE

It is obvious, of course, that the words used must amount to a promise, *i. e.*, a definite expression of intended future action conveyed to another person.[1] In formal letters of credit, no difficulty in this regard arises since, in practically every instance, a definite promise to honor the draft is expressed.[2] Many informal documents also contain such a promise.[3] Very often,

[1] 1 WILLISTON, CONTRACTS (1920) § 24; 1 AUSTIN, JURISPRUDENCE (4th Eng. ed. 1873) 456.

[2] See the standard forms of commercial letters of credit, Appendix A.

[3] *In re* Armstrong, 41 Fed. 381 (C. C. S. D. Ohio 1890); Bank of Eclectic v. Sturdivant Bank, 203 Ala. 458, 83 So. 321 (1919); Coffman v. D. C. Campbell & Co., 87 Ill. 98 (1877); Lindley v. First Nat. Bank, 76 Iowa 629, 41 N. W. 381, 2 L. R. A. 709 (1889); Nisbett v. Galbraith, 3 La. Ann. 690 (1848); Putnam Nat. Bank v. Snow, 172 Mass. 569, 52 N. E. 1079 (1899); State Bank v. Citizens Nat. Bank, 114 Mo. App. 663, 90 S. W. 123 (1905); Peoples Bank v. Stewart, 152 Mo. App. 314, 133 S. W. 70 (1911), 160 Mo. App. 643, 142 S. W. 789 (1912); Soppe v. Mechaley, 103 Neb. 264, 172 N. W. 35 (1919); Russell Grader Mfg. Co. v. Farmers' Exch. State Bank, 49 N. D. 999, 194 N. W. 387 (1923); Farmers' & Merchants' Nat. Bank v.

however, there is no stated promise to pay, but a clear indication, expressed or implied, of an intention to become bound is sufficient.[4] An authorization to draw a draft is generally recognized as implying a promise to accept the draft when drawn in accordance with the terms of the authority granted.[5] Beyond this, there is little uniformity in the cases in which the courts have considered whether an instrument contains a promise to accept. The court may feel that the language used, in one case, implies a promise and, in another, has no such implication, depending upon the attendant circumstances.[6] A statement that a check is good is generally held not to be a promise.[7] There are cases

Elizabethtown Nat. Bank, 30 Pa. Super. Ct. 271 (1906); Miln v. Prest, 4 Camp. 393 (1816); Wynne v. Raikes, 5 East 514, 102 Eng. R. 1167 (1804); Pillans v. Van Mierop, 3 Burr. 1663, 97 Eng. R. 1035 (1765); Waterston v. Edinburgh and Glasgow Bank, 20 Sess. Cas. (2d Ser.) 642 (1858).

[4] Old Colony Trust Co. v. Continental Bank, 288 Fed. 979, 982 (S. D. N. Y. 1921).

[5] Johnson v. Blakemore, 28 La. Ann. 140 (1876); Franklin Bank v. Lynch, 52 Md. 270 (1879); Barney v. Newcomb, 9 Cush. 46 (Mass. 1851); Nevada Bank v. Luce, 139 Mass. 488, 1 N. E. 926 (1885); Pollock v. Helm, 54 Miss. 1 (1876); Germania Nat. Bank v. Taaks, 101 N. Y. 442, 5 N. E. 76 (1886); Ruiz v. Renauld, 100 N. Y. 256, 3 N. E. 182 (1885); Merchants' Bank v. Griswold, 72 N. Y. 472 (1878); Merchants' Exch. Nat. Bank v. Cardozo, 3 J. & S. 162 (N. Y. 1872); Johnson v. Clark, 39 N. Y. 216 (1868); Barney v. Worthington, 37 N. Y. 112 (1867); Ulster County Bank v. McFarlan, 5 Hill 432 (N. Y. 1843), *aff'd*, 3 Denio 553 (N. Y. 1846); Sherwin & Co. v. Brigham, 39 Ohio St. 137 (1883); First Nat. Bank v. Muskogee Pipe Line Co., 40 Okla. 603, 139 Pac. 1136, L. R. A. 1916, B, 1021 (1914); Michigan State Bank v. Estate of Leavenworth, 28 Vt. 209 (1856); Michigan State Bank v. Peck, 28 Vt. 200 (1856); Jones v. Crumpler, 119 Va. 143, 89 S. E. 232 (1916); Dunspaugh v. Molsons Bank, 23 Low. Can. Jur. 57 (1878), *aff'g*, 21 Low. Can. Jur. 82 (1877); Bank of Montreal v. Thomas, 16 Ont. 503 (1888); Merchants Bank v. Winter, 8 Newf. 30 (1898). However, a general agency to purchase goods does not include an authority to draw drafts on the principal in payment for the goods unless absolutely necessary: Bank of Morganton v. Hay, 143 N. C. 326, 55 S. E. 811 (1906); Parsons v. Armor, 3 Pet. 413, 7 L. Ed. 724 (1830); Scott v. M'Lellan, 2 Greenl. 199, 203 (Me. 1823).

[6] The instrument is judged as a whole and even though formal expressions like "I shall accept" occur, if it is clear from the entire letter that no promise was intended, the writer will not be bound. Musgrove v. Hudson, 2 Stew. 464 (Ala. 1830); Reynolds v. Peto, 11 Exch. 418, 156 Eng. R. 894 (1855); see also Wilson v. Dibbs, 7 N. S. W. L. R. 310 (1886); Bullard Bros. v. Bank of Madison, 121 Ga. 527, 49 S. E. 615 (1904); McEowen & Co. v. Scott, 49 Vt. 376 (1877); Parkhurst v. Dickerson, 21 Pick. 307 (Mass. 1838).

[7] Flathead County State Bank v. First Nat. Bank, 282 Fed. 398 (C. C. A. 8th, 1922); Espy v. First Nat. Bank, 18 Wall. 604, 21 L. Ed. 947 (1873);

which take the other view, however.[8] In a case in which the letter read, "It will be satisfactory for you to honor drafts made against us . . .,"[9] the language was construed as implying a promise to accept or pay.[10] On the other hand, expressions such as "Your bill of £100 to W. shall have attention,"[11] "We have funds to pay check,"[12] or "These orders will have our attention immediately upon the sale of notes,"[13] have been held not to be sufficiently definite to constitute a promise to pay.[14]

First Nat. Bank v. Commercial Savings Bank, 74 Kan. 606, 87 Pac. 746, 8 L. R. A. (N. S.) 1148 (1906); Myers v. Union Nat. Bank, 27 Ill. App. 254 (1888), *aff'd,* 128 Ill. 478, 21 N. E. 580 (1889); Colcord v. Banco de Tamaulipas, 181 App. Div. 295, 168 N. Y. Supp. 710 (1918); see also Carmichael v. Tishomingo Banking Co., 191 S. W. 1043 (Mo. App. 1917); Kahn v. Walton, 46 Ohio St. 195, 20 N. E. 203 (1889); (1923) 32 YALE L. J. 295. When "good" is written on the face of the instrument, however, it is generally held to constitute an acceptance; see (1923) 23 COL. L. REV. 80; (1918) 16 MICH. L. REV. 546.

[8] Conn v. San Antonio Nat. Bank, 249 S. W. 1045 (Tex. Com. App. 1923), *rev'g,* 237 S. W. 353 (Tex. Civ. App. 1922); Barnet v. Smith, 30 N. H. 256 (1855).

[9] Wilson v. Niffenegger, 211 Mich. 311, 313, 178 N. W. 667 (1920).

[10] See also, where the language used was held to constitute a promise: Lamborn v. Nat. Park Bank, 240 N. Y. 520, 148 N. E. 664 (1925); Old Colony Trust Co. v. Continental Bank, *supra* note 4; Garretson v. North Atchison Bank, 51 Fed. 168 (C. C. A. 8th, 1892), *aff'g,* 47 Fed. 867 (C. C. W. D. Mo. 1891), 39 Fed. 163, 7 L. R. A. 428 (C. C. W. D. Mo. 1889); London & San Francisco Bank v. Parrott, 125 Cal. 472, 58 Pac. 164 (1899); Nat. Stock Yards v. O'Reilly, 85 Ill. 546 (1877); Golsen v. Golsen, 127 Ill. App. 84 (1906); Leach v. Hill, 106 Iowa 171, 76 N. W. 667 (1898); Commercial Bank v. First Nat. Bank, 147 La. 925, 86 So. 342, 13 A. L. R. 986 (1920); Edson v. Fuller, 22 N. H. 183 (1850); Ward v. Allen, 2 Metc. 53 (Mass. 1840); Short v. Blount, 99 N. C. 49, 5 S. E. 190 (1888); M'Kim v. Smith, 1 Am. Law J. 486 (Md. 1808); Elliott v. First State Bank, 105 Tex. 547, 152 S. W. 808 (1913); *cf.* Trevisol v. Fresno Fruit Growers Co., 195 Iowa 1377, 192 N. W. 517 (1923); Fisher v. Beckwith, 19 Vt. 31 (1846); and see Note to Ballard v. Home Nat. Bank, 91 Kan. 91, 136 Pac. 935 (1913) in L. R. A. 1916C 161, 179.

[11] Rees v. Warwick, 2 B. & Ald. 113, 106 Eng. R. 308 (1818); *cf.* Annapolis Banking & Trust Co. v. Burwell, 143 Atl. 793 (Md. 1928).

[12] Night & Day Bank v. First Nat. Bank, 150 La. 954, 91 So. 405, 26 A. L. R. 310 (1922).

[13] Murrell & Co. v. Edwards, 179 S. W. 532 (Tex. Civ. App. 1915).

[14] See also where the language used was held not to constitute a promise: McMillan v. Citizens' & Southern Nat. Bank, 37 Ga. App. 813, 142 S. E. 194 (1928); Hibbard v. Parciak, 94 Conn. 562, 109 Atl. 725 (1920); Jones v. Crumpler, *supra* note 5; Plaza Farmers' Union Warehouse & Elev. Co. v. Ryan, 78 Wash. 124, 138 Pac. 651 (1914); Home Nat. Bank v. First State Bank & Trust Co., 63 Tex. Civ. App. 533, 133 S. W. 935 (1911);

In regard to the admissibility of extrinsic facts to determine whether a promise has been made, the usual rules of parole evidence apply.[15] Where the expressions used are clear and unambiguous, no evidence can be introduced to show that the writer did not mean a promise or that he meant a different promise,[16] unless, of course, the holder took with knowledge of these limitations.[17] On the other hand, where the language used is doubtful and ambiguous, the courts will permit references to accompanying circumstances to determine whether or not a promise was made. This is clearly the rule in cases in which telegrams such as "I will,"[18] or "Yes, when cattle consigned to us,"[19] are sent. They must be referred to previous telegrams, to which they are replies, in order to be understood. They may then be shown

---

Nichols v. Commercial Bank, 55 Mo. App. 81 (1893); Atlanta Nat. Bank v. Northwestern Fert. Co., 83 Ga. 356, 9 S. E. 671 (1889), 80 Ga. 629, 5 S. E. 793 (1888); Bank of Springfield v. First Nat. Bank, 30 Mo. App. 271 (1888); Maritime Bank v. Union Bank, 4 Mont. L. R. 244 (1888); Bank of Commerce v. J. G. Shaw Blank Book Co., 22 J. & S. 83 (N. Y. 1886); Fairchild v. Feltman, 32 Hun. 398 (N. Y. 1884); State Nat. Bank v. Young, 14 Fed. 889 (C. C. D. Neb. 1883); Smith v. Milton, 133 Mass. 369 (1882); Cook v. Baldwin, 120 Mass. 317 (1876); DeLiquero & Crozier v. Munson, 11 Heisk. 15 (Tenn. 1872); Walker v. Lide, 1 Rich. L. 249 (S. C. 1845); Robbins v. Lambeth, 2 Rob. 304 (La. 1842); Martin v. Bacon, 2 Mill. Const. L. 132 (S. C. 1818); Anderson v. Heath, 4 M. & S. 303, 105 Eng. R. 847 (1815); Powell v. Jones, 1 Esp. 17 (1793). See also *supra* ch. I, note 27. In Miln v. Prest, *supra* note 3, the question of whether the oral expressions used constituted a promise was left to the jury; also *cf.* Smith v. Brown, 6 Taunt. 340, 128 Eng. R. 1066 (1815), with the above cases, though in this case the plaintiff, who was the drawer, recovered, partly at least, on the ground that the court felt that the defendant had defrauded him of the money.

[15] See also the discussion, *infra* ch. III, p. 104, of the right of purchasers to rely on the letter of credit.

[16] Pollock v. Helm, *supra* note 5; Merchants Bank v. Winter, *supra* note 5.

[17] For an example of the admissibility of extrinsic evidence where known to all parties, see also: Michigan State Bank v. Estate of Leavenworth, *supra* note 5; Michigan State Bank v. Peck, *supra* note 5; Nevada Bank v. Luce, *supra* note 5; Schimmelpennich v. Bayard, 1 Pet. 264, 7 L. Ed. 138 (1828).

[18] Oil Well Supply Co. v. MacMurphey, 119 Minn. 500, 138 N. W. 784 (1912).

[19] Sigel-Campion Live Stock Com. Co. v. Davis, 69 Colo. 511, 194 Pac. 468 (1921); see also First Nat. Bank of Dunn v. First Nat. Bank of Massillon, 210 Fed. 542 (N. D. Ohio 1913); Henrietta Nat. Bank v. State Nat. Bank, 80 Tex. 648, 16 S. W. 321 (1891).

to be, in effect, promises to pay and authorizations to draw. This is true not merely of telegrams but of any general correspondence from which a promise to pay may be gathered.[20] If, however, the attendant circumstances show no such intention, the writer cannot be held under a promise to pay.[21]

B. A Letter of Credit as a Primary Obligation

A letter of credit is a promise by a bank to accept or to purchase drafts or to pay cash upon the performance of certain conditions. It is not, therefore, a promise to pay if the buyer does not pay, a promise made collaterally to the buyer's obligation, as further security to the seller of the goods. The bank is neither a guarantor nor a surety, even though normally, as will be indicated presently, the buyer is not discharged by the issuance of a letter of credit but continues bound to the seller under the sales contract. The issuing bank has incurred a distinct, independent obligation contingent upon the performance of certain conditions contained in the letter of credit.[22] The rules governing the obligations of sureties and

[20] Ruiz v. Renauld, *supra* note 5; see also Exchange Bank v. Hubbard, 58 Fed. 530 (C. C. S. D. N. Y. 1892), 62 Fed. 112 (C. C. A. 2d, 1894), 72 Fed. 234 (C. C. A. 2d, 1896), *cert. den.*, 163 U. S. 690, 16 Sup. Ct. 1202 (1896); Smith v. Brown, *supra* note 13.

[21] First Nat. Bank v. Clark, 61 Md. 400 (1883). There the telegram sued on read: "You can draw for $750 . . . is our action satisfactory." The attendant circumstances showed that no agreement was reached and recovery was properly denied; *cf.* Trevisol v. Fresno Fruit Growers Co., *supra* note 9; Kahn v. Walton, *supra* note 6. In Nevada Bank v. Luce, *supra* note 5, the telegram sued on read: "If you decide to sell, draw $2,500 on demand; if not, draw not over $1,500." From previous telegrams, this was clearly not intended as an authority to draw but was merely a repetition of a previous telegram sent by the defendant which the addressee had already used in discounting a draft. To see, however, how the first telegram could be taken into consideration is difficult, inasmuch as the one in question was definite and complete on its face. A better basis for the decision is that the plaintiff as the addressee's bank and as the purchaser of the first draft under the original telegram should have known that the second telegram referred to the same transaction and that the second draft therefore was without authority; see *infra* ch. III, note 29.

[22] In this connection, it is immaterial whether the buyer pays cash for the opening of the credit or whether the credit is issued in reliance upon his undertaking to indemnify the bank, which may or may not require the

guarantors have no application. Accordingly, the bank is not discharged by any indulgence granted to the buyer,[23] nor can the requirements of the Statute of Frauds, with respect to promises to answer for the debt or default of another, be deemed to apply to letters of credit.[24] The distinction is also important from

---

deposit of collateral as additional security. The bank, in issuing the letter of credit, represents that it has received consideration which it considers adequate. The beneficiary of the credit is entitled to rely upon that representation. That the sales contract and the letter of credit are distinct obligations has been repeatedly recognized by the courts, *infra*, ch. VI, p. 223. As between bank and buyer, the method used by the buyer in inducing the bank to issue the credit is of great importance and has considerable bearing in determining the party ultimately bound to pay for the sale of the goods by the beneficiary of the credit to the buyer. The beneficiary, however, as a general rule, knows nothing of these details and is not a party to them. Consequently, his legal position cannot be deemed to have been altered in any way because of them. In particular instances, the bank may be substituted for the buyer, so that the beneficiary would then look only to the bank for payment, see *infra* ch. IV, p. 155. For a somewhat different approach to this problem, see McCurdy, *Commercial Letters of Credit* (1922) 35 HARV. L. REV. 715, 737.

[23] It does not follow, however, that the buyer is not discharged by any indulgence or extension granted to the issuing bank; see *infra* ch. IV, p. 157.

[24] At common law, it was accordingly recognized, as a general rule, that parol promises to accept or to pay drafts were not barred by the statute of frauds as promises to answer for the debt or default of another. BROWNE, STATUTE OF FRAUDS (5th ed. 1895) 217 *et seq.*; Barcroft v. Denny, 5 Houst. 9 (Del. 1875); Nelson v. First Nat. Bank, 48 Ill. 36 (1868); Nelson v. Ravens, 3 Ill. App. 565 (1878); Edward Hines Lumber Co. v. Anderson, 141 Ill. App. 527 (1908); Spurgeon v. Swain, 13 Ind. App. 188, 41 N. E. 397 (1895); Crowell v. Van Bibber, 18 La. Ann. 637 (1866); McCutchen v. Rice, 56 Miss. 455 (1879); Leonard v. Mason, 1 Wend. 522 (N. Y. 1828); Spaulding v. Andrews, 48 Pa. 411 (1864); Lemmon v. Box, 20 Tex. 329 (1857); Milmo Nat. Bank v. Cobbs, 53 Tex. Civ. App. 1, 115 S. W. 345 (1908); Fisher v. Beckwith, *supra* note 9; Kelley v. Greenough, 9 Wash. 659, 38 Pac. 158 (1894); Townsley v. Sumrall, 2 Pet. 170, 7 L. Ed. 386 (1829); Van Reimsdyk v. Kane, 28 Fed. Cas. No. 16,872, at p. 1071 (C. C. D. R. I. 1813), modified *sub nom.* Clark's Ex'rs v. Van Reimsdyk, 9 Cranch 153, 3 L. Ed. 688 (1815); Taylor v. Hilary, 1 C. M. & R. 741, 149 Eng. R. 1279 (1835).

While the form of the draft in question cannot always be judged from the reports, the foregoing cases are examples of the validity of parol promises to accept negotiable bills of exchange. There is no reason why this rule should not apply to non-negotiable bills of exchange or orders to pay money. If the promisor is expressing a primary liability, the principle is the same. The more closely the order approximates the normal bill of exchange, the greater is the presumption that the promisor was undertaking a primary obligation. "It has been often held that an oral acceptance of a bill of exchange is valid. . . . It seems that this rule applies equally to an oral acceptance or promise to pay made for a valuable consideration upon an order for the payment of money, which, by reason of uncertainty as to the time or amount of the payment, or of other contingencies, is not tech-

another point of view, since national banks, as well as most

---

nically a bill of exchange. . . . But this general doctrine applies only to bills of exchange and orders which are not, in reference to the purposes for which they are given, such contracts as are required to be in writing under the statute of frauds." O'Connell v. Mount Holyoke College, 174 Mass. 511, 513, 55 N. E. 460 (1899). In the following cases accordingly, parol promises to accept or pay orders which, apparently, were not negotiable, were held binding. Espalla v. Wilson, 86 Ala. 487, 5 So. 867 (1888); Ragsdale v. Gresham, 141 Ala. 308, 37 So. 367 (1904); Hughes v. Fisher 10 Colo. 383, 15 Pac. 702 (1887); Jarvis v. Wilson, 46 Conn. 90 (1878); Davis v. Rittenhouse & Embree Co., 72 Ill. App. 58 (1897); Miller v. Neihaus, 51 Ind. 401, 403 (1875); Indiana Manufacturing Co. v. Porter, 75 Ind. 428 (1881); Louisville, Evansville & St. Louis Ry. v. Caldwell, 98 Ind. 245 (1884); Comstock v. Norton, 36 Mich. 277 (1877); Lavell v. Frost, 16 Mont. 93, 40 Pac. 146 (1895); Dull v. Bricker, 76 Pa. 255, 260 (1874); Montague v. Myers, 11 Heisk. 539 (Tenn. 1872); Neumann v. Shroeder, 71 Tex. 81, 8 S. W. 632 (1888); Arnold v. Sprague, 34 Vt. 402, 410 (1861); *In re* Estate of Goddard, 66 Vt. 415, 29 Atl. 634 (1894); Shields v. Middleton, 21 Fed. Cas. No. 12,786 (C. C. D. of C. 1820); see also Gallagher v. Nichols, 60 N. Y. 438 (1875); O'Donnell v. Smith, 2 E. D. Smith 124 (N. Y. 1853).

The cases are not uniform, however, see: Plummer v. Lyman, 49 Me. 229 (1860); Manley v. Geagan, 105 Mass. 445 (1870); Preston v. Young, 46 Mich. 103, 8 N. W. 706 (1881); Pfaff v. Cummings, 67 Mich. 143, 34 N. W. 281 (1887); Williams v. Caldwell, 4 S. C. 100 (1872). Some decisions tend to limit the enforceability of oral promises to accept to cases where the promisor had funds of the drawer in his possession or received a definite consideration for the promise, see: Dunbar v. Smith, 66 Ala. 490 (1880); Chapline v. Atkinson, 45 Ark. 67 (1885); Killough v. Payne, 52 Ark. 174, 12 S. W. 327 (1889); Burkhart Mfg. Co. v. Berry, 162 Ark. 123, 257 S. W. 723 (1924); Durkee v. Conklin, 13 Colo. App. 313, 57 Pac. 486 (1899); Chicago Heights Lumber Co. v. Miller, 219 Ill. 79, 76 N. E. 52 (1905); Walton v. Mandeville, Dowling & Co., 56 Iowa 597, 9 N. W. 913 (1881); Leach v. Hill, 106 Iowa 171, 76 N. W. 667 (1898); Winburn v. Fidelity Loan & Building Ass'n, 110 Iowa 374, 81 N. W. 682 (1900); Upham v. Clute, 105 Mich. 350, 63 N. W. 317 (1895); Curle v. St. Louis Perpetual Ins. Co., 12 Mo. 578 (1849); Alberts v. Moller, 8 Am. L. Rec. 488 (Ohio 1880); Strohecker v. Cohen, 1 Spears L. 349 (S. C. 1843); Barnett v. Boone Lumber Co., 43 W. Va. 441, 27 S. E. 209 (1897); Morse v. Mass. Nat. Bank, 17 Fed. Cas. No. 9,857 (C. C. D. Mass. 1873). Part performance could, of course, have taken the promise out of the scope of the statute, see Saulsbury, Respess & Co. v. Blandy, 53 Ga. 665, 668 (1875); *cf.* Parrish v. Taggart-Delph Lumber Co., 11 Ga. App. 772, 76 S. E. 153 (1912); Lewin v. Greig, 115 Ga. 127, 41 S. E. 497 (1902). This discussion of the effect of the Statute of Frauds gives but an imperfect picture of the situation and is merely of historical interest, inasmuch as the Uniform Negotiable Instruments Law requires all acceptances to be in writing and, together with earlier similar statutes, has had a far greater influence on oral promises to accept or to pay. All cases cited above turn on that section of the Statute of Frauds relating to a promise to pay the debt of another. In a state like Georgia, where the statute specifically provided that an acceptance had to be in writing, the problems were identical with those arising when this provision was put into the laws governing bills and notes and will be discussed later when these statutes are considered in detail, *infra* ch. III, p. 117.

state banks, are not allowed to guarantee the performance of obligations of a third party.[25]

To decide what is an independent promise to pay, is often a matter of some difficulty.[26] The courts have recognized that the determination of the question lies not in the form of the promise, but in the words used, in view of the nature of the transaction. Even where the word "guaranty" is used, if the assumption of a distinct, independent obligation is indicated, it will be so held.

It is true that in the exchange of letters and telegrams the word "guarantee" is continually used; we may even assume that, if the men of affairs who composed the various writings had been asked (before the price of sugar fell and counsel were consulted) what they had done, the answer might have been that Pan-American had guaranteed payment by some one of a letter of credit. But it is clear that the legal effect of what men do is not determined by the names they affix to their deeds. The essential nature of

---

[25] 1 MORSE, BANKS & BANKING (6th ed. 1928) § 65; see also American Surety Co. v. Philippine Nat. Bank, 245 N. Y. 116, 156 N. E. 634 (1927), *cert. den.*, 275 U. S. 549, 48 Sup. Ct. 86 (1927); Stockyards Nat. Bank v. Brown, 81 Colo. 331, 255 Pac. 624 (1927). The distinction, however, between a guaranty and a letter of credit has been recognized and it has often been held that banks have the power to issue letters of credit. See *infra* notes 26 and 27, and *supra* ch. I, note 7.

[26] For cases holding promises to be primary, see: Monark Metal & S. Co. v. Schmidt, 195 Wis. 294, reported *sub. nom.*, Monark Metal & Supply Co. v. General Metal & Refining Co., 218 N. W. 179 (1928); Russell Grader Mfg. Co. v. Farmers' Exchange State Bank, 49 N. D. 999, 194 N. W. 387 (1923); Peoples Bank v. Stewart, 152 Mo. App. 314, 133 S. W. 70 (1911), 160 Mo. App. 643, 142 S.W. 789 (1912); Lyon v. Van Raden, 126 Mich. 259, 85 N. W. 727 (1901); Scribner v. Schenkel, 128 Cal. 250, 60 Pac. 860 (1900); London and San Fran. Bank v. Parrott, *supra* note 9; *infra* notes 27 and 30. For cases holding promises to be collateral, see: Moers v. Norske Handelsbank, 191 App. Div. 114, 180 N. Y. Supp. 743 (1920); Stevens v. Merchants Bank, 30 Man. 46, 59 (1919); Holmes v. Schwab & Sons, 141 Ga. 44, 80 S. E. 313 (1913); Thilmany v. Iowa Paper Bag Co., 108 Iowa 333, 79 N. W. 68 (1899); Commercial Nat. Bank v. Pirie, 82 Fed. 799 (C. C. A. 8th, 1897); Globe Printing Co. v. Bickley, 73 Mo. App. 499 (1898); Scribner, Burroughs & Co. v. Rutherford, 65 Iowa 551, 22 N. W. 670 (1885); Adams v. Jones, 12 Pet. 207, 9 L. Ed. 1058 (1838); Douglass v. Reynolds, 7 Pet. 113, 8 L. Ed. 626 (1833); see also Wakefield v. Greenhood, 29 Cal. 597 (1866). For some doubtful decisions holding promises to be collateral, see: Merchants' Bank v. Baird, 160 Fed. 642, 17 L. R. A. (N. S.) 526 (C. C. A. 8th, 1908); Bowen v. Needles Nat. Bank, 87 Fed. 430 (C. C. S. D. Cal. 1898), *aff'd*, 94 Fed. 925 (C. C. A. 9th, 1899), *cert. den.*, 176 U. S. 682, 20 Sup. Ct. 1024 (1900). For typical cases of guaranties, see: Dewey Column & Monumental Works v. Ryan, 221 N. W. 800 (Iowa 1928); Citizens' Bank v. Clements, 172 Ark. 1023, 291 S. W. 439 (1927); Bank of Buchanan County v. Continental Nat. Bank, 277 Fed. 385 (C. C. A. 8th, 1921). See also Simpson v. Dolan, 16 Ont. L. R. 459 (1908).

their acts determines, and the law has its own names for the results they achieve. Undoubtedly the names by which men describe their acts are evidence of the nature of their doings, often strong evidence; but acts control names, and that deeds speak louder than words is good law.[27]

Similarly, if the instrument taken as a whole indicates that the issuer incurred only a contingent liability, e. g., as a surety or guarantor, the courts will give it this effect, even though it contains the term letter of credit.[28]

The chief difficulty in this connection has arisen in the interpretation of promises made by banks to honor or pay drafts drawn by the seller on the buyer. Some decisions treat this type of promise as a guaranty and *ultra vires*;[29] others merely consider the form of the draft as one element in determining whether or not the bank is a primary obligor or merely a guarantor.[30]

---

[27] Pan-American Bank & Trust Co. v. Nat. City Bank, 6 F. (2d) 762, 766 (C. C. A. 2d, 1925), *cert. den.*, 269 U. S. 554, 46 Sup. Ct. 18 (1925); see also: Bridge v. Welda State Bank, 292 S. W. 1079 (Mo. App. 1927); Second Nat. Bank v. Columbia Trust Co., 288 Fed. 17, 30 A. L. R. 1299 (C. C. A. 3d, 1923); Bank of Italy v. Merchants Nat. Bank, 113 Misc. 314, 185 N. Y. Supp. 43 (1920), *aff'd*, 197 App. Div. 150, 188 N. Y. Supp. 183 (1921), 204 App. Div. 903, 197 N. Y. Supp. 897 (1922), *rev'd*, 236 N. Y. 106, 140 N. E. 211 (1923), *cert. den.*, 264 U. S. 581, 44 Sup. Ct. 331 (1924); Border Nat. Bank v. American Nat. Bank, 282 Fed. 73 (C. C. A. 5th, 1922), *cert. den.*, 260 U. S. 701, 43 Sup. Ct. 96 (1922); Bank of Plant City v. Canal-Commercial Trust & Savings Bank, 270 Fed. 477 (C. C. A. 5th, 1921); Lyon v. Van Raden, *supra* note 26; Omaha Nat. Bank v. First Nat. Bank, 59 Ill. 428 (1871); Decatur Bank v. St. Louis Bank, 21 Wall. 294, 22 L. Ed. 560 (1874); see also Commercial Trust Co. v. American Trust Co., 256 Mass. 58, 63, 152 N. E. 104, 106 (1926). For an example of undue emphasis on the word "guaranty," see Merchants' Bank v. Baird, *supra* note 26.

[28] Emerson-Brantingham Implement Co. v. Raugstad, 65 Mont. 297, 211 Pac. 305 (1922). The writer headed the instrument "letter of credit," yet the court held it to be a guaranty. Fletcher Guano Co. v. Burnside, 142 Ga. 803, 83 S. E. 935 (1914); Cheever v. Schall, 87 Hun 32, 33 N. Y. Supp. 751 (1895).

[29] "It is drafts of this character that the defendant agreed to 'accept.' Had the drafts been drawn on the defendant bank and it had agreed to pay them, its liability would be unquestioned." Nat. Bank of Brunswick v. Sixth Nat. Bank, 212 Pa. 238, 242, 61 Atl. 889, 891 (1905); Bank of Barnwell v. Sixth Nat. Bank, 28 Pa. Super. Ct. 413 (1905); First Nat. Bank v. Nat. Produce Bank, 239 Ill. App. 376 (1926); Alex Woldert Co. v. Citizens' Bank, 234 S. W. 124 (Tex. Civ. App. 1921); First Nat. Bank v. American Nat. Bank, 173 Mo. 153, 72 S. W. 1059 (1903); Groos v. Brewster, 55 S. W. 590 (Tex. Civ. App. 1900); see also Renfrow v. Citizens' State Bank, 158 N. E. 919 (Ind. App. 1927).

[30] Bridge v. Welda State Bank, *supra* note 27; Watson v. Jackson, 264 S. W. 603 (Tex. Civ. App. 1924); Bank of Plant City v. Canal-Commercial

While the distinction between guaranties and letters of credit is generally recognized today, some of the cases show much confusion in terminology. Though as a rule the correct result is reached, courts occasionally describe as a guaranty an instrument which should more properly be denominated a letter of credit.[31]

Trust & Savings Bank, *supra* note 27; Bank of Lumpkin v. Peoples Bank, 27 Ga. App. 459, 108 S. E. 835 (1921); see also Omaha Nat. Bank v. First Nat. Bank, 59 Ill. 428 (1871). This element is often made a convenient point of distinction; Lanusse v. Barker, 3 Wheat. 101, 146, 4 L. Ed. 343, 356 (1818). "Had it contained a mere guaranty of bills to be drawn on T. & Son . . . but where the defendant confers the right to draw upon himself . . . we consider it an original substantive undertaking." Generally speaking, where the seller is authorized to draw directly on the bank, the obligation is deemed primary; *cf.* however, Bowen v. Needles Nat. Bank, *supra* note 26; Merchants' Bank v. Baird, *supra* note 26.

Another solution adopted by the courts is to hold that the promise to pay a draft drawn on another is a guaranty but that the bank is estopped from denying its liability. Where the facts on which the estoppel is based are the normal facts of this type of transaction, the court is either allowing the bank to guarantee the performance of commercial transactions or else it is considering the obligation of the bank as one variety of the type incurred under a letter of credit. McCornick & Co. v. Citizens' Bank, 304 Mo. 270, 263 S. W. 152 (1924); Bank of Omega v. Wingo, Ellett & Crump Shoe Co., 19 Ga. App. 177, 91 S. E. 251 (1917); Creditors' Claim & Adj. Co. v. Northwest Loan & Trust Co., 81 Wash. 247, 142 Pac. 670, L. R. A. 1917A, 737 (1914); Farmers & Merchants Nat. Bank v. Illinois Nat. Bank, 146 Ill. App. 136 (1908); Hutchins v. Planters Nat. Bank, 128 N. C. 72, 38 S. E. 252 (1901); see also El Paso Bank & Trust Co. v. First State Bank, 202 S. W. 522 (Tex. Civ. App. 1918); York v. Farmers Bank, 105 Mo. App. 127, 79 S. W. 968 (1904); *cf.* J. L. Mott Iron Works v. Kaiser Co., 131 S. C. 394, 103 S. E. 783 (1920), *aff'd sub nom.*, First Nat. Bank v. J. L. Mott Iron Works, 258 U. S. 240, 42 Sup. Ct. 286, 66 L. Ed. 593 (1922). Where the distinction is not of importance because the bank has power to guarantee the payment of a debt or has failed to plead that the guaranty is *ultra vires,* or because the guaranty is by an individual, it is often impossible to determine whether the instrument represents a primary or a secondary obligation. Chandanmull Benganey v. Nat. Bank of India, 51 I. L. R. (Calc. Ser.) 43 (1923); Graham v. Farmers & Merchants Bank, 116 Cal. 463, 48 Pac. 384 (1897); Manatee County State Bank v. Weatherly, 144 Ala. 655, 39 So. 988 (1905); see also People's Bank v. People's Nat. Bank, 148 Va. 651, 139 S. E. 325 (1927), and *infra* note 31; see also Portuguese American Bank v. Atlantic Nat. Bank, 200 App. Div. 575, 576, 193 N. Y. Supp. 423, 424 (1922); Continental Nat. Bank v. Tremont Trust Co., 4 F. (2d) 219 (C. C. A. 1st, 1925), where the promising banks were held liable and the question of guaranty was not even mentioned by the court. Where the promise is oral, the question whether the bank has incurred a primary or a secondary obligation, *i. e.*, has issued a letter of credit or a guaranty, is always important, since the Statute of Frauds requires collateral obligations to be evidenced by written instruments, see, e. g., Simpson v. Dolan, 16 Ont. L. R. 459 (1908).

[31] Ouachita Valley Bank v. De Motte, 173 Ark. 52, 291 S. W. 984 (1927); Peoples Savings Bank & Trust Co. v. Landstreet, 80 Fla. 853, 87 So. 227

Conversely, an instrument intended to be a guaranty may be called a letter of credit.[32] In other cases, the terms are used interchangeably.[33] The reason for this confusion is that in commercial usage no clear-cut distinction is drawn between the two.[34] Where, therefore, the law relating to the two types of instruments is similar, the courts have not undertaken the labor of drawing apparently needless distinctions. This similarity in legal result was particularly noticeable in regard to the principal problems arising during the first part of the nineteenth century, e. g., rights under special and general instruments.[35] It is probable, therefore, that

(1920); Bank of Italy v. Merchants Nat. Bank, *supra* note 27; Self v. Albany Nat. Bank, 187 S. W. 982 (Tex. Civ. App. 1916); Descalzi Fruit Co. v. Bank of Italy, 73 Pitts. L. J. 954 (Pa. 1925). The distinction is not always easy to draw, particularly when there is no draft involved in the transaction or when the bank undertakes to honor a draft drawn on the buyer; *supra* notes 29 and 30. In Ouachita Valley Bank v. De Motte, the court through the use of the word, "guaranty," is led into a discussion of the law relating to guaranties, e. g., the necessity for notice to the issuer that the guaranty is being acted upon. See also Edmonston v. Drake, 5 Pet. 624, 8 L. Ed. 251 (1831).

[32] Aldricks v. Higgins, 16 Sarg. & Rawle 212 (Pa. 1827); Walsh v. Bailie, 10 Johns. 180 (N. Y. 1813); Rogers v. Warner, 8 Johns. 92 (N. Y. 1811); Robbins v. Bingham, 4 Johns. 476 (N. Y. 1809). Of course, if these had been cases of letters of credit, the decisions denying a recovery might not have been reached so easily, but since they were guaranties, the results are clear enough, even though the court calls the instruments letters of credit.

[33] See e. g., Decatur Bank v. St. Louis Bank, *supra* note 27; Lyon v. Van Raden, *supra* note 26; Wadsworth v. Allen, 8 Gratt. 174 (Va. 1851); Chandanmull Benganey v. Nat. Bank of India, *supra* note 30.

[34] See e. g., Forbes v. MacNab, Fac. Collec. 137 (1816); Chandanmull Benganey v. Nat. Bank of India, *supra* note 30. These cases illustrate the tendency of the courts to treat commercial guaranties and commercial letters of credit similarly, in the absence of legal barriers. See also Lawrence v. McCalmont, 2 How. 426, 11 L. Ed. 326 (1844), quoted *infra* note 35; First Nat. Bank v. Bowers, 141 Cal. 253, 74 Pac. 856 (1903), where the guaranty was by an individual and therefore no question of *ultra vires* arose.

[35] When a document authorizes only one person to draw under it or to rely upon it in advancing credit, no one else can recover on it even though he performs all the conditions. This is true of letters of credit as well as of guaranties. If any distinction can be found, it is merely that the courts are probably less lenient in the case of guaranties. How far the rule of *strictissimi juris* would apply to letters of credit is doubtful. See Krakauer v. Chapman, 16 App. Div. 115, 117, 45 N. Y. Supp. 127, 128 (1897), *aff'd* without opinion, 162 N. Y. 623, 57 N. E. 1114 (1900), stating that the rule does not apply; *cf.* Moss v. Old Colony Trust Co., 246 Mass. 139, 152, 140 N. E. 803, 808 (1923); see also London & San Francisco Bank v. Parrott, 125 Cal. 472, 482, 58 Pac. 164, 165 (1899). To what extent this rule applies

this distinction had not occurred to many courts of that period. In view of the present statutory limitations on the power of banks to guarantee obligations, the distinction is today of importance and is widely recognized.

Because of the credit qualifications required of a bank for the issuance of satisfactory letters of credit, another problem has arisen in this connection and has caused some discussion. The essential purpose of these instruments is, as we have seen, to add the credit of a financially more responsible party, usually a bank, to that of the buyer. A bank, to fulfill this function properly, must be one that is widely known as a responsible and trustworthy institution, particularly in the locality where the letter of credit will be used. In other words, in the typical case of international trade, it must be an international bank. A letter of credit issued by a local bank, no matter how reliable, is of little more value than the promise of the buyer himself, as no one would rely on the credit of an unknown bank. Therefore, when a local bank is requested to issue a letter of credit, it does not do so itself, but arranges for a larger bank to issue the credit. The local bank then either guarantees that the buyer will pay the issuing bank, or agrees to reimburse the bank directly, looking to the buyer for the money paid out. The former method being a guarantee is

---

to commercial guaranties is also doubtful; Lawrence v. McCalmont, *supra* note 34, at 449, 11 L. Ed. at 334 (per Story, J.): "Some remarks have been made on the argument here upon the point in what manner letters of guarantee are to be construed; whether they are to receive a strict or a liberal interpretation. We have no difficulty whatsoever in saying that instruments of this sort ought to receive a liberal interpretation. By a liberal interpretation, we do not mean that the words should be forced out of their natural meaning, but simply that the words should receive a fair and reasonable interpretation, so as to attain the objects for which the instrument is designed and the purposes to which it is to be applied. We should never forget that letters of guarantee are commercial instruments—generally drawn up by merchants in brief language—sometimes inartificial, and often loose in their structure and form; and to construe the words of such instruments with a nice and technical care would not only defeat the intentions of the parties, but render them too unsafe a basis to rely on for extensive credits so often sought in the present active business of commerce throughout the world." See also Bell v. Bruen, 1 How. 169, 11 L. Ed. 89 (1843); People's Bank v. People's Nat. Bank, *supra* note 30.

clearly *ultra vires* for most banks.[36] The latter method of solving the legal difficulty is probably the proper one.

The Federal Reserve Bulletin, in a discussion of this problem, has indicated a way out of the difficulty. The suggestion was made that the local bank appoint the issuing bank as its agent to issue the credit, the local bank acting as an undisclosed principal. It was argued that, since under the Federal Reserve Act a national bank could issue letters of credit, it could appoint an agent to do so for it. As far as the seller and other parties are concerned, the issuing bank would in practice be the only one likely to be held liable on the credit as only its name would appear on the letter of credit. Actually, the issuing bank would look for indemnification directly to the local bank as its principal, and not to the buyer. This method has the approval of the Federal Reserve Board and the Comptroller of the Currency.[37] The problem has been before the courts in several cases. In the first case the local bank wrote,

---

[36] Nowell v. Equitable Trust Co., 249 Mass. 585, 599, 144 N. E. 749, 753 (1924): "The contract of guaranty upon which this action is founded does not fall within the specific enumeration of powers conferred upon a trust company already summarized. It was not an agreement to pay drafts or bills of exchange drawn on this trust company. It was not an acceptance of such instruments already drawn or to be drawn in the future. It was not the issuance of a letter of credit. . . . There must be a dividing line between business within and business beyond the corporate powers of a trust company. This contract grew out of transactions relating to the import of goods. But it cannot by any stretch of definition or description be rightly termed a draft or bill of exchange. A guaranty of the financial obligations incurred by an importer to another banker is different in kind from the business described in the sections delimiting the corporate powers of a trust company. It is not fairly incidental to the powers there conferred." Seligman v. Charlottesville Nat. Bank, 21 Fed. Case No. 12, 642 (C. C. W. D. Va. 1879). Where the guaranty is by an individual, no question, of course, arises. Bell v. Bruen, *supra* note 35; see also Foerderer v. Moors, 91 Fed. 476 (C. C. A. 3d, 1898).

[37] (1921) 7 FEDERAL RESERVE BULLETIN 547. For another method, see WARD, AMERICAN COMMERCIAL CREDITS (1922) 152, 153. For forms see EDWARDS, FOREIGN COMMERCIAL CREDITS (1922) 207, 208. The opinion of the Federal Reserve Board also discusses the question of the effect of the statute on the power of member banks to appoint agents. It decides that inasmuch as this is for a specific purpose and not for "usual business," this method of appointment is permissible, at p. 549. See also WILLIS & STEINER, FEDERAL RESERVE BANKING PRACTICE (1926) 564.

Referring to our telephone conversation of this afternoon, we hereby guarantee the account of Messrs. S. Fisher & Co. of this city to the amount of $40,500, covering their contract with Messrs. Gordon, Woodroffe & Co., for the shipment of sugar from Java during September, 1920. We agree to pay you this amount, upon presentation of delivery order and proper document certified by transporting steamship company that the sugar is held by them subject to delivery on presentation of said order.[38]

The court held that this letter did not represent an *ultra vires* undertaking on the part of the local requesting bank but that, on the contrary, it was a letter of credit. In another case, the obligation of the requesting bank did not rest on a single letter or on the signing of a formal blank sent by the issuer, but rather on a series of exchanges of telegrams and letters. Some of the significant letters from the local requesting bank were in part:

As we now understand the matter, we have opened for account of Seago & Co. a credit through you, with your Rio de Janeiro branch in favor of Hermano Barcellos for about $815,000 . . .[39]

We now return the guarantee in the credit for account of W. E. Seago & Co. duly signed by ourselves.[40]

The court held this was not an action on a letter of credit, but an action on a promise for reimbursement:

We can therefore unhesitatingly hold that the result of the paper writings in evidence was not that Pan-American guaranteed anything; i. e., agreed to answer for the performance of some obligation in the case of another's default. On the contrary, it did undertake and promise to pay City Bank whatever it lawfully paid, the premises considered, plus one-eighth of one percent.[41]

The essential nature of the transaction becomes plain, and even simple, when its development is noted; for what Pan-American wanted to do for its customer, Seago, was to issue its own letter of credit available to Barcellos in Brazil. It yielded to the obviously truthful suggestion that its own promise for so large a

[38] Second Nat. Bank v. Columbia Trust Co., *supra* note 27, at 19, 30 A. L. R. at 1302.

[39] Pan-American Bank & Trust Co. v. Nat. City Bank, *supra* note 27, at 763.

[40] *Ibid.*, at 764.

[41] *Ibid., at 766.*

sum was hardly available in Rio de Janeiro, and it therefore procured City Bank to do for it what business, not legal disabilities prevented its doing for itself. A plainer reimbursement contract, enforceable in assumpsit, it is hard to imagine.[42]

If, then, Pan-American could issue its own letter, it could agree with City Bank to reimburse payments made by the latter on the letter actually issued; a document not differing legally from that originally proposed, but from a business standpoint more available where Pan-American wished it used.[43]

The court here evidently felt that this was an agreement to reimburse made independently and not collaterally and, therefore, not *ultra vires* for a national bank. From the language of these cases, the inference is reasonable that the courts will sanction the method proposed by the Federal Reserve Board.[44]

C. Types of Actions on a Promise to Accept or to Pay

Historically, there are two chief forms of action that must be considered in dealing with the enforceability of promises to accept or to pay. In one form of action, the promise to accept or pay is treated as an acceptance and the action is on an alleged breach of duty by an acceptor. This will be termed the action on the acceptance. It is also possible to treat the promise to ac-

---

[42] *Ibid.*

[43] *Ibid.*

[44] See also Brown v. Mt. Holly Nat. Bank, 288 Pa. 478, 136 Atl. 773 (1927); Southwark Nat. Bank v. Mt. Holly Nat. Bank, 288 Pa. 491, 136 Atl. 777 (1927). There is an able dissent by Judge Hand in the Pan-American case, *supra* note 27. He maintains that the transaction is in effect a guaranty and, therefore, *ultra vires*. The power to issue letters of credit given by the defendant's charter "meant to allow no more than the use of its credit so far as that would be accepted, and did not allow it by means of a collateral guaranty to assume far larger commitments. . . . To extend them was to offer to the defendant's officers opportunities for speculative ventures to which the shareholders never agreed when they organized the bank." (At 770.) According to this view, a bank can issue letters of credit and so extend its own obligations only so far as its own letters of credit are acceptable to merchants. Therefore, even the method suggested by the Federal Reserve Board would be *ultra vires*. This is doubtless a sound and conservative view, leading to safer banking practices. It is not sufficiently broad to meet the needs of the times in financing trade between inland states of this country and foreign nations. It is therefore probable that the majority view will prevail.

cept or pay as a promise, a term of a contract, and to bring an action for breach of the promise. This will be termed the action on the promise. Originally, at least, this was simply an action in special assumpsit. In order to avoid confusion, separate consideration of these forms of action will be necessary, and, in view of the fact that the development in the two countries has been so dissimilar in many respects, separate treatment of the development of the law in England and in America will also be desirable.

Before considering these forms of action in detail, one further distinction should be noted. As has already been suggested, a promise to pay or to accept is, in certain instances, actionable as an action on an acceptance. The use of this form of action has certain apparent legal advantages which will be considered later. At present, it is necessary only to indicate certain factual differences. When this promise to pay or to accept is written on the face of the draft, it is clearly actionable as an acceptance. This is the normal type of acceptance. If the promise is made in a separate written instrument after the draft is drawn, it is also, in most jurisdictions, actionable as an acceptance, providing it meets certain requirements. This type of acceptance is called an extrinsic acceptance. Where the promise is made in writing before the draft is drawn, it may also, under certain circumstances, be actionable as an acceptance and may be denominated a virtual acceptance.[45]

An acceptance of a draft is neither a sacrosanct concept nor a classification fixed by the law of nature. An acceptance, for the purpose in hand, is nothing more than an abridged term indicating a certain factual situation—a promise to pay written on the face of the draft—which gives rise to definite legal consequences flowing from a suit on this promise in a particular form of action. The number of facts included in this factual situation

---

[45] In the absence of statute, the terms also included oral promises to accept and to pay. As will be seen, however, statutes have uniformly required that a promise be in writing to be actionable as an acceptance.

can be increased or decreased and should be thus altered to suit the convenience of merchants.

There is no *a priori* reason for limiting this term, with its legal advantages, to promises written on the face of the draft. In this country, it has not been so limited. Likewise there is no inherent reason why this term and type of action should not be extended to all promises to accept or to pay. As will presently be indicated, at one stage in the development of the action on the acceptance in England, this extension to all types of promises to accept was clearly foreshadowed. It failed to materialize, however, and the English law of acceptances is, at present, far narrower than is the related law in this country.

D. Development of English Law Relating to Promises to Accept or to Pay

1. *Virtual and Extrinsic Acceptances*

The looseness of the early conception of the term acceptance is clearly indicated by the first English cases on the subject. The reception of the law merchant into the common law probably began sometime during the sixteenth century.[46] The law dealing with these mercantile specialties was not fully developed at that time. Commercial usages, however, seem to have become substantially crystallized. A draft was customarily accepted by writing on the face of it. Doubtless, however, it could have been accepted as well by an oral statement; [47] *a fortiori*, it could have been accepted by a writing other than on the draft itself.

No distinction can be found in the cases between promises to pay written on the face of the bill, and those contained in a sepa-

---

[46] 8 Holdsworth, History of English Law (1926) 146 *et seq.* The first case involving bills and notes was decided in the common law courts in 1602. Martin v. Boure, Cro. Jac. 6, 79 Eng. R. 6 (1602).

[47] Marius, Advice Concerning Bills of Exchange (1651, ed. of 1684) 16; 2 Street, Foundations of Legal Liability (1906) 400, 401; 8 Holdsworth, *op. cit. supra* note 46, at 138 n. 4, and at 157; Molloy, De Jure Maritimo et Navali (4th ed. 1690) 278 *et seq.*

rate instrument or made orally. The early cases in particular very obviously recognized no ground for distinction between the two types of promises. In early law, a promise to pay or to accept was an acceptance whether made before or after a bill was drawn, whether on the draft, by a separate instrument, or orally. The first case in which a promise to accept not on the face of the draft was sued on as an acceptance, arose in 1726.[48] Recovery was allowed without any comment on the fact that the promise was not written on the draft.[49] A further development in this direction is indicated by the case of *Ereskine* v. *Murray*.[50] It was there said that, in a suit on an acceptance, allegations regarding the customs of the merchants were unnecessary as the court would take judicial notice thereof.[51] *Ereskine* v. *Murray* involved an extrinsic acceptance. From the development of the law and from the case itself, however, clearly this rule was laid down for all types of acceptances. The court did not have in mind the distinction between promises to accept written on the face of the draft and those contained in another document. So well fixed was the custom of regarding oral promises to accept as acceptances that St. 3 & 4 Anne, c. 9, purporting to require all acceptances of inland bills to be in writing, was not sufficient to dislodge it. The court interpreted the statute to mean that the acceptance had to be in writing to charge the drawer with damages and costs, but that, as against the promisor, an oral promise to accept was actionable as an accep-

---

[48] Wilkinson v. Lutwidge 1 Str. 648, 93 Eng. R. 758 (1726).

[49] Though probably at this time the action on an acceptance was a form of action of assumpsit, presumably the requirements were much less rigid than in the other types of actions of assumpsit; AMES, LECTURES ON LEGAL HISTORY (1913) 160 *et seq.*; note in (1804) 1 Cranch 367, 2 L. Ed. 139; *cf.* 8 HOLDSWORTH, *op. cit. supra* note 46, at 113, 160 *et seq.*; 2 STREET *op. cit. supra* note 47, at 323, 349 *et seq.*; see also Frederick Read, *Origin of Bills of Exchange* (1926) 4 CAN. BAR REV. 440, 665; Raborg v. Peyton, 2 Wheat. 385, 4 L. Ed. 268 (1817).

[50] 2 Ld. Raym. 1542, 92 Eng. R. 500, 2 Str. 817, 93 Eng. R. 868 (1729).

[51] See also: Carter v. Downish, 1 Show. K. B. 127, 89 Eng. R. 492 (1688); Bromwich v. Loyd, 2 Lutw. 1582, 125 Eng. R. 870 (1696); Pinckney v. Hall, 1 Ld. Raym. 175, 91 Eng. R. 1013 (1696).

tance.[52] It is true that these cases all dealt with extrinsic acceptances, that is, promises to pay made after the draft was drawn. Equally true, however, is the fact that no distinction based on the time of making the promise in relation to the time of the drawing of the draft was ever made in these cases or in the writings of contemporary commentators. Neither in the law nor in the custom of the merchants can any distinction based on this fact be found.[53] This view is borne out by the case of *Pillans* v. *Van Mierop*.[54] It was there held for the first time that a promise to accept made before a draft was drawn was actionable as an acceptance. Counsel for defendant argued that "a bill cannot be accepted before it is drawn."[55] Only one of the four opinions mentioned this point, merely to dismiss it, however, without comment.

> An agreement to accept a bill "to be drawn in future" would (as it seems to me) by connection and relation, bind on account of the antecedent relation. And I see no difference between its being before or after the bill was drawn.[56]

---

[52] Ereskine v. Murray, 2 Str. 817, 93 Eng. R. 868 (1729); Lumley v. Palmer, 2 Str. 1000, 93 Eng. R. 994 (1735); see *infra* p. 50.

[53] Some authorities have taken the view that the silence of the courts and the writers of the period indicates that no promise to accept made before the draft was drawn was ever actionable as an acceptance and that the rule was intended to apply only to promises made after the draft was drawn. "The rule being thus settled that a verbal acceptance, which is merely a verbal promise to pay the bill at its maturity, is binding, it is easy to go further and say that a simple promise to accept a bill in the future is good. Marius said that words importing a promise to accept operate as an actual acceptance. 'Call on me tomorrow and you shall have it accepted', was, in his opinion, enough (*Marius' Advice*, 16). The same principle is recognized by others (*Molloy, Lib.* 2, 10, § 20). None of the writers on the *Lex Mercatoria* seem to mean more than this—that a promise to accept a bill already drawn and then actually presented is an acceptance of that bill." 2 STREET, *op. cit. supra* note 47, at 401. It is submitted however that the silence of the writers regarding a distinction of this type indicates that the possibility of the existence of such a rule had not occurred to them.

[54] 3 Burr. 1663, 97 Eng. R. 1035 (1765); see Mason v. Hunt, 1 Dougl. 297, 99 Eng. R. 192 (1779).

[55] *Ibid.*, at 1668, 97 Eng. R. at 1037.

[56] *Ibid.* at 1673, 97 Eng. R. at 1040.

The court was evidently of the opinion that "a promise 'to accept' is the same as an actual acceptance."[57] As a result of this decision, the English courts evidently awoke to the implications of this doctrine. It became clear that, unless some limitations were put on the practice of permitting promises to accept to be actionable as acceptances, eventually all promises to accept or to pay would be so actionable. Evidently, the courts felt that this was undesirable. In 1786, we find Willes, J. complaining that:

> For though formerly it was held necessary that an acceptance should be in writing, yet of late years a parol acceptance has been deemed sufficient. And indeed at present, almost anything amounts to an acceptance.[58]

However, the reproach was unjustified, since, as we have seen, parol promises to accept had previously been given the same effect as written acceptances.

A gradual limitation of this doctrine began as a result of both judicial and legislative action. Lord Mansfield himself introduced the first limitation in the case immediately following *Pillans* v. *Van Mierop,* when he held that a promise to accept was not actionable as an acceptance: "unless accompanied with circumstances which may induce a third person to take the bill by indorsement; but if there are any such circumstances, it may amount to an acceptance, though the answer be contained in a letter to the drawer."[59] In other words, Lord Mansfield introduced a new requirement—the necessity for reliance—if the promise was to be actionable as an acceptance.

In *Johnson* v. *Collings,*[60] the first case after *Pillans* v. *Van Mierop* dealing with a virtual acceptance, the court was evidently

---

[57] *Ibid.* at 1674, 97 Eng. R. at 1041.

[58] Sproat v. Matthews, 1 T. R. 182, 185, 99 Eng. R. 1041, 1043 (1786).

[59] Pierson v. Dunlop, 2 Cowp. 571, 573, 98 Eng. R. 1246, 1248 (1777). These statements were made in cases of extrinsic acceptances. The court, however, felt bound by precedent and allowed a recovery. This feeling that only promises to pay written on the face of the draft should be actionable as acceptances, expressed itself in the growing restrictions in suits on promises to pay made before the draft was drawn as acceptances, in which case it was felt that there was no binding precedent.

[60] 1 East 98, 102 Eng. R. 40 (1800).

inclined to repudiate the entire doctrine and hold that an oral promise to pay made before the bill was drawn was not actionable as an acceptance. The fact, however, that the holder had not taken the bill in reliance on the promise was also made a basis for barring a recovery. The plaintiff in the case was not the direct promisee and, the promise not being actionable as an acceptance, the action failed entirely. The court said:

> This was a promise to accept a non-existing bill, which varies this case from all those which have been decided upon the same subject; and I know not by what law I can say that such a promise is binding as an acceptance.[61]
>
> It is much to be lamented that anything has been deemed to be an acceptance of a bill of exchange besides an express acceptance in writing.[62]

Finally, it was held, in *Bank of Ireland* v. *Archer*,[63] that no promise to pay made before the bill was drawn could be actionable as an acceptance.

> For reason points out that, in order to constitute an acceptance, there ought to be a bill in existence which could be accepted; and to hold that the same act would be an acceptance or not according to the subsequent contingency of the holder of the bill having notice of it, would introduce a strange anomaly and confusion into the relation of the parties to the bill, the drawee being an acceptor as to some and not as to other endorsees.[64]

In this case, also, the plaintiff was not the direct promisee, and the action was necessarily founded on the promise as an acceptance.

The development of the rules regarding extrinsic acceptances was entirely different. The English courts were evidently of the opinion that the rule permitting promises to accept, made by separate instrument after the draft had been drawn, to be action-

[61] Johnson v. Collings, 1 East 98, 103, 102 Eng. R. 40, 42 (1800).

[62] *Ibid.;* see also Miln v. Prest, 4 Camp. 393 (1816).

[63] 11 M. & W. 383, 152 Eng. R. 852 (1843).

[64] Bank of Ireland v. Archer, 11 M. & W. 383, 390, 152 Eng. R. 852, 855 (1843).

able as acceptances, was too well established to be altered, and that they were, therefore, bound by precedent.[65] Since extrinsic acceptances were tolerated, no artificial restrictions were introduced, and they were treated as subject to the same rules as the more customary acceptances. No reliance was necessary, the suggestion made by Lord Mansfield in that regard being ignored.[66]

A promise made to any party to the bill, even after he had sold it, inured to the benefit of all holders. The state of law in regard to extrinsic acceptances can be seen from the following statement made in *Grant* v. *Hunt*,[67] one of the last cases decided before the statute abolishing them was passed:

---

[65] English courts reached the conclusion that the only workable rule was to limit the right to sue on an acceptance to those promises written on the bill itself. "It would have been much better doctrine if it had been originally determined that nothing else should amount to an acceptance than a written acceptance on the bill itself. But it is now too late to revert to that, it having been determined by many cases that an acceptance may be by parol. Whatever weight there might be in the defendant's argument, if the question were now to be agitated for the first time; yet it is material to the mercantile world that this point should not be shaken, if it have been acted upon for a long period. Now from Lord Hardwicke's time to the present it has been understood that a parol engagement to accept is an acceptance." Clarke v. Cock, 4 East 57, 72, 73, 102 Eng. R. 751, 757 (1803). Where the courts did not fear to disturb commercial practices too greatly and did not feel bound by precedent, as in the case of virtual acceptances, they followed their opinions. Virtual acceptances were abolished, extrinsic acceptances continued.

[66] *Supra* p. 47.

[67] 1 C. B. 44, 135 Eng. R. 451 (1845). For cases dealing with extrinsic acceptances and showing that no distinction was drawn between them and acceptances on the face of the draft see, in addition to the cases already cited, Cox v. Coleman, Mich. Term 6 Geo. 2 (1732) reported in 1 CHITTY, JR., BILLS OF EXCHANGE (1834) 274; Powell v. Monnier, 1 Atk. 611, 26 Eng. R. 384 (1737); Smith v. Abbot, 2 Str. 1152, 93 Eng. R. 1095 (1741); Julian v. Shobrooke, 2 Wils. K. B. 9, 95 Eng. R. 658 (1753); Pierson v. Dunlop, *supra* note 59; Sproat v. Matthews, *supra* note 58; *Ex parte* Dyer, 6 Ves. Jr., 9, 31 Eng. R. 912 (1801); Clarke v. Cock, *supra* note 65; Wynne v. Raikes, 5 East 514, 102 Eng. R. 1167 (1804); Anderson v. Hick, 3 Camp. 179 (1812); Crutchly v. Mann, 5 Taunt. 529, 128 Eng. R. 796 (1814); Anderson v. Heath, 4 M. & S. 303, 105 Eng. R. 847 (1815); Miln v. Prest, *supra* note 62; Rees v. Warwick, 2 B. & Ald. 113, 106 Eng. R. 308 (1818); Mahoney v. Ashlin, 2 B. & Ad. 478, 109 Eng. R. 1220 (1831); Mendizabal v. Machado, 6 C. & P. 218 (1833); Christie v. Peart, 7 M. & W. 491, 151 Eng. R. 859 (1841); Billing v. Devaux, 3 Man. & G. 565, 133 Eng. R. 1267 (1841); Reynolds v. Peto, 11 Exch. 418, 156 Eng. R. 894 (1855); Shepherd v. Campbells, Frazer & Co., 2 Sess. Cas. (1st Ser.) 346 (1823); Hay v. Boyd, 3 Mur. Scot. Cas. 9 (1822); *cf.* Cullen v. Maclean & Stewart, 11 Sess. Cas. (1st Ser.) 733 (1833).

On the argument before us it was not disputed by the counsel for the defendant that a foreign bill of exchange may be accepted verbally or by writing not on the face of the bill, or that a promise to accept or pay has the effect of an acceptance; nor was it disputed that such acceptance may be given to the drawer or any other party to the bill, after it has been endorsed away or even after it has become due.[68]

The legislative limitations on the doctrine of virtual and extrinsic acceptances were not based on the fortuitous distinction between promises made before and after a draft was drawn, but proceeded on a more practical basis, the distinction between inland and foreign bills. We have already indicated how the effect of St. 3 & 4 Ann., c. 9, §§ 4, 5, requiring all acceptances of inland bills to be written on the drafts themselves, was nullified by judicial interpretation.[69] Some time after the decision of *Pillans* v. *Van Mierop,* this statute was re-enacted.[70] This time the courts, being in greater sympathy with the statute, gave it its intended effect.[71] In 1856, this provision was extended to all bills of exchange[72] and was finally incorporated in the Bills of Exchange Act of 1882.[73] At present in Great Britain, therefore, no promise to accept or pay is actionable as an acceptance unless written on the draft itself.

---

[68] Grant v. Hunt, 1 C. B. 44, 58, 135 Eng. R. 451, 457 (1845). This language might equally well be applied to promises made before a bill was drawn, but the only way it can be reconciled with Bank of Ireland v. Archer, *supra* note 64, discussed *supra* p. 48, is to limit it to extrinsic acceptances. In addition, it is clear from the report of the case that the court was thinking only of extrinsic acceptances.

[69] *Supra* p. 45. St. 9 & 10 W. 3, c. 17, § 1 (1698) by implication required all acceptances to be in writing. This was never recognized by the courts.

[70] St. 1 & 2 G. 4, c. 78, § 2 (1821).

[71] "The whole effect intended by the enactment of 1 & 2 G. 4, ch. 78, s. 2, probably was to restore the true meaning of 3 & 4 Anne c. 9, s. 5 (providing that no person shall be charged by any acceptance unless written on the bill), which was departed from after it had been held in *Lumley* v. *Palmer* (2 Stra. 1000), that that section referred only to the drawer's liability for damages and costs." Mahoney v. Ashlin, *supra* note 67, at 483, 109 Eng. R. at 1222. This is an excellent example of the manner in which courts interpret out of existence a statute which, at the time of its enactment, does not meet with their approval.

[72] St. 19 & 20 Vict., c. 97, § 6 (1856).

[73] St. 45 & 46 Vict., c. 61, § 17 (1882).

2. *The Action on the Promise*

With the gradual limitation of the scope of the action on an acceptance, the action on the promise assumed greater importance. This action must be treated from two points of view, as an action either by the direct promisee, or by a subsequent purchaser of the draft. The direct promisee could, of course, sue, but he had to base his action on a special assumpsit. There are only a few reported cases of actions for breach of a promise to accept before 1867.[74] These were actions by direct promisees and were laid in special assumpsit. This is a possible method of approach though a very inconvenient one. To state transactions of this type in terms of offer, acceptance, and consideration is not always simple. The early history of the action on an acceptance is closely analogous. In the first case on an acceptance, *Martin* v. *Boure*,[75] the action was stated primarily in terms of special assumpsit. The procedure was found to be very difficult and cumbersome, as an examination of the pleadings in that case will indicate. In the very next case, therefore, *Oaste* v. *Taylor*,[76] the pleadings were greatly simplified and the action rested more or less directly on the custom of the merchants.[77]

The commercial transactions giving rise to the promise to accept expressed otherwise than in writing on the face of draft were very similar to those giving rise to the usual acceptance. The selfsame difficulty encountered in bringing actions on the latter in assumpsit would also be encountered in suing on the former in assumpsit. The direct promisee had, therefore, a very imperfect remedy. This may explain why there were before 1867 so few cases for breach of the promise to accept and why the actions were usually based on an alleged acceptance.

---

[74] Laing v. Barclay, 1 B. & C. 398, 107 Eng. R. 148 (1823); Smith v. Brown, 6 Taunt. 340, 128 Eng. R. 1066 (1815).

[75] Cro. Jac. 6, 79 Eng. R. 6 (1602).

[76] Cro. Jac. 306, 79 Eng. R. 262 (1613).

[77] See authorities cited *supra* p. 45, note 49.

The purchaser from the direct promisee was in an even more difficult position. He could not even sue in his own name at law.[78] Even if a chose in action was assignable, it was certainly not so assignable as to enable an assignee to bring an action at law in his own name. Accordingly in *Johnson* v. *Collings*,[79] where the plaintiff, a purchaser from the promisee, was denied recovery on the ground that a promise to accept made before the bill was drawn was not actionable as an acceptance, the court also denied a recovery for breach of the promise.

> As to the other ground, if we were to suffer the plaintiffs to recover on the general counts, we must say that a chose in action is assignable a doctrine to which I will never subscribe.[80]

In *Fairlee* v. *Herring* [81] involving a suit on an extrinsic acceptance, in which the plaintiff recovered, the court said in response to an argument by the defendant as to lack of privity:

> The argument on the part of the Defendants would be very good if this rested merely on a promise; but this promise is an acceptance, and an acceptance for the benefit of everybody whose name is on the bill.[82]

A purchaser from the promisee could not, therefore, recover. Even an enabling statute allowing an assignee to bring an action at law in his own name could not improve the situation materially, inasmuch as the assignee did not take free from the collateral equities between the original parties. This requirement, in view of commercial practice, is absolutely essential to any sound theory

---

[78] Whatever language may be found implying the contrary is used in reference to virtual and extrinsic acceptances; see Mason v. Hunt, 1 Dougl. 297, 299, 99 Eng. R. 192, 193 (1779); and comments on this case by Justice Story in Russell v. Wiggin, 21 Fed. Cas. No. 12,165, at p. 75 (C. C. D. Mass. 1842); see also opinions of Sir Frederic Pollock and others at p. 70.

[79] *Supra* note 61.

[80] Johnson v. Collings, *supra* note 61, at 103, 102 Eng. R. at 42; see also Parkhurst v. Dickerson, 21 Pick. 307 (Mass. 1838); Benson v. Walker, 5 Har. 110 (Del. 1848).

[81] 3 Bing. 625, 130 Eng. R. 655 (1826).

[82] Fairlee v. Herring, 3 Bing. 625, 632, 130 Eng. R. 655, 657 (1826).

upon which the holder's rights against the promisor can be based.[83] A purchaser from the promisee had to sue on an acceptance or be denied any recovery. In 1856, virtual and extrinsic acceptances were abolished by statute. After that date, therefore, promises to accept or pay not on the face of the bill were not actionable by the promisee as acceptances but were subject to the general law of contracts, with all the confusion and uncertainties that this entailed. The purchaser, if he had any right, had the uncertain and unsatisfactory one of an assignee, or, in rare cases, he could base his suit either on a novation or estoppel or else bring an action as a beneficiary of a contract. Clearly, he had no certain well defined rights, and "business men found themselves doing in reliance on each other's business honor and the banker's jealousy of his business credit."[84]

This state of affairs could not long continue and was remedied by the first case that arose after the adoption of the statute abolishing virtual and extrinsic acceptances.[85] In 1865, Agra & Masterman's Bank gave a letter of credit to Dickson, Tatham & Co., as follows:

> No. 394. You are hereby authorized to draw upon this bank at six months' sight, to the extent of £15,000 sterling, and such drafts I undertake duly to honor on presentation. This credit will remain in force for twelve months from this date, and parties negotiating bills under it are requested to indorse particulars on the back hereof. The bills must specify that they are drawn under credit, No. 394, of the 31st of October, 1865.[86]

Dickson, Tatham & Co. drew bills on the issuer and sold them to the Asiatic Banking Corporation, all the conditions of the letter

---

[83] It may be possible in isolated cases to show a novation, an estoppel, etc. The inadequacies of these theories are discussed later. It need only be stated here that, in order to preserve the holder's rights, such theories usually involve creation of fictions or straining of the facts in the case.

[84] POUND, INTRODUCTION TO THE PHILOSOPHY OF LAW (1922) 277, quoted *supra* ch. I, pp. 2, 3.

[85] *In re* Agra & Masterman's Bank, *Ex parte* Asiatic Banking Corporation, L. R. 2 Ch. App. 391 (1867).

[86] *Ibid.* at 391.

of credit being fulfilled. The issuer stopped payment. Both banks went into liquidation, and the liquidator of the Asiatic Banking Corporation brought a bill in equity to have the amount of the bills allowed as a claim against the assets of Agra & Masterman's Bank. It was defended on the ground that Dickson, Tatham & Co. owed the defendant more than was due on the bills. The defense claimed that the letter of credit did not amount to an acceptance, that there was no contract with the plaintiff, and that, if he took as assignee, he was subject to the equities between the original parties.[87]

The court found for the plaintiff. Clearly, however, it was searching for compelling reasons. The equities of the case, as well as actual commercial practice, were in the plaintiff's favor. These were the basic moving forces, even though various methods were suggested for fitting the result into the normal legal forms of action.

> The letter was written in a double form; the first part of it contains the authority which is given to Dickson, Tatham & Co. to draw the bills; the second part is evidently, though not in terms, yet in substance, addressed to the persons who are to negotiate the bills. It is plain that this letter was given by the bank with a view to its being shown to persons who were to negotiate the bills, and to make advances upon the faith of the letter; and the last passage contains these words: "Parties negotiating bills under it are requested to endorse particulars on the back hereof." It is plain that this part of the letter is in truth addressed to the person by whom the bills were to be negotiated. The whole effect of the letter is, that the *Agra Bank* held out to persons negotiating the bills a promise that it would pay the bills; and it would be impossible, according to my view of the doctrines of Courts of equity, to allow the bank, after having sent that letter into the world, addressed to the persons who were to negotiate the bills, and so held out to them that it would be answerable for their payment, to say that because there was a debt due to it from the persons to

[87] It should be noted that at the time this action was brought, the assignee of a chose in action took subject to equities of this nature against the assignor. 4 HALSBURY, LAWS OF ENGLAND (1908) 386; 25 *ibid.* (1913) 496, and cases there cited.

whom it had given the letter of credit, therefore, it would not pay the bills.[88]

If it be necessary to determine the question of the legal liability of the Agra & Masterman's Bank, I am of opinion that, upon the offer in this letter being accepted and acted on by the Asiatic Banking Corporation, there was constituted a valid and binding legal contract against the Agra & Masterman's Bank, in favor of the Asiatic Banking Corporation. . . .[89]

But assuming the contract to have been at law a contract with Dickson, Tatham & Co. and with no other, it is clear that the contract was in equity assignable, and that Dickson, Tatham & Co., must be taken to have assigned (if assignment were needed) to the Asiatic Banking Corporation, and to have been by the writers of the letter intended to assign to them, the engagement in the letter providing for the acceptance of the bills. Generally speaking, a chose in action assignable only in equity must be assigned subject to the equities existing between the original parties to the contract; but this is a rule which must yield when it appears from the nature or terms of the contract that it must have been intended to be assignable free from and unaffected by such equities. The essence of this letter is, as it seems to me, that the person taking the bills on the faith of it is to have the absolute benefit of the undertaking in the letter, and to have it in order to obtain the acceptance of the bills which are negotiable instruments payable according to their tenor and without reference to any collateral or cross claims. Unless this is done, the letter is useless; Dickson, Tatham & Co., obtain no benefit from it; the takers of the bills obtain no protection under it. In this view of the case, the Asiatic Banking Corporation are, in my opinion, assignees of the contract with Dickson, Tatham & Co., free from any equities between Dickson, Tatham & Co., and the Agra & Masterman's Bank.[90]

It is evident that the court experienced difficulty, not in obtaining the result, but rather in selecting the appropriate legal framework to be used. It was attempting to reach a commercially necessary end by the most convenient legal means. Subsequent English cases have not departed greatly from this position. Essentially, the courts are enforcing a useful and widespread commercial usage. Later cases have allowed these actions at law as well as

---

[88] *In re* Agra & Masterman's Bank, *Ex parte* Asiatic Banking Corporation, *supra* note 85, at 395.

[89] *Ibid.* at 396.

[90] *Ibid.* at 397.

in equity[91] and have extended the doctrine to the beneficiary of a letter of credit as well as to the bona fide purchaser of drafts drawn under a letter of credit.[92] We are not concerned at present with the legal theory underlying the right of the beneficiary or bona fide purchaser of the draft.[93] We are more interested in the elements necessary to support such an action. In an action on a letter of credit, apparently, both the beneficiary and the bona fide purchaser must show an acting in reliance, and the latter, to take free of equities between the original parties, must show he is a bona fide purchaser.[94]

In addition, it is quite clear that the usual rules of contract do not apply. The principles governing this type of action are much more like those relating to actions on acceptances. Slight attention is paid in the cases to problems of consideration, offer, and acceptance. Commercial customs and the expectations of mer-

---

[91] English, Scottish & Australian Bank v. Bank of South Africa, 13 Lloyd's List 21 (1922). See also Brazilian & Portuguese Bank v. British & American Exchange Banking Corp., 18 L. T. N. S. 823 (1868); Chartered Bank of India, Australia & China v. Macfayden & Co., 64 L. J. Q. B. 367 (1895); Union Bank of Canada v. Cole, 47 L. J. Q. B. 100 (1877), where the court found for the defendant on the question of substantive law involved, impliedly recognizing the procedural right of the purchaser to bring the action at law. See also Maitland v. Chartered Mercantile Bank of India, London and China, 38 L. J. Ch. 363 (1869); Nat. Bank of Egypt v. Hannevig's Bank, 1 Lloyd's List 69 (1919). See Smyth & Mandatory v. Hunter, 9 Sess. Cas. (1st Ser.) 76 (1830), which allowed a purchaser of a draft to recover against the issuer of a buyer's letter of credit, though the legal basis of the recovery is not discussed; see also Hunt v. Waugh, Hume 58 (1808); and Farrar & Rooth & Mandatory v. North British Banking Co., 12 Sess. Cas. (2d Ser.) 1190 (1850), which though distinguishable, show the tendency of the Scottish courts at that time.

[92] For actions in equity by a beneficiary see Morgan v. Larivière, L. R. 7 H. L. 423 (1875), where, though the plaintiff was denied a recovery, there was no doubt about his procedural right to bring the action. See also *In re* Barned's Banking Co., Banner & Young & Johnson, L. R. 5 H. L. 157 (1871); Larios v. Bonany y Gurety, L. R. 5 P. C. A. 346 (1873). For actions at law see: Urquhart, Lindsay & Co. v. Eastern Bank, [1922] 1 K. B. 318, 322; Stein v. Hambro's Bank, 9 Lloyd's List 433, 507 (1921); Belgian Grain & Produce Co. v. Cox & Co., 1 Lloyd's List 256, 546 (1919).

[93] See *infra* ch. VIII.

[94] See M. A. Sassoon & Sons v. International Banking Corp., [1927] A. C. 711, 729. It is assumed, of course, that all the conditions of the letter of credit are fulfilled.

chants are the elements upon which emphasis is placed. This is neither the usual approach of the courts in adjudicating rights under the orthodox type of contract, nor their normal legalistic attitude toward the action of special assumpsit. On the contrary, it is very similar to the attitude which resulted in the introduction of the principles of the law merchant into the common law. A new type of action has grown up. Before considering its implications, however, it is necessary to indicate its development in this country.

E. DEVELOPMENT OF AMERICAN LAW RELATING TO VIRTUAL AND EXTRINSIC ACCEPTANCES

The development in this country of the action for breach of the promise to accept or to pay and the action on the promise as a virtual or extrinsic acceptance has been entirely different from that which we have just been tracing. The reasons for this difference are mainly the influences of *Coolidge* v. *Payson*[95] and the New York Revised Statutes.[96] Chief Justice Marshall wrote the opinion in *Coolidge* v. *Payson* in 1817 and based it largely on the English cases. The English law at that time had not yet been clarified.[97] The last English case decided before *Coolidge* v. *Payson*

[95] 2 Wheat. 66, 4 L. Ed. 185 (1817).

[96] See *infra* note 107. 3 REVISERS' NOTES, NEW YORK REVISED STATUTES (1827) Part II, ch. IV, p. 13. "The sections proposed, also vary from the British statute, in not requiring, as a necessary condition of the validity of an acceptance, that it be written on the bill itself. The revisers have been led to make this change, not only from the evident propriety of conforming to the decisions of the Supreme Court of the United States (2 Wheat. 66) but also because it is not perceived, that there can be any danger in admitting a written acceptance not on the bill itself, where, upon the faith of the acceptance, the bill was negotiated."

[97] "But it seems doubtful, whether a mere *promise* to accept a *non-existing* (foreign) bill, even upon an executed consideration, can be considered an acceptance, except perhaps where the bill is taken by a third person, *bona fide*, upon the faith and credit, and with the knowledge, of such promise, communicated by letter." 1 CHITTY, JR., BILLS OF EXCHANGE (1834) 13; see also BAYLEY, BILLS OF EXCHANGE (4th ed. 1822) 142 *et seq.* The texts generally are not very helpful. The treatment given the topic of extrinsic and virtual acceptances is both inadequate and, particularly in the later texts, confusing. Early writers reflected the

son involving this problem was *Miln* v. *Prest.*[98] It represented the English tendency previously discussed, *i. e.*, the attempt to limit virtual acceptances while allowing the doctrine of extrinsic acceptances to expand normally. As has been indicated, this tendency was due to the growing opinion at the time that no promise should be actionable as an acceptance unless written on the face of the draft itself. Marshall accepted this basic principle and recognized its commercial utility. He felt, however, that some promises should be actionable as acceptances so that the purchaser of a draft in reliance on the promise would be enabled to recover freely and easily. The arbitrary distinction between promises made before and after a draft was drawn, adopted by the English courts, chiefly for historical reasons, did not recommend itself to his keen insight. He recognized that there was as much reason in one case as in the other for allowing a recovery on a promise as an acceptance.

> The court can perceive no substantial reason for this distinction. The prevailing inducement for considering a promise to accept, as an acceptance, is that credit is thereby given to the bill. Now, this credit is given as entirely by a letter written before the date of the bill as by one written afterwards.[99]

---

undeveloped state of the law. Later ones have not only failed to treat all the distinctions made but, to a great extent, have failed to treat any in sufficient detail. See in addition, CHITTY, BILLS AND NOTES (2d ed. 1807) 73, 74; *cf.* (12th Am. ed. 1854) 322 *et seq.* (11th Eng. ed. 1878) 205; BAYLEY, BILLS OF EXCHANGE (2d ed. 1799) 48, 49; *cf.* Bayley, *loc. cit.* (4th ed.); MARIUS, ADVICE CONCERNING BILLS OF EXCHANGE (4th ed. 1684) 16; KYD, BILLS AND NOTES (2d Eng. ed. 1791) 45 *et seq.*; 3 KENT, COMMENTARIES (13th ed. 1884) 83 *et seq.*; STORY, BILLS OF EXCHANGE (1st ed. 1843) §§ 242-250; 1 PARSONS, BILLS & NOTES (2d ed. 1879) ch. 9, § 2 and p. 286; 2 AMES, CASES ON BILLS & NOTES (1894) 788; EATON AND GILBERT, COMMERCIAL PAPER (1903) §§ 147, 148; 1 DANIEL, NEGOTIABLE INSTRUMENTS (6th ed. 1913) §§ 504-507a, ch. 19, 2 *ibid.* §§ 1797, 1799; NORTON, BILLS AND NOTES (4th ed. 1914) §§ 51, 52, 53; 1 BELL, PRINCIPLES OF THE LAW OF SCOTLAND (8th ed. 1885) 198; F. Thulin, *The Form of the General Acceptance* (1916) 14 MICH. L. REV. 455.

[98] 4 Camp. 393 (1816). It is hardly likely of course that Marshall had heard of this decision at the time he wrote the opinion in Coolidge v. Payson. It is not cited in his opinion. The cases he cites however indicate the same tendency as Miln v. Prest.

[99] Coolidge v. Payson, 2 Wheat. 66, 75, 4 L. Ed. 185, 188 (1817). The opinion also points out that in no case had the English court rested a

Instead, he created a totally different group of requirements for allowing promises to accept or to pay not on the face of the draft to be actionable as acceptances. One of these, the requirement of definiteness, was entirely new. The other major requirement, reliance, can be traced to English cases. The effect of these requirements will be considered later in detail. At this point we need note only that the result of this decision was effectually to abolish the distinction between the virtual and extrinsic acceptance so laboriously built up in England. Even the various statutes on the subject which have attempted to preserve the distinction have failed to influence the courts.

The first statute on the subject in this country was enacted in New York in 1827 as part of the Revised Statutes of that year.[100] The framers of this statute were also influenced by the English conception of the period that an extrinsic acceptance was a "real" acceptance while a virtual acceptance was merely a promise to accept and should therefore be actionable as an acceptance only on certain conditions.[101] This theory, as has been pointed out, is based on a metaphysical distinction involving the inherent nature of an acceptance, the argument being that one cannot accept what does not exist.[102] To repeat what has already been indicated, the

decision on that distinction. "It is true, in the case of Clark v. Cock the bill was made before the promise was given, and the judges, in their opinions, use some expressions which indicate a distinction between bills drawn before and after the date of the promise; but no case has been decided on this distinction; and in Pillans and Rose v. Van Mierop and Hopkins, the letter was written before the bill was drawn." At 74, 4 L. Ed. at 188. Marshall therefore felt free to repudiate the distinction as undesirable and unnecessary.

[100] See *infra* note 107.

[101] It is interesting to note that Section 7 of the Revised Statutes dealing with extrinsic acceptances is headed "Effect of acceptance on separate paper," while Section 8 relating to virtual acceptances is headed "Written promises to accept." Similarly the Uniform Negotiable Instruments Law heads the section referring to extrinsic acceptances: "Acceptance by Separate Instrument," § 134, and the section on virtual acceptances: "Promise to accept—when equivalent to acceptance," § 135.

[102] See Bank of Ireland v. Archer, 11 M. & W. 383, 390, 152 Eng. R. 852, 855 (1843): "For reason points out that, in order to constitute an acceptance, there ought to be a bill in existence which could be accepted."

fallacy lies in the fact that the concept of the "inherent nature of an acceptance" is essentially erroneous. No inherent reason exists why an acceptance cannot be defined so as to include a promise to accept a draft made before the draft is drawn. As the term is used in the business world, it is a technical word, and its meaning in the law should be governed by such usage. No distinction can validly be made between promises made before and after a bill is drawn, unless based on differences in commercial practice. As will be seen, the general opinion is that there are no such commercial differences. A distinction based on purely metaphysical grounds has no place in the law.[103]

Fortunately, Chief Justice Marshall's view has prevailed and the differentiation made between virtual and extrinsic acceptances has been largely broken down in this country—cases of virtual acceptances being cited as authorities for extrinsic acceptances and cases of extrinsic acceptances being cited when the courts are considering virtual acceptances.[104] To determine whether the promise was made before or after the draft was drawn is, from the statement of a case, often impossible. Occasionally, courts state that that fact is of no significance[105] or even fail to mention it. It is a factor only in a few decisions. All the cases dealing with these problems may, therefore, be considered together, the distinction being pointed out when necessary.[106]

---

[103] See discussion *supra* pp. 43, 44.

[104] For an example of this, see *infra* note 181 in reference to Massachusetts Law, and also the rule in Read v. Marsh, 5 B. Mon. 8, 10 (Ky. 1844), as applied in Anderson County Deposit Bank v. Turner-Looker Co., 2 Ohio N. P. 73 (1894).

[105] See quotation from Coolidge v. Payson, *supra* note 99, at p. 58. M'Kim v. Smith, 1 Am. Law J. 486 (Md. 1808); Howland v. Carson, 15 Pa. 453 (1850); Bank of Morganton v. Hay, 143 N. C. 326, 55 S. E. 811 (1906); Nimocks v. Woody, 97 N. C. 1, 2 S. E. 249 (1887); Goodrich v. Gordon, 15 Johns. 6 (N. Y. 1818); see also: Bank of Michigan v. Ely, 17 Wend. 508 (N. Y. 1837); Carrollton Bank v. Tayleur, 16 La. 490 (1840); Iowa State Savings Bank v. City Nat. Bank, 183 Iowa 1347, 1353, 168 N. W. 148, 150, L. R. A. 1918F, 169, 172 (1918).

[106] The Uniform Negotiable Instruments Law attempts to preserve the distinction. See Section 134, *Acceptance by Separate Instrument:* "Where an acceptance is written on paper other than the bill itself, it does not bind

One more consideration must be mentioned. The revisers of the New York statutes, under the influence of the peculiar English theories of the nature of an acceptance, introduced, in addition to the general requirements for both types of acceptances, an additional requirement for virtual acceptances. A promise made before a draft was drawn if it were to be actionable as an acceptance, had to be "unconditional" as well as comply with other provisions common to both virtual and extrinsic acceptances.[107] Since this statute was widely followed, this requirement was introduced generally.[108] As a result of the influence of *Coolidge* v. *Payson* in

the acceptor except in favor of a person to whom it is shown and who, on the faith thereof, receives the bill for value." Section 135: *Promise to accept—when equivalent to acceptance:* "An unconditional promise in writing to accept a bill before it is drawn is deemed an actual acceptance in favor of every person who, upon the faith thereof, receives the bill for value." Section 135 of the Illinois Negotiable Instruments Law, however, reads as follows: "An unconditional promise in writing to accept a bill before or after it is drawn." This would include both extrinsic and virtual acceptances. Section 134 is also included, despite the fact that under Section 135 as altered it is unnecessary.

[107] The statute in New York was first passed with the Revised Statutes in 1827. The relevant provisions are: 1 Rev. St. 768, Part II, c. IV, Title 2, §§ 6, 7, 8, 10. § 6. Acceptances of bills to be in writing, &c.: "No person within this state shall be charged as an acceptor on a bill of exchange, unless his acceptance shall be in writing, signed by himself, or his lawful agent." § 7. Effect of acceptance on separate paper: "If such acceptance be written on a paper, other than the bill, it shall not bind the acceptor, except in favor of a person to whom such acceptance shall have been shown, and who, on the faith thereof, shall have received the bill for a valuable consideration." § 8. Written promises to accept: "An unconditional promise, in writing, to accept a bill before it is drawn, shall be deemed an actual acceptance, in favor of every person who, upon the faith thereof, shall have received the bill for a valuable consideration." § 10. Rights of drawers in certain cases, not to be affected: "The four last sections shall not be construed to impair the right of any person, to whom a promise to accept a bill, may have been made, and who, on the faith of such promise, shall have drawn or negotiated the bill, to recover damages of the party making such promise, on his refusal to accept such bill."

[108] Before the Negotiable Instruments Law, there were three general types of statutes. The first merely required an acceptance to be in writing, e. g., Alaska, Maine, Michigan, New Mexico, Oregon, Pennsylvania and Wisconsin. In Georgia this was included under the Statute of Frauds. The second had additional provisions governing the enforcement of virtual and extrinsic acceptances, e. g., Idaho, Montana, Mississippi, North Dakota, Oklahoma, South Dakota, Utah and Wyoming. The statute in Mississippi, after providing that an acceptance must be in writing, went on to say, "but an unconditional promise in writing duly subscribed by the promisor, or his agent, to accept a bill, before it is drawn,

destroying the distinction between virtual and extrinsic acceptances, the requirement was often applied indiscriminately to both virtual and extrinsic acceptances, despite the wording of the statute.

Three major problems must, therefore, be considered in discussing the action on a promise to accept or to pay as an acceptance, namely, lack of conditions, definiteness, and reliance. The first two are entirely American developments, the last, however, having played an incidental part in the growth of the English law on the subject.

1. Conditions

The requirement in Section 135 of the Uniform Negotiable Instruments Law that a promise to accept, made before the draft was drawn, be unconditional, can be traced to the New York Revised Statutes of 1827 and, from there, to the statutes of various other states.[109] Though this requirement has been limited in

---

shall amount to an acceptance of it." Miss. Code (1906), c. 116, § 4012. The third had in addition a curious provision saving the common law right of a direct promisee who had drawn or negotiated the bill in reliance on the promise, e. g., New York, *supra* note 107. Among the followers of New York were Alabama, Arkansas, California, Kansas, Missouri, Nevada and Washington.

[109] At common law there was no such requirement. Promises to pay not written on the face of the bill, when held to be actionable as acceptances, were in regard to conditions, subject to the rules applicable to the usual type of acceptance. Since a promise to pay on the face of the bill was held to be valid and binding after the performance of the condition, the same was held to be true of promises not on the face of the bill. Pierson v. Dunlop, 2 Cowp. 571, 98 Eng. R. 1246 (1777); Anderson v. Hick, 3 Camp, 179 (1812); Crutchly v. Mann, 5 Taunt. 529, 128 Eng. R. 796 (1814); Miln v. Prest, *supra* note 62; Smith v. Brown, 6 Taunt. 340, 128 Eng. R. 1066 (1815); Mendizabal v. Machado, 6 C. & P. 218 (1833). Most of the cases merely allow recovery after the conditions have been performed, without discussing the effect of the conditions in the acceptance. In a few, however, the question is considered. In Anderson v. Hick, *ibid.*, Lord Ellenborough in allowing a recovery on an oral extrinsic acceptance, after the condition was performed said, at 179, "This was only a conditional promise to accept and could not operate as an acceptance, till the bill was sent back to the counting house." The condition was the return of the bill to the counting house. The common law of this country was similar. Coolidge v. Payson, *supra* note 99; Goodrich v. Gordon, *supra* note 105; Williams v. Winans, 14 N. J. L. 339 (1834); see also Hickman's Ex'r. v. R. W. King & Co., Chev. L. 132 (S. C. 1840); Walker v. Lide, 1 Rich. L. 249 (S. C. 1845); Stevens v. Androscoggin Water Power Co., 62 Me. 498 (1874); Exchange Bank v. Rice, 98 Mass. 288, 289 (1867), 107 Mass. 37 (1871).

these statutes to virtual acceptances, it has been applied more or less indiscriminately to extrinsic acceptances as well.

In considering this statutory requirement regarding conditions, we are not concerned with the problem of the sufficiency of certain acts as constituting performance of conditions. That question is of no significance here but will be discussed later. At this point, we are interested only in two matters relating to conditions. The first is the type of promise held to be conditional, and the other is the effect of the subsequent performance, or excuse for non-performance, of a condition.

The answer to the first question depends to a large extent on the manner in which the term condition is defined. In the law of contracts, the term condition is used to describe those operative events, not certain to occur, the occurrence of which affects the rights and duties of the parties to the contract.[110] So used, the term does not include acts or promises given in exchange for the promise of the offeror. The performance of these acts is part of the acceptance of the offer. The offeror may make these as complex as he pleases. He is free to dictate the terms and manner of the acceptance. If, after all the acts constituting the acceptance have been performed, the duty of the offeror is still not absolute, but is conditioned upon the happening of certain other events; then, the resulting obligation is conditional, these operative events constituting the conditions.[111] In this sense, therefore, a promise to accept a draft, if a bill of lading is attached calling for a "carload of pigs at 8¼ cents," is an offer looking to an un-

---

[110] CORBIN'S ANSON ON CONTRACTS (4th ed. 1924) 427 *et seq.*

[111] CORBIN'S ANSON ON CONTRACTS (4th ed. 1924) 428. "In the law of contract it is sometimes used in a very loose sense as synonymous with 'term,' 'provision,' or 'clause.' In such a sense it performs no useful service. In its proper sense the word 'condition' means some operative fact subsequent to acceptance and prior to discharge, a fact that affects the rights and duties of the parties." See also: Corbin, *Conditions in the Law of Contract* (1919), 28 YALE L. J. 739, 743; 1 BOUVIER, LAW DICTIONARY (8th ed. 1914) 581 Condition, in common law: "a clause . . . which has for its object to suspend, rescind, or modify the principal obligation." Merchants' Bank v. Griswold, 72 N. Y. 472 (1878).

conditional obligation upon acceptance. It is fairly clear, however, that, with certain limited exceptions to be presently considered, courts will hold that the same promise, where it amounts to an acceptance of a draft, is merely a conditional acceptance.[112]

As has been noted, the term condition is sometimes used to include the acts required by the offeror as acceptance. So used, a promise to honor a draft "for three months sight for $300.00 in favor of *X*" is conditional upon the drawing of a draft meeting these requirements.[113] Yet no court will hold a promise of this type, which fulfills the requirements of the statute in other respects, not to be an acceptance because it is conditional. The term as used in § 135 of the Uniform Negotiable Instruments Law must be given a meaning differing from either of the foregoing, and lying somewhere between them. Obviously, obligations which are conditional, as the word is used in contracts, are also conditional in the meaning of the term as used in § 135. In addition, when the acceptor in his promise to accept requires the performance of certain acts as part of the acceptance of his offer, the acceptance is also held to be conditional. As indicated, this does not extend to all acts requested in exchange for the promise to accept. The problem, therefore, is to determine which types of acts may be required in return for the promise without making the acceptance conditional.

The addition of words describing the terms of the draft to be accepted obviously will not make the promise conditional.[114] A

---

[112] Wallace State Bank v. Corn Exchange Bank, 220 Mo. App. 1062, 282 S. W. 86 (1926); *cf.* James v. E. G. Lyons Co., 134 Cal. 189, 195, 66 Pac. 210, 212 (1901), 147 Cal. 69, 81 Pac. 275 (1905).

[113] Corbin, *Supervening Impossibility of Performing Conditions Precedent* (1922), 22 Col. L. Rev. 421, 423. "A fact, the existence or future occurrence of which is uncertain, and in the absence of which certain contemplated legal relations will not exist." See also *supra* note 111.

[114] Seaboard Nat. Bank v. Burleigh, 74 Hun 400, 26 N. Y. Supp. 587 (1893), *aff'd* without opinion, 147 N. Y. 720, 42 N. E. 726 (1895); Merchants' Exchange Nat. Bank v. Cardozo, 3 J. & S. 162 (N. Y. 1872); Burns v. Rowland, 40 Barb. 368 (N. Y. 1863); Johnson v. Clark, 39 N. Y. 216 (1868); Michigan State Bank v. Peck, 28 Vt. 200 (1856); Ulster County

similar conclusion must be reached where the phrase used apparently lays down requirements additional to those usually mentioned in describing the draft, but actually adds nothing to the acts necessary to constitute performance of the terms of those promises which merely describe the draft. Expressions such as "we will honor J. W.'s check for $5,000 *when properly signed,*" are in this class.[115] No duty to pay arises in any event unless the check is properly signed. Promises, therefore, which merely specify the terms of the draft are unconditional within the meaning of the statute. How is the following promise to be treated however? "Will pay H.'s draft $2,300.00 for stock."[116] Apparently, it is similar to the requirement of a draft for a "carload of pigs at 8¼ cents," which was held to be conditional. But, under the Uniform Negotiable Instruments Law and similar earlier statutes, the former type of promise has been held to be unconditional.[117] It has been interpreted as merely a statement of

Bank v. McFarlan, 5 Hill 432 (N. Y. 1843), *aff'd,* 3 Denio 553 (N. Y. 1846); see also: Van Reimsdyk v. Kane, 28 Fed. Cas. No. 16, 872 (C. C. D. R. I. 1813), where recovery was allowed though the terms had not been strictly performed; and also: Glover v. Tuck, 1 Hill 66 (N. Y. 1841); Allen v. Leavens, 26 Oreg. 164, 37 Pac. 488, 26 L. R. A. 620 (1894); Pake v. Wilson, 127 Ala. 240, 28 So. 665 (1899). In the last three cases recovery was denied because the terms had not been fulfilled.

[115] Selma Savings Bank v. Webster County Bank, 182 Ky. 604, 206 S. W. 870, 2 A. L. R. 1136 (1918); Hough v. Loring, 24 Pick. 254 (Mass. 1837); Bank of Michigan v. Ely, *supra* note 105; Clarke v. Gordon, 3 Rich. L. 311 (S. C. 1832); Grant v. Shaw, 16 Mass. 341 (1820); see also Gates v. Parker, 43 Me. 544 (1857); Greele v. Parker, 5 Wend. 414 (N. Y. 1830).

[116] Coffman v. D. C. Campbell & Co., 87 Ill. 98 (1877). Compare the effect upon the negotiability of bills and notes of the inclusion of such phrases as "as per contract." BRANNAN, NEGOTIABLE INSTRUMENTS LAW (4th ed. 1926) 38 *et seq.;* Ralph W. Aigler, *Conditions in Bills and Notes* (1928), 26 MICH. L. REV. 471, 485.

[117] State Bank of Beaver County v. Bradstreet, 89 Neb. 186, 130 N. W. 1038, 38 L. R. A. (N. S.) 747 (1911). The promise read: "Will pay M's draft on me two-fifty for horses." In Ensign v. Clark Bros. Cutlery Co., 195 Mo. App. 584, 193 S. W. 961 (1917), the telegram read: "Will honor your draft $1,500 telegram attached." The court said in part: "Of course, if the defendant's telegram is a conditional acceptance, then plaintiff cannot recover unless he shows he complied with the condition." At 588, 193 S. W. at 962. See also: Huston v. Newgass, 234 Ill. 285, 84 N. E. 910 (1908), and *infra* p. 66, note 118. An excellent case in point is Merchants' Bank v. Griswold, *supra* note 111. Here the promise was contained in the following instrument, at 476: "This is to certify that I

the transaction giving rise to the draft and not as requiring any additional act of the drawer or purchaser. Even a promise containing so comparatively complex a phrase as "provided drafts have bills of lading or express receipts attached" has been held to be unconditional.[118] One suggested explanation has been that this type of condition has become so common in commercial transactions that it is regarded as a term of the promise, much as the provisions for the draft itself are treated.[119]

In other words, a promise is unconditional within the meaning of the statute if it describes the draft and requires certain other acts very commonly performed in this type of transaction. How far the courts will go in this direction and how many types of phrases and additional requirements will be included under the term unconditional, remains to be seen.

These decisions are based, to some extent, on a desire to throw the responsibility for the performance of this kind of condition on the promisor rather than on the bona fide purchaser. In order to effectuate this, however, it is unnecessary to allow a recovery as on an acceptance. A recovery in an action for breach of the promise to accept or pay would accomplish the same result.[120] A

---

hereby authorize H. L., as my agent, to make drafts on me, from time to time, as may be necessary for the purchase of lumber." This was interpreted as a limitation of authority and not a condition and therefore as an unconditional promise within the meaning of the statute. At 477: "There is a distinction, I think, between a conditional authority to draw and a limitation of authority. . . . In all the cases where the authority to draw has been held absolute, the authority was limited in amount, time or otherwise. In such cases the authority is absolute to draw within the limit prescribed. In this case the power cannot be said to be general and unlimited. It is restricted to the amount necessary to purchase lumber for the defendant, but within that limit is absolute and unqualified." Louisiana Nat. Bank v. Schuchardt, 15 Hun 405 (N. Y. 1878), is a similar case. The additional words may occasionally be so vague as to be properly ignored. Bissel v. Lewis, 4 Mich. 450 (1857). The letter read, in part, "You are at liberty to make drafts on us in amounts necessary for such operations." See also Posey v. Denver Nat. Bank, 7 Colo. App. 108, 42 Pac. 684 (1895), *aff'd*, 24 Colo. 199, 49 Pac. 282 (1897); James v. E. G. Lyons Co., *supra* note 112. See also cases *supra* note 115.

[118] Wilson & Co. v. Niffenegger, 211 Mich. 311, 178 N. W. 667 (1920).

[119] (1925) 25 Col. L. Rev. 819, 821.

[120] This consideration operates irrespective of any statute. Coffman v. D. C. Campbell & Co., *supra* note 116, was decided before Illinois had

similar group of cases is found where a recovery is allowed, even though the conditions have not been remedied, on the theory that the holder cannot be responsible for the performance of the type of condition under consideration.[121] What has been said above applies here as well. These cases represent only a further step along the same road. The fiction is here destroyed and the decision rested on its real basis, the non-responsibility of the holder for the performance of the conditions. As a step toward clarification, it is welcome, but there can be no doubt that it is an obvious straining of the term unconditional.

There are decisions denying a recovery in an action on an acceptance on the ground that the promise was conditional where the conditions had not been remedied.[122] The real bases of these de-

---

adopted a statute. It applies of course only to requirements of the promise which do not result in having documents attached, since where documents are attached, the purchaser can examine them and judge of their adequacy for himself. The bases for the decisions in this type of case must be found in the other considerations mentioned, e.g., that the phrases are merely statements of the transactions, and that they are so widely used that they are to be treated similarly to those terms of the promise that describe the draft. The problem is considered later, *infra* ch. V, p. 206.

[121] Adoué v. Fox, 30 Mo. App. 98 (1888); Merchants' Bank v. Griswold, *supra* note 111; Bissell v. Lewis, *supra* note 117. But see Stough v. Healy, 75 Kan. 526, 89 Pac. 898, 10 L. R. A. (N. S.) 918 (1907). In this case, recovery was denied because no hogs or cattle were shipped. The promise read "in reply will say we will honor Mr. Payne's draft for $1,000 on hogs or cattle." Coffman v. D. C. Campbell & Co., *supra* note 116, is distinguished as not being a case of conditions at all. But the language is so similar in these two cases, that if the promise in one case is not conditional, neither is it in the other. The real basis of distinction is that in Coffman v. D. C. Campbell & Co. the plaintiff reasonably supposed that the cattle were shipped, while in the Kansas case the plaintiff knew that they were not. Coffman v. D. C. Campbell & Co. holds that the plaintiff is not responsible for the performance of a condition of this sort, but this does not imply that he can recover when he knows the conditions have not been performed.

[122] Banco Nacional Ultramarino v. First Nat. Bank, 289 Fed. 169 (D. Mass. 1923); Brown, Graves & Co. v. Ambler, 66 Md. 391, 7 Atl. 903 (1887); Germania Nat. Bank v. Taaks, 101 N. Y. 442, 5 N. E. 76 (1886); Shaver v. Western Union Telegraph Co., 57 N. Y. 459 (1874); the order here was non-negotiable, but the court treated it as subject to the provisions of the New York Revised Statutes relating to acceptances. First State Bank v. Thuet, 88 Minn. 364, 93 N. W. 1 (1903). It is not perfectly clear here that the action was on an acceptance, as distinguished from a promise to accept.

cisions are, of course, that the conditions were not performed as required. All else is mere dictum and is incorporated to sustain the result.

New York seems to be the only jurisdiction where a recovery has been denied, even though the conditions had been performed at the time suit was brought, on the theory that the promise was conditional and, therefore, not an acceptance under the statute.[123] Other jurisdictions have not only failed to follow the New York rule, but have even allowed a recovery after the performance of various requirements in the promise of the acceptor, which requirements, even under the strained interpretations of Section 135 which have been considered, must be deemed to have made the promise conditional.[124]

The interpretation of the statutory requirement that the promise be unconditional, is varied and loose. Promises which merely specify the terms of the draft are uniformly held to be unconditional.[125] Many jurisdictions hold that promises which, in addition, specify certain very common requirements, are also unconditional. Others hold that requirements in the acceptance for the performance of which the purchaser or payee is not responsible do not make the promise conditional within the meaning of the

[123] Harrison v. Smith, 2 Sweeny 669 (N. Y. 1870); New York & Va. State Stock Bank v. Gibson, 5 Duer 574 (N. Y. 1856); see also Germania Bank v. Taaks, *supra* note 122; Muller v. Kling, 149 App. Div. 176, 180, 133 N. Y. Supp. 614, 617 (1912), *aff'd,* 209 N. Y. 239, 103 N. E. 138 (1913). The law, in New York at least, seems to be that a conditional promise, even when the condition has been performed, is not actionable as an acceptance. To offset this there is great freedom in interpreting provisions, either as not properly constituting conditions, or as being merely terms or limitations of the promise and therefore not to be classed as conditions. See the New York citations *supra* notes 114, 115; *cf.* Starr v. Murchison, 1 City Ct. 413 (N. Y. 1878).

[124] Whilden v. Merchants' & Planters' Nat. Bank, 64 Ala. 1 (1879); see also Soppe v. Mechaley, 103 Neb. 264, 172 N. W. 35, 175 N. W. 658 (1919); Barnsdall v. Waltemeyer, 142 Fed. 415 (C. C. A. 8th, 1905), *cert. den.*, 201 U. S. 643, 26 Sup. Ct. 759 (1906); Southern Creosoting Co. v. Chicago & Altoona R. R., 205 S. W. 716 (Mo. 1918).

[125] To have regarded promises containing terms, other than such as are regarded as stating the nature of the transaction, as conditional, would have been functionally not only most convenient, but also most logical by analogy to the normal acceptance on the face of the draft.

statute. Finally, a few jurisdictions interpret the provision of the statute as meaning cured of conditions.

It is to be regretted that the Uniform Negotiable Instruments Law, by continuing the use of the term unconditional in Section 135 without further explanation, has permitted the development of the confusion arising under the earlier statutes.[126]

2. *Definiteness*

The origin of the requirement that the acceptance be definite can be traced directly to the rule laid down by Marshall in *Coolidge* v. *Payson*. He says there:

> Upon a review of the cases which are reported, this court is of opinion that a letter written within a reasonable time before or after the date of a bill of exchange, describing it in terms not to be mistaken, and promising to accept it, is, if shown to the person who afterwards takes the bill on the credit of the letter, a virtual acceptance binding the person who makes the promise.[127]

This lays down clearly the requirement of definiteness for both virtual and extrinsic acceptances. The cases upon which the Chief Justice states he relied in formulating this rule have not been ascertained. The English decisions, certainly, say nothing about it. On the contrary, they allow a recovery on an acceptance where

[126] Under the Uniform Negotiable Instruments Law, there is nothing to prevent a promise to pay after the draft is drawn, even though this promise be conditional, from being actionable upon the performance of the condition, Section 134. Generally, however, this fact has not been commented upon. In only one case does it seem to be recognized, Citizens Bank v. Willing, 109 Wash. 464, 468, 186 Pac. 1072, 1073 (1920); see also Wallace State Bank v. Corn Exchange Bank, *supra* note 112; Lehnhard v. Sidway, 160 Mo. App. 83, 141 S. W. 430 (1911). There is a tendency, however, to treat extrinsic acceptances, in regard to conditions, as subject to the same rules as virtual acceptances, see State Bank of Beaver County v. Bradstreet, *supra* note 117; Selma Savings Bank v. Webster County Bank, *supra* note 115. New York & Va. State Stock Bank v. Gibson, *supra* note 123, decided in New York under the Revised Statutes, treated an extrinsic acceptance as though it were a virtual acceptance and denied recovery under Section 8 because the promise was conditional, even though the condition had been performed.

[127] 2 Wheat. 66, 75, 4 L. Ed. 185, 188 (1817).

the loosest phraseology is used.[128] The American cases decided before 1817, the year of *Coolidge* v. *Payson,* are equally silent on the question.[129] In addition, the New York Revised Statutes, passed ten years later, though they include the requirement as to lack of conditions, omit all mention of definiteness.[130] As has been suggested, the Chief Justice probably tried to lay down a rule that would settle the question for all time. Accordingly he brought together a number of requirements which he thought would make a working rule, some of which have their justification in precedent, others being justifiable if at all, only in expediency. This rule has been followed in the federal courts with fair consistency.[131] Many other jurisdictions, on the other hand, have

[128] Smith v. Brown, *supra* note 109; Miln v. Prest, 4 Camp. 393 (1816); Bank of Ireland v. Archer, 11 M. & W. 383, 152 Eng. R. 852 (1843). For the acceptance of a series of drafts see Billing v. Devaux, 3 Man. & G. 565, 133 Eng. R. 1267 (1841); Wynne v. Raikes, 5 East 514, 102 Eng. R. 1167 (1804). It is interesting to note that one of the letters offered in evidence in Clarke v. Cock, 4 East 57, 102 Eng. R. 751 (1803), was written by the defendant to the plaintiff, before the action was begun expressing surprise that the plaintiff should have discounted a bill for £1,200 on the faith of a letter so vague that it did not mention the sum for which the writer was liable. This is a commentary on the soundness of Marshall's rule. Yet the English courts do not seem to have been influenced by it during the period when virtual and extrinsic acceptances were permitted.

[129] M'Evers v. Mason, 10 Johns. 207 (N. Y. 1813); M'Kim v. Smith, 1 Am. Law J. 486 (Md. 1808); Storer v. Logan, 9 Mass. 55 (1812); Banorgee v. Hovey, 5 Mass. 11 (1809); Wilson v. Clements, 3 Mass. 1 (1807); Havens v. Griffin, N. Chipman 42 (Vt. 1789).

[130] *Supra* note 107. It has been suggested that the language of the statute, "to accept a bill," limits the promise to a single bill rather than a series. See Ulster County Bank v. McFarlan, *supra* note 114, and *infra* p. 73. This is not forceful: "a bill," might just as well mean any bill as one bill, in fact, logically it would signify the former. The Missouri court, for example, in limiting the doctrine to a definite promise did not proceed on this ground, but held that the statute was silent on the question; *infra* p. 77. The Negotiable Instruments Law uses similar language; therefore the same considerations apply to it.

[131] Coolidge v. Payson, *supra* note 127, allowed a recovery where the amount, but not the time, was mentioned. The court evidently felt that this was a broad enough rule as the following few cases, in which looser language was used than in Coolidge v. Payson, were held to be too indefinite to be acceptances: Schimmelpennich v. Bayard, 1 Pet. 264, 7 L. Ed. 138 (1828); Boyce v. Edwards, 4 Pet. 111, 7 L. Ed. 799 (1830); Cassel v. Dows, 5 Fed. Cas. No. 2502 (C. C. S. D. N. Y. 1848); see also: Exchange Bank v. Hubbard, 62 Fed. 112, 115 (C. C. A. 2d, 1894); *cf.* Bayard v. Lathy, 2 Fed. Cas. No. 1, 131 (C. C. D. Ill. 1841); Ogden v. Gillingham, 18 Fed.

failed to follow the federal courts in the requirements laid down by Chief Justice Marshall.

New York is an excellent illustration of a jurisdiction that is liberal in this regard. There is practically no requirement as to definiteness in that state. Anything definite enough to be a promise is definite enough to be an acceptance. The first case in New York permitting recovery on a virtual acceptance was *Goodrich* v. *Gordon*.[132] The letter, there, promised to honor a draft at not more than $2,000.00. This was held to be an acceptance. The requirement of definiteness was not mentioned. The case was decided, however, only one year after *Coolidge* v. *Payson*, which case does not appear to have been mentioned by the attorneys on argument or by the court in its opinion.[133] In the next case that arose, a promise couched in the following terms was held actionable as an acceptance:

> I have no objection to accepting for you at three and four months for $2500.00 on the terms you propose.[134]

Since both time and amount were mentioned, this bill would probably have been held sufficiently described in any jurisdiction,

Cas. No. 10,456 (C. C. E. D. Pa. 1829); *In re* Armstrong, 41 Fed. 381 (C. C. S. D. Ohio 1890); North Atchison Bank v. Garretson, 51 Fed. 168 (C. C. A. 8th, 1892), *aff'g*, 47 Fed. 867 (C. C. W. D. Mo. 1891), 39 Fed. 163, 7 L. R. A. 428 (C. C. W. D. Mo. 1889); First Nat. Bank of Dunn v. First Nat. Bank of Massillon, 210 Fed. 542 (N. D. Ohio 1913). The promises in these cases were much more definite than in the former cases. That they were held to be acceptances, therefore, does not mean that the federal courts are departing in any way from the rule as laid down and interpreted by Marshall.

[132] 15 Johns. 6 (N. Y. 1818); M'Evers v. Mason, *supra* note 129, the first case on the subject, involved a virtual acceptance. Recovery was denied partly because there was no reliance and partly because the court felt that there could be no acceptance of a bill which was still to be drawn, and the plaintiff was held not to have any rights on the promise as he was not the direct promisee. This case, however, seems to have had little influence in the development of New York law, in view of the fact that the court, in Goodrich v. Gordon, which was decided only five years later, allowed recovery on a virtual acceptance without hesitation.

[133] Coolidge v. Payson is reported for the February term of 1817, and Goodrich v. Gordon for January, 1818. It is doubtful whether the former case had been heard of at the time the latter case was decided. It is, however, mentioned by the reporter in a note to Goodrich v. Gordon, at 13. The volume was printed in 1819.

[134] Greele v. Parker, *supra* note 115, at 417.

but the significant fact is that, while Marshall's rule is mentioned, the chief emphasis in both majority and minority opinions is laid on the problem of conditions. The next case goes further. The language there used was:

> If you want more funds, you can make drafts on me; due in August next; make them in sums of $1000.00 each and spread the time of their payment through the month—to the amount of $10,000.00.[135]

This was an action against the defendant as acceptor. The court discusses it only under the statute and holds it to be an acceptance. A virtual acceptance of a series of drafts is, therefore, permissible. An even more indefinite promise can be found in *Ulster County Bank* v. *McFarlan.*[136] In that case, defendant wrote a letter as follows:

> I hereby authorize you to draw on me at ninety days from time to time for such amount as you may require, provided that the whole amount running and unpaid shall not exceed $3000.00. The above letter of credit to be good and binding for one year from this date.[137]

The lower court held this to be "an unconditional promise to accept within the meaning of the statute"[138] and after citing *Bank of Michigan* v. *Ely*[139] and *Greele* v. *Parker,*[140] the court stated:

> These cases show also that the written promise to accept need not contain a particular description or identification of the bill to be drawn. It is enough that it be drawn in pursuance of the authority.[141]

Recovery, however, was denied on the ground that the terms of the promise had not been performed. On appeal, the opinions of four senators are reported. Of these, two are for affirmance,

---

[135] Bank of Michigan v. Ely, 17 Wend. 508, 509 (N. Y. 1837).

[136] 5 Hill 432 (N. Y. 1843), *aff'd,* 3 Denio 553 (N. Y. 1846).

[137] 3 Denio at 556.

[138] 5 Hill at 434.

[139] *Supra* note 135.

[140] *Supra* note 115.

[141] Ulster County Bank v. McFarlan, *supra* note 138.

and two, for reversal. The latter agree with the lower court that this was an acceptance within the meaning of the statute.[142] Of the former, one bases his opinion solely on the ground of non-performance of the terms of the promise,[143] while the other emphasizes the fact that the promise was too indefinite to be an acceptance[144] and maintains that an acceptance of a series of bills is impossible, that all previous cases speak only of single transactions, and that "our statute speaks in the singular number 'to accept a bill'—'shall have received a bill,' etc."[145] He also says:

> But the ground upon which I put this part of the case is, that by the law of this country, irrespective of the statute, the promise must *point to the particular bills and describe them in terms not to be mistaken,* and that the statute has in no way enlarged that rule. On the contrary, if it has changed it at all, it has limited it more strictly than before.[146]

Finally, he also rests his opinion on the ground of the commercial undesirability of allowing indefinite promises to be actionable as acceptances. In spite, however, of this opinion and the dissenting opinion in *Greele* v. *Parker,*[147] this stand was clearly contrary to the general opinion prevalent in New York at the time—that a promise of this sort, though to accept a series of bills and though for no definite amount on each bill, was sufficient to constitute an acceptance. The Michigan court, in a case where the New York law was held to govern, held the following to be an acceptance:

> You are at liberty to make drafts on us in amounts necessary for such operations, on such times as you can make advantageously for us.[148]

---

[142] 3 Denio at 561, 563 (N. Y. 1846).

[143] *Ibid.* at 559.

[144] *Ibid.* at 556.

[145] *Ibid.* at 557.

[146] *Ibid.* at 558.

[147] 5 Wend. 414, 416 (N. Y. 1830).

[148] Bissell v. Lewis, 4 Mich. 450, 451 (1857).

After reviewing the cases above mentioned and ending with *Ulster County Bank* v. *McFarlan,* the last case decided at that time, the Michigan court added:

> From this review of the decisions of the State of New York, there can be no doubt as to what is the rule of the commercial law of that State in regard to this important class of contracts, however the weight of authority may be in regard to the American law.[149]

This view as to the rule in New York was sustained in *Merchants' Bank* v. *Griswold,*[150] in which case the following was held to be an acceptance:

> To whom it may concern: This is to certify that I hereby authorize H. L., as my agent, to make drafts on me, from time to time, as may be necessary for the purchase of lumber for my account.[151]

Laxity could go no further. No time, no amount, not even the number of drafts or the period for which the credit is to run is mentioned; yet the instrument is held to amount to an acceptance. The question of definiteness is completely ignored. The same tendency characterizes succeeding cases, and there is no reason to suppose that the rule has since been narrowed in any way.[152]

New York is not the only jurisdiction which takes this view of the law; California is another. In that jurisdiction, the court cites and discusses all the New York cases and bases its interpretation of the California statute, for all practical purposes identical with the New York statute, on the New York rule. It sees the conflicting rules and definitely chooses the more liberal one:

---

[149] *Ibid.* at 463.

[150] 72 N. Y. 472 (1878).

[151] *Ibid.* at 476.

[152] See particularly Ruiz v. Renauld, 100 N. Y. 256, 3 N. E. 182 (1885); see also: Burns v. Rowland, 40 Barb. 368 (N. Y. 1863); Barney v. Worthington, 37 N. Y. 112 (1867); Merchants' Exchange Nat. Bank v. Cardozo, 3 J. & S. 162 (N. Y. 1872); Molson's Bank v. Howard, 8 J. & S. 15 (N. Y. 1875); Louisiana Nat. Bank v. Schuchardt, 15 Hun 405 (N. Y. 1878); Seaboard Nat. Bank v. Burleigh, 74 Hun 400, 26 N. Y. Supp. 587 (1893), *aff'd* without opinion, 147 N. Y. 720, 42 N. E. 726 (1895).

We are aware that there are cases which take a view of the questions involved, opposed to those hereinbefore expressed, but we prefer to stand by the cases cited herein as presenting the true rule governing the question.[153]

There are many states, however, which follow the federal rule much more closely. Missouri, for example, was at first inclined to be rather liberal and allow a recovery where the amount and time could easily be computed though, perhaps, they might not be mentioned.[154] The courts of that jurisdiction, however, hesitated to allow a recovery on an acceptance where the letter was a general letter of credit authorizing drafts for three-fourths of

[153] James v. E. G. Lyons Co., 134 Cal. 189, 196, 66 Pac. 210, 212 (1901), 147 Cal. 69, 81 Pac. 275 (1905); see also Naglee v. Lyman, 14 Cal. 450 (1859). If we may judge from the language of the courts in a single instance and from the type of promise held to be sufficiently definite to be an acceptance, the following jurisdictions tend to follow the New York and California rule; *Mich.;* Wilson & Co. v. Niffenegger, 211 Mich. 311, 318, 178 N. W 667, 669 (1920); see also: Bissell v. Lewis, *supra* note 148; *Ind.;* Beach v. State Bank, 2 Ind. 488, 492 (1851); *Maine;* Gates v. Parker, 43 Me. 544 (1857); *Minn.;* James River Nat. Bank v. Thuet, 135 Minn. 30, 159 N. W. 1093 (1916); *Kan.;* Milwaukee Corrugating Co. v. Traylor, 95 Kan. 562, 565, 148 Pac. 653, 654 (1915); and *Ala.;* Whilden v. Merchants' and Planters' Nat. Bank, 64 Ala. 1, 29, 32 (1879); *cf.* Kennedy v. Geddes & Co., 8 Porter 263 (Ala. 1839), 3 Ala. 581 (1842). The effect of the silence of the statute in Alabama was practically to nullify the requirements as to definiteness. This is unusual. As far as the cases go, the courts generally followed the tendency that had been indicated before the adoption of any statute; *cf.* the development of this rule in California *infra* p. 77. The attitude of the court in Illinois as illustrated in the case of Nelson v. First Nat. Bank, 48 Ill. 36 (1868), is interesting. After rejecting the distinction between an action on an acceptance and an action for breach of contract to accept, the court says, in referring to the rule in Coolidge v. Payson. At 39: "It seems to us, a fair construction of the language of Chief Justice Marshall would require, not that the promise should describe the bill to be drawn and accepted, by its date and amount, and the name of the drawee, as that would be generally impossible; but merely in such a mode that there could be no possible doubt as to the application of the promise to the bill to be drawn." This is merely giving lip service to the rule and violating its spirit. See also Wilson & Co. v. Niffenegger, *ibid.* From the later Federal cases, decided by Marshall himself, it can be seen that at least some of these items were meant; clearly the amount had to be specified before the promise could be actionable as an acceptance. This is due to the feeling of the Supreme Court that the doctrine of virtual acceptances is an undesirable one and should be limited as much as possible. See also: Huston v. Newgass, 234 Ill. 285, 84 N. E. 910 (1908); Golsen v. Golsen, 127 Ill. App. 84 (1906); and Hall v. Cordell, 142 U. S. 116, 12 Sup. Ct. 154, 35 L. Ed. 956 (1891), applying the Illinois law.

[154] Lathrop v. Harlow, 23 Mo. 209 (1856); see also Brinkman v. Hunter, 73 Mo. 172, 180 (1880).

all shipments although the time was specified.[155] The next case, where the time was stated and the amount easily inferable, allowed a recovery on an acceptance.[156]

The Missouri rule regarding definiteness, however, was apparently laid down in the case of *Bank of Atchison County* v. *Bohart Commission Co.*[157] The instrument there was:

> We told Mr. G. we would pay his drafts for cost of cattle, or hogs, not to exceed two car loads at a time, made on day of shipment.[158]

This was held to be too indefinite to be an acceptance. In view of the preceding cases, there is nothing startling in this result *per se.* The significant fact lies in the tone of the opinion. *Coolidge* v. *Payson,*[159] and *Boyce* v. *Edwards*[160] are dwelt upon, and *Lathrop* v. *Harlow*[161] in effect, is ignored. In *State Bank of Iowa Falls* v. *American Hardwood Lumber Co.,*[162] a promise to accept stating the amount definitely, but the time only by reference, was held to be an acceptance. Missouri is clearly a follower of the federal rule and requires that the promise be limited to one bill, that the amount be stated, and, most probably, that the time be also stated or, at least, clearly inferable.[163]

---

[155] Vallé v. Cerré, 36 Mo. 575 (1865).

[156] Adoué v. Fox, 30 Mo. App. 98 (1888).

[157] 84 Mo. App. 421 (1900).

[158] *Ibid.* at 422.

[159] 2 Wheat. 66, 4 L. Ed. 185 (1817).

[160] 4 Pet. 111, 7 L. Ed. 799 (1830).

[161] *Supra* note 154.

[162] 121 Mo. App. 324, 98 S. W. 786 (1906).

[163] Similar jurisdictions seem to be *Md.;* Franklin Bank v. Lynch, 52 Md. 270 (1879); First Nat. Bank v. Clark, 61 Md. 400 (1883). The former case was recognized as going too far. There, a telegram giving the amount, and the time by inference, was held too indefinite to be an acceptance. This aspect of the case was disapproved in the latter decision. *La.*; Von Phul v. Sloan, 2 Rob. 148 (La. 1842); Carrollton Bank v. Tayleur 16 La. 490 (1840). *Ohio*; Lonsdale & Gray v. Lafayette Bank, 18 Ohio 126 (1849), the time was fixed and the amount for the series but not for each bill. *Fla.*; Wauchula Development Co. v. Peoples Stock Yards State Bank, 86 Fla. 298, 98 So. 220 (1923), neither time nor amount was fixed. In the remaining jurisdictions, the cases are of such

In general, the effect of the lack of statutory provisions concerning the requirement of definiteness for virtual and extrinsic acceptances seems to have been slight. Two interpretations of the silence of the statutes are possible, and both have been taken. One is that it has left the courts free to legislate on this subject. This view, of course, has been taken by the closer followers of Marshall's rule, as, for example, Missouri:

> But what will be considered to be such acceptance, save only that it must be unconditional and in writing, is left for judicial construction.[164]

The other view is that the silence of the statute is to be interpreted as requiring no particular definiteness. This construction is naturally taken by the more liberal jurisdictions, such as New York and California, where the discussion tends to center around the requirement of writing and the lack of conditions, which are both mentioned in the statute.

> We cannot concur in respondent's position that the promise, to be binding under the Statute must relate to and describe a particular bill or *the* particular bill referred to in the complaint. It is

---

a character, *i. e.*, the promises are so definite, that they cannot indicate the policy of the courts. Farmers Bank v. Stapleton, 118 Kan. 755, 236 Pac. 828 (1925); Kahn v. Walton, 46 Ohio St. 195, 20 N. E. 203 (1889); Atlanta Nat. Bank v. Northwestern Fertilizing Co., 83 Ga. 356, 9 S. E. 671 (1889); Parrish v. Taggart-Delph Lumber Co., 11 Ga. App. 772, 76 S. E. 153 (1912); Nimocks v. Woody, 97 N. C. 1, 2 S. E. 249 (1887); Read v. Marsh, 5 B. Mon. 8 (Ky. 1844); Vance v. Ward, 2 Dana 95 (Ky. 1834); Elliott v. First State Bank, 105 Tex. 547, 152 S. W. 808 (1913); Henrietta Nat. Bank v. State Nat. Bank, 80 Tex. 648, 651, 16 S. W. 321 (1891): "Whether according to the rules laid down the correspondence should show any more than the amount and character of the bill as to the time of payment we need not here inquire, though it would seem that such a description ought to be sufficient according to the most rigid rule recognized by any court." Bank of Morganton v. Hay, 143 N. C. 326, 55 S. E. 811 (1906); Steman, Baker & Co. v. Harrison, 42 Pa. 49 (1862); Farmers' and Merchants' Nat. Bank v. Elizabethtown Nat. Bank, 30 Pa. Super. Ct. 271 (1906). It is clear that Massachusetts does not go so far as New York in holding a general authority to draw under a letter of credit to be an acceptance of all bills drawn under it; Carnegie v. Morrison, 2 Metc. 381 (Mass. 1841). How far the Massachusetts courts will go is doubtful; Exchange Bank v. Rice, 98 Mass. 288 (1867), 107 Mass. 37 (1871); Central Savings Bank v. Richards, 109 Mass. 413 (1872).

[164] Bank of Atchison County v. Bohart Commission Co., 84 Mo. App. 421, 424 (1900).

sufficient if it can be fairly inferred from the language of the promise that it was intended to include the bill of exchange upon which the action is based.[165]

The effect of the statutes, therefore, seems to be nil. New York and California, having similar statutes, are liberal. Missouri, also with a similar statute, is a strict jurisdiction. Illinois and Indiana, without any statute, are liberal. Maryland and Louisiana, also without statutes, are strict. The rule seems to have been arrived at independently of any statute. The Uniform Negotiable Instruments Law also does not affect the rule as previously laid down in various jurisdictions. In the few cases that have arisen, the treatment under the Negotiable Instruments Law has been similar to that previously given. There is no reason to suppose that this tendency will cease or that each court will not continue along the lines indicated.[166]

Generally, therefore, we may say that there are two broad classes of jurisdictions. Those which have a tendency to confine the doctrine of virtual and extrinsic acceptances to promises, definite as to time and amount and limited to a single draft, constitute one type, of which Missouri and the federal courts are the best illustrations. New York, California, and Illinois represent the other type; these jurisdictions are very liberal, treating as an acceptance almost anything which amounts to a promise. Perhaps there is an intermediate class which would be satisfied with a specification of the amount or the limitation to a single draft.

---

[165] James v. E. G. Lyons Co., *supra* note 153, at 194, 66 Pac. at 211.

[166] The following cases have allowed a recovery under the Negotiable Instruments Law as being sufficiently definite: Wilson & Co. v. Niffenegger, *supra* note 153; James River Nat. Bank v. Thuet, *supra* note 153; Huston v. Newgass, *supra* note 153; Farmers & Merchants' Nat. Bank v. Elizabethtown Nat. Bank, *supra* note 163; State Bank of Iowa Falls v. American Hardwood Lumber Co., 121 Mo. App. 324, 98 S. W. 786 (1906). The following two cases have denied a recovery: Wauchula Development Co. v. Peoples Stock Yards State Bank, *supra* note 163; Bank of Morganton v. Hay, *supra* note 163. A glance at these cases will show that the treatment before and after the adoption of the Negotiable Instruments Law is similar. Indeed it does not appear that the statutes passed before the Negotiable Instruments Law, on the model of the New York Revised Statutes, had any effect upon this question, with the possible exception of Alabama, *supra* note 153.

Massachusetts and Georgia may be examples of this type. The determination of this last type must wait on the further development of the rule.

3. *Reliance*

The requirement that the draft be taken in reliance on the promise to accept was first laid down in the English case of *Pierson* v. *Dunlop*[167] and represented a phase of the attempt to limit the number of promises to accept or pay made before the draft was drawn, which could be actionable as acceptances. That early English law was rather inclined in this direction for a time has already been indicated. With the development of the law, however, the requirement was abolished as to extrinsic acceptances, while the doctrine of virtual acceptances was wholly repudiated.[168]

In this country, on the other hand, the requirement for reliance was laid down generally both in statutes and decisions. The first case on the subject was decided in Pennsylvania.[169] It was a case of an alleged virtual acceptance, and recovery was allowed. The draft was taken in reliance on the promise. The next case was *M'Evers* v. *Mason.*[170] Here recovery was denied on a virtual acceptance partly on the ground of no reliance. The court was evidently also of the opinion that a promise to accept a non-existing bill could never be actionable as an acceptance. This was followed by *Coolidge* v. *Payson.*[171] In this case, as we have seen, the distinction between virtual and extrinsic acceptances was repudiated, and the rule as laid down for both required that the bill be taken in reliance on the promise.[172] While no decision has been

[167] 2 Cowp. 571, 573, 98 Eng. R. 1246, 1248 (1777).

[168] See discussion *supra* p. 47 *et seq.*

[169] M'Kim v. Smith, 1 Am. Law J. 486 (Md. 1808).

[170] M'Evers v. Mason, 10 Johns. 207 (N. Y. 1813).

[171] *Supra* note 159.

[172] *Supra* pp. 58, 69.

based on this point, the federal courts have mentioned the fact that there was a taking in reliance on the promise, as one ground for allowing a recovery.[173] Before the New York statutes of 1827, only one other case in point was decided in New York,[174] and this involved a written virtual acceptance. Recovery was allowed, the court pointing out that there was actual reliance. Illinois, which had no statute on the subject until the passage of the Uniform Negotiable Instruments Law in 1907, seems to have preserved the distinction between virtual and extrinsic acceptances in this respect. In regard to extrinsic acceptances, the court states:

> A promise by the drawee to pay an existing bill is an acceptance, or, in law, amounts to an acceptance, whether the bill was taken upon the faith of the promise or not. A promise to any person interested in having a bill paid inures to the benefit of the holder.[175]

In regard to virtual acceptances, it was held:

> A promise to Allen to pay his checks, if it had not come to the knowledge of appellant, and been the basis of the sale made by him to Allen, would have created no privity between him and the bank, and as the promise would have been without benefit to the bank, and without injury to the appellant, if unaware it had been made, it would have been absolutely without consideration as between these parties, and therefore not binding.[176]

While this logic would have applied just as well to extrinsic acceptances, it was not so applied, and the distinction was continued until the Uniform Negotiable Instruments Law was adopted.[177]

---

[173] Ogden v. Gillingham, 18 Fed. Cas. No. 10,456 (C. C. E. D. Pa. 1829); Boyce v. Edwards, *supra* note 160; Bayard v. Lathy, 2 Fed. Cas. No. 1, 131 (C. C. D. Ill. 1841); *In re* Armstrong, 41 Fed. 381 (C. C. S. D. Ohio 1890); North Atchison Bank v. Garretson, 51 Fed. 168 (C. C. A. 8th, 1892), *aff'g*, 47 Fed. 867 (C. C. W. D. Mo. 1891), 39 Fed. 163, 7 L. R. A. 428 (C. C. W. D. Mo. 1889); First Nat. Bank of Dunn v. First Nat. Bank of Massillon, 210 Fed. 542 (N. D. Ohio 1913).

[174] Goodrich v. Gordon, 15 Johns. 6 (N. Y. 1818).

[175] Jones v. Council Bluffs Branch of the State Bank of Iowa, 34 Ill. 313, 319 (1864).

[176] Nelson v. First Nat. Bank, 48 Ill. 36, 37 (1868).

[177] For cases on extrinsic acceptances, see: Mason v. Dousay, 35 Ill. 424 (1864); Jones v. Council Bluffs Branch of the State Bank of Iowa, *supra* note 175; Dillon v. Moratz, 109 Ill. App. 17 (1902); Golsen v. Golsen, 127 Ill. App. 84 (1906). For virtual acceptances; Coffman v.

The law in Massachusetts, on the other hand, was not entirely clear. To recover as on a virtual acceptance, a taking in reliance was required.[178] The law as to extrinsic acceptances was much more doubtful. There is the case of *Exchange Bank* v. *Rice*,[179] holding that an extrinsic acceptance is not binding unless the holder took the draft in reliance on the promise. Later cases, however, allowed a recovery where there was no such reliance.[180] The distinction between virtual and extrinsic acceptances, moreover, was not maintained.[181] The law remained in this uncertain state until the Uniform Negotiable Instruments Law was adopted.

Though the language of the courts is confusing, the results reached at common law in this country are for the most part clear. In regard to extrinsic acceptances, a sharp conflict exists. Some states seem to require reliance at the time of purchase,[182] others,

D. C. Campbell & Co., 87 Ill. 98 (1877); First Nat. Bank v. Pettit, 41 Ill. 492 (1866), especially as interpreted by Nelson v. First Nat. Bank, *supra* note 176. See also: Coffman v. Clarinda Nat. Bank, 33 Ill. App. 641 (1889), and Hall v. First Nat. Bank, 133 Ill. 234, 24 N. E. 546 (1890), which are probably actions for breach of promise to accept, but which were treated in the same manner by the courts; and also Springfield Marine Bank v. Mitchell, 48 Ill. App. 486, 491 (1892), for a dictum implying the contrary. The importance of this decision, however, is problematical.

[178] Banorgee v. Hovey, 5 Mass. 11, 29 (1809); Storer v. Logan, 9 Mass. 55, 58 (1812); Carr v. Nat. Security Bank, 107 Mass. 45, 46 (1871); Central Savings Bank v. Richards, *supra* note 163; see Putnam Nat. Bank v. Snow, 172 Mass. 569, 576, 52 N. E. 1079 (1899).

[179] *Supra* note 163.

[180] Pierce v. Kittredge, 115 Mass. 374 (1874). But *cf.* Clement v. Earle, 130 Mass. 585n (1879). The Clement case was decided on the ground that the oral promise to pay did not amount to an acceptance. There are also cases before Exchange Bank v. Rice not requiring reliance, see: Grant v. Shaw, 16 Mass. 341 (1820); Hough v. Loring, 24 Pick. 254 (Mass. 1837); Ward v. Allen, 2 Metc. 53 (Mass. 1840).

[181] See, e.g., Central Savings Bank v. Richards, *supra* note 163, and Carr v. Nat. Security Bank, *supra* note 178; both cite Exchange Bank v. Rice as their authority for requiring reliance. Yet the former were cases of virtual acceptances, while the latter involved an extrinsic acceptance.

[182] Read v. Marsh, *supra* note 163, at 10; Howland v. Carson, 15 Pa. 453 (1850); see also: Lugrue v. Woodruff, 29 Ga. 648 (1860); Strohecker v. Cohen, 1 Spears L. 349 (S. C. 1843); Pynetree Paper Co. v. Wilkinson County Bank, 24 Ga. App. 260, 100 S. E. 753 (1919); Overman v. Hoboken City Bank, 30 N. J. L. 61, 68 (1862), 31 N. J. L. 563 (1864).

by their decisions and the language of the opinions, do not.[183] If we examine those cases where reliance is not required, it will be seen that they are for the most part cases where the promise was made directly to the holder who kept the draft in reliance on the promise. While these are not cases of a taking in reliance on the promise, they are nevertheless instances of a certain type of reliance.[184] The language used in these opinions, however, generally goes beyond this point and implies that no reliance is necessary. Since the decisions, as a rule, draw no distinction between virtual and extrinsic acceptances, logically, no reliance should have been required in cases of virtual acceptances. Only two cases, one decided in Pennsylvania and the other in Kentucky, state this in so many words.[185] Both of them, however, deal with extrinsic acceptances and the statements are therefore merely dicta. No case of a virtual acceptance without reliance has arisen in either state, so that whether the court would apply the rule as stated was never settled. A lower court in Ohio, in applying Kentucky law, did decide that a virtual acceptance was binding

[183] Stockwell v. Bramble, 3 Porter 428 (Ind. 1852); Edson v. Fuller, 22 N. H. 183 (1850); Clarke v. Gordon, 3 Rich. L. 311 (S. C. 1832); Neumann v. Shroeder, 71 Tex. 81, 8 S. W. 632 (1888); Barnet v. Smith, 30 N. H. 256 (1855); Milmo Nat. Bank v. Cobbs, 53 Tex. Civ. App. 1, 115 S. W. 345 (1908); Read v. Marsh, *supra* note 163; Spaulding v. Andrews, 48 Pa. 411 (1864). But *cf.* Howland v. Carson, *supra* note 182. See also Hatcher v. Stalworth, 25 Miss. 376 (1853). The promise, however, would have to be made to some party to the bill; see Martin v. Bacon, 2 Mill. Const. L. 132 (S. C. 1818); also the English rule as expressed in Grant v. Hunt, quoted *supra* page 50, and Spaulding v. Andrews, *ibid.*

[184] Milmo Nat. Bank v. Cobbs, *supra* note 183, is an excellent example of this. There, a written promise to the drawer after the sale to the plaintiff was held insufficient, but an oral promise to the plaintiff himself was held sufficient as an acceptance.

[185] Howland v. Carson, *supra* note 182; Read v. Marsh, 5 B. Mon. 8 (Ky. 1844). In these cases the promise was made to the drawer either after he had sold the draft to the plaintiff (Ky. case), or before sale where it was bought without knowledge of the promise (Pa. case). The court was therefore forced into the position that no reliance was necessary in order to allow the plaintiff to recover. However, it went further than necessary in extending this rule in terms to virtual acceptances.

without reliance.[186] This is apparently the only decision definitely reaching this conclusion. All the other cases either require reliance or find it there as a fact.[187]

Under statutes similar to that of New York, the law in this regard is clear. Reliance at the time of taking the draft is required for both virtual and extrinsic acceptances. In this state and in those that had adopted its statute, the cases are uniform[188] even though the distinction between the two types of acceptances is not maintained or pointed out.[189] In the type of statute re-

---

[186] Anderson County Deposit Bank v. Turner-Looker Co., 2 Ohio N. P. 73 (1894).

[187] Mercantile Bank v. Cox, 38 Me. 500, 507 (1854); Lewis v. Kramer, 3 Md. 265, 289 (1852); Smith v. Ledyard, 49 Ala. 279 (1873); Whilden v. Merchants' & Planters' Nat. Bank, 64 Ala. 1, 32 (1879); Parrish v. Taggart-Delph Lumber Co., 11 Ga. App. 772, 76 S. E. 153 (1912); Woodard v. Griffiths-Marshall Grain Com. Co., 43 Minn. 260, 45 N. W. 433 (1890); Steman, Baker & Co. v. Harrison, 42 Pa. 49 (1862); Williams v. Winans, 14 N. J. L. 339 (1834); Kendrick v. Campbell, 1 Bail. L. 522 (S. C. 1830); Vance v. Ward, 2 Dana 95 (Ky. 1834); Allentown Nat. Bank v. Kimes, 12 Phila. 329 (Pa. 1878); Beach v. State Bank, 2 Ind. 488 (1851); Gates v. Parker, 43 Me. 544 (1857); Nimocks v. Woody, 97 N. C. 1, 2 S. E. 249 (1887); Havens v. Griffin, N. Chipman 42 (Vt. 1789).

[188] Greele v. Parker, 5 Wend. 414 (N. Y. 1830); Bank of Michigan v. Ely, 17 Wend. 508 (N. Y. 1837); Burns v. Rowland, 40 Barb. 368 (N. Y. 1863); Barney v. Worthington, 37 N. Y. 112 (1867); Johnson v. Clark, 39 N. Y. 216 (1868); Molson's Bank v. Howard, 8 J. & S. 15 (N. Y. 1875); Louisiana Nat. Bank v. Schuchardt, 15 Hun 405 (N. Y. 1878); Merchants' Bank v. Griswold, 72 N. Y. 472 (1878); Seaboard Nat. Bank v. Burleigh, 74 Hun 400, 26 N. Y. Supp. 587 (1893), *aff'd* without opinion, 147 N. Y. 720, 42 N. E. 726 (1895). For cases barring recovery partly on the ground of no reliance at the time of purchase see: Worcester Bank v. Wells, 8 Metc. 107 (Mass. 1844) applying New York law; M'Evers v. Mason, 10 Johns. 207 (N. Y. 1813); Ontario Bank v. Worthington, 12 Wend. 593 (N. Y. 1834); Fairchild v. Feltman, 32 Hun 398 (N. Y. 1884). In the last case there was a written promise made directly to the plaintiff after he had received the bill. This was held not to be sufficient reliance (at p. 400). At common law this would probably have been sufficient, *supra* notes 183, 184. See also Southwick v. First Nat. Bank, 84 N. Y. 420, 426, 433 (1881), where a discounting of the draft without knowledge of the promise was held not to be a taking "upon the faith" of the promise. For cases in jurisdictions that have adopted the New York Statute see: Naglee v. Lyman, 14 Cal. 450 (1859); James v. E. G. Lyons Co., 134 Cal. 189, 66 Pac. 210 (1901), 147 Cal. 69, 81 Pac. 275 (1905); Lathrop v. Harlow, 23 Mo. 209 (1856); Adoué v. Fox, 30 Mo. App. 98 (1888); see also Eakin v. Citizens' State Bank, 67 Kan. 338, 72 Pac. 874 (1903), denying recovery on the ground that there was no reliance.

[189] Of course there is no reason for drawing a distinction in this instance as both sections require reliance. *Supra* note 107.

quiring that the acceptance be in writing but saying nothing about reliance, the confusion that had arisen under the American common law continued until the Uniform Negotiable Instruments Law was adopted[190] under which statute, reliance, at the time of taking or drawing the draft is required.[191]

In regard to reliance, there is one difference between the two sections of the Negotiable Instruments Law. Section 134 requires the extrinsic acceptance to be shown to the buyer, while, according to Section 135, the virtual acceptance is sufficient if merely

[190] Ravenswood Bank v. Reneker, 18 Pa. Super. Ct. 192, 198 (1901). "A contract which would have constituted a valid acceptance before the enactment of the statute, will if in writing and signed by the party or his agent still do so." This decision was rendered after Pennsylvania had adopted a statute requiring merely that acceptances be in writing, but before the Uniform Negotiable Instruments Law became effective.

[191] Commercial Bank v. First Nat. Bank, 147 La. 925, 86 So. 342, 13 A. L. R. 986 (1920); Wilson & Co. v. Niffenegger, 211 Mich. 311, 178 N. W. 667 (1920); Illinois Trust & Savings Bank v. Northern Bank & Trust Co., 214 Ill. App. 440, 445 (1919), *rev'd* on other grounds, 292 Ill. 11, 126 N. E. 533 (1920); Swenson Bros. Co. v. Commercial State Bank, 98 Neb. 702, 705, 154 N. W. 233, 234, L. R. A. 1917F 1096, 1099 (1915); First Nat. Bank v. Muskogee Pipe Line Co., 40 Okla. 603, 139 Pac. 1136, L. R. A. 1916B, 1021 (1914). For cases denying recovery on the ground of no reliance at the time of taking the draft, see: Citizens' Bank v. Willing, 109 Wash. 464, 186 Pac. 1072 (1920); Jones v. Crumpler, 119 Va. 143, 89 S. E. 232 (1916); McMillan v. Citizens' & Southern Nat. Bank, 37 Ga. App. 813, 142 S. E. 194 (1928); *cf.*, however, Bulliet v. Allegheny Trust Co., 284 Pa. 561, 131 Atl. 471, 42 A. L. R. 1133 (1925), where the court allowed a recovery on a promise as a certification though made after the check had been deposited in escrow. See also Southern Creosoting Co. v. Chicago & A. R. R., 205 S. W. 716 (Mo. 1918). A very interesting question also arises as to what constitutes reliance. Discounting a draft after seeing the letter containing the promise is, of course, sufficient. Where sight of the instrument containing the promise is not necessary, the holder is bound by its terms, whether he sees it or not, and cannot recover unless all the terms and conditions of the acceptance are performed, whether or not he is informed of them, see Jones v. Crumpler, *ibid.* It has also been held that allowing a holder to draw against a draft previously taken for collection, on the production of the letter with the promise in it, is a taking in reliance, see Commercial Bank v. First Nat. Bank, *ibid.;* see also Louisiana Nat. Bank v. Schuchardt, 15 Hun 405 (N. Y. 1878). Retaining a draft previously taken or performing other acts such as sending a straight bill of lading to the consignee in reliance on the promise has been held not to be reliance within the meaning of §§ 134 and 135 of the Uniform Negotiable Instruments Law, see Citizens' Bank v. Willing, *ibid.*, and Jones v. Crumpler, *ibid.;* see also Lugrue v. Woodruff, 29 Ga. 648 (1860), decided at common law. Compare the foregoing with the discussion of what constitutes reliance in an action on the promise, *infra* p. 110.

relied on. This is obviously borrowed from the similar provision of the New York Revised Statutes. Of that provision, the New York court has said:

> No reason can be perceived for a distinction in this respect between the two cases and we do not believe that any was intended by the legislature and that the difference in the phraseology is altogether accidental. . . . The language "shall have been shown" means nothing more than to express the idea, that the holder must know of the acceptance; this is, indeed, the only effect of it. All this is undoubtedly implied in the next sentence and the clause, therefore, might as well have been omitted altogether, as it is in the next section.[192]

The English common law did not require sight of the promise in cases in which it was held that reliance was necessary,[193] and such American cases as require reliance also do not require an actual sight of the instrument.[194] That this useless and meaningless requirement was continued in the Uniform Negotiable Instruments Law is unfortunate,[195] and when the problem arises, the courts are almost certain to disregard it as an accidental difference in phraseology.

This requirement for reliance raises a curious problem as regards both virtual and extrinsic acceptances, in the case where one holder who has taken the draft in reliance on the promise sells it to another who has no knowledge of the promise. What are the rights of the subsequent holder against the promisor, in the event that he is subsequently informed of the promise? A proper appreciation of the desiderata in regard to the free passage of negotiable paper would allow a recovery. To give different

---

[192] Bank of Michigan v. Ely, *supra* note 188, at 511.

[193] Clarke v. Cock, 4 East 57, 102 Eng. R. 751 (1803).

[194] It is true that the rule in Coolidge v. Payson, quoted *supra* p. 69, requires actual sight of the writing. This has not been very strictly construed or followed. Lewis v. Kramer, 3 Md. 265, 289 (1852). See Woodard v. Griffiths-Marshall Grain Com. Co., *supra* note 187, where the court shows clearly the undesirability of the rule; *cf.* Jones v. Crumpler *supra* note 191.

[195] The Illinois and South Dakota statutes omit that requirement. BRANNAN, NEGOTIABLE INSTRUMENTS LAW (4th ed. 1926) 826.

holders different rights on the same paper would only add to the confusion of the law on the subject. In addition, it should be noticed that, under the Negotiable Instruments Law, there is no instance where a purchaser is deprived of a right that a previous holder had, against an acceptor or maker, except as a result of the purchaser's own act.[196] This is, of course, not conclusive but it is a strong indication of the tendency of the law and should be followed since there are no weighty reasons to the contrary. Opposed to this is the express language of the statute allowing a recovery by a holder only when he has taken in reliance on the promise.[197] In the absence of any case on this point, the prevail-

[196] In cases of defences against the payee or endorsee, when the drafts once get into the hands of a bona fide purchaser, then even a subsequent purchaser with knowledge can recover; UNIFORM NEGOTIABLE INSTRUMENTS LAW, § 58. This is a wise rule as otherwise the acceptor can through publicity in the proper places, where paper is usually discounted, destroy the value of the paper to the bona fide purchaser. It is notorious that merely a slight rumor will considerably impair the negotiability of a draft or note. The bona fide purchaser is buying, not a law suit, but a paper that is freely negotiable.

[197] It has been argued that Sections 58 and 37 (2), would tend to give the subsequent endorsee a right even though he took without reliance. These are general sections and it may well be maintained that Sections 134 and 135 are exceptions to the general rule there laid down. It has also been suggested that the purchaser be deemed to be an assignee of all the holder's rights, or the grantee of an irrevocable power of attorney coupled with an interest. There are several objections to this approach, particularly where the acceptor has defenses against the holder. The purchaser would take subject to the equities available against the holder. This is undesirable. The purchaser should be given rights on the acceptance similar to those of the usual bona fide purchaser. In addition, in view of the facts, this interpretation is in the nature of a fiction inasmuch as an endorsement is not a grant of a power of attorney and is seldom so intended. Finally, it is well recognized that parties have not the power to grant the right to sue on an instrument unless sanctioned by law. "Who may maintain a suit is a matter of law, not subject to be controlled by the private conventions of parties." Mackay v. Randolph Macon Coal Co., 178 Fed. 881, 884 (C. C. A. 8th, 1910). If the law not only does not permit, but actually denies, the purchaser a recovery, any efforts of the parties to avoid this result must be ineffectual. Bank of Manhattan Co. v. Morgan, 242 N. Y. 38, 47, 150 N. E. 594, 597 (1926), quoted *supra* ch. I, note 2. It is submitted that the simplest method of reaching the desired result is to hold that, in view of commercial desirabilities, Sections 134 and 135 could not have been intended to cover the type of case under discussion. Since, therefore, these sections are not applicable, the usual rules of mercantile custom and convenience must be allowed to control, and the purchaser can therefore recover against the acceptor.

ing opinion of the commentators in this country seems to be that the holder cannot recover.[198] In England, the courts realized that confusion would result from the adoption of such a rule, and they avoided the difficulty by entirely abolishing the requirement of reliance.[199] Strictly speaking, the more logical rule would be to hold that a subsequent purchaser, who takes without reliance on the promise, cannot recover. Yet, if the courts in this country were to take the opposite view when the problem arises, it would not be surprising. It would not be the first time that statutory language was strained to reach what appears to be a desirable conclusion.

4. *Miscellaneous Requirements*

There are other requirements of the Uniform Negotiable Instruments Law. The promise must be in writing. At common law, apart from the rule in *Coolidge* v. *Payson,* this was not the rule.[200] But all the earlier statutes on the subject included such a requirement.[201] Other requirements, not incorporated into statutes, were also enunciated. Justice Story, following the policy of the federal courts in limiting as far as possible the extent to which promises to accept not written on the face of the bill were actionable as acceptances, attempted, more or less arbitrarily, to limit the recognition of such promises as acceptances to time bills

[198] BRANNAN *op. cit. supra* note 195, at 830.

[199] Bank of Ireland v. Archer, 11 M. & W. 383, 390, 152 Eng. R. 852, 855 (1843). "And to hold that the same act would be an acceptance or not according to the subsequent contingency of the holder of the bill having notice of it, would introduce a strange anomaly and confusion into the relation of the parties to the bill, the drawee being an acceptor as to some and not as to other indorsees."

[200] See *supra* p. 33, note 24, and *infra* ch. III, p. 118, note 59, p. 119, note 60.

[201] This is not only true of states that followed the New York statutes, but of others as well. *Supra* p. 61, note 108; *infra* p. 119.

only.[202] His rule was not widely followed by the courts.[203] The distinction was not incorporated into the Negotiable Instruments Law nor into any previous statute. It will probably not be followed.[204] And, finally, as we have seen in discussing the question of reliance, it does not matter to whom the promise is made. As long as reliance exists, the holder may sue though he is not the addressee, as in the case of the usual acceptance. The bill is an accepted bill and can be treated as such.

A requirement of Marshall's rule that has not been incorporated into any statute is that the draft be drawn not more than a reasonable time after the date of the promise. The statutes are silent as to this requirement and no case directly in point has arisen under them.[205] It is very likely, however, that mere lapse of time will of itself cause any promise to become ineffective even

[202] Wildes v. Savage, 29 Fed. Cas. No. 17, 653 (C. C. D. Mass. 1839). Justice Story, in view of the fact that English opinion at the time was against the doctrine of virtual acceptances and in view of its commercial inconvenience, took advantage of the distinction between Coolidge v. Payson and this case to narrow the rule.

[203] Maryland seems to be the only jurisdiction which has followed Story's distinction. Brown, Graves & Co. v. Ambler, 66 Md. 391, 7 Atl. 903 (1887); Franklin Bank v. Lynch, 52 Md. 270 (1879).

[204] Under New York and similar statutes holding a virtual acceptance of a sight draft possible, see Adoué v. Fox, *supra* note 188; Merchants' Exchange Nat. Bank v. Cardozo, 3 J. & S. 162 (N. Y. 1872), *cf.* Nimocks v. Woody, *supra* note 187; Scudder v. Union Nat. Bank, 91 U. S. 406, 23 L. Ed. 245 (1875), applying Illinois Law. In Ulster County Bank v. McFarlan, 3 Denio 553 (N. Y. 1846), the question arose whether the authority granted was to draw sight or time bills. The court held that the authority applied to only the former type of bill and that an action on a time bill could therefore not be maintained. The question was purely one of the extent of the authority granted. *Cf.* Seaboard Nat. Bank v. Burleigh, *supra* note 188. There is nothing to indicate that the doctrine of virtual and extrinsic acceptances does not equally apply to both time and sight bills. *Cf.* however, BRANNAN *op. cit.*, *supra* note 195, at 831.

[205] But at common law, in Parrish v. Taggart-Delph Lumber Co., *supra* note 187, two days, and in Nimocks v. Woody, *supra* note 187, six or seven days, were held to be reasonable intervals, while in First Nat. Bank v. Bensley, 2 Fed. 609, 615 (C. C. N. D. Ill. 1880), a delay of a year was held to be unreasonable. See also Davidson v. Keyes, 2 Rob. 254 (La. 1842); State Nat. Bank v. Young, 14 Fed. 889 (C. C. D. Neb. 1883); Kendrick v. Campbell, *supra* note 187, at 525; Wilson v. Clements, 3 Mass. 1 (1807); Leach v. Hill, 106 Iowa 171, 76 N. W. 667 (1898). See also Union Bank v. Shea, 57 Minn. 180, 186, 58 N. W. 985, 987 (1894); Posey v. Denver Nat. Bank, 24 Colo. 199, 49 Pac. 282 (1897).

without any statutory provision to that effect.[206] This requirement would be equally true of an action on a promise to accept. It is therefore of no particular significance at this point.[207] There have been suggestions in some of the cases that the promisor must be notified that the draft has been drawn and negotiated.[208] This does not seem ever to have become a rule.[209] Under the Negotiable Instruments Law, there is no such requirement.

Another requirement of the Negotiable Instruments Law is that the holder must take the bill for value. This applies both to virtual and to extrinsic acceptances. It is also a provision of the earlier New York statute.[210] Marshall, however, does not mention it in his rule. This requirement raises two problems, first, whether the holder has any right, and second, under what circumstances he takes free from defenses that are available against a previous holder. In the case of an acceptance written on the draft itself, it is clear that the payee or endorsee has a right against the acceptor even though he is a donee. The effect of a taking for value is to make defenses available against a pre-

[206] Johnson v. Clark, *supra* note 188; Starr v. Murchison, 1 City Ct. 413 (N. Y. 1878). In the law of negotiable instruments, for example, the rule is that when a negotiable instrument payable on demand is purchased an unreasonable time after its issue, the taker cannot be considered a bona fide purchaser. UNIFORM NEGOTIABLE INSTRUMENTS LAW, § 53.

[207] The problem is unimportant generally, since nearly every modern letter of credit specifically mentions the date upon which it expires, see forms Appendix A.

[208] Kendrick v. Campbell, 1 Bail. L. 522 (S. C. 1830).

[209] It is not often mentioned in the cases, but see Allentown Nat. Bank v. Kimes, 12 Phil. 329 (Pa. 1878). This is one of the additional distinctions between a letter of credit and a guaranty, since under the latter instrument, particularly when it is a general guaranty, the rule usually is that notice of action taken in reliance on the guaranty must be given. See 1 BRANDT, SURETYSHIP AND GUARANTY (3d ed. 1905) § 205 *et seq.*; SPENCER, SURETYSHIP (1913), § 38; *cf.* CAL. CIV. CODE (Deering, 1923), § 2865, and similar provisions of other states, *supra* ch. I, note 41; London & San Francisco Bank v. Parrott, 125 Cal. 472, 58 Pac. 164 (1899). In the case of a buyer's letter of credit, there can be no requirement for notice, as the buyer is merely making an offer to honor drafts upon certain conditions, including the delivery of the goods and documents that he desires. Therefore, unless required by the terms of the offer, no notice is necessary. Union Bank v. Shea, 57 Minn. 180, 58 N. W. 985 (1894). But see Edmonston v. Drake, 5 Pet. 624, 8 L. Ed. 251 (1831).

[210] The New York Statute says "for a valuable consideration." *Supra* p. 61, note 107.

vious holder inadmissible against the bona fide purchaser. At common law, since the promise to accept or pay contained in a separate instrument was treated like a promise to pay written on the draft itself, the same rules would seem to apply. A donee, therefore, logically should have been allowed to recover under a virtual acceptance against the acceptor. He was, however, subject to defenses against the drawer or previous holder.[211]

Under the New York statute and the Negotiable Instruments Law, the purchaser, if he gave value, would obviously also take free from all equities which the acceptor may have against the drawer and all previous holders.[212] However, it would seem that one who had not given value could not recover under the statute, even though the acceptor had no defense against an action by the

---

[211] There is no case which allows a donee from a drawer or endorser to recover against a virtual or extrinsic acceptor, nor has any dictum to that effect been found. There is a general, uneasy feeling that some sort of consideration must be present. Usually it is found in one form or another. Occasionally, however, recovery is denied where the consideration is not clear. What constitutes value is not entirely certain. Under the statutes, the rules applicable to the normal acceptance would seem to apply, see *infra* note 212. At common law the rules appear to have been much the same. If the holder discounted the draft he could of course recover: Parrish v. Taggart-Delph Lumber Co., 11 Ga. App. 772, 76 S. E. 153 (1912); Central Savings Bank v. Richards, 109 Mass. 413 (1872); Jones v. Council Bluffs Branch of the State Bank of Iowa, 34 Ill. 313 (1864); Kendrick v. Campbell, *supra* note 208. A past debt was usually good consideration, especially in view of the fact that the holder forebore to sue the drawer. Pierce v. Kittredge, 115 Mass. 374 (1874); Coolidge v. Payson, 2 Wheat. 66, 4 L. Ed. 185 (1817); M'Kim v. Smith, 1 Am. Law J. 486 (Md. 1808). But this was not always so, especially if the holder had not taken the draft in reliance on the promise. Morse v. Massachusetts Nat. Bank, 17 Fed. Cas. No. 9,857 (C. C. D. Mass. 1873); Lugrue v. Woodruff, 29 Ga. 648 (1860). It was also held that unless value was actually given the drawer in reliance on the promise no recovery was possible. Strohecker v. Cohen, 1 Spears L. 349 (S. C. 1843). Usually, even if the holder gave the drawer consideration, there was an attempt to show that the promisor received something, such as a reliance on his promise. Where the draft was taken for a past debt, the fact that the payee forebore to sue the drawer is mentioned, as well as the reliance on the promise.

[212] Under Section 25 of the Uniform Negotiable Instruments Law, this would also include a pre-existing debt. This was also the law under the New York and similar statutes, though the fact that the holder refrained from suing the drawer is mentioned as consideration. Naglee v. Lyman, 14 Cal. 450 (1859); Molson's Bank v. Howard, 8 J. & S. 15 (N. Y. 1875); Burns v. Rowland, 40 Barb. 368 (N. Y. 1863); Bank of Michigan v. Ely, 17 Wend. 508 (N. Y. 1837); But *cf.* Ontario Bank v. Worthington, 12 Wend. 593 (N. Y. 1834).

drawer, and had funds of the drawer in his possession. A strict construction of the statute also would seem to require that the donee of a bona fide purchaser be denied a recovery under the statute. This is analogous to the problem in reliance, *i. e.*, whether a subsequent purchaser in ignorance of the virtual or extrinsic acceptance can recover when he takes from one who bought relying on the acceptance.[213] Whether the courts will take this technical position or a more common sense view and hold that once the bill is in the hands of a bona fide purchaser all subsequent holders can recover, remains to be seen.

Another problem arises under the statutory requirement that the holder shall have given value. In cases where the value given is not money but goods, the promisor may assert that the goods delivered were not those contracted for by the drawer. In New York it was held that where the seller who was the holder of the draft, admits that such was the fact, he cannot recover.[214]

This is but one aspect of the question of how far an acceptor or a promisor to accept may introduce as a defense facts which raise problems that deal essentially with the relation between drawer and payee or endorser and endorsee. This question will be considered in detail later.[215] At present it is necessary only to notice that the functional category into which the promisor falls is of some significance. If he is a banker making many such promises, one set of considerations may apply. If, on the other hand, he is engaged in an occupation which does not call for many such promises, the factors involved may be entirely different. The solution to the problem cannot be found by considering merely the words of the statute. A strict interpretation of these terms would necessitate the conclusion that the giving of any value, no

---

[213] *Supra* p. 85.

[214] Lemon Importing Co. v. Garfield Savings Bank Co., 105 Misc. 627, 173 N. Y. Supp. 551 (1919), *aff'd* without opinion, 187 App. Div. 932, 174 N. Y. Supp. 910 (1919); *cf.* Bulliet v. Allegheny Trust Co., 284 Pa. 561, 131 Atl. 471, 42 A. L. R. 1133 (1925).

[215] *Infra* ch. VI, p. 257 *et seq.*

matter how slight, would be sufficient, as the statute does not mention any definite amount. It is clear, however, that obtaining the draft by such fraud as to amount to the giving of no value at all would properly bar the holder. But short of that, if some value be given, the requirements of the statute are apparently complied with and a recovery on this ground cannot be denied.

These constitute all the requirements of any significance that have been mentioned in connection with virtual and extrinsic acceptances. Briefly, they are that the words used amount to a promise which must be in writing, unconditional, and definite in form; that the promise be relied on by the holder at the time of taking the draft; and that value be given. The interpretation and application of these requirements and the manner in which they have been affected by the different statutes have been considered in detail. It is apparent, of course, that the Uniform Negotiable Instruments Law has completely failed in its attempt to make the law in this regard uniform throughout the various states of the Union. In addition, by omitting to define the terms, unconditional and in reliance, by neglecting to take cognizance of the various rules regarding definiteness of the promise to accept, and by continuing the requirement for actual sight of the instrument containing the promise in the case of a virtual acceptance, the law has been left in an uncertain, doubtful, and confused state.

Chapter III

FORMS OF ACTION ON LETTERS OF CREDIT—(*Continued*)

F. Development of American Law relating to the Action on the Promise

1. Rights of the Direct Promisee
Special and General Letters of Credit

As can be seen from the previous discussion, the law relating to virtual and extrinsic acceptances has been worked out in this country in far greater detail than was possible in England. Doubtless, this was due to the fact that this type of action was before the courts with greater frequency in this country, because of the greater use made of the early form of letter of credit issued by the buyer himself. For the same reason, it will be found that the rights of various parties in the action on the promise to accept have also been considered in greater detail.

The action on the promise to accept must be considered from several angles and must be distinguished from the normal orthodox assumpsit action for breach of a promise. In the first place, the action should be viewed as affected by the various statutes relating to virtual and extrinsic acceptances.[1] In addition, the factual distinction between the direct promisee and a subsequent purchaser and the differences in their respective legal relations are important and often difficult of determination.[2] It is in this con-

[1] Discussed *infra* p. 117 *et seq.*

[2] This distinction is not always maintained by the courts; see, e. g., Banco Nacional Ultramarino v. First Nat. Bank, 289 Fed. 169, 174 (D. Mass. 1923).

nection that the terms general letter of credit and special letter of credit come into use and are of significance.

Letters of credit may be special in several ways. The term is generally used to signify, however, that the letter may be relied and acted upon by only one person or by a limited group of people. When a letter of credit is special in this sense, no one but the direct promisee may recover on it because, by the terms of the letter, all others are excluded. This distinction between general and special letters of credit has been clearly recognized by courts and commentators.

> It is called a general letter of credit when it is addressed to all persons in general requesting such advance to a third, and a special letter of credit when addressed to a particular person by name.[3]

> Letters of credit are of two kinds, general and special. A special letter of credit is addressed to a particular individual by name, and is confined to him and gives no other person a right to act upon it. A general letter, on the contrary, is addressed to any and every person, and therefore gives any person to whom it may be shown authority to advance upon its credit.[4]

Letters of credit may be special or general in other respects. The authority to draw drafts and likewise the power to purchase the draft from the person who is advancing the credit may be restricted to one person or extended generally. Since early letters of credit in this country were usually given to an agent, the authority to draw was generally limited to this agent.[5] The courts, therefore, took for granted and did not concern themselves with this phase of general and special letters of credit. On the other hand, before the middle of the nineteenth century, whether the purchaser of a draft had any right against the issuer of the credit

---

[3] 2 DANIEL, NEGOTIABLE INSTRUMENTS (6th ed. 1913) 2009.

[4] Union Bank v. Coster, 3 N. Y. 203, 214 (1850). See also the statutory definition adopted by several states, *supra* ch. I note 41.

[5] Sometimes the power to draw was given the seller, Cassel v. Dows, 5 Fed. Cas. No. 2,502 (C. C. S. D. N. Y. 1848), where the defendant's agent was authorized to have the seller himself draw on the defendant, the buyer. See also First Nat. Bank v. Black Hills Trust & Savings Bank, 44 S. D. 414, 184 N. W. 236 (1921).

is doubtful because of the view then held by the courts that there was no privity between him and the issuer.[6] As a result, this aspect of the distinction between special and general letters of credit did not arise.[7] We, therefore, find that commentators, in discussing the differences between general and special letters of credit, have expatiated merely upon the extent of the authority to rely on the letter when giving credit to the agent or the issuer because of it.[8]

These distinctions hold true today. In formal letters of credit, the authority to draw is ordinarily special, *i. e.*, limited to the seller. The authority to rely on the credit in advancing goods is also special, being limited in most cases to the seller under the sales contract.[9] On the other hand, the authority to buy the draft from the seller in reliance on the letter of credit is normally general, so that any party may buy it and thus obtain rights against the issuer of the credit.[10] It is clear that there is no reason at the present time, why a letter of credit may not be issued without a definite beneficiary, giving any one the power

---

[6] If, however, the promise was held to amount to a virtual or extrinsic acceptance any holder could recover.

[7] For an illustration of a letter held special as to purchasers, see Sherwin & Co. v. Brigham, 39 Ohio St. 137 (1883). When the distinctions became of importance, the courts often failed to notice them. For a typical case where they are confused, see Evansville Nat. Bank v. Kaufmann, 93 N. Y. 273 (1883). The basis of this decision is discussed *infra* ch. IV, note 38.

[8] In addition to the definitions quoted, see STORY, BILLS OF EXCHANGE (4th ed. 1860) § 459, p. 577; Birckhead v. Brown, 5 Hill 634, 642 (N. Y. 1843); American Steel Co. v. Irving Nat. Bank, 266 Fed. 41, 43 (C. C. A. 2d, 1920); Bissell v. Lewis, 4 Mich. 450 (1857); Monroe v. Pilkington, 14 How. Pr. 250, 255 (N. Y. 1857); Pollock v. Helm, 54 Miss. 1, 5 (1876); Regis v. Hébert, 16 La. Ann. 224, 225 (1861); see also BEAWES, LEX MERCATORIA (2d ed. 1761) 447; CAL. CIV. CODE (Deering, 1923) §§ 2861, 2862, 2863 and similar provisions of other states, *supra* ch. I, note 41.

[9] This does not dispose of the problem of whether the seller may assign the letter of credit, in the consideration of which other factors must be taken into account, see *infra* p. 142.

[10] In the formal letters of credit this is usually expressly stated. See forms, Appendix A. The courts have recognized however that it may be limited, see Banco Nacional Ultramarino v. First Nat. Bank, *supra* note 2, at 173.

to make himself beneficiary by selling goods to the buyer in reliance on the credit and by otherwise fulfilling its conditions.[11] Whether the letter of credit is general or special depends on the intention of the parties as expressed in it. This distinction was of importance during the first half of the nineteenth century. In the last thirty years, however, it has ceased to be of serious consequence owing to the gradual change in the method of trading and doing business.[12]

The question of the rights of a party who is not the addressee is but another aspect of the same problem of special and general letters of credit. If the letter is special, then only the addressee can recover on it, since it is meant to apply only to him.[13] If it

---

[11] For an early form of this type issued by an English firm, see the letter of credit in Russell v. Wiggin, 21 Fed. Cas. No. 12,165 at p. 68 (C. C. D. Mass. 1842). For early forms in which there was a special beneficiary, see Carnegie v. Morrison, 2 Metc. 381 (Mass. 1841); Birckhead v. Brown, *supra* note 8, at 635.

[12] Better and more rapid methods of communication are largely responsible for this result. It is now possible for a buyer in one country to deal directly with a seller in another, reaching an agreement with him and having some bank by a letter of credit authorize this particular seller to draw. Previously, it was the custom to send an agent abroad, or to large cities, to deal with sellers. The authority to draw was naturally given to him. This was true of both England and America, the only difference being that in this country, for domestic trade, buyers issued their own letters of credit, while for foreign commerce, which was financed mainly in England, letters of credit were issued by well-known English financial houses through their agents in this country on behalf of the buyers. For a typical transaction of that time, see Russell v. Wiggin, *supra* note 11; Carnegie v. Morrison, *supra* note 11; Birckhead v. Brown, 5 Hill 634 (N. Y. 1843), *aff'd*, 2 Denio 375 (N. Y. 1845).

[13] De Tastett v. Crousillat, 7 Fed. Cas. No. 3,828 (C. C. D. Pa. 1807); Grant v. Naylor, 4 Cranch 224, 2 L. Ed. 603 (1808); Robbins v. Bingham, 4 Johns. 476 (N. Y. 1809); Walsh v. Bailie, 10 Johns. 180 (N. Y. 1813); Penoyer v. Watson, 16 Johns. 100 (N. Y. 1819); Carrollton Bank v. Tayleur, 16 La. 490 (1840); Lyon v. Van Raden, 126 Mich. 259, 85 N. W. 727 (1901). Of course, it is conceivable that the letter of credit may be special to others than the addressee, but this must have been very rare, as it is mentioned neither in the cases nor in the texts. The modern letter of credit is, however, very often not addressed to the seller, but to a correspondent bank. This practice raises no legal difficulty inasmuch as the correspondent is usually expressly authorized to notify the seller; see forms Appendix A, the advice being given by the correspondent, as agent, on behalf of the issuer, as principal. And where such is not the case, the promise contained in the letter of the issuing bank though addressed to the correspondent must be deemed to be directed to the seller, within the rules we have been discussing.

is general, then all others who rely on it may also recover on it. During the first part of the nineteenth century, courts in this country tended to favor the interpretation of such instruments as special.[14] Later, influenced by commercial needs, they were inclined to hold such instruments to be general.

Accordingly, where a lumber company wrote a contractor agreeing to pay all of his employees who remained throughout the season, one who continued to work in reliance on the letter was held entitled to recover against the company, though the letter was not addressed to the plaintiff.[15] A similar result was reached where a letter was addressed by the buyer to a particular seller and was relied upon by another merchant in selling goods to the buyer's agent.[16] Likewise, where a letter of credit was written by the agent of an issuing bank at the request of a buyer, it was held that the seller could recover where the letter was addressed by the issuer's agent to his principal and mentioned the seller as the special beneficiary.[17] The same result was reached in a case in which the letter was not addressed to any one and mentioned no particular seller.[18] The effect of these decisions seems to have been that, unless the language of the promise expressly prohibited it, any person who advanced credit in reliance on the

[14] A letter that was clearly general would be limited in other ways. See Aldricks v. Higgins, 16 Sarg. & Rawle 212 (Pa. 1827), where a letter addressed "To any gentleman in the City of New York" was limited to only one transaction.

[15] Toohey v. Comstock, 45 Mich. 603, 8 N. W. 564 (1881).

[16] Bleeker v. Hyde, 3 Fed. Cas. No. 1,537 (C. C. D. Mich. 1843); see also Duval v. Trask, 12 Mass. 154 (1815). In the latter case, the letter is clearly general by its language. It is doubtful, otherwise, whether the plaintiff could have recovered at that time. In neither case is an authority to draw given, so that no question of the rights of drawers or holders of drafts could have arisen. See also Dorland v. Mulhollan, 10 Ohio St. 192 (1859).

[17] Carnegie v. Morrison, *supra* note 11; Lafargue v. Harrison, 70 Cal. 380, 9 Pac. 259, 11 Pac. 636 (1886); see also Ouachita Valley Bank v. DeMotte, 173 Ark. 52, 57, 291 S. W. 984, 986 (1927), where a telegram addressed to a bank in the seller's vicinity was held to entitle the seller to rely upon it.

[18] See Russell v. Wiggin, *supra* note 11, where the authority to draw was in the buyer's agent.

letter could recover against the issuer no matter to whom the letter was addressed, providing he had complied with its terms.[19]

In discussing the development in England of the action for breach of promise, it was indicated that the direct promisee had, in most cases, an orthodox contract action but that to state and prove a valid cause of action in strict assumpsit was often very difficult and sometimes impossible. In the interests of trade and commerce, with the growing recognition of the necessity of giving the promisee, who had made advances relying on the promise, an adequate and simple remedy against the promisor, these obstacles were gradually removed. In effect, this process resulted in the creation of a new form of action midway between the action on an acceptance and the orthodox action of assumpsit. Since this development began earlier in this country than in England, the growth was more gradual, and the greater latitude allowed to the direct promisee in stating and proving his cause of action cannot, therefore, be traced to the authority of any one case. From the language of the courts, however, the conclusion can clearly be drawn that the action on the promise to accept was considered more nearly akin to an action on an acceptance than to the normal action for breach of contract.

This point of view allowed the promisee greater liberty in stating his cause of action by freeing him from the necessity of conforming to all the technical requirements of the action of assumpsit. To what extent the doctrine of the presumption of consideration applied to an action on the promise to accept, is not certain. As will be seen in discussing the requirements of reliance and consideration in the action on the promise to accept, the cases are by no means consistent, definite, or clear. This much, however, can be inferred: that the promisee, after prov-

[19] See, however, Bank of Buchanan County v. Continental Nat. Bank, 277 Fed. 385 (C. C. A. 8th, 1921). The telegram was addressed to one bank and the draft was purchased by another. Recovery was denied on the ground that the purchaser was no party to the obligation of the issuing bank. The instrument, in this case, was apparently a guaranty, which fact probably accounts for the attitude of the court.

ing that he has acted in accordance with general business usage, will find that the rules of consideration, applicable to contracts generally, are applied much less stringently in his case.[20]

2. *Rights of the Subsequent Purchaser*

In the cases we have been discussing, whether the authority was special or general, the plaintiff proceeded on the theory that he was the direct promisee of the letter, even though it was formally addressed to another.[21] This assumption was sound and accurate. It did not, however, affect the problem of whether or not the purchaser of the draft could recover against the writer

[20] For the general position of the promisee in actions on promises made by banks, see, *inter alia:* Citizens Bank v. Singer, 109 Okla. 27, 234 Pac. 708 (1925), 79 Okla. 267, 193 Pac. 41 (1920); Moravek v. First Nat. Bank, 119 Kan. 84, 237 Pac. 921 (1925); Maurice O'Meara Co. v. Nat. Park Bank, 239 N. Y. 386, 146 N. E. 636, 39 A. L. R. 747 (1925); Lamborn v. Nat. Park Bank, 240 N. Y. 520, 148 N. E. 664 (1925); Second Nat. Bank v. Lash Corp., 299 Fed. 371 (C. C. A. 3d, 1924); Moss v. Old Colony Trust Co., 246 Mass. 139, 140 N. E. 803 (1923); Lamborn v. Nat. Bank of Commerce, 276 U. S. 469, 48 Sup. Ct. 378, 72 L. Ed. 657 (1928); Russell Grader Mfg. Co. v. Farmers' Exch. State Bank, 49 N. D. 999, 194 N. W. 387 (1923); Conn v. San Antonio Nat. Bank, 249 S. W. 1045 (Tex. Com. App. 1923); Scoby v. Bird City State Bank, 112 Kan. 135, 211 Pac. 110 (1922); American Steel Co. v. Irving Nat. Bank, 266 Fed. 41 (C. C. A. 2d, 1920), 277 Fed. 1016 (C. C. A. 2d, 1921), *cert. den.,* 258 U. S. 617, 42 Sup. Ct. 271 (1922); Saylors v. State Bank, 99 Kan. 515, 163 Pac. 454 (1917); Goeken v. Bank of Palmer, 100 Kan. 177, 163 Pac. 636 (1917); Pile v. Bank of Flemington, 187 Mo. App. 61, 173 S. W. 50 (1915). For actions on promises made by buyers, see *inter alia:* Citizens Bank v. Perkins Co., 250 Mass. 156, 145 N. E. 280 (1924); Sigel-Campion Live Stock Com. Co. v. Davis, 69 Colo. 511, 194 Pac. 468 (1921); Moro Supply Co. v. Griffis-Newbern Co., 142 Ark. 231, 218 S. W. 370 (1920); American Nat. Bank v. Pillman, 176 Mo. App. 430, 158 S. W. 433 (1913); Peoples Bank v. Stewart, 152 Mo. App. 314, 133 S. W. 70 (1911), 160 Mo. App. 643, 142 S. W. 789 (1912); Huston v. Newgass, 234 Ill. 285, 84 N. E. 910 (1908).

[21] Toohey v. Comstock, *supra* note 15, at 606, 8 N. W. at 565. "Courts may refine upon such agreements, at the expense of justice, and render them a mere snare to mislead men. . . . This was not a promise made to some third persons for their benefit. It was made to the men directly." Occasionally, the promise may be made to the purchaser directly, e. g., to a bank which is expected to purchase the drafts, Bank of Buchanan County v. Continental Nat. Bank, *supra* note 19. In this situation, the purchaser is the direct promisee and can recover on the grounds previously indicated. See Union Bank v. Shea, 57 Minn. 180, 58 N. W. 985 (1894); Baeschlin v. Chamberlain Banking House, 67 Neb. 196, 93 N. W. 412 (1903); Zacharie & Co. v. Rogers & Harrison, 19 La. 218, 223 (1841).

of the letter. Owing to the great use in this country of the informal letter of credit issued by the buyer himself, this question arose and was decided here about twenty-five years earlier than in England. The first case directly in point denied this right to the subsequent purchaser:

> The defendants requested Messrs. Brown & Co. to give a certain credit to Smith & Town. . . . If Brown & Co. had made the advance, and the principal debtors had failed to put them in funds, they might have had an action against the defendants on the letters of credit. But how can the plaintiffs sue? They were not requested to give a credit to Smith & Town either by paying the bills or in any other form. They have stepped in and advanced money as mere volunteers, and they can only sue upon the contracts to which they are parties, to wit, the bills of exchange.[22]

On the other hand, in *Russell* v. *Wiggin,* Justice Story, in an able opinion, laid down the rule that anyone who relied on the letter of credit in purchasing the draft could recover. He based this on the commercial practices and necessities of the times.

> On the contrary, I have understood, and always supposed that, in the commercial world, letters of credit of this character were treated as in the nature of negotiable instruments, and that the party, giving such a letter, held himself out to all persons who should advance money on bills drawn under the same, and upon the faith thereof, as contracting with them an obligation to accept

---

[22] Birckhead v. Brown, *supra* note 12, 5 Hill at 643, 644. See also: Carrollton Bank v. Tayleur, *supra* note 13; Worcester Bank v. Wells, 8 Metc. 107 (Mass. 1844); Exchange Bank v. Rice, 107 Mass. 37 (1871), 98 Mass. 288 (1867); Henrietta Nat. Bank v. State Nat. Bank, 80 Tex. 648, 651, 16 S. W. 321 (1891); Second Nat. Bank v. Diefendorf, 90 Ill. 396, 407 (1878); and Bay City Bank v. Lindsay, 94 Mich. 176, 179, 54 N. W. 42, 43 (1892), where, however, the promise was oral. Compare these cases with Kendrick v. Campbell, 1 Bail. L. 522 (S. C. 1830). In Birckhead v. Brown, the court recognized the different view prevailing in other jurisdictions but elected to differ with it. The court was also obviously influenced by the financial depressions of the years immediately preceding the decision, caused, it thought, by the overexpansion of credit. "I am aware that a great effort has been made within the last few years to have everything in the form of paper credit turned into a circulating medium, or, at the least, placed upon the footing of bills of exchange and promissory notes; and if our overstrained credit system had held out a few years longer, I am not sure that the courts would have been able to resist the current which was setting so strongly in favor of negotiability. But now that the bubble has exploded, I trust the common law, which declares that choses in action are not assignable, will not be overturned." 5 Hill at 646.

and pay the bills. And I confess myself totally unable to comprehend, how, upon any other understanding, these instruments could ever possess any general circulation and credit in the commercial world.[23]

Though this was said in a case where the plaintiff was the seller of the goods, it is fairly clear from the forceful language of the opinion that the subsequent purchaser of the draft from the first party to rely thereon would also be entitled to recover on it.[24] Such, of course, is the present law.[25]

---

[23] Russell v. Wiggin, *supra* note 11, at p. 74. For an attempted distinction between this case and Birckhead v. Brown, *supra* note 12, see Monroe v. Pilkington, 14 How. Pr. 250, 253, 254 (N. Y. 1857). An examination will reveal no sound commercial basis for the suggested difference. The cases represent different points of view. This difference is recognized by the court in Birckhead v. Brown: "Mr. Justice Story is evidently disposed to extend the doctrine of negotiability to letters of credit and commercial guaranties. (See Russell v. Wiggin, 5 Law Reporter 533, and Story on Bills, 534, 545.) But with us the rule is settled the other way, and we must take the law as we find it." 5 Hill at 646.

[24] This case seems to have been generally recognized as an authority for the rule that the subsequent bona fide purchaser could recover. Even Birckhead v. Brown, *supra* note 12, decided the following year, fails to distinguish Russell v. Wiggin, *supra* note 11, as a case of a beneficiary who had a right to rely on a general letter of credit, while Birckhead v. Brown was obviously a case of a bona fide purchaser. This is probably due to the strong language in the opinion of Justice Story, which clearly covers the case of a bona fide purchaser as well. The attempt in Birckhead v. Brown to distinguish the case as one involving a virtual acceptance is inaccurate, as Justice Story says specifically that it is not an action on an acceptance, Russell v. Wiggin, *supra* note 11, at 72, 73. The authority of Russell v. Wiggin was a very important factor in enlarging the right to recover of those who relied on letters of credit in advancing money or credit. See the cases cited *supra* note 20, decided after Russell v. Wiggin; also cases *infra* note 25.

[25] "In such case the import and meaning of the promise is that it is not made exclusively to the drawer of the bill, but is a promise made to any person into whose hands the bill may come *bona fide* for value; that the same shall be accepted and paid according to its tenor and effect; and such person may maintain an action for the breach of the promise." Franklin Bank v. Lynch, 52 Md. 270, 281 (1879). For other cases of promises made by buyers see, *inter alia:* Belton Nat. Bank v. Armour & Co., 11 F. (2d) 929 (C. C. A. 5th, 1926), *cert. den.*, 271 U. S. 678, 46 Sup. Ct. 630 (1926), 22 F. (2d) 727 (C. C. A. 5th, 1927); Oil Well Supply Co. v. MacMurphey, 119 Minn. 500, 138 N. W. 784 (1912); Parrish v. Taggart-Delph Lumber Co., 11 Ga. App. 772, 76 S. E. 153 (1912); Putnam Nat. Bank v. Snow, 172 Mass. 569, 52 N. E. 1079 (1899); Merchants Bank v. Winter, 8 Newf. 30 (1898); Posey v. Denver Nat. Bank, 24 Colo. 199, 49 Pac. 282 (1897), *aff'g*, 7 Colo. App. 108, 42 Pac. 684 (1895); Exchange Bank v. Hubbard, 62 Fed. 112 (C. C. A. 2d, 1894), *rev'g*, 58 Fed. 530 (C. C. S. D. N. Y. 1892); 72 Fed. 234 (C. C. A. 2d,

The real basis for the extension of the right to holders, not direct promisees, to sue on the promise, where the letter contains

---

1896), *cert. den.*, 163 U. S. 690, 16 Sup. Ct. 1202 (1896); Seaboard Nat. Bank v. Burleigh, 74 Hun 400, 26 N. Y. Supp. 587 (1893), *aff'd* without opinion, 147 N. Y. 720, 42 N. E. 726 (1895); Bank of Montreal v. Thomas, 16 Ont. 503 (1888); Dunspaugh v. Molsons Bank, 23 Low. Can. Jur. 57 (1878), *aff'g*, 21 Low. Can. Jur. 82 (1877); Smith v. Ledyard, 49 Ala. 279 (1873); Scott v. Pilkington, 15 Abb. Pr. 280 (N. Y. 1861); Barney v. Newcomb, 9 Cush. 46 (Mass. 1851); Lonsdale and Gray v. Lafayette Bank, 18 Ohio 126 (1849); Nisbett v. Galbraith, 3 La. Ann. 690 (1848); see also Murdock v. Mills, 11 Metc. 5, 10 (Mass. 1846). As has already been indicated, *supra* ch. I, p. 22, in this type of instrument, it is often impossible to determine whether the plaintiff is to be treated technically as the beneficiary of the credit or as the purchaser of the draft. In the cases cited, however, his position seems to have been analogous to that of the purchaser of the draft. In no case was he the addressee of the letter of credit.

For cases dealing with promises made by banks see: Muentzer v. Los Angeles Trust and Savings Bank, 3 F. (2d) 222 (C. C. A. 7th, 1924); Bank of Taiwan v. Union Nat. Bank, 1 F. (2d) 65 (C. C. A. 3d, 1924); Bank of America v. Whitney-Central Nat. Bank, 291 Fed. 929 (C. C. A. 5th, 1923); Border Nat. Bank v. American Nat. Bank, 282 Fed. 73 (C. C. A. 5th, 1922), *cert. den.*, 260 U. S. 701, 732, 43 Sup. Ct. 96 (1922); Nat. City Bank v. Seattle Nat. Bank, 121 Wash. 476, 209 Pac. 705, 30 A. L. R. 347 (1922); Bank of Plant City v. Canal-Commercial Trust and Savings Bank, 270 Fed. 477 (C. C. A. 5th, 1921); Bank of Lumpkin v. Peoples Bank, 27 Ga. App. 459, 108 S. E. 835 (1921); Pierceville State Bank v. Gray County Bank, 113 Kan. 352, 214 Pac. 788 (1923); Midwest Nat. Bank & Trust Co. v. Niles & Watters Sav Bank, 190 Iowa 752, 180 N. W. 880 (1921); Bank of Eclectic v. Sturdivant Bank, 203 Ala. 458, 83 So. 321 (1919); Elliott v. First State Bank, 105 Tex. 547, 152 S. W. 808 (1913); Bank of Seneca v. First Nat. Bank, 105 Mo. App. 722, 78 S. W. 1092 (1904); Pollock v. Helm, 54 Miss. 1 (1876); Cassel v. Dows, 5 Fed. Cas. No. 2,502 (C. C. S. D. N. Y. 1848); *cf.* cases cited *supra* note 22.

The influence of Birckhead v. Brown, *supra* note 12, has not been very great. On appeal, the upper court, the state senate at that time, was divided evenly on the question of the right of the purchaser to sue. The verdict therefore was not reversed. Almost immediately, however, this court showed a tendency to limit the extent of the rule laid down in that case. See Ulster County Bank v. McFarlan, 3 Denio 553, 556 (N. Y. 1846); Evansville Nat. Bank v. Kaufmann, 93 N. Y. 273, 286 (1883): "The case of *Birckhead* v. *Brown* not only on account of the reasoning by which it is supported, but because it is a decision of a court distinguished for learning and ability, is entitled to great weight, although some of the reasons urged in support of the judgment are no longer tenable, owing to the provisions of our Code and the principles adopted in later cases." See also the opinion of the court below, 24 Hun 612 (1881). For a discussion of this case, see *infra* ch. IV, note 38.

That the purchaser of a draft drawn under the formal letter of credit, which contains an express undertaking to purchasers to honor the draft, can recover against the issuer is clear, Appendix A. This result would follow even under Birckhead v. Brown, *supra* note 12. Even in the absence of an express promise to purchasers it is fairly clear that at the present time a purchaser can recover in New York. See in addition to the cases cited *ibid.* Ruiz v. Renauld, 100 N. Y. 256, 3 N. E. 182

no express undertaking directed to purchasers, has been a recognition of the universal commercial usage that the drawer of the draft uses the letter to discount the draft with third parties who take it in reliance on the letter. Clearly, the letter is useless to the beneficiary unless he can so use it, and to enable him to so use it, the purchaser of the draft must be given a right against the issuer of the credit. The custom being so universal, the assumption now is that the writer intends the letter to be used in that fashion, and that he impliedly requests the third party to buy the draft and look to him for reimbursement.

> But it [the letter of credit] is drawn for the express purpose of being shown to others, and of inducing them to make advancements of money for the object contemplated in it; and after the purpose has in this way been accomplished, to withhold a remedy against the writers, would seem to be giving a direct countenance, by law, to the perpetration of a fraud. It would be strange if authorities could not be found to obviate the difficulty supposed to exist in a case like the present, from the want of a privity of contract.[26]

> Defendant appears to be an intelligent professional man, and it is safe to assume that he was not unacquainted with business methods. Hence he must have inferred from the telegram that Hukill wished to negotiate the draft on the strength of defendant's agreement to honor it. That defendant so understood the purport of the telegram admits of no doubt, when the subsequent correspondence between him and plaintiff is considered.[27]

(1885); and Scott v. Pilkington, *ibid.* quoted *infra* p. 106; Barney v. Worthington, 37 N. Y. 112 (1867); Monroe v. Pilkington, *supra* note 23; Germania Nat. Bank v. Taaks, 101 N. Y. 442, 450, 5 N. E. 76, 80 (1886), quoted *infra* p. 248; Portuguese American Bank v. Atlantic Nat. Bank, 200 App. Div. 575, 193 N. Y. Supp. 423 (1922). In the last two cases recovery was denied to the purchasers on the ground that the conditions had not been performed. The whole tenor of the opinions, however, recognizes and rests upon the assumption that purchasers of drafts can recover against the issuer of the credit. See also Muller v. Kling, 209 N. Y. 239, 103 N. E. 138 (1913), *aff'g*, 149 App. Div. 176, 180, 133 N. Y. Supp. 614, 617 (1912), quoted *infra* note 53. It is interesting to note that the dissenting opinion in the lower court seemed inclined to take the view that the purchaser of a draft in reliance on a promise to accept acquired no rights against the promisor.

[26] Lonsdale and Gray v. Lafayette Bank, *supra* note 25, at 141.

[27] Oil Well Supply Co. v. MacMurphey, *supra* note 25, at 502, 138 N. W. at 785; see also: Dunspaugh v. Molsons Bank, *supra* note 25; Wells v. Western Union Telegraph Co., 144 Iowa 605, 620, 123 N. W. 371, 377, 24 L. R. A. (N. S.) 1045, 1052 (1909).

The purchaser has a right, on reading a promise to pay, to infer that the promisor wishes him to rely on it in purchasing the draft. If, therefore, the promisor does not so desire, it is only reasonable to require him to indicate this clearly in his letter. Any understandings with the addressee of which the purchaser is unaware or which he cannot reasonably infer from reading the letter, cannot relieve the promisor of the obligation. The representation of a grant of authority to purchase upon the terms mentioned in the letter is still implied.

Even if it were true that the defendants had no intention that Wickham should shew the message to the Bank or any other person, or use it as it was used, still the defendants' conduct in sending such a telegram is such that any reasonable man would take the representation to which it amounts to be true, and believe it was meant that he should act upon it.[28]

On the other hand, if the purchaser knows that the promise is not intended to be relied on, either because he has knowledge of the fact that the promisor meant it to apply only to the addressee or because of some other circumstance which indicates that the words used are not to be given their ordinary meaning, then he is bound by that knowledge. He cannot force the promisor into any obligation which he knew the promisor did not intend to undertake.[29]

[28] Merchants Bank v. Winter, *supra* note 25, at 41; Pollock v. Helm, 54 Miss. 1 (1876); Monroe v. Pilkington, *supra* note 23, at 252. In Belton Nat. Bank v. Armour & Co., *supra* note 25, the court held, however, that the problem of whether promises contained in a letter and a telegram were intended to be shown to third parties was a question of fact for the jury. The instruments in this case were unusual in form and content. It is submitted therefore that the usual presumptions did not apply and that evidence as to the real intent of the parties was admissible and became a question for the jury. If the instruments had been in usual form, it would seem that the presumption that they were intended to be shown to and relied upon by third parties should have been conclusive, in the absence of proof of knowledge to the contrary on the part of the plaintiff. On appeal, after a trial where the jury found that the instruments were intended to be shown to third parties, the court sustained the judgment. 22 F. (2d) 727 (C. C. A. 5th, 1927).

[29] See Sherwin & Co. v. Brigham, 39 Ohio St. 137 (1883) where the court doubted whether a friendly letter to a brother containing a promise to pay was the type of letter which entitled a third party to rely on it without further question; see Parlin v. Hall, 2 N. D. 473, 52 N. W. 405

The effect of this view of the promisor's liability is to base the holder's right of recovery on the theory that he is in direct privity with the promisor, that there is an independent contract between the two and that the holder does not obtain his rights from the addressee in any way.

In the Supreme Court of the United States the doctrine has been directly affirmed on several occasions that the Letter writer is positively and directly bound to any party making the advance upon the faith of the Letter; . . . And it has been further held, that, if the engagement be, to accept and pay any Bills, not exceeding a limited amount, drawn by the person, to whom and for whose benefit, the advance is to be made; in such a case, the per-

---

(1892); and *infra* notes 51 and 52; see also Bank of Morganton v. Hay, 143 N. C. 326, 55 S. E. 811 (1906); Exchange Bank v. Rice, 107 Mass. 37, 44 (1871), 98 Mass. 288 (1867); *cf.* Barney v. Newcomb *supra* note 25, at 54, where the court held that there was no evidence that a business letter was intended to be confidential, and Barney v. Worthington, 37 N. Y. 112 (1867). The fact that the drafts are given in payment of a personal debt of the drawer does not constitute notice to the taker that it is outside the terms of the credit, in the absence of any limitations in the letter of credit. Oriental Banking Corp. v. Lippert, 5 Buch. 152 (S. A. 1875).

See also: Maitland v. Chartered Mercantile Bank of India, London and China, 38 L. J. Ch. 363 (1869); Watson v. Jackson, 264 S. W. 603 (Tex. Civ. App. 1924); Hutchinson v. Mitchell & Co., 15 La. Ann. 326 (1860); Forman v. Walker, 4 La. Ann. 409 (1849); Davidson v. Keyes, 2 Rob. 254 (La. 1842); and Hoe and Harrison v. Oxley and Hancock, 1 Wash. 19, 24 (Va. 1791); to the effect that the bona fide purchaser of a draft can recover against the issuer of a credit, even though the draft is drawn for unauthorized purposes or in violation of conditions not contained in the letter of credit and of which the purchaser is unaware at the time he takes the draft. See also Naglee v. Lyman, 14 Cal. 450 (1859); Burns v. Rowland, 40 Barb. 368 (N. Y. 1863); Palmer v. Rice, 36 Neb. 844, 55 N. W. 256 (1893); Bank of America v. Whitney Central Nat. Bank, 291 Fed. 929, 935 (C. C. A. 5th, 1923); Bissell v. Lewis, 4 Mich. 450, 454 (1857); *infra* ch. V, p. 000. See however, Michigan State Bank v. Estate of Leavenworth, 28 Vt. 209 (1856). Here, the defendant signed as joint issuer of a letter of credit. Between the parties, he was considered only a surety. The plaintiff knew this at the time he took the drafts and the court held that he was bound by that knowledge. See also: Baeschlin v. Chamberlain Banking House, 67 Neb. 196, 93 N. W. 412 (1903); Graham v. Farmers & Merchants Bank, 116 Cal. 463, 48 Pac. 384 (1897); Saulsbury, Respess & Co. v. Blandy, 53 Ga. 665 (1875), 60 Ga. 646 (1878), 65 Ga. 45 (1880); Schimmelpennich v. Bayard, 1 Pet. 264, 7 L. Ed. 138 (1828); Ford v. Angelrodt, 37 Mo. 50 (1865); Union Bank of Canada v. Cole, 47 L. J. Q. B. 100 (1877); Storer v. Logan, 9 Mass. 55 (1812); Nevada Bank v. Luce, 139 Mass. 488, 1 N. E. 926 (1885), *infra* ch. V, note 66. For the application of these principles to the revocability of letters of credit, see *infra* ch. IV, p. 159. Compare the discussion *supra* ch. II, p. 31, of whether an instrument can be held to contain a promise. See also *infra* ch. V, p. 175.

son, taking such Bills, and making the advance upon the faith thereof . . . is entitled to treat it as a direct promise to accept and pay such bills, which promise he may enforce, accordingly, in an action in his name, founded upon such a Letter of Credit, against the writer thereof.[80]

3. *Reliance*

From this conception of the nature of the rights of the holder, whether direct promisee or purchaser, against the issuer of the letter of credit, as well as from the language of the courts in many cases, the element of reliance is clearly a very important factor in aiding the courts to reach their conclusions.

Such facts make a case of a promise made to one party for the benefit of another (anyone who might, on the faith of it, take such bill); and our books are full of cases holding that such third party, though a stranger to the actual promise, may recover in a suit directly against the promisor and founded on the promise.[81]

The reasons for this point of view are clear. It was obviously felt that one who had acted in accordance with a well recognized commercial usage and in reliance on a promise made by one who was or should have been aware of this usage[82] was, at least equitably, entitled to recover. The courts were, therefore, prepared to make every effort to insure a recovery on this type of instrument.[83] These considerations apply whether the holder is the beneficiary of the letter of credit or a subsequent purchaser from him. In England, as previously shown, these equitable considerations influenced the court in giving the subsequent holder rights.

There are four types of reliance. The purchaser of the draft or the promisee of the letter of credit may take the draft or

[80] STORY, BILLS OF EXCHANGE (4th ed. 1860) § 462, p. 580.

[81] Scott v. Pilkington, *supra* note 25, at 284; see also Nelson v. First Nat. Bank, 48 Ill. 36, 37 (1868), quoted *supra* p. 80; Boyce v. Edwards, 4 Pet. 111, 123, 7 L. Ed. 799, 803 (1830).

[82] Oil Well Supply Co. v. MacMurphey, *supra* note 25, at 502, 138 N. W. at 785, quoted *supra* p. 103.

[83] See Scudder v. Union Nat. Bank, 91 U. S. 406, 414, 23 L. Ed. 245, 249 (1875), quoted *infra* p. 139, note 109.

advance credit generally in reliance on the promise already made. It is obvious from the foregoing discussion[34] that whether or not the promise is made directly to the party advancing credit is of no significance in this connection. In a second type of situation, the party advancing the credit may have acted without knowledge of a promise already made, and subsequently learn of it. A third possibility is that the party advancing the credit may act before a promise has been made and later learn of a promise made to another after he has acquired the draft. Finally, the promise may be made directly to him after he has acted.[35] In each of these four illustrations, the holder may retain the draft in reliance on the credit or otherwise permit credit previously extended to continue. From the language of the courts, it would seem that the first type of reliance is meant, but whether they will insist on it is another matter. The equitable considerations underlying the requirement for reliance of the first type apply to the other types of reliance, when the promise induces the holder to keep the draft or otherwise to continue the credit.[36] And from this point of view, the distinction between these categories becomes in its essence more formal than real. If all the other conditions of the promise are performed, what possible difference can it make to the promisor whether or not the holder knew and relied on the promise at the time he took the draft? If there is no knowledge and reliance, the holder is, of course, obtaining something he never anticipated at the time he took the draft or otherwise extended the credit. But there can be no serious objection to that, especially in cases where the holder's subsequent knowledge influences his future activity.

[34] *Supra* p. 102 *et seq.*

[35] The holder may, in reliance upon a promise made to him after he has purchased the drafts, release bills of lading or other documents of title which he might otherwise have retained. Watson v. Jackson, *supra* note 29, at 612.

[36] "It is true that a person who takes a bill for an antecedent debt may thereby be induced to relax his exertions to obtain other security." Ontario Bank v. Worthington, 12 Wend. 593, 600 (N. Y. 1834).

The common law in this country relating to virtual acceptances, as we have seen, probably required reliance at the time of purchase, while, in regard to extrinsic acceptances, reliance on the promise even after purchase was sufficient in many jurisdictions. As already indicated, the Uniform Negotiable Instruments Law has substantially clarified the entire problem of reliance in so far as it relates to virtual and extrinsic acceptances. The law relating to actions on the promise, however, continues in confusion. It is intimately connected with the similar problem in virtual and extrinsic acceptances. The cases often fail to indicate whether the action is on an acceptance or for breach of the promise to accept and some expressly repudiate any distinction.[37] Therefore, the same uncertainty exists as to the precise kind and amount of reliance necessary to support an action for breach of promise, as was found in regard to actions on virtual and extrinsic acceptances at common law.

One who takes a bill in reliance on the promise can obviously recover against the issuer of the credit. In cases in which the promise is made directly to him, the holder of the bill may occasionally spell out a cause of action under the usual rules of contract. The difficulties of stating an action on the promise to accept or pay in the usual action in assumpsit have already been suggested.[38] It is more likely, therefore, that the rights of the direct promisee will also be classed with those arising in cases where the holder takes the bill in ignorance of the promise and retains it either because of subsequently acquired knowledge of a promise previously made or because of a promise made to a third person after the holder has taken the bill. In the first third of the nineteenth century, it is doubtful whether these latter types of reliance would have supported an action. Later developments, in view of the growing recognition of the fact that the equities in all the various types of reliance are practically alike, make it

[37] See *supra* p. 58, *infra* p. 140, note 110.

[38] *Supra* p. 51 *et seq.*

more probable that they would be sufficient.[39] If the subsequent discovery that a promise has been made, induces the holder to keep the draft, presumably a recovery in an action on the promise should also be allowed, since the obligation is merely that which, in view of the language of the instrument, the promisor expected to assume. On the other hand, any other result would defeat the rights of the holder who, in reliance on the promise, retains the draft or continues the advance of credit.[40] To broaden the rule regarding reliance so as to include retaining the draft in reliance on the promise, would be practically to abolish the requirement, in view of the readiness of the holder to modify his conduct, on learning of the promise. This is not however an unusual method of procedure for common law courts in cases in which they feel the desired results require it. Traditionally, in view of the conduct

---

[39] See Watson v. Jackson, *supra* note 29, at 612. It is difficult to reconcile this prediction with the language of the courts in some cases, e. g., Scudder v. Union Nat. Bank, *supra* note 33, quoted *infra* p. 140, note 109. The authority of these cases, however, must be accepted with caution. Most of the early cases were actions on virtual or extrinsic acceptances. We have seen that, in the former group, reliance was strictly insisted upon, with almost no exceptions, and that, in the latter type, greater latitude was permitted. Cases dealing with actions on the promise are fewer, and in most of them there was reliance at the time of taking the draft, a fact which the courts notice more or less casually. Opposed to this, there are the practical considerations mentioned above, as well as the fact that the courts were more lenient in regard to actions on the promise than they were to actions on virtual or extrinsic acceptances. Finally, no case has been found resting solely, or even mainly on the fact that there was no reliance, in an action on the promise as such. See, however, Bank of Seneca v. First Nat. Bank, *supra* note 25. In addition, there is at least one case which allowed a recovery where the promise was made to the holder after he had purchased the draft, Watson v. Jackson, *supra* note 29; *cf.* an earlier decision, Morse v. Massachusetts Nat. Bank, 17 Fed. Cas. No. 9,857 (C. C. D. Mass. 1873).

[40] This is true only when the holder has given value for the draft or has taken it for a past debt. If he is a mere donee, he has nothing to lose. The rights of a donee are based on a totally different theory. In its essence, the right of action of one who has given value in any way rests on the commercial customs and expectations of the community. These customs extend only to business transactions. A donee, therefore, if he has any rights, must proceed on the theory that the gift was some sort of assignment. This is sufficient basis for a donee's rights. In the case of a holder for value, it is important that the right of action be distinct and independent of the drawer's or indorser's rights. The reason for this is the necessity for barring unknown equities between the original parties. This aspect of the problem is discussed in connection with the doctrine of consideration, *infra* p. 112.

of courts in similar situations, it is much more likely to occur than is a formal abrogation of the rule.

Reliance can be shown only by certain external behavior. Accordingly, courts have been inclined to infer it from certain courses of conduct. Taking a draft with knowledge of, and after seeing, a lètter of credit is held in most cases to be conclusive of the fact of reliance.[41] Also taking a draft with knowledge of a letter of credit, even though it is not actually seen, would be sufficient.[42] In this case, of course, the purchaser is bound by the contents of the letter of credit, and, if the letter is so worded as to give no basis for the reliance, he cannot recover.[43] If, however, he takes the draft before the letter of credit was written or without knowledge of it, clearly his action cannot be held to constitute reliance at the time of taking the draft.[44] On the other

[41] Putnam Nat. Bank v. Snow, 172 Mass. 569, 52 N. E. 1079 (1899); Pollock v. Helm, *supra* note 28; Scott v. Pilkington, 15 Abb. Pr. 280 (N. Y. 1861); Barney v. Newcomb, 9 Cush. 46 (Mass. 1851); Cassel v. Dows, *supra* note 25; Nisbett v. Galbraith, 3 La. Ann. 690 (1848); Boyce v. Edwards, *supra* note 31. Because of the insistence upon this type of requirement in the modern formal letter of credit the problem of reliance has become academic. The present forms contain two provisions, among others, which are significant in this connection: that the draft state it is drawn under a certain letter of credit, and that the party purchasing the draft endorse on the letter of credit the details of the negotiation. See Appendix A. To recover against the issuer, the conditions of the letter of credit must be fulfilled. When these conditions are fulfilled, the holder not only knows of the existence of the letter of credit but has actually seen it at the time he took the draft. The question of reliance therefore settles itself. In the cabled credits and telegrams containing promises to pay the problem of reliance still remains.

[42] Smith v. Ledyard, 49 Ala. 279 (1873).

[43] McClung v. Means, 4 Ham. 196 (Ohio 1829); see also Woodward v. Griffiths-Marshall Grain Com. Co., 43 Minn. 260, 263, 45 N. W. 433, 434 (1890). Likewise, he cannot recover if the conditions are not fulfilled even though he does not know of them. Jones v. Crumpler, 119 Va. 143, 89 S. E. 232 (1916).

[44] There are no clear holdings on this point, but see: Parlin v. Hall, 2 N. D. 473, 52 N. W. 405 (1892); Lugrue v. Woodruff, 29 Ga. 648 (1860); Milmo Nat. Bank v. Cobbs, 53 Tex. Civ. App. 1, 115 S. W. 345 (1908). See also Guaranty State Bank v. Sumner, 278 S. W. 459 (Tex. Civ. App. 1926), where the holder retained a draft previously taken in reliance on an oral promise to pay. There was no discussion of the problem of reliance. The holder was allowed to recover on a theory of an assignment of the amount of the check to him by the drawer. See *infra* note 67. In Overman v. Hoboken City Bank, 30 N. J. L. 61, 68 (1862), 31 N. J. L. 563 (1864), however, the court took the position that unless

hand, if he is informed of the promise after he has taken the draft, there may be a reliance, though of a different kind, *i. e.*, a reliance in keeping the draft. As we have seen, the law in regard to this type of case is still doubtful.[45]

4. *Consideration*

From the foregoing discussion of the requirement for reliance, there can be no doubt that one who purchased a draft or advanced money or credit in reliance on a promise to accept or pay, could recover without difficulty in an action which, while perhaps superficially resembling the normal assumpsit action, actually was a different type lying midway between the usual contract action and the action on an acceptance. The basis of this action was the custom of the merchants. To look at it, therefore, from the point of view of the requirements of the strict contract action—consideration, offer and acceptance—would be to adopt a false perspective. In the usual business transaction, consideration was present. Since the early letter of credit used in this country was generally issued by the buyer as promisor to the seller as beneficiary, the consideration for the promise contained in the letter must be considered to have moved directly from the seller to the buyer. In modern commercial letters of credit, issued by banks, the consideration for the issuance moves from the buyer to the bank, the former acting in pursuance of a contract made with the seller.[46]

there was reliance at the time of taking the draft, the usual rules of contract applied.

[45] Another problem in this connection arises when the first holder who took in reliance on the promise sells the draft to another who takes without knowledge of the promise. Can the latter recover? There are no cases on the subject. In discussing the analogous problem in virtual and extrinsic acceptances, it was indicated that it was commercially desirable to allow such an action, *supra* p. 85. The identical considerations apply here. And as there are no statutory difficulties in the way of the desired result in this case, it is very probable that, when the problem arises, the action will be allowed.

[46] The inference is not to be drawn that the right of action of the seller or beneficiary rests on this basis. The legal theories underlying his right of action are considered later, see ch. VIII, p. 279.

The effect of failure or lack of consideration through fraud, mistake, or in other ways, upon the rights of parties, will later be considered in detail, particularly as relating to modern commercial letters of credit.[47] At this point, since we are primarily interested in indicating how closely this form of action was governed by rules applying mainly to actions on acceptances rather than by the usual contract rules, only certain results need be mentioned. Though the consideration between buyer and bank failed, the seller could still recover. Even if the consideration failed between buyer and bank and buyer and seller or, in the case of the early buyer's letter of credit, between issuer and beneficiary, a bona fide purchaser of the draft could still recover against the promisor. In all these cases, the equities between the original parties gave the promisor no defenses against one advancing credit. That this was due primarily to commercial considerations cannot be doubted.

> And it would be impossible, according to my view of the doctrines of Courts of equity, to allow the bank, after having sent that letter into the world, addressed to the persons who were to negotiate the bills, and so held out to them that it would be answerable for their payment, to say that because there was a debt due to it from the persons to whom it had given the letter of credit, therefore it would not pay the bills.[48]

Of course, a donee would take subject to the equities against his donor in accordance with the usual rule of negotiable instruments. As the action on the promise was never clearly recognized, its limits were never definitely marked, and no conclusion can be reached as to whether the donee could have used this loose and nebulous form of action or whether he would have been compelled to sue in strict assumpsit. At present, the question is

---

[47] See generally *infra* ch. VI, p. 224 *et seq.*

[48] *In re* Agra & Masterman's Bank, *Ex parte* Asiatic Banking Corporation, L. R. 2 Ch. App. 391, 395 (1867); Coolidge v. Payson, 2 Wheat. 66, 73, 4 L. Ed. 185, 188 (1817); *cf.* Sherwin & Co. v. Brigham, *supra* note 29; Ontario Bank v. Worthington, *supra* note 36, at 600. See also Pollock v. Helm, *supra* note 28; Nisbett v. Galbraith, *supra* note 41; and cases cited *infra* ch. VI, p. 251 *et seq.*

practically academic, in view of the development of the modern law governing assignments of *choses in action,* which has enabled a donee to assert rights as assignee subject always, however, to the equities between the original parties. Finally, from the tenor of opinions which consider promises to accept, it is fairly certain that a past debt was good consideration.

Then, again, as to the consideration, it can make no difference in law, whether the debt for which the bill is taken is a pre-existing debt, or money then paid for the bill. In each case there is a substantial credit given by the party to the drawer, upon the bill, and the party parts with his present rights at the instance of the promisee.[49]

One of the conclusions to be drawn from an examination of the cases involving actions on the promise to accept is that the questions of reliance and consideration are really two aspects of one problem. Where there has been reliance, courts in their attempts to fit the action on the promise into the usual contract form are compelled to exert themselves to find a consideration and will mention the fact of reliance, the forbearance to sue and the giving of value.[50] The resulting legal confusion is illustrative of the difficulties encountered in basing this action on

[49] Townsley v. Sumrall, 2 Pet. 170, 182, 7 L. Ed. 386, 390 (1829); see also Burns v. Rowland, 40 Barb. 368 (N. Y. 1863); Russell v. Wiggin, 21 Fed. Cas. No. 12, 165, at p. 77 (C. C. D. Mass. 1842); *cf.* Lugrue v. Woodruff, 29 Ga. 648 (1860). In some jurisdictions, in the case of oral promises, a new consideration was required, see, e. g., Strohecker v. Cohen, 1 Spears L. 349 (S. C. 1843), see also cases cited, *supra* ch. II, note 24. This rule was based on the interpretation given to the requirements of the Statute of Frauds. In the cases where the holder takes the bill without reliance on the promise, but is later informed of a promise made either before or after he had purchased the draft, it would seem that equities between the original parties should not be considered in determining whether he has a right to recover. This view is more in harmony with the rule that a past debt is good consideration, as the purchaser would merely have to request the drawer or endorser to re-deliver the draft after the former had learned of the promise to bring himself within the rule of taking the draft in reliance on the promise and for a past consideration.

[50] Of course, there is usually no express agreement to forbear, but such an implied agreement might be found, especially if the holder refrained from suing the drawer, as would generally be the case, until maturity of the draft. Certainly, where the draft is taken in conditional payment of an antecedent debt, the holder cannot sue on the old debt at least until the draft is dishonored at maturity by a refusal to accept or to

the usual contract theory. The real basis, as the language of the cases clearly indicates, is the recognition of a widespread commercial custom. Cognizance of this fact will dismiss as superfluous all problems of consideration arising in assumpsit.

5. *Scope of Action on the Promise.*

The action on the promise applies primarily to commercial letters of credit, and has as its basis well recognized commercial customs. The form of action obviously includes not only promises to accept made by a bank but also all types of promises contained in a letter of credit, e. g., to pay cash or that another bank will accept or pay cash. It includes certain types of bank credit. Other kinds of bank credit, such as the promise implied in receiving a deposit, are clearly not included. The depositor must spell out his cause of action in a normal contract action, and his assignee does not take free from equities between the original parties.

In this country, it is clear from the cases that the rights arising in connection with the use of the informal early letter of credit issued by the buyer are also enforceable in an action on the promise. The basic principles of the form of action in this country originated and were developed as a result of problems arising from the use of that instrument. In England, the matter

pay, see Burns v. Rowland, *supra* note 49. There is no reason why this type of analysis cannot be used in those cases where the holder takes in reliance on the promise. American courts have been inclined to do so. The promise to accept is considered as an offer to any one who takes in reliance on it, with the consideration moving from the holder to the promisee. This is fairly sound and adequate as far as it goes. However, when applied to cases where the promise is made after the holder has the bill or where he takes in ignorance of the promise, difficulties arise. It seems, therefore, more accurate as well as more useful not to rest these cases on the common law theory of contracts, with all its arbitrary limitations, but on the basis of commercial practice and custom. To do this would not be to make a theory out of whole cloth since, even from a casual reading of the cases, there can be no doubt that their commercial aspects influenced the courts greatly in reaching the desired results. Naturally, the courts attempted, whenever possible, to fit these cases into traditional legal categories, rather than to create precedents.

is more doubtful, as there are few cases involving this type of instrument. But, if the English courts should recognize a customary use in that country of the buyer's letter of credit similar to that which has existed in America, they might apply the same rules as apply generally to commercial letters of credit.

Promises made by merchants not in the form of letters of credit are, however, not included.[51] The position of the promisee in this case is analogous to that of a depositor in a bank. From the analysis given previously, this must be viewed as a totally different kind of credit situation. Where the promise of this type is to accept, if it should amount to an acceptance, then it inures to the benefit of all, and the purchaser has the usual rights of a bona fide purchaser. In England, where this type of promise is no longer actionable as an acceptance, or, in this country, if the promise does not satisfy the requirement for a virtual or extrinsic acceptance, its function and form determine whether or not it is subject to the rules governing actions on the promise. A promise not in the form of and not fulfilling the functions of a commercial letter of credit, is subject to the rules relating to ordinary contract obligations, and rights arising as a result of the promise are transferable only by the usual method of assignment.[52]

---

[51] Nicholson v. Ricketts, 2 El. & El. 497, 528, 121 Eng. R. 187, 199 (1860). "There is, however, great difficulty in saying that the facts shew any authority from the defendants to S & Co. to shew third persons the defendants' letter of credit." See also Wauchula Development Co. v. Peoples Stock Yards State Bank, 86 Fla. 298, 98 So. 220 (1923); Belton Nat. Bank v. Armour & Co., *supra* note 25. Whether the rules would apply in cases where the modern commercial letter of credit is issued by a party other than a bank is doubtful, see pp. 15, 293. If the issuer should bring himself within the principle of the commercial considerations previously discussed, either by the large number of letters of credit issued by him or otherwise, these rules might logically be applied also to credits issued by him. Otherwise, in view of the foundation for these rules, it is hardly likely that they will be so applied. Even if the holder of a draft under this type of credit is allowed to recover on the principles that have been discussed, it is clear that the rules as to performance of conditions may be different, as well as the nature of the defenses that an issuer may set up for refusing to honor its letter of credit. This aspect of the problem will be considered later. See *infra* ch. VI, p. 260.

[52] In Wauchula Development Co. v. Peoples Stock Yards State Bank, *supra* note 51, the defendant, by one clause of a long and involved contract, authorized the promisee to draw. The latter did so and sold the

The conclusions to be deduced from this discussion are hardly satisfactory. No definite result can be reached, no fixed rules laid down. In the cases, no comforting sense of security can be found.[53] This much is clear; the action for breach of the promise to accept, made in the usual course of business, is recognized as being much more freely actionable than is at present, or ever was, permissible in the orthodox contract action. It is a form of action that tends to adopt the rules governing the action on an acceptance.[54] Its basis is the custom of the merchants, and its prerequisites are the taking of a draft for value and in reliance on a promise. This being shown, the courts have felt inclined to allow a recovery. While no formal rules have ever been laid down, e. g., a presumption of consideration, as in an action on an acceptance, there can be no doubt that the burden of pleading and proving consideration, as well as the other requirements of the usual assumpsit action, weighs much less heavily on the holder of the draft who brings an action on the promise than on the plaintiff in an action for the breach of an ordinary type

---

draft to the plaintiff, who sued as purchaser of the draft. No formal assignment was ever made. The court held the promise too indefinite to be an acceptance and denied a recovery for breach of the promise. "The declaration only states a breach of the defendant's agreement to accept, and as such a breach affords no cause of action to the holder of the draft, a third person, no cause of action is stated by the declaration and the demurrer should be sustained." At 305, 98 So. at 223.

[53] "It is frequently a nice question to what extent a promise to accept a bill not in existence binds the promisor to third parties who have acted on the faith of it." Muller v. Kling, 149 App. Div. 176, 180, 133 N. Y. Supp. 614, 617 (1912), *aff'd*, 209 N. Y. 239, 103 N. E. 138 (1913).

[54] It is significant to note in this connection that in a recent decision the federal court adopted the rule of negotiable instruments relating to delay in presentment for payment as being applicable also to letters of credit. The letter of credit, in that case, required presentment on or before February 1st. Plaintiff mailed the draft so that in normal course it would have reached New York, the place of presentment, in due time. There was a delay in the mails and the draft arrived after the credit had expired. The court held that the rule of negotiable instruments excusing the holder for delay, owing to circumstances beyond his control, applied also to similar situations under letters of credit. Second Nat. Bank v. M. Samuel & Sons, 12 F. (2d) 963, 53 A. L. R. 49 (C. C. A. 2d, 1926), *cert. den.*, 273 U. S. 720, 47 Sup. Ct. 110 (1926).

of contract, and that, generally, a letter of credit "partakes of the nature of a negotiable instrument."[55]

6. *The Effect of the Requirements of Virtual and Extrinsic Acceptances on the Action on the Promise*

We have seen that, influenced by commercial practice, courts have tended to apply the rules of an action on an acceptance to an action on the promise. This close relation between the two forms of action is admirably illustrated by a consideration of the influence of the statutes governing virtual and extrinsic acceptances on the action on the promise.

Two interpretations of these statutes are possible. If they were intended to cover the whole field of the enforceability of promises to accept, then a promise to accept must comply with their provisions or must remain legally ineffectual. If, however, they merely state the requirements which make a promise to accept actionable as an acceptance, then there is nothing to prevent an action for breach of the promise as such, whether or not it complies with the requirements of the statutes. Our previous discussion of these statutes has shown that many promises cannot be actionable as acceptances because they are too indefinite within the meaning of the rule laid down by *Coolidge* v. *Payson*,[56] or too conditional within the purview of the statutes,[57] as these requirements have been interpreted by the courts. Apparently, therefore, the latter interpretation would be the one universally adopted.[58]

---

[55] *Ibid.* at 966, 53 A. L. R. at 54.

[56] *Supra* note 49, *supra* ch. II, p. 69.

[57] *Supra* ch. II, p. 62. See the provisions of the statutes supra ch. II, notes 106, 107, 108.

[58] The Canadian courts have recognized that their statute, which is similar to the English statute, was not intended to cover the whole field of actionable promises to accept, see Dunspaugh v. Molsons Bank, 23 Low. Can. Jur. 57, 58 (1878). "The Code takes away the negotiable character of acceptance which is not written on the bill, and this effect is not destroyed by holding that the appellants are liable in this action." Whether this principle would be extended to oral promises to accept, has never been decided.

As will be seen, however, the courts generally have inconsistently taken both views, depending on their opinion of the commercial *desiderata* involved in each problem. No better illustration can be found of the influence of commerce and trade on the action of the promise.

One principal requirement of the statutes is that the promise be in writing in order to be actionable as an acceptance. At common law, an oral extrinsic acceptance was usually held to be actionable as an acceptance.[59] As to oral virtual acceptances, there was more doubt. But the majority view seems to have

[59] **Gt. Brit.**: Ereskine v. Murray, 2 Str. 817, 93 Eng. R. 868 (1729); Lumley v. Palmer, 2 Str. 1000, 93 Eng. R. 994 (1735); Julian v. Shobrooke, 2 Wils. K. B. 9, 95 Eng. R. 658 (1753); Sproat v. Matthews, 1 T. R. 182, 99 Eng. R. 1041 (1786); Miln v. Prest, 4 Camp. 393 (1816); Fairlee v. Herring, 3 Bing. 625, 130 Eng. R. 655 (1826); Hay v. Boyd, 3 Mur. Scot. Cas. 9 (1822); *cf.* Cullen v. Maclean & Stewart, 11 Sess. Cas. (1st Ser.) 733 (1833); **U. S.**: Scudder v. Union Nat. Bank, 91 U. S. 406, 23 L. Ed. 245 (1875); **Conn.**: Dougal v. Cowles, 5 Day 511 (Conn. 1813); **Ill.**: Jones v. Council Bluffs Branch of the State Bank of Iowa, 34 Ill. 313 (1864); Mason v. Dousay, 35 Ill. 424 (1864); Phelps v. Northup, 56 Ill. 156 (1870); Nat. Stock Yards v. O'Reilly, 85 Ill. 546 (1877); Crumb v. Phettiplace, 53 Ill. App. 337 (1893); Heitschmidt v. McAlpine, 59 Ill. App. 231 (1894); Golsen v. Golsen, 127 Ill. App. 84 (1906); **Ind.**: Stockwell v. Bramble, 3 Porter 428 (Ind. 1852); Bird v. McElvaine, 10 Ind. 40 (1857); **La.**: Kane v. Robertson, 26 La. Ann. 335 (1874); **Mass.**: Grant v. Shaw, 16 Mass. 341 (1820); Peck v. Cochran, 7 Pick. 34 (Mass. 1828); Ward v. Allen, 2 Metc. 53 (Mass. 1840); Wells v. Brigham, 6 Cush. 6 (Mass. 1850); Pierce v. Kittredge, 115 Mass. 374 (1874); Dunavan v. Flynn, 118 Mass. 537 (1875); Smith v. Milton, 133 Mass. 369 (1882); Putnam Nat. Bank v. Snow, *supra* note 41; **Neb.**: Farmers & Merchants Bank v. Dunbier, 32 Neb. 487, 49 N. W. 376 (1891); **N. H.**: Edson v. Fuller, 22 N. H. 183 (1850); Barnet v. Smith, 30 N. H. 256 (1855); **N. J.**: McPherson v. Walton, 42 N. J. Eq. 282, 11 Atl. 21 (1886); **N. C.**: Wylie, Roddie & Ames v. Bryce, 70 N. C. 422 (1874); Short v. Blount, 99 N. C. 49, 5 S. E. 190 (1888); **Pa.**: Spaulding v. Andrews, 48 Pa. 411 (1864); Saylor v. Bushong, 100 Pa. 23 (1882); Ecker v. Snowden, 2 Miles 275 (Pa. 1838); **S. C.**: Clarke v. Gordon, 3 Rich. L. 311 (S. C. 1832); **Tenn.**: Farmers' & Traders' Bank v. Carter, 88 Tenn. 279, 12 S. W. 545 (1889); **Tex.**: White v. Dienger, 25 S. W. 666 (Tex. Civ. App. 1894); Milmo Nat. Bank v. Cobbs, *supra* note 44; Seguin Milling & Power Co. v. Guinn, 137 S. W. 456 (Tex. Civ. App. 1911); First Nat. Bank v. San Juan State Bank, 189 S. W. 745 (Tex. Civ. App. 1916); Farmers' Guaranty State Bank v. Burrus Mill & Elevator Co., 207 S. W. 400 (Tex. Civ. App. 1918); **Vt.**: Vermont Marble Co. v. Mann, 36 Vt. 697 (1864); McEowen v. Scott, 49 Vt. 376 (1877); First Nat. Bank v. Merchants' Nat. Bank, 7 W. Va. 544 (1874). See also Strohecker v. Cohen, 1 Spears L. 349 (S. C. 1843); Walker v. Lide & McLauchlin, 1 Rich. L. 249 (S. C. 1845); Overman v. Hoboken City Bank, *supra* note 44.

been that if the proper reliance were present, they were equally enforceable as acceptances.[60]

Under the Uniform Negotiable Instruments Law or any of the various types of statutes in effect before that law was adopted, it is clear that no promise to pay or accept is now, or ever could have been, actionable as an acceptance except when in writing.[61] Courts have assumed that these statutes were

---

[60] Townsley v. Sumrall, *supra* note 49; Nelson v. First Nat. Bank, 48 Ill. 36 (1868); Sturges v. Fourth Nat. Bank, 75 Ill. 595 (1874); see Hall v. Cordell, 142 U. S. 116, 12 Sup. Ct. 154, 35 L. Ed. 956 (1891), and Bank of Laddonia v. Bright-Coy Com. Co., 139 Mo. App. 110, 120 S. W. 648 (1909), applying Illinois Law; Williams v. Winans, 14 N. J. L. 339, 343 (1834); Hull v. First Guaranty State Bank, 199 S. W. 1148 (Tex. Civ. App. 1917); Kennedy v. Geddes, 8 Porter 263 (Ala. 1839), 3 Ala. 581 (1842); Havens v. Griffin, N. Chipman 42 (Vt. 1789); see also Putnam Nat. Bank v. Snow, 172 Mass. 569, 576, 52 N. E. 1079 (1899); Gates v. Parker, 43 Me. 544, 551 (1857); Storer v. Logan, 9 Mass. 55, 57 (1812); Banorgee v. Hovey, 5 Mass. 11, 23, 29, 38 (1809); Wilson v. Clements, 3 Mass. 1, 9 (1807); Van Reimsdyk v. Kane, 28 Fed. Cas. No. 16,872, at p. 1070 (C. C. D. R. I. 1813), modified on other grounds, *sub nom.*, Clark's Ex'rs v. Van Reimsdyk, 9 Cranch 153, 3 L. Ed. 688 (1815). Maine seems to have been the only jurisdiction definitely holding oral virtual acceptances invalid. Plummer v. Lyman, 49 Me. 229 (1860); Mercantile Bank v. Cox, 38 Me. 500, 507 (1854); see also, Scott v. M'Lellan, 2 Greenl. 199, 203 (Me. 1823); Edson v. Fuller, *supra* note 59, at 188. In New York, it is extremely doubtful whether such a promise was actionable as an acceptance, even before the Revised Statutes. See Ontario Bank v. Worthington, 12 Wend. 593 (N. Y. 1834); M'Evers v. Mason, 10 Johns, 207 (N. Y. 1813). See also the cases cited, *supra* ch. II, note 24, where the effect of the Statute of Frauds on oral acceptances and promises to accept is considered.

[61] See *supra* ch. II, notes 106, 107, and 108; Bank of Magazine v. Friddle, 14 S. W. (2d) 238 (Ark. 1929); Bailey & Co. v. Southwestern Veneer Co., 136 Ark. 583, 207 S. W. 34, 132 Ark. 63, 200 S. W. 280 (1918), 126 Ark. 257, 190 S. W. 430 (1916); Lewin v. Greig, 115 Ga. 127, 41 S. E. 497 (1902); Ingle v. Davis, 81 Ga. 766, 8 S. E. 192 (1888); Whitewater Com. & Sav. Bank v. United States Bank, 224 Ill. App. 26, 32 (1922); Mansfield v. Goldsmith Bank, 82 Ind. App. 224, 145 N. E. 586 (1924); Interstate Nat. Bank v. Ringo, 72 Kan. 116, 83 Pac. 119, 3 L. R. A. (N. S.) 1179 (1905); Ewing v. Citizens Nat. Bank, 162 Ky. 551, 172 S. W. 955 (1915); Lawless v. Temple, 254 Mass. 395, 150 N. E. 176, 48 A. L. R. 758 (1926); Corinth, etc., Turnpike Co. v. Gooch, 113 Miss. 50, 73 So. 869 (1916); Hanna v. McCrory, 19 N. M. 183, 141 Pac. 996 (1914); Quin v. Hanford, 1 Hill 82 (N. Y. 1841); Ontario Bank v. Worthington, *supra* note 60; Adams' Estate, 24 Pa. Co. Ct. 444 (1900); Bank of Rutland v. Woodruff, 34 Vt. 89 (1861), applying the New York law; Seattle Shoe Co. v. Packard, 43 Wash. 527, 86 Pac. 845 (1906); see Wakefield v. Greenhood, 29 Cal. 597 (1866) for the necessary allegations under the statute. See also cases, *infra* note 64.

Under the statutes previous to the Negotiable Instruments Law, since they often applied to all bills of exchange and not merely negotiable instruments, this rule was held to apply to non-negotiable bills as well; see Hoyt

intended to prevent an oral promise from becoming legally effective and have accordingly held that they barred an action for breach of a promise based on an oral promise to accept. To allow such an action would therefore be to avoid the effect of the statute.

Section 134 relates to rights and duties, and not to form of remedy. It means that the drawee is not obligated to pay the holder unless and until he accepts, and the plaintiffs gain nothing by saying that they do not sue "on the bill." Neither do they gain anything by saying that they ground their action upon equitable considerations, since equity must follow the law in all cases in which the legislature has intervened and prescribed rules of law which govern the rights of the parties.[62]

---

v. Lynch, 2 Sandf. 328 (N. Y. 1849); Weinhauer v. Morrison, 49 Hun. 498, 2 N. Y. Supp. 544 (1888); Dickinson v. Marsh, 57 Mo. App. 566 (1894); *cf.* however, Curle v. St. Louis Perpetual Ins. Co., 12 Mo. 578 (1849). Since the Uniform Act applies only to negotiable instruments, it would seem that non-negotiable bills of exchange could be accepted orally. Some courts, however, still tend to hold oral acceptances of such instruments invalid. Faircloth-Byrd Mercantile Co. v. Adkinson, 167 Ala. 344, 52 So. 419 (1910); Sheets v. Coast Coal Co., 74 Wash. 327, 133 Pac. 433 (1913); Clayton Townsite Co. v. Clayton Drug Co., 20 N. M. 185, 147 Pac. 460 (1915); *cf.* however, Simpson v. E. C. Payne Lumber Co., 17 Ala. App. 159, 82 So. 649 (1919), *rev'd sub nom., Ex parte* E. C. Payne Lumber Co., 203 Ala. 668, 85 So. 9 (1920), 87 So. 876 (Ala. 1921); Dumbeck v. Walsh, 179 Ill. App. 239, 241 (1913); Clay-Butler Lumber Co. v. W. H. Pickering Lumber Co., 276 S. W. 664 (Tex. Com. App. 1925), *aff'g*, 264 S. W. 267 (Tex. Civ. App. 1924); Ahrens & Ott Mfg. Co. v. George Moore & Sons, 131 Tenn. 191, 174 S. W. 270 (1914); and cases cited in BRANNAN, NEGOTIABLE INSTRUMENTS LAW (4th ed. 1926) 1 and 215. But see Southern Creosoting Co. v. Chicago & A. R. R., 205 S. W. 716 (Mo. 1918). See also Ulrich v. Hower, 156 Pa. 414, 27 Atl. 243 (1893); Moeser v. Schneider, 158 Pa. 412, 27 Atl. 1088 (1893), where the court was of the view that the objection that an acceptance was not in writing could only be set up by the acceptor. This is apparently the minority view, see Erickson v. Inman, Poulson & Co., 34 Oreg. 44, 54 Pac. 949 (1898), and cases there cited. In view of the public policy generally found by courts behind the prohibition against oral acceptances, it certainly seems more desirable to hold that the objection to an oral acceptance can be raised by any interested party. An interesting decision in this connection is Kramer v. Mid-City Trust & Savings Bank, 225 Ill. App. 575 (1922). A depositor sued the bank for charging against his account two drafts drawn on him by his agent. The bank pleaded, *inter alia*, an oral acceptance. The court held that the statute against oral acceptances did not apply as it was not a suit on a draft. Under this decision, an oral authority by a drawee to another to pay a draft, would bind the drawee to the payor. The recovery would not be on the draft, but under the usual rules of agency.

[62] Rambo v. First State Bank, 88 Kan. 257, 259, 128 Pac. 182 (1912); Accord: Kohn v. First Nat. Bank, 15 Kan. 428 (1875); Anderson & Co. v. Jones, 102 Ala. 537, 14 So. 871 (1893); Sands & Co. v. Matthews, Finley & Co., 27 Ala. 399 (1855); Van Buskirk v. State Bank, 35 Colo. 142, 146, 83 Pac. 778, 779 (1905); Baer v. English, 84 Ga. 403, 11 S. E.

In the jurisdictions which had adopted the earlier New York

453 (1889); Parrish v. Taggart-Delph Lumber Co., 11 Ga. App. 772, 76 S. E. 153 (1912); Mansfield v. Goldsmith Bank, *supra* note 61; Upham v. Clute, 105 Mich. 350, 63 N. W. 317 (1895); Pfaff v. Cummings, 67 Mich. 143, 34 N. W. 281 (1887); Elliott v. Miller, 8 Mich. 132 (1860); Flato v. Mulhall, 4 Mo. App. 476, 477 (1877), *aff'd*, 72 Mo. 522 (1880): "It is contended for the plaintiff that, while under the statute an actual parol acceptance, whether upon valuable consideration or otherwise, is invalid, yet a parol promise to accept, if supported by a consideration, may be enforced as a common law obligation. Thus, the promise to assume an undertaking is made more effectual than the undertaking itself. The statement of the proposition seems to furnish its own refutation. . . . It will follow that while the liabilities of an actual acceptance can result from a promise to accept only when this is reduced to writing, yet, if there be no writing, the same liabilities will arise under a different name." See also Rousch v. Duff, 35 Mo. 312 (1864); Bank of Laddonia v. Bright-Coy Com. Co., *supra* note 60; Dickinson v. Marsh, 57 Mo. App. 566 (1894); Nichols v. Commercial Bank, 55 Mo. App. 81 (1893); First Nat. Bank v. Gordon, 45 Mo. App. 293 (1891); Bank of Springfield v. First Nat. Bank, 30 Mo. App. 271 (1888); Luff v. Pope, 5 Hill 413, 417 (N. Y. 1843), *aff'd* without opinion, 7 Hill 577 (N. Y. 1844): "He must take his remedy against the drawer. . . . It is a chose in action which cannot be transferred so as to give the assignee a right to sue in his own name, except in the form of an accepted bill of exchange. To give a parol promise to pay the effect of a written acceptance of the bill would be no better than a device to get round the statute and defeat all the valuable ends which it was designed to accomplish." See also: Risley v. Phoenix Bank, 83 N. Y. 318 (1881), *aff'd*, 111 U. S. 125, 4 Sup. Ct. 322, 28 L. Ed. 374 (1884); Loonie v. Hogan, 9 N. Y. 435 (1854); Nagle v. Richards, 134 App. Div. 25, 118 N. Y. Supp. 53 (1909); Weinhauer v. Morrison, 49 Hun 498, 2 N. Y. Supp. 544 (1888); Fairchild v. Feltman, 32 Hun 398 (N. Y. 1884); Matteson v. Moulton, 11 Hun 268, 270 (1877), *aff'd* memo. opinion, 79 N. Y. 627 (1880); Pike v. Irwin, 1 Sandf. 14 (N. Y. 1847); Gruber v. Bank of America, 127 Misc. 132, 215 N. Y. Supp. 222 (1926); Hunt v. Security State Bank, 91 Oreg. 362, 179 Pac. 248 (1919); Maginn v. Dollar Savings Bank, 131 Pa. 362, 18 Atl. 901 (1890); Nat. State Bank of Camden v. Lindeman, 161 Pa. 199, 28 Atl. 1022 (1894); Croyle v. Guelich, 35 Pa. Super. Ct. 356 (1908); Howes v. McCrea, 21 Pa. Super. Ct. 592 (1902); Huffman v. Farmers' Nat. Bank, 10 S. W. (2d) 753 (Tex. Civ. App. 1928); First Nat. Bank v. Sanford, 228 S. W. 650 (Tex. Civ. App. 1921); 255 S. W. 644 (Tex. Civ. App. 1923); Hall v. Cordell, *supra* note 60, at 119, 12 Sup. Ct. at 155, 35 L. Ed. at 458; *cf.* Saylor v. Bushong, *supra* note 59, decided before the Pennsylvania statute went into effect. See also: Kelley v. Greenough, 9 Wash. 659, 38 Pac. 158 (1894), *infra* note 64; Citizens' Bank v. Mabray, 90 Okla. 63, 66, 215 Pac. 1067, 1069 (1923): "This rule is not in conflict with the rule that the holder of a check cannot maintain an action against the drawee on the check until it has been accepted, for the liability is not predicated upon the unaccepted check, but upon the breach of the contract to accept and pay the debt, and such a promise is an original promise and not a promise to answer for the debt of another." The rule in Coolidge v. Payson also required the acceptance to be in writing. But this was not held to apply to actions on the promise. Townsley v. Sumrall, 2 Pet. 170, 7 L. Ed. 386 (1829). See also Curle v. St. Louis Perpetual Ins. Co., *supra* note 61; Light v. Powers, 13 Kan. 96 (1874); Bay City Bank v. Lindsay, 94 Mich. 176, 54 N. W. 42 (1892), and cases *infra* note 64.

statute, an additional consideration existed against allowing a purchaser of the bill this type of action on an oral promise to accept, because of the provision preserving the rights of a direct promisee even, apparently, where the promise was oral.[63] From the inclusion of this section, it is reasonable to infer that no other than the direct promisee could acquire rights under an oral promise.[64]

In this connection, it is desirable to lodge a *caveat*. There are many cases in which there is no written acceptance, where the holder of a draft recovers against the drawee.[65] The recovery may be based on a constructive acceptance because of acts of the drawee, e. g., his failure to return on demand, or his willful destruction of the draft.[66] In addition, the recovery may be

---

[63] Section 10, New York Revised Statutes, quoted *supra* ch. II, p. 61, note 107.

[64] Blakiston v. Dudley, 5 Duer 373 (N. Y. 1856); Light v. Powers, 13 Kan. 96 (1874); Flato v. Mulhall, *supra* note 62; Nichols v. Commercial Bank, *supra* note 62; Sands v. Matthews, 27 Ala. 399 (1855); New York & Va. State Stock Bank v. Gibson, 5 Duer 574 (N. Y. 1856). See, however, Kelley v. Greenough, *supra* note 62, where, though recovery was allowed a direct promisee, the language of the court indicated that a holder not the direct promisee could also recover. The statute identical with that of New York was not mentioned. What the effect of Section 10 was and how far it extended, is not clear. An oral promise to the holder of a check after he had taken it gave him no rights. See Duncan v. Berlin, 60 N. Y. 151 (1875). But what, for example, was meant by "any person to whom a promise to accept a bill may have been made," or by "negotiated"? New York, for instance, seemed to confine the latter word to the seller of the draft, Blakiston v. Dudley, *ibid.* See also Flato v. Mulhall, 72 Mo. 522, 526 (1880); Brinkman v. Hunter, 73 Mo. 172, 181 (1880). Alabama held that it included the buyer as well as the seller, Smith v. Ledyard, 49 Ala. 279, 282 (1873): "He who receives the bill for value, negotiates it as well as he from whom it is received. It requires at least two to make a negotiation." But see Hall v. Cordell, *supra* note 60. The Alabama courts also seemed to imply that a buyer from the direct promisee would have come under the words, "any person to whom a promise . . . may have been made." Naturally, New York assumed a contrary position. New York & Virginia State Stock Bank v. Gibson, 5 Duer 574, 585 (N. Y 1856); see also Ontario Bank v. Worthington, 12 Wend. 593 (N. Y. 1834).

[65] See on this subject Aigler, *Rights of Holder of Bill of Exchange Against the Drawee* (1925) 38 HARV. L. REV. 857.

[66] UNIFORM NEGOTIABLE INSTRUMENTS LAW, § 137; L. W. Feezer, *Acceptance of Bills of Exchange by Conduct* (1928) 12 MINN. L. REV. 129. Under the Uniform Act, it is also clear that the holder of an unaccepted draft cannot recover against the drawee in the absence of additional facts,

based on the theory that the drawer has assigned a claim against the drawee to the holder,[67] that the drawee is estopped from

§§ 127, 189. Leach v. Mechanics Savings Bank, 202 Iowa 899, 211 N. W. 506, 50 A. L. R. 388 (1926); Union State Bank v. Peoples State Bank, 192 Wis. 28, 211 N. W. 931 (1927); see also BRANNAN, NEGOTIABLE INSTRUMENTS LAW (4th ed. 1926) 814, 902, and cases there cited.

[67] For cases holding that the facts show an equitable assignment see, *inter alia:* Fourth Street Nat. Bank v. Yardley, 165 U. S. 634, 17 Sup. Ct. 439, 41 L. Ed. 855 (1897); Pope v. Huth, 14 Cal. 403 (1859); Wheatley v. Strobe, 12 Cal. 92 (1859); Indiana Mfg. Co. v. Porter, 75 Ind. 428 (1881); Merchants' Nat. Bank v. State Bank, 172 Minn. 24, 214 N. W. 750 (1927); Carlson v. Stafford, 166 Minn. 481, 208 N. W. 413 (1926); First Nat. Bank v. Rogers-Amundson-Flynn Co., 151 Minn. 243, 186 N. W. 575 (1922); Risley v. Phoenix Bank, *supra* note 62; Lowery v. Steward, 25 N. Y. 239 (1862); Bell v. Pletscher, 32 Misc. 746, 65 N. Y. Supp. 669 (1900); Moeser v. Schneider, *supra* note 61; Trumbower v. Ivey & Rapp, 2 Pa. Co. Ct. 470 (1886); People's Nat. Bank v. Swift, 134 Tenn. 175, 183 S. W. 725 (1916); Hatley v. West Texas Nat. Bank, 284 S. W. 540 (Tex. Com. App. 1926), *rev'g*, 272 S. W. 571 (Tex. Civ. App. 1925); Clay-Butler Lumber Co. v. W. H. Pickering Lumber Co., *supra* note 61; Webb v. O'Geary, 145 Va. 356, 133 S. E. 568 (1926); Boyle v. Vivian State Bank, 226 N. W. 579 (S. D. 1929).

Compare the foregoing cases with the following, where the court held that the facts did not warrant holding that an assignment had been made: Equitable Trust Co. v. First Nat. Bank, 275 U. S. 359, 48 Sup. Ct. 167, 72 L. Ed. 313 (1928), *rev'g*, *In re* Gubelman, *Ex parte* First Nat. Bank, 13 F. (2d) 732 (C. C. A. 2d, 1926); Eastman Kodak Co. v. Nat. Park Bank, 231 Fed. 320 (S. D. N. Y. 1916), *aff'd* without opinion, 247 Fed. 1002 (C. C. A. 2d, 1917); Sands v. Matthews, *supra* note 64; Baer v. English & Co., 84 Ga. 403, 11 S. E. 453 (1889); El Dorado Nat. Bank v. Butler County State Bank, 120 Kan. 109, 242 Pac. 475 (1926); Hall v. Flanders, 83 Me. 242, 22 Atl. 158 (1891); Superior Nat. Bank v. Nat. Bank of Commerce, 99 Neb. 833, 157 N. W. 1023 (1916); First Nat. Bank v. Clark, 134 N. Y. 368, 32 N. E. 38, 17 L. R. A. 580 (1892); Loonie v. Hogan, *supra* note 62; Izzo v. Ludington, 79 App. Div. 272, 79 N. Y. Supp. 744 (1903), *aff'd* without opinion, 178 N. Y. 621, 70 N. E. 1100 (1904); Weinhauer v. Morrison, *supra* note 62; Citizens' Bank v. Mabray, *supra* note 62; First Nat. Bank v. School Dist. No. 4, 31 Okla. 139, 120 Pac. 614, 39 L. R. A. (N. S.) 655 (1912); Erickson v. Inman, Poulson & Co., *supra* note 61; see also: Ford v. Angelrodt, 37 Mo. 50 (1865); Carmichael v. Tishomingo Banking Co., 191 S. W. 1043 (Mo. App. 1917); N. Y. & Va. State Stock Bank v. Gibson, *supra* note 64; Jones v. Crumpler, 119 Va. 143, 89 S. E. 232 (1916); De Liquero & Crozier v. Munson, 11 Heisk. 15 (Tenn. 1872); and *supra* note 66.

Some decisions permit a recovery on the theory that a special deposit has been made for the benefit of the holder of a check. This is but a special form of the theory that there has been an assignment by the drawer to the holder of the check; see: Eshbach v. Byers, 164 Ill. App. 449 (1911); Dolph v. Cross, 153 Iowa 289, 133 N. W. 669 (1911); First Nat. Bank v. Barger, 115 S. W. 726 (Ky. 1909); State *ex rel.* Roberts v. Trimble, 316 Mo. 354, 289 S. W. 796 (1926); Walls v. Crocker State Bank, 205 Mo. App. 323, 220 S. W. 671 (1920); Pile v. Bank of Flemington, 187 Mo. App. 61, 173 S. W. 50 (1915); Cotulla State Bank v. Herron, 191 S. W. 154 (Tex. Civ. App. 1917); Hitt Fireworks Co. v. Scandinavian American Bank, 114 Wash. 167, 195 Pac. 13, 196 Pac. 629

denying his liability,[68] possibly that a novation has occurred,[69] or for other similar reasons.[70]. In each of these cases, there

(1921); *cf.* however, Andrew v. Waterville Sav. Bank, 219 N. W. 53 (Iowa 1928). The above citations also include cases dealing with non-negotiable drafts. No distinction has been drawn between the two, as the principle involved is generally the same whether or not the draft is negotiable. See also (1926) 5 TEX. L. REV. 99.

[68] See Pope v. Bank of Albion, 59 Barb. 226, 238 (1871), *rev'd*, 57 N. Y. 126 (1874); Rambo v. First State Bank, *supra* note 62; Ballen & Friedman v. Bank of Kremlin, 37 Okla. 112, 130 Pac. 539, 44 L. R. A. (N. S.) 621 (1913); Brennan v. Merchants' & Manufacturers' Nat. Bank, 62 Mich. 343, 28 N. W. 881 (1886); *cf.* Hitt Fireworks Co. v. Scandinavian American Bank, *supra* note 67.

[69] In the following cases, the court found that the facts did not indicate that there had been a novation; Corinth, etc., Turnpike Co. v. Gooch, *supra* note 61; Izzo v. Ludington, *supra* note 67; Haeberle v. O'Day, 61 Mo. App. 390 (1895); Lee v. Porter, 18 Mo. App. 377 (1885); Pfaff v. Cummings, *supra* note 62; Farquhar v. Zwicker, 42 N. S. 525 (1908); Ahrens & Ott Mfg. Co. v. George Moore & Sons, 131 Tenn. 191, 174 S. W. 270 (1914).

[70] (1926) 26 COL. L. REV. 459. In most jurisdictions it is difficult to delimit with any accuracy the nature of the facts necessary to allow a holder to recover. Kansas, for example, seems to have worked out a rule that, where there is an express understanding between drawer and bank to honor certain checks, the holder can recover. This case differs from the one under discussion, as the promise is not directed to the holder. On what basis the holder of a check can recover against the drawee when a special arrangement exists, is not clear. In every deposit, the bank impliedly undertakes to honor checks when it is in funds. Inasmuch as the holder, in order to recover, need not necessarily have knowledge of any special arrangement between drawer and bank, at the time he takes the check, it is difficult to see how any distinction, on the basis of commercial customs, can be drawn between the two types of deposits. It probably represents an attempt to limit, to a large extent, the doctrine that a check is not an assignment. See Humpert v. Citizens' State Bank, 122 Kan. 101, 250 Pac. 1077 (1926); Moravek v. First Nat. Bank, 119 Kan. 84, 237 Pac. 921 (1925); Pierceville State Bank v. Gray County Bank, 113 Kan. 352, 214 Pac. 788 (1923); Scoby v. Bird City State Bank, 112 Kan. 135, 211 Pac. 110 (1922); Goeken v. Bank of Palmer, 100 Kan. 177, 163 Pac. 636 (1917); Saylors v. State Bank of Allen, 99 Kan. 515, 163 Pac. 454 (1917); Ballard v. Home Nat. Bank, 91 Kan. 91, 136 Pac. 935, L. R. A. 1916C, 161 (1913); Chanute Nat. Bank v. Crowell, 6 Kan. App. 533, 51 Pac. 575 (1897); Northcraft v. Home State Bank, 120 Kan. 572, 245 Pac. 114 (1926). See also Joy v. Grasse, 173 Minn. 289, 217 N. W. 365 (1927). *Cf.* however, El Dorado Nat. Bank v. Butler County State Bank, *supra* note 67, at 112, 242 Pac. at 476: "If the rule that an ordinary check is not to be regarded as an assignment is to be given any considerable practical effect, its operation should not be suspended by a conversation such as that here pleaded, for almost any talk between the drawer and payee conveying assurance of the check being good could be urged to that end with equal force, and cases of the application of the ordinary rule would be rare." First Nat. Bank v. Pettit and Smith, 41 Ill. 492 (1866). See also: J. T. Fargason Co. v. Furst, 287 Fed. 306 (C. C. A. 8th, 1923); Second Nat. Bank v. Averell, 2 App. D. C. 470, 25 L. R. A. 761 (1894); Burkhart Mfg. Co. v. Berry, 162 Ark. 123,

may be an oral promise by the drawee to accept or pay. It should be noted, however, and some courts are careful to indicate, that the recovery is not on the promise or on the negotiable instrument but is on the special facts which result in giving the holder a right based on one theory or another.[71] The check or draft and the promise are merely incidental considerations and additional evidence of these facts. The drawee may not have

---

257 S. W. 723 (1924); Dumbeck v. Walsh, *supra* note 61; Lewis v. McMahon & Co., 307 Mo. 552, 271 S. W. 779 (1925); Johnson-Brinkman Com. Co. v. Central Bank, 116 Mo. 558, 22 S. W. 813 (1893); Nagle v. Richards, *supra* note 62; Gruber v. Bank of America, *supra* note 62; Gruenther v. Bank of Monroe, 90 Neb. 280, 133 N. W. 402 (1911); Saylor v. Bushong, 100 Pa. 23 (1882); Howes v. McCrea, *supra* note 62; Webster v. First State Bank, 50 S. D. 159, 208 N. W. 774 (1926); 46 S. D. 460, 193 N. W. 675 (1923); Gibbs v. Commercial & Savings Bank, 50 S. D. 134, 208 N. W. 779 (1926); Thompson v. Commercial & Savings Bank 50 S. D. 154, 208 N. W. 780 (1926); Payne Bros. v. Burnett, 151 Tenn. 496, 269 S. W. 27, 39 A. L. R. 1125 (1925); Bank of Rutland v. Woodruff, 34 Vt. 89 (1861); *cf.* First Nat. Bank v. Gordon, *supra* note 62. See also York v. Farmers Bank, 105 Mo. App. 127, 79 S. W. 968 (1904); Singer v. Citizens Bank, 79 Okla. 267, 193 Pac. 41 (1920), 109 Okla. 27, 234 Pac. 708 (1925); Hawley v. Exchange State Bank, 97 Iowa 187, 66 N. W. 152 (1896); Springfield Marine Bank v. Mitchell, 48 Ill. App. 486 (1892).

[71] Nagle v. Richards, 134 App. Div. 25, 27, 118 N. Y. Supp. 53, 55 (1909): "If the action is to be considered as founded entirely upon these orders no case was made out. There was no written promise to accept them, and they were not accepted in writing after they were drawn and presented." J. T. Fargason Co. v. Furst, *supra* note 70, at 310: "Clearly then this contention of Fargason Co. might be so far correct as to be decisive of the point, if the action were one upon the draft. But it is not such a suit. It is a suit to establish a lien, and thereupon to charge Fargason Co., as a junior lienor, for the conversion of property on which a prior and senior lien existed." Lowery v. Steward, *supra* note 67, at 242, 244: "The draft was not a bill of exchange requiring acceptance to bind the drawers, but a specific draft or order upon a particular fund. . . . It was equivalent to an assignment in equity to Lowery & Co. of so much of the proceeds of the cotton. . . . The draft or order was necessary only for a voucher. They were not bound to accept the draft; acceptance was entirely unnecessary." Risley v. Phoenix Bank, 83 N. Y. 318 (1881), *aff'd,* 111 U. S. 125, 4 Sup. Ct. 322, 28 L. Ed. 374 (1884); Gruber v. Bank of America, 127 Misc. 132, 215 N. Y. Supp. 222 (1926); Burkhart Mfg. Co. v. Berry, *supra* note 70; Pope v. Huth, *supra* note 67; Wheatley v. Strobe, *supra* note 67; Dolph v. Cross, *supra* note 67; Goeken v. Bank of Palmer, *supra* note 70; Ballard v. Home Nat. Bank, *supra* note 70; First Nat. Bank v. Rogers-Amundson-Flynn Co., *supra* note 67; Gruenther v. Bank of Monroe, *supra* note 70; Howes v. McCrea, 21 Pa. Super. Ct. 592 (1902); Trumbower v. Ivey & Rapp, *supra* note 67; Hatley v. West Texas Nat. Bank, *supra* note 67; Bank of Rutland v. Woodruff, *supra* note 70; see also: Van Buskirk v. State Bank, 35 Colo. 142, 146, 83 Pac. 778, 779 (1905); U. S. Nat. Bank v. First Trust & Savings Bank, 60 Oreg. 266, 271, 119 Pac. 343, 345 (1911); Lynch v. First Nat. Bank, 107 N. Y. 179, 184, 13 N. E. 775, 777 (1887).

made any promise and also, except in the case of the constructive acceptances, there may not be any check or draft in existence. Often there are both. As a result, the case is apparently an illustration of a recovery by a holder against a drawee on a promise that is either oral or in other ways not in accordance with the statute. This should not mislead us. These cases proceed on a totally different theory and have additional and different facts as part of the cause of action. They are merely mentioned here that they may be distinguished from the action on the promise or on the acceptance.

No case, decided after the adoption of a statute requiring acceptances to be in writing, has been found which allows a recovery on an oral promise to accept as such. Several decisions have been handed down which allow a recovery on an assignment or some similar theory and which are based merely on a state of facts which would permit a recovery on an oral acceptance except for the requirements of the statute.[72] In these cases, a problem similar to the one under discussion arises, *i. e.*, the basis for allowing a recovery in another form of action, when the statute prohibits it in one form. From a commercial point of view the imposition of a liability upon the drawee of an unaccepted draft or check seems to be undesirable except in cases where the additional

[72] Guaranty State Bank v. Sumner, 278 S. W. 459, 462 (Tex. Civ. App. 1926): "This being correct, we hold that, by the bank's promise to appellee that the bank would pay the check, there was an assignment of such funds then in the bank, pro tanto, and the appellant thereby became liable for the payment of such funds, and that its appropriation of same to the payment of its own debt was unlawful." See also cases, *supra* notes 66 to 70. It has been recognized however that to allow the holder to recover on any theory based on facts amounting merely to an oral promise to accept, is to that extent defeating the aim of the statute, assuming that it was intended that no oral promise to accept should give rise to legal liability. Nichols v. Commercial Bank, 55 Mo. App. 81, 91 (1893): "He cannot invoke the doctrine of an estoppel to validate a promise which the statute declares absolutely void." See also Ballen & Friedman v. Bank of Kremlin, *supra* note 68; Superior Nat. Bank v. Nat. Bank of Commerce, *supra* note 67; Corinth, etc. Turnpike Co. v. Gooch, 113 Miss. 50. 60, 73 So. 869, 871 (1916): "The contention that, if the drawee of a bill of exchange be the debtor of the drawer, then an oral acceptance would be binding, would abrogate and nullify section 4012 above quoted. Such is not the law."

facts are certain and obviously adequate to support the theory upon which the recovery is based.

> I think it an extremely pernicious thing to throw doubt upon the scope of doctrines governing negotiable paper which, though a mere skeleton of expression, is among the most useful inventions of mankind. To seek too readily for exceptions from the well-settled rules upon this branch of the law in pursuit of a supposed equity, which incidentally does not exist here, is an evidence of insufficient understanding of the economies of finance and their immense value to industry.[73]

Some courts, however, have, with little hesitation, tended to seize upon a few additional facts as a basis for holding that the drawee of a draft was bound to the holder, particularly in those jurisdictions where, before the adoption of the Uniform Negotiable Instruments Law, a check was held to be an assignment of the amount for which it was drawn.[74]

Despite these apparent exceptions, it may be stated as a formal rule that oral promises to accept are entirely without legal effect as promises or as acceptances because they violate the statutory requirement that acceptances are to be in writing. To this extent, therefore, the relevant sections of the Negotiable Instruments Law cover the entire field of enforceable promises to accept. Such promises, however, may be unenforceable as acceptances for other

---

[73] Eastman Kodak Co. v. Nat. Park Bank, *supra* note 67, at 324.

[74] *In re* Gubelman, *Ex parte* First Nat. Bank, *supra* note 67, 13 F. (2d) at 734: "For whatever reasons courts have gone far to find indications in such cases of an independent agreement to assign an interest in the funds." See, e. g., *Equitable Assignment of Bank Deposits* (1928) 37 YALE L. J. 626; *Iowa Legal Problems: Checks as Assignment of Funds* (1923) 9 IOWA L. BULL. 64, 210; McEwen v. Sterling State Bank, 5 S. W. (2d) 702, 704 (Mo. App. 1928); McClain & Norvet v. Torkelson, 187 Iowa 202, 174 N. W. 42, 5 A. L. R. 1665 (1919) and cases cited, *supra* notes 67 to 70. It may perhaps be well to indicate that these forms of action, based on facts in addition to the oral promise and interpreted as constituting an assignment or an analogous legal result, bear no relation to the usual action on a letter of credit or similar type of promise. The plaintiff's rights in the former case are usually derivative and, especially in the case of assignment, subject to equities between the original parties. Generally, the objections against using this approach in actions on a letter of credit are similar to those indicated in the previous discussion against compelling the holder of a draft to sue the promisor in the usual assumpsit action.

reasons, e. g., that they are too conditional within the meaning of the statutes or too indefinite under the rule in *Coolidge* v. *Payson*.[75] Some courts which have required definiteness may have proceeded on the theory that this is also a requirement of the statutes. If this view that the statutes cover the entire field of enforceable promises to accept be carried to a logical conclusion, promises too indefinite or too conditional, as these terms have been interpreted, to be actionable as acceptances would also be unenforceable in the action on the promise. Such, however, has not been the case.

The federal courts, though adopting the rule in *Coolidge* v. *Payson*, have subsequently clearly indicated that despite the fact that a promise is too indefinite to be considered a virtual acceptance, a count on a promise to accept will be sustained.[76] Chancellor Kent, in a case decided in New York before the adoption of the Revised Statutes,[77] implied that, in his opinion, no action was ever possible on a virtual acceptance, the proper form being an action on a promise to accept.[78] The same distinction was attempted later in England.[79] Otherwise, no attempt was made to draw a distinction in this connection between virtual and extrinsic acceptances and promises to accept. The effect of conditions was the same in both forms of action at common law. There was no requirement of definiteness, except in those states that followed the federal rule, where, uniformly, an action on the promise was allowed where the promise was held to be too indefinite to be an acceptance.[80]

---

[75] 2 Wheat. 66, L. Ed. 185 (1817).

[76] Boyce v. Edwards, 4 Pet, 111, 122, 7 L. Ed. 799, 803 (1830).

[77] *Supra* ch. II, p. 79.

[78] M'Evers v. Mason, 10 Johns. 207 (N. Y. 1813).

[79] Bank of Ireland v. Archer, 11 M. & W. 383, 389, 152 Eng. R. 852, 855 (1843).

[80] Kennedy v. Geddes & Co., 8 Porter 263 (1839), 3 Ala. 581 (1842); Johnson v. Blakemore & Co., 28 La. Ann. 140 (1876); Kendrick v. Campbell, 1 Bail. L. 522 (S. C. 1830); Franklin Bank v. Lynch, 52 Md. 270 (1879); First Nat. Bank v. Clark, 61 Md. 400 (1883); Hen-

Another interesting phase of the relation between the statutes dealing with virtual and extrinsic acceptances and actions on the promise can be found in Section 10, Chapter 4, Part 2, of the New York Revised Statutes relating to the rights of the direct promisee. We have seen that until about 1840 no action in this country on a promise to accept was possible save by the direct promisee. New York, at the time of the adoption of the Revised Statutes in 1827, codified this rule,[81] the right of the direct promisee being saved by Section 10.[82] After 1850, the pressure of business forced a broader interpretation of this provision in order to protect subsequent purchasers of drafts under promises which were not actionable as virtual or extrinsic acceptances. Section 10, which had been adequate up to this point, as declaratory of the law in regard to an action on the promise, was now a barrier in the way of legal development. We therefore find the courts holding that:

> The statute of this state making a promise to accept an actual acceptance does not oust the common law remedy to which the facts of any particular case may entitle a party.[83]

The action on the promise was allowed or denied without any reference being made to Section 10.[84] By being tacitly ignored the rule had become inoperative, except of course in connection with oral promises to accept.

In states that had statutes merely requiring that the acceptance be in writing, no reason existed why actions on the promise should

---

rietta Nat. Bank v. State Nat. Bank, 80 Tex. 648, 16 S. W. 321 (1891); Carrollton Bank v. Tayleur, 16 La. 490 (1840); Nisbett v. Galbraith, 3 La. Ann. 690 (1848).

[81] This was first suggested in M'Evers v. Mason, *supra* note 78; Ontario Bank v. Worthington, 12 Wend. 593 (N. Y. 1834), and was finally decided in Birckhead v. Brown, 5 Hill 634 (N. Y. 1843), *aff'd*, 2 Denio 375 (N. Y. 1845). See also New York & Va. State Stock Bank v. Gibson, 5 Duer 574, 583, 584 (N. Y. 1856).

[82] *Supra* ch. II, p. 61, note 107.

[83] Scott v. Pilkington, 15 Abb. Pr. 280, 285 (N. Y. 1861).

[84] Monroe v. Pilkington, 14 How. Pr. 250 (N. Y. 1857); Germania Nat. Bank v. Taaks, 101 N. Y. 442, 5 N. E. 76 (1886); see also Harrison v. Smith, 2 Sweeny 669 (N. Y. 1870).

not have been allowed at common law. There can be no doubt that actions on the promise were allowed in the first instance to the direct promisee and later to the purchaser in reliance on the promise. Even in jurisdictions which adopted the New York rule, including Section 10, we find that where the question arose, an action on the written promise was allowed, though not within the provisions of that Section.[85]

Under the Negotiable Instruments Law, actions on the promise in writing are not prohibited in any jurisdiction.[86] No other result is possible. Letters of credit contain promises to accept that are much too conditional and, in many jurisdictions, too indefinite, to be acceptances under the Negotiable Instruments Law. Yet, recovery is constantly allowed on them. There may as yet be no unanimity as to the underlying basis of the right of the holder of a draft against the promisor, but it is clear that the Negotiable Instruments Law has no bearing on his right to sue, whether or not he is the direct promisee. It is hardly even mentioned in that connection.[87]

The varied means used and the results indicated are an interesting illustration of the effect of our business life on statutes, of the inability of the latter to control the former, and of the inevitable failure of any such attempt. Doubtless, the sections of the New York Revised Statutes which we have been discussing represented the state of the common law at the time of their adoption. Provision was made for virtual and extrinsic acceptances.[88] Chan-

---

[85] Vallé v. Cerré, 36 Mo. 575 (1865). Alabama attempted to reach this result by stretching the meaning of the statute to include the purchaser from the promisee under the head "to whom a promise to accept a bill may have been made" and "negotiated," *supra* note 64, Smith v. Ledyard, 49 Ala. 279 (1873). This is, of course, interpreting the statute out of existence.

[86] Midwest Nat. Bank & Trust Co. v. Niles & Watters Sav. Bank, 190 Iowa 752, 180 N. W. 880 (1921) and cases there cited. For various forms of letters of credit, see *supra* ch. I, p. 16 *et seq.*

[87] See e. g. Banco Nacional Ultramarino v. First Nat. Bank, 289 Fed. 169, 176 (D. Mass. 1923).

[88] The additional requirement that the promise be unconditional was probably new, *supra* ch. II, p. 62.

cellor Kent was evidently of the opinion in *M'Evers* v. *Mason* that an action on the promise was valid only between the immediate parties to the promise. This right was saved by Section 10. Chancellor Kent's view was for a time broad enough to meet commercial needs. With the rising importance of New York's commerce and trade, it became imperative to allow a recovery in cases where the holder could not recover in an action on an acceptance and was not the direct promisee. A series of decisions like *Birckhead* v. *Brown*[89] would have gone far toward seriously injuring the development of commerce and trade, particularly in New York City. The scope of the statute was therefore limited. Originally, Sections 6, 7, 8, and 10 were intended to cover all instances in which a holder could sue on a promise to accept as an acceptance or for breach of the promise. This was the early interpretation placed upon those sections.[90] Later, the courts changed this interpretation of the statute so that it did not interfere with any common law remedy the holder was supposed to have had. The courts disregarded the fact that the holder at the time of the adoption of the Revised Statutes not only had no rights other than those specified in the statute but also that the statute was intended to supersede the common law. What was done in effect was to create a new right in the guise of perpetuating one which was presumed to have existed at common law.

In regard to oral promises to accept, there was no such commercial pressure. They were not used in the usual conduct of business. The law in regard to them, therefore, continued the rules of the first half of the nineteenth century. The holder could not recover unless he came within the provisions of Section 10.

The commissioners, in drawing up the Negotiable Instruments Law, omitted Section 10. The effect of this omission, appar-

---

[89] *Supra* note 81, *supra* p. 100.
[90] New York & Va. State Stock Bank v. Gibson, *supra* note 81, at 583 *et seq.*

ently, would be to make it clear that the statute does not intend to cover the whole field of promises to accept, but merely refers to that type of promise which is held to be an acceptance.[91] This has been recognized and is a fair and reasonable interpretation.[92] The only difficulty that arises is in connection with oral promises to accept. If the Negotiable Instruments Law does not cover the whole field, there is no reason why oral promises should not be actionable as promises, especially as Section 10 has been omitted. Yet, under the Negotiable Instruments Law, these oral promises have not been held to be so actionable. The answer lies again with the commercial considerations involved. Not only has there been no commercial pressure for the recognition of oral promises but the courts have felt that business *desiderata* were against their enforcement.[93] Therefore, despite the omission of Section 10 and regardless of the general proposition that the Negotiable Instruments Law does not pretend to cover the whole field of actionable promises to accept, the oral promise to accept is generally held not to give the holder any right when he is not the direct promisee. Whether the direct promisee can recover is also doubtful. Under Section 10, it is clear that he could do so. Under the Negotiable Instruments Law, there is authority to the effect that he cannot. Probably, however, the courts will allow him to recover on one theory or another.[94] Because of the commercial

---

[91] Commercial custom as expressed in the law merchant might therefore result in making promisors liable to holders of drafts for breach of their promises under the rules we have been discussing. See Bank of Manhattan v. Morgan, 242 N. Y. 38, 47, 150 N. E. 594, 597 (1926), quoted *supra* ch. I, p. 2, note 2.

[92] "To be sure, the Negotiable Instruments Law only covers the case of an unconditional promise to accept, doubtless because, in general, conditions attached to commercial paper deprive it of the attribute ot negotiability." Muller v. Kling, 149 App. Div. 176, 181, 133 N. Y. Supp. 614, 617 (1912), *aff'd,* 209 N. Y. 239, 103 N. E. 138 (1913).

[93] "By this it is not meant that a bank can never contract itself out of the N. I. L. but we might require a business approach to a business situation, e. g. some writing or other equivalent for the letter of credit used in similar transactions evidencing an intent that the payee should acquire new rights." (1926) 26 Col. L. Rev. 459, 462.

[94] See cases cited, *supra* note 71.

considerations involved, therefore, we find the law continuing in its illogical position, permitting promises in writing which for one reason or another cannot be considered as acceptances under the Negotiable Instruments Law, to be actionable as promises to accept, while denying a recovery on oral promises to accept either as acceptances or as promises to accept.

G. Diversity in Legal Results between an Action on an Acceptance and an Action on the Promise

From the point of view of the most desirable commercial practice, presumably a promise should not be considered as an acceptance unless written on the instrument itself. A limitation of this kind would lessen confusion and make instruments pass more freely. It may be doubted whether drafts, accepted by a writing other than on the instrument itself, are as readily negotiable in practice as the more usual form of accepted draft unless, perhaps, the promise is contained in a document attached to the draft.

In commercial practice, a distinction is usually made between promises to pay written on the face of the draft, *i. e.*, the usual acceptances, and other promises to accept or to pay. While both types of promises to accept or to pay have their place in the financing of trade, they are to be distinguished in function and usage. This distinction in practice should be reflected in the law. In England, this has been done, and the statute there, accordingly, provides that only promises to pay written on the face of the draft are actionable as acceptances and that all other promises to accept or to pay are actionable only as promises.

This is a simple and workable rule and, in the absence of any reason to the contrary, should be adopted. The problem, therefore, is to ascertain whether there are any desirable legal results reached by an action on a promise as a virtual or extrinsic acceptance, that are not reached, or could not be reached, just as easily by an action on the promise.

The distinction most often quoted in support of the doctrine of virtual and extrinsic acceptances is the one stated in *Boyce* v. *Edwards*.

> The distinction between an action on a bill as an accepted bill, and one founded on a breach of promise to accept, seems not to have been adverted to. But the evidence necessary to support the one or the other is materially different. To maintain the former, as has been already shown, the promise must be applied to the particular bill alleged in the declaration to have been accepted. In the latter, the evidence may be of a more general character and the authority to draw may be collected from circumstances, and extended to all bills coming fairly within the scope of the promise.[95]

This distinction, based on the type of evidence that is admissible, can, it will be noticed, be made only in jurisdictions like Missouri or the federal courts which require that the promise definitely describe the draft in order to be actionable as a virtual or extrinsic acceptance.[96] In states like New York and California, where there is no requirement of definiteness, this distinction would not apply. Furthermore, the differentiation made in *Boyce* v. *Edwards* merely results in the requirement that, in an action on a virtual or extrinsic acceptance, proof be of a more definite character than is necessary in an action on a promise. The distinction can therefore hardly be considered as a reason for perpetuating the action on the acceptance, as the same facts can be shown more easily in an action on the promise. Finally, this rule of evidence is merely a difference in the method of proving an allegation. It is one result of the distinction between virtual and extrinsic acceptances and promises to accept, and cannot be set up as the basis for a continuation of the distinction upon

[95] *Supra* note 76, at 122, 7 L. Ed. at 803; see also Exchange Bank v. Hubbard, 62 Fed. 112 (C. C. A. 2d, 1894); Von Phul v. Sloan, 2 Rob. 148 (La. 1842); Henrietta Nat. Bank v. State Nat. Bank, *supra* note 80, at 651, 16 S. W. at 321.

[96] *Supra* ch. II, p. 69 *et seq.*

which it rests. Even in jurisdictions which follow the distinction made in *Boyce* v. *Edwards* and require definiteness, promises which are definite can be shown in an action on the promise as readily as in an action on the acceptance. From this point of view therefore, the recognition of virtual and extrinsic acceptances is unnecessary.

Though the desirability of the distinction is assumed, the court itself indicates that there is no basis upon which the rule can be rested.[97] The reasoning of this opinion, therefore, is of no aid at this point. Only when the usefulness of the distinction has been determined, does a discussion of methods of proof become relevant.

To treat the promise to accept or to pay as though it were an acceptance, brings with it at least three apparent commercial advantages for the holder of the drafts: ease of transfer by endorsement and delivery; the power to convey good title to a bona fide purchaser irrespective of any defect in the title of the transferor; and the presumption of consideration. However, these advantages are more apparent than real. We have seen that at present a purchaser of the draft can sue for breach of the promise to accept or to pay.[98] The indorsement and delivery of the draft therefore gives the holder the same rights against the promisor for breach of the promise that he would have against the promisor as acceptor. It has also been shown that, as a result of the same development, the purchaser's rights are independent of any equities between the original parties.[99]

Finally, though the presumption of consideration, which applies in an action on an acceptance, would not apply if the action for

[97] "As it respects the rights and the remedy of the immediate parties to the promise to accept, and all others who may take bills upon the credit of such promise, they are equally secure, and equally attainable by an action for the breach of the promise to accept, as they could be by an action on the bill itself." Boyce v. Edwards, 4 Pet. 111, 123, 7 L. Ed. 799, 803 (1830).

[98] *Supra* p. 99 *et seq.*

[99] *Supra* p. 104.

breach of the promise to accept were treated as an ordinary action in special assumpsit, yet in this regard also the courts have been much more lenient in dealing with the action on the promise to accept than they have been with the orthodox assumpsit action. The former type of action has tended more and more to assume the attributes of the action on an acceptance. While no formal rule to the effect that a presumption of consideration applies in favor of the holder of a draft, has ever been laid down in a case of an action on the promise, it is reasonable to infer, from what has already been indicated, that the courts have favored this type of action and that the tendency has been toward a presumption of consideration.[100] There can likewise be little doubt, that this tendency will eventually resolve itself into a formal presumption of consideration, as the action for breach of a promise to accept becomes more and more highly specialized.

The only other legal difference that might justify the special doctrine of virtual and extrinsic acceptances is a difference in the measure of damages. If the measure of damages is such that the holder of a draft can recover a larger sum when he sues on an acceptance than when he sues for breach of the promise to accept, then, at least from his point of view, the doctrine should be continued.[101] This will be discussed later in some detail.[102] It will be seen that not only does the action on the promise allow a greater recovery, but that it is also a much more flexible action, in this regard at least, that the rule of

---

[100] *Supra* p. 111. Likewise, there is little doubt that past consideration is as effective to support an action for breach of promise, as it is an action on an acceptance. See ch. III, p. 113.

[101] Another argument might be made for this doctrine if it enabled the acceptor to set up additional defenses. Except for the commercially undesirable requirements of definiteness and lack of conditions, however, the defenses available to the promisor are identical whether the action is on a promise or on an acceptance. See *infra* ch. VI, p. 255 *et seq.*

[102] See *infra* ch. VII, p. 271.

damages is not arbitrarily fixed and can be adjusted to the actual intentions of the parties and needs of the case.[103]

Intrinsically, there is no reason why the term acceptance cannot be deemed to include all promises to accept or pay, of whatever tenor.[104] If this view had been adopted there would have been no need for an action on the promise.[105] But, in view of commercial convenience, it has been felt that an acceptance should be limited to those promises that are very definite and easily ascertainable.[106] In England, this view has been carried to its logical conclusion and only promises to pay written on the

---

[103] Another illustration of the greater flexibility of the action on the promise to accept can be found in Scott v. Pilkington, 15 Abb. Pr. 280 (N. Y. 1861), where the plaintiff bought a draft in reliance on a letter from the defendant promising to accept. The defendant refused to accept and the plaintiff brought this action. Counsel for defendant argued that the promise was an acceptance and that the action was premature, having been brought before the date of maturity, (at 282). The court did not discuss this point but found for the plaintiff, thus overruling the objection. Under the Uniform Negotiable Instruments Law, Section 133, the same result would follow, regardless of which form of action was used, since a refusal to write the acceptance on the draft itself would be grounds for treating it as dishonored. At common law, the result was not so clear.

[104] See Parrish v. Taggart-Delph Lumber Co., 11 Ga. App. 772, 76 S. E. 153 (1912), where the court, in discussing the enforceability of a written promise to accept made before the draft was drawn, makes no distinction between the action on the promise and one on the acceptance. The limitations fixed by this court on actionable promises are those usually found in actions on virtual acceptances, and not in actions on promises to accept. Under this decision, therefore, many promises to accept, which do not conform to these requirements and are generally treated as giving rise to liability, would be totally unenforceable. See also State Nat. Bank v. Young, 14 Fed. 889 (C. C. D. Neb. 1883), *supra* ch. I, p. 16, note 27.

[105] Where the letter of credit contains a promise other than to accept, e. g., to pay cash or that a correspondent will accept, the problem would still exist as to such promises, since by no stretch of the imagination can they be deemed "acceptances."

[106] This is particularly true in the early decisions of the federal courts; "Courts have latterly leaned very much against extending the doctrine of implied acceptances, so as to sustain an action upon the bill. For all practical purposes, in commercial transactions in bills of exchange, such collateral acceptances are extremely inconvenient, and injurious to the credit of the bills; and this has led judges frequently to express their dissatisfaction, that the rule had been carried as far as it has; and their regret that any other act, than a written acceptance on the bill, had ever been deemed an acceptance." Boyce v. Edwards, *supra* note 97, at 122, 7 L. Ed. at 803.

face of the draft are actionable as acceptances. In this country, the tendency toward the abolition of the doctrine of virtual and extrinsic acceptances was arrested primarily through inertia and a blind following of earlier cases and statutes. Some promises to pay not on the face of the draft, are actionable as acceptances; others are not. We have seen the practical impossibility of drawing a satisfactory line between the two, and, also, that any distinction made is arbitrary and inconvenient in practice.

One commentator has suggested as a reason for perpetuating the doctrine of virtual and extrinsic acceptances, the fact that the rights of the parties can be determined easily and simply.

The American doctrine of virtual acceptance, moreover, is not without certain advantages. In England the modern cases have kept the two sorts of liability distinct, and the trouble there experienced in working out a satisfactory theory by which to protect those who advance money on the bill is illustrated in *In re Agra, etc., Bank* (1867), (L. R. 2 Ch. 391), where a bill was negotiated on the faith of a letter of credit given by a bank to the drawer. The letter was unquestionably a general offer, and when it was acted upon by any bank to which it was presented, a binding contract resulted. In order to protect such a bank the English court was compelled to treat this contract right as being negotiable to the extent of cutting off all equities existing between the bank and its customers. Where such a contract is treated as an acceptance, as is done by the majority of the American courts, no difficulty is experienced in reaching this end at once.[107]

The answer to all this is that, if all promises to accept were actionable as acceptances, this view might be sound, but such is not the situation. The result is that the theories of the *Agra and Masterman's Bank* case, which in effect created a new form of action, had to be evolved in order to protect purchasers of drafts under promises not actionable as acceptances.[108] Now

[107] 2 STREET, FOUNDATIONS OF LEGAL LIABILITY (1906) 402, 403.

[108] In the federal courts, for example, the letter in the Agra case would have been held to contain too indefinite a promise to be an acceptance. In addition, most letters of credit must be deemed conditional, as that term is interpreted within the meaning of Section 135 of the Negotiable Instruments Law, so that they could not be actionable as acceptances. Finally, as indicated previously, *supra* p. 17, not all of them contain promises to accept.

that this form of action has been developed, there is no reason why it should not be used to the fullest extent, so that the distinction between the two forms may be made with two objectives in view, namely, ease in applying the distinction to the facts and commercial convenience. It is submitted that the distinction between acceptances on the bill and those not on the bill achieves both of these objectives.

The suggestion has also been made that since the actions on virtual and extrinsic acceptances have already been developed, there is at present no pragmatic reason why they should not be continued. It is submitted, however, that, in view of the foregoing analysis of the law on the subject, these actions are obviously in a state of confusion. Not only do the various jurisdictions differ seriously, but, even within each jurisdiction, it can seldom be definitely determined whether a particular promise will or will not be held actionable as an acceptance. In addition, this confusion can hardly be remedied if the present artificial lines of demarcation are used as bases in the decision of cases. The action on virtual or extrinsic acceptances is therefore of little value. Either it should be eliminated entirely, thus ending the confusion; or its limits should be greatly extended by the removal of arbitrary limitations. Finally, it is submitted that the former alternative is preferable, in view of the fact that the action on the promise is much more flexible than the action on the acceptance and results in, or can easily be made to result in, as simple and as direct, a determination of the rights of various parties.

The rule permitting the action on virtual and extrinsic acceptances arose because of procedural difficulties which have long since been removed. Undoubtedly, the origin of the rule is to be found in the fact that the subsequent endorsee had not adequate remedy unless he brought an action on an acceptance.[109] Since

---

[109] The courts recognized the fundamental necessity, both ethical and commercial, of imposing liability upon one who had promised to accept a bill, in favor of a person who had bought relying on that promise, when in view of the commercial practices of the times, it was

this procedural gap is now filled by the action on the promise, which fulfills this function at least as well as the action on an acceptance, there is no reason for maintaining the latter form and attempting to draw a legal distinction for which there is no practical need.[110] The conclusion must be reached, therefore, that the English rule limiting acceptances to promises to pay written on the draft itself, is preferable.

It is unfortunate that in this country the commissioners, at the time of the drawing of the Uniform Negotiable Instruments Law, did not seize the opportunity to clarify the law by abolishing virtual and extrinsic acceptances and thus eliminate a confusing problem from the law. In this respect at least, the Uniform Negotiable Instruments Law has failed in its purpose and has done little "to render certain and unambiguous that which had theretofore been doubtful and obscure, so that the business of the commercial world, largely transacted through the agency of negotiable paper, might be conducted in obedience to a written law emanating from a source whose authority admits of no question."[111]

In view of this failure, less desirable substitutes must be considered. At present, the law is in a highly unsatisfactory state. Attempts at compromise have resulted in unworkable rules. One

---

obviously intended to be so acted upon, e. g., Scudder v. Union Nat. Bank, 91 U. S. 406, 414, 23 L. Ed. 245, 249 (1875); "It is a sound principle of morality, which is sustained by well considered decisions, that one who promises another, either in writing or by parol, that he will accept a particular bill of exchange, and thereby induces him to advance his money upon such bill, in reliance upon his promise, shall be held to make good his promise. The party advances his money upon an original promise, upon a valuable consideration; and the promisor is, upon principle, bound to carry out his undertaking."

[110] This lack of any real distinction between the two has been often indicated. Boyce v. Edwards, *supra* note 97; Brown, Graves & Co. v. Ambler, 66 Md. 391, 398, 7 Atl. 903, 905 (1887); Bissell v. Lewis, 4 Mich. 450, 463 (1857); Nelson v. First Nat. Bank, 48 Ill. 36 (1868); Scudder v. Union Nat. Bank, *supra* note 109, at 414, 23 L. Ed. at 249; Pillans v. Van Mierop, 3 Burr. 1663, 1673, 97 Eng. R. 1035, 1040 (1765).

[111] Baltimore & Ohio R. R. v. First Nat. Bank, 102 Va. 753, 757, 47 S. E. 837, 839 (1904); see also Union Trust Co. v. McGinty, 212 Mass. 205, 206, 98 N. E. 679, 680 (1912).

alternative is to adopt the policy of broadening as far as possible the doctrine of virtual and extrinsic acceptances so that, in effect, the action on the promise and the action on the acceptance become co-extensive, and the distinction between the two negligible and thus unnecessary.[112] But for the requirement in the Negotiable Instruments Law that the promise, to be held a virtual acceptance, must be unconditional, this result might easily be accomplished. Even under the present statute, it is not impossible if unconditional be interpreted as meaning unconditional at the time suit is brought, or in other words cured of conditions. The other alternative is to limit narrowly the doctrine of virtual or extrinsic acceptances by making the requirements as to definiteness and absence of conditions as rigid as possible. This interpretation would make cases coming under those sections comparatively rare and so would eliminate most of the confusion.[113] Either of these positions, if definitely taken, would do much to clarify the problems and to settle the law more satisfactorily.

Finally, it need hardly be repeated that the Negotiable Instruments Law has failed in every way in its attempt to make the law on this subject uniform among the several states. The divergent constructions placed upon Marshall's requirement of definiteness is sufficient to indicate this failure, and it will become increasingly apparent as problems of the nature of reliance and taking for value arise. That a majority of the states will independently reach any greater accord on these points, than they have on the others is hardly likely. The only practicable way to achieve uniformity would be by an amendment to the Negotiable Instruments Law entirely abolishing the doctrine of virtual and extrinsic acceptances.

---

[112] Bissell v. Lewis, *supra* note 110, at 463.

[113] The federal courts adopted this policy with the result that their early law on this subject is clearer than that of any of the states.

H. Assignability of Letters of Credit

A problem often confused with the question of general and special letters of credit, is that of the assignability of letters of credit. As already indicated, in the case of a general letter of credit, any one may accept the offer contained in the letter. A special letter of credit limits it to one or to several persons. Any one else who performs the acts required in the letter acquires no rights against the issuer. This is not because the letter is not assignable, but because the offer is not made to such person. It involves no question of assignability.

Another distinction should be made. A letter of credit is not negotiable, within the meaning of the term as applied to commercial instruments. Nor is it desirable to have it so. A mere endorsing of the letter of credit to another gives the endorsee no rights against the issuer.[114] It clearly gives him no rights without the drawing of drafts, as that is usually a condition precedent to the bank's liability, and even the direct beneficiary has no claim without first presenting a draft for honor.[115]

---

[114] Allen v. Leavens, 26 Oreg. 164, 37 Pac. 488, 26 L. R. A. 620 (1894); see also Jacques-Cartier Bank v. The Queen, 25 Can. S. C. 84, 93 (1895): "Finally, it seems to me that the bank could not deal in such securities as the one sued upon in the present instance. The letter of credit is conditional, . . . therefore, it cannot be held to be a negotiable instrument either within the Bills of Exchange Act of 1890, or within the Bank Act then in force." In Struthers v. Commercial Bank, 4 Sess. Cas. (2d Ser.) 460 (1842), the court indicated that the endorsement of the letter of credit gave the endorsee certain rights in respect of the letter of credit, though the members of the court differed as to the basis for these rights. At 466, "I think that a letter of credit is not a document transferable by indorsation so as to put it in the power of the indorsee to draw the money himself as in his own right. But I think that the person to whom the credit is granted putting the name upon the back of the letter, is just the same as his drawing." At 468, "I should have difficulty in holding that the indorsation was equivalent to a draft by the indorser on Sir W. Forbes and Company." The case did not involve the relations of the endorsee and the issuer so that the nature of the rights of the former against the latter was not decided.

[115] See *infra* ch. V, note 5. In the subsequent discussion it is indicated that the right of the purchaser of a draft from the beneficiary may be occasionally put on the basis of an assignment, *infra* p. 277. Union Bank of Canada v. Cole, 47 L. J. Q. B. 100 (1877). This alleged assignment is of a different type from the one under discussion here. It is not an assignment of the letter of credit, but of a particular chose in action arising under

The assignability of letters of credit raises the question as to whether the beneficiary can transfer his rights to a third party so as to enable the latter to acquire a claim against the bank upon the drawing of a draft by the assignee, in his name, and upon the performance of all other conditions.[116] Banks naturally claim that this is impossible and hesitate to pay any such assignee on the ground that such payment is not in accordance with their instructions from the buyer. Sellers, on the other hand, maintain that letters of credit should be assignable.[117] Clearly this is a matter on which the nature of the sales contract has an important bearing. If the latter is non-personal and freely assignable, there is no reason why the former should not likewise be as freely assignable. As far as the seller and the bank are concerned, nothing in the letter of credit can be deemed personal.[118] It makes no difference to the bank whom it pays so long as the draft and the accompanying documents are in order. A very sound suggestion has been made that, after an attempted assignment, the issue should be determined in equity where the assignee can join all the necessary parties and show that the sales contract was assign-

---

it, and raises a totally different problem. The purchaser of a draft claims one limited sum and takes free from equities between the original parties. The assignee of a letter of credit attempts to assert all the rights of his assignor, subject to the usual rules of assignment. The problem is whether a normal assignment, not a negotiation, of a letter of credit is ever possible.

[116] A word should be said here in reference to a peculiar form of assignment. The beneficiary may assign the letter of credit to his bank and then also draw a draft and attach documents and sell it to the bank. This is an assignment for security only. The mere possession of the letter of credit is of great importance to the beneficiary as he cannot negotiate or present his drafts without it. Banks will therefore take it as security for a loan; Old Colony Trust Co. v. Lawyers' Title & Trust Co., 297 Fed. 152 (C. C. A. 2d, 1924), *cert. den.*, 265 U. S. 585, 44 Sup. Ct. 459 (1924), or on purchasing a draft under it to prevent the seller's using it again, Old Colony Trust Co. v. Columbia Trust Co., 210 App. Div. 705, 206 N. Y. Supp. 257 (1924). In neither case is this a real assignment. The bank does not assert the right to draw drafts. It is rather to be treated as a bona fide purchaser. See also Old Colony Trust Co. v. Continental Bank, 288 Fed. 979 (S. D. N. Y. 1921).

[117] (1921) 7 FED. RES. BULL. 686.

[118] See, however, Lyon v. Van Raden, 126 Mich. 259, 85 N. W. 727 (1901).

able.[119] Some such rule is necessary, inasmuch as it is clear that, generally speaking, letters of credit should not be assignable.[120] Which rule is finally adopted is not of much practical consequence. Business men and bankers would hesitate to take drafts not drawn by the designated beneficiary even if letters of credit were assignable. Such a practice would introduce an element of uncertainty and confusion into a branch of the law that, as much as the law of bills and notes, requires definiteness and clarity.

---

[119] See McCurdy, *Commercial Letters of Credit* (1922) 35 HARV. L. REV. 715, 738, 741.

[120] See, however, Old Colony Trust Co. v. Continental Bank, *supra* note 116. If any necessity for assignment is anticipated, provision can be made for it expressly in the letter of credit, giving the beneficiary the right to appoint another to draw drafts under the credit on written notice to the bank. See the form of credit in Duncan v. Edgerton, 6 Bosw. 36, 38 (N. Y. 1860). To protect the buyer a provision might be inserted that his consent in writing be also attached. These variations show how generally unsatisfactory is the entire scheme of assignments of commercial letters of credit. A letter of credit, like a bill or note, should carry all its information within itself, if outsiders are to rely upon it freely and safely. Provisions for arrangements such as suggested here will lead only to doubt and confusion and lessen the acceptability of drafts under this type of credit.

Chapter IV

LEGAL RELATIONS BETWEEN RESPECTIVE PARTIES TO COMMERCIAL LETTER OF CREDIT TRANSACTIONS

Consideration has been given to the economic and commercial functions of the letter of credit, its relation to other types of credit instruments, and to certain related legal problems which have been analyzed primarily from a historical and procedural point of view. These questions, however, are not of primary importance since they seldom arise in connection with the modern letter of credit, in the use of which new problems have developed. These problems fall into three general groups, which will be considered in turn: (1) legal relations between the respective parties to the letter of credit transaction; (2) performance of conditions; and (3) the relation between the letter of credit and the sales contract in connection with which the former is usually issued. The examination of the legal relations between the parties to letter of credit transactions is essentially an analysis of the rights, duties, and powers arising from the use of various types of letters of credit.

The simplest type of the modern letter of credit, and therefore the most convenient as a model, though perhaps not the most usual, is an irrevocable letter of credit issued by a bank on behalf of a buyer to a beneficiary or seller, addressed to the latter and authorizing him to draw on the issuing bank. There are, then, three parties to this type of transaction, the buyer or indemnitor, the seller or beneficiary, and the bank, usually called the issuing bank, in this case also the drawee bank.[1]

[1] These terms are used throughout. The buyer is the party who, by one means or another, induces the bank to issue the letter of credit.

A. The Duty of the Issuing Bank to the Beneficiary as a Measure of the Bank's Rights against the Buyer

The series of transactions which culminates in the issue of the letter of credit is usually begun by the seller and buyer coming to

---

Since this is a commercial letter of credit, it is usually issued in connection with a sale of goods of which he is the buyer; he is also called the accredited buyer, importer, indemnitor, etc. The most accurate term, in view of the discussion *supra* ch. I, p. 14, is probably, indemnitor. Since, however, he is also as a rule the buyer of goods, the term buyer is, for practical purposes, equally descriptive, and since it is a less awkward expression, it is more desirable for constant usage. The seller is the party in whose favor the letter of credit is issued. Almost always, he is a seller of goods, and is often called the beneficiary or accreditee. Here the term accreditee is perhaps the more accurate. Beneficiary, however, has been recognized as conveying substantially the same implications and is the term more generally used. The use of the word seller is also legitimate for considerations similar to those suggested in connection with the term buyer. The bank which issues the letter of credit, may be denominated the opening or issuing bank. The bank on which the draft is to be drawn is the drawee bank. In the illustration above it is the same as the issuing bank. It may be and often is another bank which is designated by the issuing bank. If this or any other bank should notify the seller of his right to draw it is called the notifying or advising bank; if, in addition, it confirms the letter of credit, it is the confirming bank. The term confirmation has until recently been a source of some confusion, see *infra* p. 154. There are two more possible parties, the purchaser who buys the draft from the seller and also the intermediate bank which enters the transaction in cases where the buyer does not ask the issuing bank directly to issue the letter of credit but applies to an intermediate bank, which in turn requests the issuing bank to issue the credit. The intermediate bank is often called the requesting bank or the local or inland bank. From a technical point of view it is in much the same position as the buyer and could therefore also be termed the accredited party or, to distinguish it from the buyer, the accredited bank. The term requesting bank is more desirable, however, as more accurately portraying the situation. See Ward, American Commercial Credits (1922) 30 *et seq.;* McCurdy, *Commercial Letters of Credit* (1922) 35 Harv. L. Rev. 539, 544, 545.

That the possible forms the commercial letter of credit may take vary widely, has already been indicated, *supra* ch. I, p. 16. It should also be noticed that more than one instrument may be issued in connection with one letter of credit transaction. In addition to the instrument of the issuing bank, there may be additional documents issued by the requesting bank or by the correspondent. In so far as the terms commercial letter of credit or letter of credit can be used with any accuracy, they should be limited to instruments issued by the issuing bank. The correspondent, when it acts merely as an advising bank, issues a letter of advice, or advises of the credit opened. If it acts as a confirming bank, it issues a letter of confirmation or confirms the credit. In substance, a letter of confirmation represents two instruments, a letter of advice that the issuing bank has opened an irrevocable credit and an irrevocable letter of credit issued by the confirming bank and containing the same terms as the issuing bank's credit. Any one of

some sort of agreement for the sale of goods.[2] Often one of the terms of this agreement is that the buyer procure a letter of credit from a bank, the identity of which may or may not be specified. Usually the contract also recites in a general way the terms of the letter of credit. The buyer or indemnitor then applies to the particular bank and signs an application requesting that the letter of credit be issued as he specifies.[3] Among other things, it is important to note at this point that this application contains the conditions upon which the bank is to pay the seller. The bank then issues a letter of credit specifying these terms.[4] In other words,

these "letters" may be, of course, a telegram, a cable, or even an oral communication, instead of a formal letter. There is at present no recognized form to be used by the requesting bank in requesting the issuance of a letter of credit. Any such communication however may well be termed a letter of request or a letter of authorization. The Commercial Credit Conference, composed of representatives of New York banks, in preparing standard forms of commercial letters of credit, used the term letter of credit as applying to instruments issued by correspondents as well as by issuing banks. It attempted to differentiate between instruments of the issuing bank and those of the correspondent by adding the word "correspondent's." This type of nomenclature, it is submitted, leads to confusion. The opening bank may also issue an authority to purchase. This evidences an authority granted by the buyer to the opening bank to purchase from the beneficiary drafts drawn on the buyer, upon an understanding between bank and buyer that the latter will honor such drafts. It is generally regarded as revocable, except in Far Eastern credits; WARD, *ibid.* at 59 *et seq.* There is also the authority to pay, which is issued by the opening bank and is a suggested substitute for the revocable letter of credit, see *infra* p. 153.

[2] If the issuance of a documentary letter of credit is contemplated by the parties, as is generally the case, the contract is in effect a cash against documents contract, acceptance of a draft being often substituted, however, in place of the cash requirement. The agreement is almost always a c.i.f. contract as well, *infra* ch. V, note 6.

[3] After the application is approved, he is generally requested to sign an additional document usually called an agreement to reimburse. In many instances this is incorporated as part of the application. For forms see Appendix A.

[4] It is not *ultra vires* for the cashier to issue the letter of credit; Bridge v. Welda State Bank, 292 S. W. 1079 (Mo. App. 1927); see also Muentzer v. Los Angeles Trust & Savings Bank, 3 F. (2d) 222 (C. C. A. 7th, 1924); J. L. Mott Iron Works v. Kaiser Co., 103 S. E. 783 (S. C. 1920); Bank of Omega v. Wingo Ellett & Crump Shoe Co., 19 Ga. App. 177, 91 S. E. 251 (1917); *cf.* Cotulla State Bank v. Herron, 191 S. W. 154 (Tex. Civ. App. 1917); see however, Brown v. Mt. Holly Nat. Bank, 288 Pa. 478, 136 Atl. 773 (1927); Southwark Nat. Bank v. Mt. Holly Nat. Bank, 288 Pa. 491, 136 Atl. 777 (1927), holding that it was an *ultra vires* act for the cashier to appoint another bank to issue a

the buyer requests the bank to pay when certain conditions are fulfilled and to indicate to the seller that it has assumed such an obligation. The bank in turn promises the seller to pay him when these same conditions are complied with. Therefore, if the conditions are found to have been performed as between seller and bank, it necessarily follows that as between the bank and the buyer, if the question should arise, courts will hold that the conditions have also been performed.[5] Also, if the question arises in the first instance between bank and buyer, after the former has paid the seller, the court, in making its decision, will, in effect, be considering whether the seller had performed the conditions when the bank paid him.

> We hold that, under contract made, the usages of the trade, and Brazilian law, the Rio branch, regarded as an independent purchaser of the drafts, bought a good claim against the City Bank, and that therefore that bank has a good claim against the Pan-American.[6]
>
> While it is true that the plaintiff seeks to recover, the question is really whether it could have been forced to pay Barcellos.[7]

This was said in an action by an issuing bank against a requesting bank, at whose instance the letter of credit had been issued. The problem, however, is identical in this respect with the case of a suit against the buyer by an issuing bank. The requesting bank had merely acted in place of the buyer in requesting the issuing bank to issue the letter of credit. In this connection, therefore, its rights and liabilities are similar to those of the buyer. From the point of view of the issuing bank, it is merely substituted in place of the buyer.

From the foregoing, no conclusion can be drawn, however, that

---

letter of credit as agent of his own bank; see also *In re* Southport & West Lancashire Banking Co., 1 T. L. R. 204 (1885).

[5] This applies of course only where the letter of credit was issued as the buyer directed and where the bank did not err in issuing the credit.

[6] Pan American Bank & Trust Co. v. Nat. City Bank, 6 F. (2d) 762, 769 (C. C. A. 2d, 1925), *cert. den.*, 269 U. S. 554, 46 Sup. Ct. 18 (1925).

[7] *Ibid.* at 772, dissent by Judge Hand.

where the issuing bank is under no duty to pay the seller,[8] it may not recover against the buyer in the event that it should honor the letter of credit.[9] The legal relations between the holder of the draft and the issuing bank must be kept distinct from those between the issuing bank and the buyer.[10] The rights, powers, and duties of the bank are not necessarily co-extensive in both instances.[11] In certain limited cases, as will be seen, while it has the privilege of refusing payment, the issuing bank may nevertheless elect to honor the draft and thus acquire a right to reimbursement from the indemnitor.

Between requesting bank and buyer, the problem is similar to that arising between issuing bank and buyer or requesting bank. If the issuing bank is bound to pay the seller, then the requesting bank must pay the issuing bank, and accordingly the buyer is obligated to pay the requesting bank. If the letter of credit is confirmed by a correspondent bank, the same principle holds

---

[8] It is obvious that the problems in this connection are identical, whether the holder of the draft is the seller or the bona fide purchaser.

[9] Courts generally have a tendency to dispose of the question of the right to reimbursement against the buyer by deciding that the bank was under a duty to pay the holder of the drafts. See in addition to the language in the Pan-American case quoted *supra* p. 148, Farmers Bank v. Stapleton, 118 Kan. 755, 236 Pac. 828 (1925); Laudisi v. American Exch. Nat. Bank, 239 N. Y. 234, 239, 146 N. E. 347, 348 (1924); Bank of Montreal v. Recknagel, 109 N. Y. 482, 488, 17 N. E. 217, 219 (1888); Camp v. Corn Exchange Nat. Bank, 285 Pa. 337, 132 Atl. 189 (1926); First Wisconsin Nat. Bank v. Forsyth Leather Co., 189 Wis. 9, 17, 206 N. W. 843, 846 (1926), quoted *infra* ch. VI, note 13. The rule does not work the other way, however. If the conclusion is reached that the bank was not under a duty to pay the holder of the draft, the question still remains whether the bank was empowered to pay and recover against the buyer. The problem can be settled only by considering the relations between the buyer and the bank, as distinct from those between the seller and the bank.

[10] Camp v. Corn Exch. Nat. Bank, *supra* note 9, at 342, 132 Atl. at 191; (1926) 74 U. of Pa. L. Rev. 501.

[11] This distinction has been recognized, see dissenting opinion of Judge Cardozo in Maurice O'Meara Co. v. Nat. Park Bank, 239 N. Y. 386, 401, 146 N. E. 636, 641, 39 A. L. R. 747, 754 (1925). "I assume that no duty is owing from the bank to its depositor which *requires* it to investigate the quality of the merchandise. I dissent from the view that if it chooses to investigate and discovers thereby that the merchandise tendered is not in truth the merchandise which the documents describe, it may be forced by the delinquent seller to make payment of the price irrespective of its knowledge."

true between the correspondent and the issuing bank. If this confirming bank is under a duty to pay, it has a right to reimbursement against the issuing bank. Whether the seller presents the draft himself or negotiates it to a bona fide purchaser, does not matter in this connection. The fundamental question is whether or not there has been performance of the conditions of the duty to pay of that party to whom the holder of the draft first looks for payment of those obligated on the credit. Once it is decided that this party is liable, the question of reimbursement is, in effect, settled for all subsequent parties.[12]

B. The Beneficiary

Under all types of letters of credit, where the obligation of the issuing bank is irrevocable, the beneficiary acquires rights against the bank, assuming, of course, that all conditions have been properly performed.[13] Only where the credit is revocable does any problem arise in connection with the right of the beneficiary against the issuing bank, after there has been compliance with the terms of the credit. At what point a revocable credit ceases to be revocable, if it ever does, is a nice question and one of some importance. If it is still revocable at the time the seller presents

[12] This, of course, assumes that the letter was issued according to the instructions of the indemnitor and that all the conditions of the different agreements are the same. Where a variation occurs, a different set of problems arises. These will be considered later.

[13] We are not concerned at this point with the theoretical basis for that right; for a discussion of this problem, see *infra* ch. VIII. The only point raised here is whether the beneficiary has a right. Though the theoretic bases vary widely, it is uniformly agreed that he has such a right, *supra* pp. 56, 97-99. The credit obviously establishes no trust fund in favor of the beneficiary, since it is merely a promise to honor drafts or to pay cash up to a stated amount. Upon insolvency of the issuing bank, therefore, the beneficiary of the credit or the purchaser of the draft ranks merely as a general creditor and is not entitled to a preference. His position is analogous to that of the holder of an accepted draft or certified check, 1 Morse, Banks and Banking (6th ed. 1928) 926; 2 Michie, Banks and Banking (1913) 1181; see also *In re* Barned's Banking Co., Banner & Young & Johnson, L. R. 5 H. L. 157 (1871); Florian, Jr. v. Bank of Gothenberg, 69 N. Y. L. J., July 14, 1923, at 1344; *cf. Ex parte* Dever, *In re* Suse, L. R. 13 Q. B. D. 766 (1884); and *infra* ch. VIII, note 15.

his draft, then, of course, he has no rights, as the bank may refuse to pay even though it concedes that the seller has performed his share of the bargain. On the other hand, if the letter of credit has, at that time, ceased to be revocable, it must be classed as an irrevocable credit and treated as such.[14]

In dealing with revocation, the courts usually treated that early form of letter of credit which was issued by the buyer himself as an offer looking to an acceptance, consisting of an act or series of acts, generally the delivery of goods and the presentation or negotiation of a draft. In some cases, these forms of letters of credit were regarded as evidencing the creation of revocable agencies, subject to revocation at any time before the agent had fully performed those acts upon the performance of which his principal's obligation to honor drafts rested.[15] Naturally, therefore, where the letter was addressed to the beneficiary authorizing him to draw, the mere drawing of the draft was no acceptance. The

---

[14] Whether a letter of credit is revocable or irrevocable at the time of issuance is seldom a question of great doubt. The modern standard form of irrevocable credit uses the word irrevocable, and so avoids any confusion; see Appendix A. Even without this, the type of letter intended is usually clear. It is the substance of the transaction and the general form of the credit, not merely the words used that control. See First Wisconsin Nat. Bank v. Forsyth Leather Co., *supra* note 9; *cf.* Ernesto Foglino & Co. v. Webster, 217 App. Div. 282, 296, 216 N. Y. Supp. 225, 237 (1926), *modified,* 244 N. Y. 516, 155 N. E. 878 (1926). "I reach the conclusion that by the weight of authority and reason the letter in question was a commercial letter of credit, and, containing no words stipulating the possibility of revocation before its limit of maturity, it was irrevocable as well." See also Albert De Bary, Jr., Inc. v. Agar-Bernson Corp., 208 App. Div. 645, 647, 204 N. Y. Supp. 18, 19 (1924). The fact that a letter has a time limit at which it expires does not necessarily make it irrevocable if the intention of the parties is otherwise. "A letter of credit, whether revocable or not, so far as we know, is always given a limited duration; at least, it is natural to give it one, and there is no reason to infer that a letter is irrevocable merely because it has a limit. It may or may not be." Federal Coal Co. v. Royal Bank of Canada, 10 F. (2d) 679, 681 (C. C. A. 2d, 1926); see, however, Chandanmull Benganey v. Nat. Bank of India, 51 I. L. R. (Calc. Ser.) 43 (1923). A letter of credit containing no time limit would have to be used within a "reasonable time," see pp. 88, 89, 201.

[15] Moro Supply Co. v. Griffis-Newbern Co., 142 Ark. 231, 218 S. W. 370 (1920); Ilsley v. Jones, 78 Mass. 260 (1858); see also Lanusse v. Barker, 3 Wheat. 101, 143, 4 L. Ed. 343, 355 (1818); De Tastett v. Crousillat, 7 Fed. Cas. No. 3,828 (C. C. D. Pa. 1807). This was apparently true also of the early forms of the modern credit, Lienow v. Pitcairn, 15 Fed. Cas. No. 8,341 (C. C. D. Conn. 1832).

offer, together with the resulting power in the offeree, was revocable until the draft had been presented to the buyer as issuer of the credit or had been negotiated to a bona fide purchaser.[16] The promise contained in the letter was subject to the usual rules relating to offers and to agents.[17] The revocation was effective from the date it was received by the offeree or agent.[18] Death, insanity, or bankruptcy of the issuer would normally terminate the power.[19] Likewise, this type of letter of credit could be revoked at any time before the completion of the total series of acts, contemplated by it as an acceptance. If, therefore, the exercise of the power granted was conditioned upon the actual presentation of the draft, it could be revoked at any time before the draft was presented. Apparently, however, the power could not be revoked at the moment of presentation, as all the acts necessary for acceptance would at that time have been completed.[20] In other words, the issuer of the credit could not wait until the draft was presented and then say that he revoked the credit. He would have to revoke at some time previous to the moment of presentation and, of course, give proper notice in order to effect such revocation.

The question of revocation is also of importance in modern revocable letters of credit which uniformly require that the seller present or negotiate the draft. At what stage the issuer of the

---

[16] "If the letter of the defendants of October 29th, 1856, reached the plaintiff before the second draft was presented by Jackson to the defendants for their acceptance, Jackson having no interest in the draft, and acting only as the agent or messenger of the plaintiff to get the acceptance of the defendants, the withdrawal of the offer was made before the plaintiff had signified his assent to the proposition made by the defendants to accept. The mere writing of the draft, so long as it remained in the plaintiff's possession or under his control, did not make such assent. If, when the draft was presented by his agent, he knew the offer to accept it had been withdrawn, the defendants clearly were not bound to accept." Ilsley v. Jones, *supra* note 15, at 264.

[17] Lapse of time or similar facts accordingly terminated the offer or power, Wilson v. Clements, 3 Mass. 1 (1807); Aldricks v. Higgins, 16 Sarg. & Rawle 212 (Pa. 1827); *cf. supra* note 14.

[18] De Tastett v. Crousillat, *supra* note 15. See also Gelpcke v. Quentell, 74 N. Y. 599 (1878), *rev'g*, 59 Barb. 250 (N. Y. 1871).

[19] See Michigan State Bank v. Estate of Leavenworth, 28 Vt. 209 (1856); 1 WILLISTON, CONTRACTS (1920) §§ 62, 279.

[20] *Supra* note 16.

credit must give due notice of revocation, if it is to be effective, has not been determined. Technically, a revocable letter of credit is an offer requiring for its acceptance the performance of a series of acts. Since the usual revocable letter of credit promises to pay only on presentation of the draft, this presentation is the last act necessary for acceptance. Theoretically, the offer can, therefore, be revoked at any time before presentation.[21] In actual practice, however, great difference of opinion exists among bankers as to when a revocable credit becomes irrevocable.[22] Many banks avoid the difficulty by inserting a provision that the credit may be revoked without notice to the beneficiary.[23] The general confusion on the subject led the New York Bankers' Commercial Credit Conference to suggest the total abolition of the revocable letter of credit and the substitution of the advice of authority to pay.[24]

The rights of the beneficiary against the issuing bank remain the same whether the simple buyer-bank-beneficiary form of

---

[21] There is no reason why the usual rule of unilateral contracts should not apply. See 1 WILLISTON, CONTRACTS (1920) § 60.

[22] See a study made by Dr. George W. Edwards for the Federal Reserve Board, 7 FED. RES. BULL. 170 (1921).

[23] For an excellent discussion of this whole problem see WARD, AMERICAN COMMERCIAL CREDITS (1922) ch. IX. This type of credit opens the door to many frauds. The seller after receiving the notice of revocation may fraudulently discount a draft to a bona fide purchaser showing him the letter of credit but not the notice. Who is to bear the loss in this case, assuming the seller absconds or is bankrupt? If it is to be the purchaser, the revocable letter of credit is useless as no banker could rely on it, unless he telegraphed the issuing bank to find out if the credit had been revoked. The liability must, therefore, rest upon the issuing bank. The latter can and usually does protect itself to a large extent by requiring the seller to present the draft to a particular correspondent, to whom a notice is also sent in the event of revocation. This, of course, does not cover the case where the seller discounts to a bona fide purchaser who presents the draft to the correspondent. If, however, the correspondent is in the same town as the seller, there is no reason why the seller should be given the power to discount the draft, and if he does so without authority, the issuing bank is obviously under no duty to honor the draft.

[24] The essential difference between the revocable letter of credit and the authority to pay is that the former is good until proper notice of revocation is given while the latter represents no obligation of any type on the part of the issuing bank and can therefore be cancelled and modified without notice. WARD, AMERICAN COMMERCIAL CREDITS (1922) 159-62.

credit which we have been considering is employed, or, as is common, a more complex form of credit is used, in which a correspondent of the issuing bank enters into the credit transaction. This may be effected in one of several ways, usually by requesting the correspondent either to confirm the credit[25] or to advise the beneficiary of the opening of the credit by the issuing bank.[26] When the correspondent bank confirms the credit, usually by a communication addressed to the beneficiary, the latter obviously acquires rights against it similar to his rights against the issuing bank under an irrevocable credit. Where the credit is unconfirmed, the beneficiary obtains no rights against the correspondent bank.[27] The letter of advice is merely a notification to

---

[25] The term confirmation is used to indicate that a correspondent has added, to that of the issuing bank, its own like irrevocable obligation to honor a certain credit; see in this connection WARD, *op. cit. supra* note 24, ch. V, "The Confusion Concerning Confirmation." See also *supra* note 1.

[26] The correspondent may also issue an instrument containing a revocable promise, which would be similar to the revocable letter of credit of the issuing bank. However, this seldom occurs. Where it does, the position of the correspondent is similar to that of the bank issuing a revocable letter of credit. The correspondent may also become involved in a credit as drawee of the drafts without issuing any instrument. Obviously, in this case, the correspondent is under no duty to the beneficiary.

[27] Even where the correspondent bank merely advises the seller of the issuance of the letter of credit and does not confirm it, there is an understanding between the advising bank and the issuing bank that the former is to honor or to purchase the draft, inasmuch as no bank can afford to risk the loss of prestige that would result from the dishonor of its letter of credit by a designated correspondent. It has been suggested that wherever this arrangement amounts to a contract, the holder of a draft is the beneficiary of this contract and can therefore recover from the advising bank if this contract is broken by the latter. This view, it is submitted, is both legally and factually unsound. The holder of a draft under a letter of credit is no more a beneficiary of the contractual arrangement described than is the holder of a check a beneficiary of the agreement between the depositor and the bank. It is well recognized that before the adoption of the Uniform Negotiable Instruments Law, some jurisdictions allowed a payee of a check to recover against the drawee bank in cases where the drawer had sufficient funds on deposit. That rule has been repudiated in all states by the adoption of the Uniform Act, § 189. It is now uniformly settled that the holder of a check cannot ordinarily sue the drawee bank for its failure to honor the check; see, however, discussion *supra* p. 122. Any other rule would not only be contrary to the intentions of the parties, but also very inconvenient commercially. The analogy to the problem under discussion is a close and compelling one. Nothing can be clearer than that the intention of the issuing bank as well as of the advising bank is that

the beneficiary of the creation of a credit by the issuing bank and the notifying bank usually expressly states that its letter creates no obligation on its part to pay the draft.[28] It has therefore been held that the notifying bank may refuse to pay without previous notice to the seller, whether or not express language limiting its liability has been used.[29]

Whether a seller may look to the buyer for payment after the

---

the latter, as far as the holders are concerned, is not to be bound in the absence of confirmation to honor any drafts drawn under a letter of credit. The device of confirmation exists for the particular purpose of indicating when an obligation to the beneficiary is intended and an extra charge will be made by the confirming bank for incurring such obligation. The letter of advice is issued primarily for the benefit and in the interest of the issuing and advising banks. And it is important to note that the advising bank enters no obligation on its books upon advising the seller of the credit; WARD, *op. cit. supra* note 24, at 133, 177. To hold, under these circumstances, that the holder can recover against the advising bank, on any theory, would not only be to ignore the very definite intentions of the parties but also seriously to interfere with a well settled and recognized method of financing trade. There is another objection. The only theory on which a holder could recover would be as beneficiary of a contract. The conflicting rules among the various jurisdictions on this question would result in making rights on drafts under this type of letter of credit very uncertain. Inasmuch as letters of credit by their very nature are intended for use in various states and countries other than those in which they are issued, it is important that the rules of law relating to them be made as nearly uniform as possible.

[28] For forms see Appendix A. If the notification was intentionally false, the beneficiary would, it is submitted, have an action in tort for fraud and deceit. Where the notifying bank issues what may be termed a revocable letter of confirmation and thus makes a revocable promise of its own, it is then in the position of the issuer of a revocable letter of credit. See Gelpcke v. Quentell, *supra* note 18. Generally, the letter of confirmation, the revocable letter of confirmation, and the letter of advice differ from one another in the same manner as do the irrevocable letter of credit, the revocable letter of credit, and the authority to pay.

[29] Chicago Roller Skate Co. v. New York Produce Exchange Bank, 146 App. Div. 818, 131 N. Y. Supp. 430 (1911); Cape Asbestos Co. v. Lloyds Bank, [1921] Weekly Notes 274; see also United States Steel Prod. Co. v. Irving Bank Columbia Trust Co., 9 F. (2d) 230 (C. C. A. 2d, 1925), where the court doubts whether the advice of credit opened is a credit in any real sense of the term. The court also held that since the advice of credit opened could be entirely revoked, therefore, on the theory that "the greater includes the less" (at 232), its conditions could be changed. See also Giddens v. Anglo-African Produce Co., 14 Lloyd's List 230 (1923). The credit contained the following provision: "Negotiations of drafts under these credits are subject to the bank's convenience. All drafts hereunder are negotiated with recourse against yourselves." Of this provision the court stated: "How that can be called an established credit in any sense of the word absolutely passes my comprehension."

issuance of a letter of credit depends on the expressed intentions of the parties which must be gathered primarily from the terms of the sales contract.[30] If the contract states that the seller is to look only to the bank for payment, obviously he has no rights against the buyer, as the letter of credit is taken in absolute satisfaction of the buyer's obligation. The usual contract is silent on the subject and merely requires that the seller be furnished with a letter of credit. Probably, however, the seller does not intend a substitution of the bank's liability for that of the buyer. He desires additional security without the surrender of any rights that he may have against the buyer. This interpretation has been the one generally recognized.

> A credit with a banker is not payment, but a means of payment, more or less secure, according to the solidity of the depositary; and the greater or less certainty of the security cannot affect the question of its character: it is but a security still.[31]

---

[30] For an excellent discussion of this problem see (1926) 40 HARV. L. REV. 294.

[31] Bell v. Moss, 5 Whart. 189, 203 (Pa. 1840); Lamborn v. Allen Kirkpatrick & Co., 288 Pa. 114, 135 Atl. 541 (1927); Dickerman v. Ohashi Imp. Co., 63 Cal. App. 101, 104, 218 Pac. 458, 460 (1923). "The first contention of the defendant is that there was a custom among shippers, importers, exporters, and merchants that where a contract is entered into by telegram and the buyer established a letter of credit, the obligation to present the draft with proper documents was a condition precedent, the non-performance of which excused performance by defendant. . . . This was an additional guarantee to them and in no way restricted the obligation of defendant under a contract such as in the case at bar." See also Birckhead v. Brown, 5 Hill 634, 640 (N. Y. 1843), *aff'd*, 2 Denio 375 (1845); Alcock v. Hopkins, 6 Cush. 484 (Mass. 1850); *cf.* however, Hindley & Co. v. Tothill, Watson & Co., 13 N. Z. L. R. 13, 23 (1894). After the letter of credit expires it is clear that the buyer is liable on the original sales contract, provided that the seller can perform within the terms of that contract, see Dickerman v. Ohashi Imp. Co., *ibid.*, and Hindley & Co. v. Tothill, Watson & Co., *ibid.* Courts have recognized that the analogy here is not to the certification of a check at the request of the holder which relieves the drawer of liability, but rather to certification at the request of the drawer which makes him liable equally with the bank after presentation and dishonor. "We are considering not a check certified at the request of the holder but a credit established by a debtor in favor of his creditor." Lamborn v. Allen Kirkpatrick & Co., *ibid.*, at 118, 135 Atl. at 543. Whether or not the buyer has actually paid cash for the letter of credit is immaterial in this connection. This factor affects only the relation between the bank and buyer as to which party is ultimately obligated to pay, and is of no significance in considering the rights of the seller

Normally, therefore, the seller can proceed against the buyer after the bank dishonors the credit.[32]

In the various instances where one bank requests another to issue a letter of credit on its behalf, whether a seller acquires any rights against the requesting bank, depends on the form the transaction takes. If the practice suggested by the Federal Reserve Board is followed, the requesting bank becomes the undisclosed principal for the issuing bank.[33] In that event, the seller, on discovering the existence of the requesting bank, may

---

who is bound in this respect by the terms of the sales contract, see *supra* ch. II, p. 32, note 22.

[32] The effect of an extension or other indulgence granted by the seller to the issuing bank is not entirely clear. Where the bank's promise amounts to an acceptance, the buyer, in the unusual case where he is the drawer of the draft, would be discharged not only by an extension, but even by a failure to present the draft within a reasonable time; UNIFORM NEGOTIABLE INSTRUMENTS LAW, §§ 120, 144. Similar rules would also apply to those drafts that are deemed to have been accepted to which the buyer is not a party, whether drawn by the seller or otherwise, 3 WILLISTON, CONTRACTS (1920) § 1922a; (1926) 40 HARV. L. REV. 294, 297. It is submitted that the same result should apply even where the letter of credit does not amount to an acceptance. The principles underlying both types of transactions are the same. The buyer, at least where he has paid cash for the letter of credit, has, in each case, assumed for a certain period of time the risk of the solvency of the issuing bank. He should not be compelled to assume the risk for a further period without his consent. While these conclusions are fairly certain where the buyer has paid cash for the opening of the credit, it would seem that the same result should follow even where the buyer has merely promised to reimburse the issuing bank. The buyer usually is obligated to, and does, put the bank in funds before the bank comes under a duty to pay the seller, and therefore in this case also assumes the risk of the solvency of the bank. That this risk is borne for a shorter period of time is all the more reason why it should not be prolonged without his consent. Secondly, it has been seen that as a general rule the rights of the seller are not influenced by any arrangements made between the bank and the buyer. It is desirable in the interest of simplicity and uniformity that these rights should not be so affected in this case. Finally, it is submitted, that the seller is, in this instance, in a position like that of the holder of a check who has elected to have it certified rather than to receive cash. That the drawer of the check is discharged under these circumstances is well settled; UNIFORM NEGOTIABLE INSTRUMENTS LAW § 188. Similar considerations, leading to a similar result, should also apply to the buyer when the seller extends the time of payment to the issuing bank under its letter of credit or fails to act with reasonable promptness in demanding payment, and the bank becomes insolvent, even in the case where the buyer is not obligated to reimburse the bank until after the latter has paid the seller.

[33] See *supra* p. 40.

elect to sue it rather than the issuing bank.[34] If, however, the requesting bank merely guarantees to the issuing bank the payment of the amount due from the buyer, it is difficult to see how there is any legal relation between the requesting bank and the seller. This guaranty extends only to the issuing bank in order to give it the additional security it desires. The seller as a rule neither requests nor has knowledge of any additional security. Clearly, the requesting bank has not intended to extend its guaranty to the seller. It is submitted, therefore, that the seller cannot recover against the requesting bank. The entire problem is not, however, of serious consequence, as the seller will rarely elect to sue the requesting bank, usually a small inland bank, in preference to the issuing bank, generally a well-known seaboard bank.[35]

C. The Purchaser of the Draft

If the beneficiary sells his draft, the rights of a new party, the purchaser of the draft, must be considered. That the position of the purchaser should be in all respects identical with that of the seller does not necessarily follow. It is well, therefore, to consider the legal relations of the purchaser to the other parties to the credit transaction, viz., the issuing bank, the correspondent bank, the requesting bank, the buyer, and seller, in a manner similar to that in which the legal relations of the beneficiary to these parties have been examined.

Clearly the purchaser has rights against the issuing bank on

---

[34] TIFFANY, AGENCY (2d ed. 1924) 273 *et seq.*

[35] See Federal Coal Co. v. Royal Bank of Canada, 10 F. (2d) 679 (C. C. A. 2d, 1926). The defendant bank requested a local bank of Jacksonville, Fla., to issue a credit to the plaintiff. The defendant did not itself communicate with the plaintiff, so that it was not the usual case of an issuing bank with a correspondent confirming. It was similar to the case under discussion, a request by an intermediate bank to an issuing bank, only in this instance the facts were reversed, as the request came from the international bank to the local institution. The court intimated that in its opinion the plaintiff had no cause of action against the defendant. It did not choose, however, to rest its decision on that ground, at 681.

its irrevocable letter of credit.[36] Has he any rights in the case of a revocable letter of credit? The early buyer's letter of credit used in this country was generally considered to be revocable. It was held, however, that the issuer could revoke only with reference to those drafts which had not been negotiated at the time of revocation.[37] The general opinion was also that where the purchaser bought without notice of the revocation, the issuer was bound, if the terms of the letter had been fulfilled.[38] On the

[36] *Supra* ch. III, p. 101 and cases there cited. It should be noted that the purchaser is under no duty to the issuing bank or to the buyer. Scanlon v. First Nat. Bank, 249 N. Y. 9, 13, 162 N. E. 567, 568 (1928); "When a bank buys or discounts a draft relating to a letter of credit it owes no duty to the drawee or the drawee's customer. No contractual relation exists between it and the drawee who has delivered to it the letter of credit. It may buy or refuse to buy as it chooses. It may buy after the passage of the expiry date of the letter without violating any duty resting in contract or otherwise. . . . Equally must it be true that it owes no contractual duty toward the person for whose benefit the letter is written to discount or purchase any draft drawn against the credit." See also Bank of Italy v. Colla, 118 Ohio St. 459, 161 N. E. 330 (1928). The purchaser discounts the draft and assumes the responsibility for its conformance to the requirements of the letter of credit. If the conditions have not been complied with, he has no rights against the issuing bank. See Courteen Seed Co. v. Hong Kong & Shanghai Banking Corp., 245 N. Y. 377, 157 N. E. 272, 56 A. L. R. 1186 (1927), *aff'g*, 216 App. Div. 495, 215 N. Y. Supp. 525 (1926), quoted *infra* note 45. As in the case of a beneficiary, *supra* note 13, the purchaser is not a preferred creditor upon the insolvency of the issuing bank, see Kuehne v. Union Trust Co., 133 Mich. 602, 95 N. W. 715 (1903); *Ex parte* Dever, *In re* Suse, L. R. 13 Q. B. D. 766 (1884).

[37] Seaboard Nat. Bank v. Burleigh, 74 Hun 400, 26 N. Y. Supp. 587 (1893), *aff'd* without opinion, 147 N. Y. 720, 42 N. E. 726 (1895); Johnson v. Clark, 39 N. Y. 216 (1868); Union Bank v. Coster, 3 N. Y. 203 (1850); see also Lanusse v. Barker, 3 Wheat. 101, 143, 4 L. Ed. 343, 355 (1818); Robbins v. Lambeth, 2 Rob. 304 (La. 1842); Baeschlin v. Chamberlain Banking House, 67 Neb. 196, 93 N. W. 412 (1903); *cf.* however, First Nat. Bank v. Clark, 61 Md. 400 (1883).

[38] In view of the impossibility of giving notice of revocation to all possible purchasers of drafts, general letters of credit would become in fact practically irrevocable. "I can see no object which the drawers should have for limiting the party for whose benefit the letter was issued to a single bank. It is said that it would enable them more readily to revoke the authority. But these letters are not issued without either undoubted confidence in the persons for whose benefit they are drawn, or upon ample security. The idea of giving notice of revocation to any party but that for whose benefit they are drawn, is never entertained by the guarantors in cases of general letters. When they wish to provide for any such contingency the letters are framed accordingly." Union Bank v. Coster, *supra* note 37, at 215. One method of avoiding this result would be to make the letter of credit special as to purchasers of the drafts drawn under it. See *supra* ch. III, p.

other hand, if the purchaser was in a position where he could be expected to know that the offer had been revoked or had lapsed, he, of course, acquired no rights.[39]

Under an irrevocable letter of credit, the rights of the purchaser against the confirming bank are similar to his rights against the issuing bank. On the other hand, like the seller, he also acquires no rights against a notifying bank, as there is no promise or undertaking of any sort.

The purchaser, obviously, acquires no rights of any kind under the letter of credit against the buyer.[40] He is discounting the draft in reliance on the bank's promise to pay[41] and, at the time

94 *et seq.* The few parties given the power to rely on the letter of credit in purchasing the drafts, could be notified of the revocation at the same time as the drawer. There could therefore be no possibility of a bona fide purchaser without knowledge of the revocation. An interesting case in this connection is Evansville Nat. Bank v. Kaufmann, 93 N. Y. 273 (1883), where the court went astray in an attempt to prevent a letter of credit, general as to purchasers, from becoming practically irrevocable. The letter there read as follows: "Messrs. Bingham Bros. . . . Any drafts you may draw on Mr. . . . we guarantee to be paid at maturity." (At 274). The court held that the letter gave merely the addressee, not the purchaser, a right. The letter was held to be special. The motivating reason for the decision was that the broad terms of the letter and the unlimited credit that was granted, made it unlikely that the writer intended to enable all purchasers of drafts to acquire rights against him (at 281 *et seq.*). If the court had adopted the distinction between the different types of general and special letters of credit suggested previously, it would have recognized that the letter was special as to the drawer of the draft, but general as to purchasers. It is true that in the instant case this interpretation would have resulted in putting the defendant at the drawer's mercy. As indicated, however, in the language quoted from Union Bank v. Coster. *ibid.*, letters of credit are not, and should not, be issued without either collateral security or confidence in the parties to whom they are given. The issuer, not the purchaser, should bear the risk of letters poorly dawn and issued without proper safeguards. It is particularly important in this type of case, where the entire method of financing trade in this manner becomes imperiled unless the purchaser feels he can discount drafts with safety in reliance upon the letter of credit, that courts should not yield to the temptation of allowing hard cases to make poor law.

[39] Wilson v. Clements, 3 Mass. 1 (1807); see also Aldricks v. Higgins, 16 Sarg. & Rawle 212 (Pa. 1827). This is an illustration of the principle that a purchaser is bound only by facts of which he has, or is presumed to have, knowledge at the time of purchase, *supra* p. 104.

[40] Similarly the purchaser of the draft is under no duty to the buyer; nor can the latter recover against the purchaser after he has been paid although the conditions have not been performed; *supra* note 36.

[41] Accordingly the buyer cannot be held as the undisclosed principal of the issuing bank. In the first place, he is usually mentioned in the letter of

of purchase, is looking only to the bank for payment.[42] On the other hand, however, he has rights against the seller as the drawer of the draft. The seller remains secondarily liable until the draft is actually paid. In practice, of course, this is not of great moment as the purchaser relies on the credit standing of the bank in discounting the draft.[43] This liability does exist,

---

credit, which states for whose account it has been issued. Secondly, if the buyer is held as principal, the issuing bank can hardly be liable, since it is a mere agent. This obviously is not the intention of the parties, nor should the occasional failure to disclose the identity of the buyer affect the normal interpretation given to the instrument.

[42] See Bank of Taiwan v. Gorgas-Pierie Mfg. Co., 273 Fed. 660, 663 (C. C. A. 3d, 1921). In a recent case, it was held that where the buyer induced the issuing bank not to honor the draft, the purchaser, in addition to his right against the bank, had a right against the buyer for inducing a breach of contract. Second Nat. Bank v. M. Samuel & Sons, 12 F. (2d) 963, 53 A. L. R. 49 (C. C. A. 2d, 1926), *cert. den.*, 273 U. S. 720, 47 Sup. Ct. 110 (1926). This action was not on the letter of credit, but rather in the nature of an action in tort for inducing breach of contract. The court also pointed out that the defendant received goods for which it never paid and was thus unjustly benefited.

[43] See WARD, AMERICAN COMMERCIAL CREDITS (1922) 159 62 and ch. XIII. The purchaser may also have rights against the seller because of additional representations and warranties that the latter may be deemed to have made as beneficiary of the letter of credit in a sale of the draft under it. Does the seller warrant that the conditions have been performed, that the documents conform, that they are genuine and have not been procured fraudulently? The bona fide purchaser may, of course, recover against the bank unless, subject to certain exceptions, the conditions have not been performed or the documents do not conform, *infra* ch. V, pp. 177, 200 *et seq.* But regardless of whether or not he has rights against the bank, may he nevertheless sue the seller for breach of warranty? The purchaser does not expect to buy a lawsuit. What he bargains for is an instrument which the bank will promptly honor. It may well be that the seller will by analogy to the Negotiable Instruments Law be held to warrant that the documents are genuine, that the conditions of the letter of credit have been performed, and that the documents conform, even where he draws or endorses the draft without recourse. This warranty may not apply, however, where the seller thinks the documents do conform and the purchaser has had an opportunity to compare the documents with the requirements of the letter of credit, since in this type of case he is on an equal footing with the seller.

The seller may remove all risk of liability on the draft by drawing it without recourse. NEGOTIABLE INSTRUMENTS LAW, §§ 38, 61. This tends to impair its negotiability, unless expressly authorized by the letter of credit, and also makes it ineligible for rediscount or purchase by a federal reserve bank. WARD, *ibid.*, at 196, 197. This practice is generally followed only in Far Eastern credits, where the draft usually goes abroad immediately after purchase, so that neither consideration is of con-

however, and should be borne in mind. The rights of the purchaser against the local requesting bank, when one enters the transaction, are similar to those of the seller which have already been considered.[44]

D. THE CORRESPONDENT BANK

The rights of the correspondent bank, when one enters the transaction, depend not only on the nature of the obligation it incurs to the holder of the draft but also, to some extent, on the form of the draft. If the draft is drawn on the issuing bank, it is submitted that the correspondent, where it has merely advised the beneficiary of the opening of the credit, should, in the event that it purchases the draft, acquire the same rights as the usual purchaser against the beneficiary as drawer, and against all endorsers.

The advising bank is also in the same general position as the purchaser in relation to the issuing bank, subject, of course, to the terms of the special agreement usually existing between them.[45] If the draft is drawn on the notifying bank as drawee,

---

sequence. When the draft is drawn on the bank, the seller, as drawer, is not liable to the purchaser, unless there has been a proper presentation of the draft to, and dishonor by, the issuing bank as drawee. UNIFORM NEGOTIABLE INSTRUMENTS LAW §§ 70, 71, 186. The same rule should also apply in the case of an irrevocable authority to purchase, and the seller should not be liable until the bank has dishonored its credit, even though it is not the drawee of the draft. Accordingly, where the purchaser has knowledge of the credit and has received no instructions authorizing him to present the draft to the buyer, the presentation of the draft to the latter as drawee, instead of to the issuing bank, should not subject the seller, as drawer, to any liability to the purchaser. And if any such liability is held to arise, the seller should have a counterclaim against the purchaser because of the latter's failure to present the draft to the bank. *Cf.* M. A. Sassoon & Sons v. International Banking Corp., [1927] A. C. 711, 728 *et seq.*

Normally, the purchaser may release the documents to the bank upon the latter's acceptance of the draft and may nevertheless look to the seller as drawer if the draft is not paid at maturity. Nat. Bank of India v. Saleh Mahomed, 25 I. L. R. (Bom. Ser.) 706 (1901).

[44] *Supra* p. 157.

[45] Accordingly, the advising bank is under no duty to the buyer or, in the absence of an express agreement, to the issuing bank. "When a bank buys a draft relating to a letter of credit it does not act as the agent of the

clearly, after paying the draft is has no rights against the issuing bank on the draft as such, since the latter does not appear on the instrument in any capacity. In addition, after such payment, the liability of the seller as drawer as well as that of all endorsers, ceases to exist.[46] The rights of the advising bank against the issuing bank in this case are not based on the draft as such but on an agreement to reimburse expressly or impliedly entered into by the issuing bank. In the absence of any such agreement, an action would lie in general assumpsit on the count of money paid at the request of the issuing bank. The draft and the letter of credit are merely evidence of this payment.

Where the credit is revocable, the notifying bank has a claim against the issuing bank for all payments or acceptances made up to the time that it receives notice of revocation. In cases where the advising bank, upon authority from the issuing bank, has made a revocable promise of its own, it may pay or accept, with right to reimbursement, until it has had an opportunity to relieve itself of liability under such revocable promise by giving notice to the beneficiary or otherwise.[47]

The rights of the confirming bank in cases where the draft is drawn on itself are similar to those of the notifying bank. Where the draft is drawn on the issuing bank, however, it is submitted

---

drawee. The transaction is at its own risk. It owes no duty to the drawee or the drawee's customer. It buys commercial paper relying on the credit of the drawer and the security that is offered. No contractual relation exists between the drawee's customer and the purchasing bank. Therefore no breach of contract arises out of the purchase of a draft after the expiry date of the letter of credit." Courteen Seed Co. v. Hong Kong & Shanghai Banking Corp., *supra* note 36, at 379, 157 N. E. at 273; *cf.* Banque Belge pour L'Etrange v. Nat. City Bank, 74 N. Y. L. J., Dec. 26, 1925, at 1228; Descalzi Fruit Co. v. Bank of Italy, 73 Pitts. L. J. 954 (Pa. 1925). See also *supra* note 36. As indicated in the opinion of the lower court in the Courteen Seed Co. case, the advice is often sent by the notifying bank, in the absence of a special agreement with the issuing bank, to afford the advising bank the opportunity of purchasing the draft and thus of earning the commission or fee involved.

[46] Payment by the party primarily bound on a negotiable instrument discharges it. UNIFORM NEGOTIABLE INSTRUMENTS LAW §§ 51, 119.

[47] Gelpcke v. Quentell, 74 N. Y. 599 (1878), *rev'g*, 59 Barb. 250 (N. Y. 1871).

that the confirming bank has no rights against the seller and the endorsers on drafts purchased by it.[48]

The confirmation of the credit is essentially an undertaking that the issuing bank will accept and pay. Moreover, an undertaking to purchase from the holders drafts drawn under the credit is generally included. Necessarily implied in the confirmation is an assurance that the holder and his predecessors are to be held harmless regardless of whether or not the drafts will eventually be paid.[49] Any other interpretation would make the confirmation practically valueless. While the confirming bank might technically have a claim on the draft if it is dishonored, the defendant would have a counterclaim for an equal amount, for breach of the agreement contained in the letter of confirmation. The result would be that the drawer and endorser would ultimately not be liable in any way for the amount of the draft.[50] The rights

---

[48] This is also true in the case of a draft on the buyer which the issuing bank irrevocably promises to buy. This form of credit is used particularly in Far Eastern transactions; see WARD, *op. cit. supra* note 43, at 43, 200, and *infra* note 49; *cf.* Second Nat. Bank v. Diefendorf, 90 Ill. 396, 408 (1878).

[49] It has been held that where a bank buys a draft from the beneficiary under an irrevocable authority to purchase and the draft is dishonored by the buyer, the beneficiary is under no duty to take up the draft, and that the usual rule of a drawer's obligation on dishonor by the drawee does not apply. Bank of East Asia v. Pang, 140 Wash. 603, 612, 249 Pac. 1060, 1063 (1926): "Our attention is called to Rem. Comp. Stat., § 3452, (P. C. § 4132), which provides that the drawer of a negotiable instrument, if dishonored, is required to pay the amount thereof to the holder or any subsequent endorser who may be compelled to pay it, but that the drawer may insert in the instrument any express stipulation negativing or limiting his liability. The general provision of that statute which permits the holder or any subsequent endorser of a negotiable instrument dishonored to maintain an action thereon against the drawer is not applicable in the present case, because the drafts here involved specifically state that they are drawn under the irrevocable letter of credit and by that the bank was required to pay when a draft and other documents specified were presented." See also Chandanmull Benganey v. Nat. Bank of India, 51 I. L. R. (Calc. Ser.) 43, 60 (1923): "And while it may be possible to give a meaning to the warning that the drawers were not released from liability consistent with a guarantee of the bills by the defendant bank, such a warning in a printed form intended to convey such a guarantee is at least remarkable."

[50] See M. A. Sassoon & Sons v. International Banking Corp., [1927] A. C. 711. For a different approach reaching the same result see WARD, *op. cit. supra* note 43, at 200, 201.

of the confirming bank against the issuing bank would be based either on the draft, on the agreement to reimburse, or on the counts for money paid at the request and for the use of the issuing bank.[51]

In all these cases, whether the advising or the confirming bank has rights against the buyer depends on the provisions of the agreement signed by him. As confirmation by the correspondent bank is usually requested by the buyer who is often required to pay an increased commission for this additional assurance to the seller, the position may well be taken that there is an implied request to the confirming bank, particularly if it is designated, to pay and look to the buyer as surety for the issuing bank.[52] Practically, of course, this is of very slight consequence, since the confirming bank relies solely on the credit of the issuing bank and, in case of doubt, will refuse to confirm.[53] Conceivably, how-

[51] Whether the suit is on the letter of credit or on the general agreement to reimburse, often inferred from the running account between the parties, might make a difference in some cases. Regis v. Hébert, 16 La. Ann. 224 (1861). In that case, the correspondent sued the issuing bank. The court held that the suit was on the general account and was therefore barred by the three year statute of limitations. The statute for suits on letters of credit was ten years.

[52] The buyer may, at times, contract directly with another bank that it is to buy drafts drawn against the issuing bank. In this situation, the second bank obtains rights against the buyer and, conversely, comes under a duty to the buyer. Royal Card & Paper Co. v. Dresdner Bank, 27 F. (2d) 791 (C. C. A. 2d, 1928). In this case, no letter of confirmation was issued, the agreement being oral. The beneficiary was the agent of the buyer, but the contract was apparently made with him as agent of the buyer and not as beneficiary under the credit.

[53] Kunglig Jarnvagsstyrelsen v. Nat. City Bank, 20 F. (2d) 307, 309 (C. C. A. 2d, 1927). "The relation between the Swedish Bank and the defendant bank arose by instructions to open a special letter of credit and the carrying out of this instruction. The defendant bank was paid a commission. There was no expressed contract between the plaintiff and defendant bank. The bank's contract was to open a letter of credit for another bank, which made it its correspondent bank, and it was from it alone that it took instructions. The defendant bank never communicated with the customer of the foreign bank, who was the buyer of the goods, and indeed did not investigate the credit of such foreign buyer. It looked to the correspondent foreign bank for reimbursement. The plaintiff, under these circumstances, could not recover upon any contract made by the correspondent bank, acting, apparently, for and in the name of the buyer of the coal." The plaintiff in this case was the purchaser of the goods from the buyer. Clearly, he had no rights of any kind against the defendant, the correspondent bank. The court was also, apparently, of the opinion

ever the question may become of importance in isolated cases.

In the case of the notifying bank, it is more difficult to see how that bank has any rights against the buyer. Whether the issuing bank authorizes the seller to draw on itself or on the notifying bank is usually a matter of convenience and arrangement between the two banks concerned. The notification is normally sent by the notifying bank merely as a courtesy, as a matter of record, or for the purpose of inducing the beneficiary to discount with the advising bank the drafts drawn under the letter of credit.[54] Such notification is seldom expressly requested by the buyer. In the usual case, therefore, the notifying bank is, in regard to the buyer, in much the same position as the bona fide purchaser of the draft and can therefore have no claim against the buyer.[55]

---

that the buyer was in no contractual relation with the correspondent bank. It is a fair inference from the facts in the case that the buyer requested the issuing bank to act through a correspondent, which would confirm the credit to the seller. That the court felt the buyer had no relation with the correspondent, seems to indicate that, in its opinion, there is a presumption that no such relationship arises. This was an action against the confirming bank, but the problems of relation are identical with the case where a correspondent bank sues the buyer, see *infra* note 68.

[54] *Supra* p. 162, note 45.

[55] It is instructive to note that the considerations determining who is to bear the payment of commissions in letter of credit transactions, support generally the various suggested analyses of the legal relations between the respective parties. When a purchaser discounts the draft, the discount is normally paid by the seller who receives the face value of the draft less the discount, thus reinforcing the conclusion that the purchaser has no relation to the buyer, *supra* p. 160. When the credit is confirmed, the commission of the confirming bank is paid by the buyer, through the medium of the issuing bank. Accordingly, it may well be argued that the confirming bank has rights against the buyer, *supra* p. 165. When the notifying bank purchases the draft from the beneficiary, the latter may receive the face value of the draft while the buyer pays no additional charge, the charge of the advising bank would therefore be borne by the issuing bank. Though this is not as clear a case as that of the bona fide purchaser, it seems to be in accord with the view that the notifying bank has no claim against the buyer. In the more usual case, where the buyer pays an additional commission for the issuance of a letter of advice, the notifying bank might have a claim against the buyer similar to that of the confirming bank. The rights of the notifying or confirming bank against the local requesting bank are also based on an analysis similar to that of the seller's rights against the requesting bank, already discussed, *supra* p. 157.

E. The Buyer

That the issuing bank has rights against the buyer on the agreement to reimburse is obvious.[56] The rights of the other parties against the buyer have been discussed.[57] On the other hand, however, in certain cases, the buyer has rights against the seller,[58]

---

[56] See in this connection *Ex parte* Agra Bank, *In re* Barber & Co., L. R. 9 Eq. 725 (1870). Whether it has any such rights in case the buyer acts through a local requesting bank, particularly where the buyer has not designated the issuing bank, is not so clear. See Basse & Selve v. Bank of Australasia, 90 L. T. N. S. 618 (1904), where the court refused to pass on the question. If requesting bank merely guarantees that the buyer will reimburse the issuing bank, it is submitted that the latter must have an action against the buyer on an agreement to reimburse expressed or implied. If the issuing bank acts as agent for an undisclosed principal, *i. e.*, requesting bank, it is more doubtful whether it has any rights against the buyer, see *supra* p. 39 *et seq.*

[57] See pp. 155, 160, 165. An important element in the relation between buyer and bank is the question of commission. In the modern formal letter of credit, this is usually provided for in the agreement to reimburse. The terms allow the bank a certain percentage for such part of the credit as is used, with provision for a minimum commission in any event, see Appendix A for a form of agreement to reimburse. This is sound both from a commercial and a legal point of view. There are two stages involved in the use of letters of credit, the issuance of the credit and the acceptance of the draft. Commercially, the bank is entitled to payment for each of these operations. Legally, two stages of liability are represented in these operations. The issuance of the credit involves a contingent, and the acceptance of the draft creates an absolute, liability. The bank is entitled to commission for the use of its credit at either or both of these stages. The same result should be reached in the absence of any formal agreement. The bank should be entitled to an initial commission upon the opening of the credit and to an additional sum for such part of the credit as is used. In the only case on the subject, Baring v. Lyman, 2 Fed. Cas. No. 983 (C. C. D. Mass. 1841), it was held that the right to commission arose upon the drawing of the bills even though these were never presented or negotiated. "The commission was a commission not accruing upon the payment of the bills, but designed as an indemnity and compensation for the risk run, and responsibility incurred by Messrs. Baring & Co. and their duty to accept and pay the bills if drawn under the letter of credit." (At 801.) This seems to be a pointless distinction and is certainly difficult of application. The mere drawing of the draft alters the position of the bank in no way. Its liability is affected at two points, the issuance of the credit, and the presentation of the draft. Its commission should therefore be fixed at these points. The risk and responsibility mentioned by the court attach upon the issuance of the credit and not upon the drawing of the draft. It is the former act therefore that should be important in fixing the point at which the bank becomes entitled to commission. As can be seen from the quotation, the case is not an actual holding opposed to this point of view, since the rule was there laid down in disposing of the contention of counsel that the bank was not entitled to any commission before acceptance, and no holding on the effect of the drawing of drafts was necessary.

[58] The rights of the buyer against the seller are more logically consid-

the issuing bank, and various parties to the transaction.[59] Where the buyer has deposited money with the bank and the latter has agreed to open a credit, clearly the bank cannot thereafter dishonor its credit and apply the amount deposited to the payment of an indebtedness of the buyer to the bank. Any such attempt renders it not only liable to the beneficiary,[60] but to the buyer as well.[61]

---

ered under the law of sales, except in the few cases where the issuance of the letter of credit raises peculiar problems. It has been held, for example, that where the buyer sued the seller for shipping more goods than were ordered and collecting from the issuing bank the purchase price for the larger amount, no action would lie while the goods were in the possession of the bank, which had a lien against them for the advances under the credit. The court took the view that the buyer had not been damaged until he had paid the bank and freed the goods of the lien and was in a position either to resell or to return them to the seller. E. E. Huber & Co. v. Lalley Light Corp., 242 Mich. 171, 218 N. W. 793 (1928).

[59] The buyer has rights against the issuing bank in the event that it should fail to issue the letter of credit as agreed upon or if it should fail to honor drafts drawn under the letter after it had been issued. These rights are based on the preliminary agreement to issue and honor the credit, and not on the letter of credit itself. Kronman & Co. v. Public Nat. Bank, 218 App. Div. 624, 218 N. Y. Supp. 616 (1926). They are similar in their nature to rights arising from the failure of a bank to fulfill its obligation to establish a credit, see Richard v. American Union Bank, 241 N. Y. 163, 149 N. E. 338, 43 A. L. R. 512 (1925), 225 App. Div. 634, 234 N. Y. Supp. 177 (1929); Richard v. Credit Suisse, 242 N. Y. 346, 152 N. E. 110, 45 A. L. R. 1041 (1926); see also Bank of British North America v. Cooper, 137 U. S. 473, 11 Sup. Ct. 160, 34 L. Ed. 759 (1890); or to take proper steps in collecting a draft deposited for collection, Bown Brothers v. Merchants Bank, 243 N. Y. 366, 153 N. E. 493 (1926); or to honor checks, see authorities cited *infra* ch. VII, p. 263, note 7. As indicated previously, the buyer has no rights against the purchaser of the draft after the latter has received payment, even though the conditions of the letter of credit had not been performed when the draft was purchased. See cases cited *supra* note 36. Whether the buyer has rights against the correspondent bank depends entirely on the nature of the transaction. Where the credit is confirmed, it is probable that the confirming bank comes under a duty to the buyer similar to that of the issuing bank, since the confirmation is usually specifically requested and an additional charge is made for it, see discussion *supra* p. 165 and note 55. If the correspondent merely advises of the opening of the credit, its position, as a general rule, is similar to that of the purchaser, and the buyer has no rights against it, p. 165 and notes 36, 45, 55.

[60] *Supra* ch. III, p. 123, note 67, ch. IV, p. 150, ch. VI, p. 250.

[61] Laing v. First Nat. Bank, 138 Wash. 227, 244 Pac. 679 (1926); Smith v. Sanborn State Bank, 147 Iowa 640, 126 N. W. 779, 30 L. R. A. (N. S.) 517 (1910). See also Payne Bros. v. Burnett, 151 Tenn. 496, 269 S. W. 27, 39 A. L. R. 1125 (1925); Graham v. Mahoney, 1 Irish Law Rec. (1st Ser.) 385 (1828). But *cf.* Ellis v. Bank of Australasia, 3 N. S. Wales L. R. 96 (1882). This is but an illustration of the general rule that any

Where the buyer pays cash for the letter of credit, he has, of course, no right to the funds deposited until the credit has expired or is returned, and then only to an amount representing the unused portion of the credit.[62] In the event that the bank becomes insolvent, the buyer is merely a general creditor and has no preference in respect to the funds covering the unused portion of the credit. The credit is very similar in this respect to an ordinary deposit which does not establish a trust fund, but merely a debtor and creditor relationship.[63] The same rule should apply in the case of the unused portion of a letter of credit. No case directly in point has been found, though several strong analogies support this conclusion. It has been held that the holder of a traveler's letter of credit, returned partially unused, is merely a general creditor of the insolvent issuing bank;[64] that the drawer of a check, dishonored because the bank is insolvent, is merely a gen-

money or credits received by the bank for a specific purpose must be used for that purpose, 1 MORSE, BANKS AND BANKING (6th ed. 1928) ch. XIV and § 325. This rule would apply whether the debt was incurred before or after the credit was issued. If, however, the buyer returns the letter of credit or if it expires unused, there is no reason why the bank should not then be permitted to set off its own debt. The money becomes a general debt due the buyer which the bank should be permitted to set off against a debt due it from the buyer. In modern formal letters of credit, the problem of set off in regard to other claims is expressly dealt with in the agreement to reimburse. By the terms of the usual form, the bank can apply the money or collateral deposited to any pre-existing debt or to one contracted subsequently, see modern form of agreement for reimbursement in Appendix A. This provision may protect it against any action by the buyer. The beneficiary, however, would still retain his right to be paid, once he has been notified of the credit, as he is no party to this agreement and as his rights generally are not conditioned by the state of the accounts between bank and buyer, *infra* ch. VI, p. 250.

[62] See Cutler v. American Exchange Nat. Bank, 113 N. Y. 593, 21 N. E. 710, 4 L. R. A. 328 (1889). Where the letter of credit is lost, the buyer may well be required to put up a bond securing the bank against loss before the bank becomes obligated to return collateral or money deposited with it. In the case of travelers' letters of credit or circular notes, such would more clearly be the rule. Conflans Stone Quarry Co. v. Parker, L. R. 3 C. P. 1 (1867).

[63] 2 MORSE, BANKS AND BANKING (6th ed. 1928) § 589.

[64] Taussig v. Carnegie Trust Co., 156 App. Div. 519, 141 N. Y. Supp. 347 (1913), *aff'd* without opinion, 213 N. Y. 627, 107 N. E. 1086 (1914); see also Kuehne v. Union Trust Co., 133 Mich. 602, 95 N. W. 715 (1903); Equitable Trust Co. v. Rochling, 275 U. S. 248, 48 Sup. Ct. 58, 72 L. Ed. 264 (1927); Latzko v. Equitable Trust Co., 275 U. S. 254, 48 Sup. Ct. 60, 72 L. Ed. 267 (1927).

eral creditor of the bank;[65] and that the party depositing money to be cabled to Europe is merely a general creditor where the depositary fails to cable the money and becomes insolvent.

To establish a rule that in a case like this the plaintiff becomes a preferred creditor; that the transaction is in the nature of a trust, and that checks deposited with banks upon the purchase of credit are trust funds held for certain and specified purposes, is apt to lead to much confusion especially when those who have developed this method of doing business into a well-established custom have never treated them as such.[66]

Where the credit is issued merely against the promise of the buyer to indemnify the bank, the former can in no way control the discretion of the bank in paying out its funds under the credit.[67] The buyer can only refuse to indemnify the bank and then defend any action that may be brought against him.[68] This

---

[65] Beecher v. Cosmopolitan Trust Co., 239 Mass. 48, 131 N. E. 338 (1921).

[66] Legniti v. Mechanics & Metals Nat. Bank, 230 N. Y. 415, 424, 130 N. E. 597, 599, 16 A. L. R. 185, 190 (1921). See also Equitable Trust Co. v. First Nat. Bank, 275 U. S. 359, 48 Sup. Ct. 167, 72 L. Ed. 313 (1928), *rev'g*, *In re* Gubelman, *Ex parte* First Nat. Bank, 13 F. (2d) 732 (C. C. A. 2d, 1926), and overruling in effect, *In re* Zimmerman & Forshay, *Ex parte* Gray, 14 F. (2d) 527 (C. C. A. 2d, 1926).

[67] There is another possible form of action that may arise after the bank has paid the holder. If the buyer has paid the bank at the time of the opening of the credit, or if he does not learn of the non-performance of certain conditions until after he has paid the bank, he may sue the latter at law to recover the money paid. See Basse & Selve v. Bank of Australasia, *supra* note 56; Borthwick v. Bank of New Zealand, 17 T. L. R. 2 (1900); Munroe v. Bonanno, 16 App. Div. 421, 45 N. Y. Supp. 61 (1897). Except in the case where the buyer can be considered to have waived the non-performance of certain conditions, this type of action involves substantially the same considerations as an action by the bank against the buyer, and therefore need not be considered separately at this point.

[68] When a correspondent bank wrongfully pays a draft, there is authority for the proposition that the buyer, where he has entered into a contract with the correspondent, may have an action against it. Royal Card & Paper Co. v. Dresdner Bank, *supra* note 52, at 793: "If it [the buyer] rejected them [the goods], it could hold defendant [the correspondent] responsible for paying out plaintiff's money—or, more accurately, causing plaintiff to incur an obligation to reimburse the Irving National Bank on its letter of credit—contrary to defendant's contract obligation." It is submitted that the general applicability of this rule is somewhat doubtful. If the correspondent paid the draft contrary to the terms of the credit, the issuer was under no duty to pay the correspondent. And if the issuer honored the credit under these conditions, it would seem under the rules we have been considering that the buyer would come under no

should also hold true where the buyer has paid cash for the issuance of the credit. Since the buyer is only a general creditor, he can claim no specific assets and, even if the bank is insolvent, it is submitted that he cannot enjoin the bank from improperly paying a draft drawn under the credit, since the latter cannot be deemed to be paying out funds of the buyer.[69] Courts, however, have been inclined at the instance of the buyer to enjoin the bank from honoring its credit where the conditions have not been performed, when the buyer can show prospective irreparable damage or similar grounds for equitable relief.[70]

In this situation, the problem created is similar to that which arises where the bank sues the buyer on the agreement to reimburse. If, in the latter case, the buyer would have a valid defense, then, in the former, he can enjoin the bank from paying certain parties.[71] If the buyer would be under no duty to reimburse the

---

duty to pay the issuing bank. In the instant case, however, defendant made a special contract with the buyer to purchase the drafts. *Supra* note 52. This contract contained additional terms not in the letter of credit. The defendant, therefore, might have purchased documents that fully complied with the requirements of the letter of credit and yet, in so doing, have violated the buyer's instructions.

[69] *Cf.* (1921) 34 HARV. L. REV. 533, 535, n. 13.

[70] Even under this view, the instances where the buyer is entitled to an injunction are rare. In the first place, the buyer should not be able to obtain an injunction when the bank issues the credit in reliance only on the promise of the buyer to idemnify the bank, as he cannot show irreparable damage. If conditions are not performed, he is simply under no duty to pay the bank. It is the bank that suffers the loss. Only when the buyer has deposited cash or collateral, can he possibly prove irreparable damage. In this situation, he must show that the bank is in danger of insolvency. Frey & Son v. E. R. Sherburne Co., 193 App. Div. 849, 184 N. Y. Supp. 661 (1920); Central Sugar Co. v. Lamborn, 200 N. Y. Supp. 499 (1921), *aff'd* without opinion, 195 App. Div. 909, 186 N. Y. Supp. 936 (1921); Ideal Cocoa & Chocolate Co. v. De Magalhaes, 64 N. Y. L. J., Jan. 18, 1921, at 1324; Sun Herald Corp. v. Maurice O'Meara Co., 64 N. Y. L. J., Jan. 26, 1921, at 1426; El Reno Grocery Co. v. Lamborn, 64 N. Y. L. J., Dec. 15, 1920, at 908; Shapiro Candy Mfg. Co. v. Reiter, 64 N. Y. L. J., Dec. 13, 1920, at 855; see also: J. Hungerford Smith Co. v. Lamborn, 200 N. Y. Supp. 292, 294 (1921).

[71] "Unless and until the plaintiff shall establish its rights under the contract on the law side of the court, it is not entitled to the equitable remedy of injunction pendente lite." Central Sugar Co. v. Lamborn, *supra* note 70, at 500. As previously indicated, *supra* p. 149, the bank may have a right to reimbursement when it pays the holder of a draft, even though it could justifiably have refused to do so. In this situation also, some courts are of the opinion that, these equitable circumstances existing, the

bank in the event that it should pay the seller, he can enjoin the bank from paying the seller and the seller from presenting or discounting the draft. Where the buyer would have a valid defense after the bank paid a purchaser with notice, he can obtain a similar injunction against the bank and the purchaser with notice. In no case, however, can he obtain an injunction preventing the bank from paying purchasers generally, since unless the defense is apparent from the contents of the letter of credit, the draft may fall into the hands of a bona fide purchaser.[72] In this event, the bank would be obligated to honor the draft and, by so doing, would acquire a right to reimbursement against the buyer. The buyer cannot therefore be granted an injunction so comprehensive in its terms.[73]

F. The Issuing Bank and the Requesting Bank

The rights and duties of the issuing bank and the requesting bank, when the latter enters the transaction, have been pointed out in the discussion of the relations of the other parties. It need

buyer can enjoin the bank from paying the draft to any holder with notice. Therefore we find the court saying that, "the plaintiff's right in equity to stop payment depends upon the obligation of the Union National Bank to honor the draft drawn on faith of its letter of credit." Bank of Taiwan v. Gorgas-Pierie Mfg. Co., 273 Fed. 660, 663 (C. C. A. 3d, 1921). The court is also of the opinion, apparently, that the buyer is not entitled to an injunction until the rights between the immediate parties have been adjudicated at law. See also Williams Ice Cream Co. v. Chase Nat. Bank, 210 App. Div. 179, 205 N. Y. Supp. 446 (1924); Frey & Son v. E. R. Sherburne Co., *supra* note 70; C. A. Gambrill Mfg. Co. v. American Foreign Banking Corp., 194 App. Div. 425, 185 N. Y. Supp. 502 (1920); see also Higgins v. Steinhardter, 106 Misc. 168, 175 N. Y. Supp. 279 (1919), overruled by Frey & Son v. E. R. Sherburne Co., *supra* note 70.

[72] See e. g., Maitland v. Chartered Mercantile Bank of India, London and China, 38 L. J. Ch. 363 (1869).

[73] Frey & Son v. E. R. Sherburne Co., *supra* note 70, at 854, 184 N. Y. Supp. at 664: "Interests of innocent parties who may hold drafts upon the letter of credit should not be made to suffer by reason of rights that may exist between the parties to the contract of sale in reference to which the letter of credit was issued. It would be a calamity to the business world if for every breach of a contract between buyer and seller a party may come into a court of equity and enjoin payment on drafts drawn upon a letter of credit issued by a bank which owed no duty to the buyer in respect of the breach."

only be added that in any case where the requesting bank is obligated to pay the issuing bank, its rights against the buyer are similar to those of the issuing bank against the requesting bank or the buyer, as the case may be.[74]

---

[74] *Supra* p. 167.

Chapter V

CONDITIONS IN THE LETTER OF CREDIT

Commercial letters of credit are most frequently used in connection with the sale of goods. Two of the functions of the instrument have been indicated, the security it furnishes the seller that payment will be made, and the convenience to both parties as the most economical and most expedient method of financing transactions. In discussing the conditions[1] of the letter of credit, two other functions come into the foreground—the protection afforded the buyer against the non-performance or fraudulent performance of the contract by the seller before payment, and the assurance to the seller, not only that he will be paid, but that he will be paid promptly and without hesitation. The relative importance and weight of these functions and tendencies will be more clearly apprehended when the problems have been considered.

Another factor to be noted is that the beneficiary of a credit not only takes subject to the terms and conditions of the credit, but also may take subject to conditions communicated to him orally or in writing in another instrument, contingent, of course,

[1] The term conditions is used in this chapter in its broadest sense, to mean all those acts which must be performed by the seller or purchaser before the bank comes under a duty to honor drafts drawn under the letter of credit. Its use in this connection is to be distinguished from the meaning given it previously; *supra* ch. II, p. 62. Normally the duty of the bank to the seller is to accept and to pay drafts, or to purchase drafts. There may be additional duties as well, e. g., that the bank will not release documents to the buyer except upon payment of the balance of the purchase price, to be delivered to the seller, where the bank upon receipt of the documents had paid the seller only a part of the purchase price. See Gordon v. Irving Bank-Columbia Trust Co., 210 App. Div. 186, 205 N. Y. Supp. 522 (1924) where the bank was held liable to the seller for breaching this type of condition.

upon the admissibility in evidence of these extrinsic provisions.[2] While a purchaser can ordinarily acquire no rights against the issuer unless all the conditions contained in the credit are performed, nevertheless his rights against the issuer cannot be affected by conditions of which he is ignorant. The responsibility lies with the issuer to insert the conditions directly or at least by reference into the letter of credit, if he desires to limit the rights of all holders of drafts by their performance. The bona fide purchaser, therefore, can recover without the performance of those conditions of which he is ignorant and of which he cannot reasonably be presumed to have knowledge. As already indicated, the basis of this rule is the *bona fides* of the purchaser, and this becomes clear from its limitations. If the purchaser should discover the existence of those conditions before or at the time of taking the draft, his rights immediately become subject to their performance. Similarly, in accordance with the principle which underlies the general test of a bona fide purchaser, if the purchaser is in such a relationship to the various parties that, in view of his previous dealings or otherwise, he may reasonably be presumed to have knowledge of these additional limitations, or at least to have been put on inquiry as to their existence, then he cannot recover independently of the performance of those conditions.[3]

---

[2] In this connection, it may be well to notice that it is quite customary to alter the terms of commercial credits with the consent of all parties concerned, after they have been issued and before they have been acted upon. The contents of a credit are not, therefore, fixed and determined as irrevocably as in the case of bills and notes. For an illustration, see E. E. Huber & Co. v. Lalley Light Corp., 242 Mich. 171, 218 N. W. 793 (1928). It is clear that after a credit has been relied upon, even though no drafts have been drawn, the bank cannot ordinarily change the terms of the credit without the consent of the seller. Lamborn v. Nat. Park Bank, 240 N. Y. 520, 148 N. E. 664 (1925).

[3] It is assumed that these additional terms are admissible in evidence, either because the language of the credit itself is ambiguous or for other reasons. See the discussion and cases cited, *supra* ch. III, p. 104, *et seq.* Compare this with the discussion of the question as to whether a promise had been intended. *Supra* ch. II, p. 31. It will be seen that identical principles are involved. The same result should therefore be reached in all these instances, *i. e.*, that the purchaser is never subjected in the exercise of his rights to terms and conditions not contained in the letter of

The rights of other parties, such as the notifying, the negotiating, or the confirming bank, depend on similar considerations, *i. e.*, on whether or not they have actually been informed of, or can reasonably be presumed to have been put on inquiry as to, the additional limitations. The only difference here is one of degree. These parties are more likely to be in a position in which they can reasonably be expected to know of the existence of these limitations, than is a casual bona fide purchaser. However, this difference in degree does not constitute a difference in the rule that is applied or in the theory that is used. The test in all cases is essentially one of *bona fides*.

The rights of the issuing bank against the buyer or the requesting bank are fixed generally, in accordance with the analysis already suggested, by the considerations determining the duty of the bank to the party presenting the draft. Since the bank need not honor its credit when the seller presents the draft unless all conditions of the credit are performed, it should not be permitted to recover against the buyer in the absence of such performance. If the draft is in the hands of a bona fide purchaser, however, the issuing bank may recover against the party requesting the credit on the performance of such conditions as obligate it to pay the draft in the hands of such bona fide purchaser.[4]

---

credit of which he had no knowledge, and as to which he was not put on inquiry. On the other hand, if the secret limitations make the promise more liberal than appears on the face of the letter of credit, the purchaser without notice should be allowed to take advantage of that fact upon discovering it.

[4] It is assumed that there is no variance between the instructions of the buyer to the bank and the terms inserted into the letter of credit. Where, for example, the buyer requests a credit to be opened and, before it is issued, specifies certain conditions which the bank puts into another instrument, not the letter of credit, a bona fide purchaser should not have his rights subjected to the performance of those conditions if they have not been incorporated into the credit at least by reference. As will be seen, however, it is doubtful whether the bank can recover against the buyer unless the additional conditions have been performed. There is an exception to this, of course, in some situations presently to be considered, where the bank is under no duty to pay the holder of the draft, but has the power by so doing to subject the buyer to a duty to reimburse it.

A. Conformity of Documents

Conditions contained in letters of credit may be usefully classified according to the nature of their requirements. The almost universal custom now is to insert those conditions which require the attaching of documents to the draft. Conditions which do not require the attaching of documents are also occasionally included, particularly in the more informal instruments. These two groups raise many different considerations and can most effectively be dealt with separately. The principal problem raised by the former is the question as to whether the documents presented conform to the requirements of the letter of credit, a problem usually considered under the head of conformity of documents.[5]

These requirements as to documents are usually inserted in the letter of credit itself. There is, normally, no difference between the position of the seller and that of the subsequent bona fide purchaser, and their rights may therefore be considered together.

---

[5] It is hardly necessary to note that normally in addition to the performance of the conditions, an actual tender of the draft with the necessary documents is required before the holder has a right of action against the bank. The rule is similar under c.i.f. contracts. Cohen v. Wood & Selick, 214 App. Div. 175, 212 N. Y. Supp. 31 (1925); Kunglig Jarnvagsstyrelsen v. Dexter & Carpenter, 32 F. (2d) 195 (C. C. A. 2d, 1929). *Cf.* Richard v. Royal Bank of Canada, 23 F. (2d) 430 (C. C. A. 2d, 1928), holding the drawing and presentation of a draft unnecessary under the provisions of the particular letter of credit. See also Struthers v. Commercial Bank, 4 Sess. Cas. (2d Ser.) 460 (1842). Where the draft is lost, presumably the holder could recover in equity upon tender of an indemnity bond. Savannah Nat. Bank v. Haskins, 101 Mass. 370 (1869); see also *supra* ch. IV, note 62. Waiver or subsequent impossibility of performance of conditions is considered *infra* p. 207. For the effect of an anticipatory breach of a letter of credit, see *infra* ch. VII, p. 267. The suspension of payment however by the issuing bank is no such anticipatory breach as to give the holder a right of action without a tender, as the trustee might decide to accept the draft to avoid such an action. *In re* Agra Bank, *Ex parte* Tondeur, L. R. 5 Eq. 160 (1867). Though of course the drafts would have to be sold at a much higher rate of discount, this would merely mean that the beneficiary obtained less credit than he expected under the letter of credit. But that is no breach of contract by the bank. "All it comes to is, that the applicants have not got the extent of credit they hoped to have got. They might have complained in the same way, although there had been no stoppage, if there has been disastrous rumors about the losses of the bank and that there was great probability of a suspension of payment." At 166; see also *Ex parte* Agra Bank, *In re* Barber & Co., L. R. 9 Eq. 725 (1870).

The position of the seller, when he tenders documents to the bank under a letter of credit, is analogous to that in which he is placed when he is tendering documents to the buyer under a c.i.f. contract.[6] A brief analysis of the underlying basis of the rights of the seller in that peculiar form of contract will greatly aid, not only in showing the changes created by the introduction of the letter of credit, but also in clarifying the essential functions of the latter instrument.

A c.i.f. contract may be defined as a contract for the sale of goods by the terms of which the seller becomes entitled to the purchase price on the delivery to the buyer of certain specified documents which are prima facie evidence of performance on his part.[7] The purchase price, therefore, is to be paid against documents. The main question is naturally whether the documents presented fulfill the terms of the contract. If they do, the buyer must pay even though the goods have not as yet arrived and though he does not know whether or not they are the goods he desires.[8] On the other hand, if the documents do not meet the

---

[6] What is meant is a contract calling for payment against documents. Not all c.i.f. contracts call for payment against documents, nor are all "payment-against-documents contracts," c.i.f. contracts. But since to a great extent and in most matters they are co-extensive, the term c.i.f. contract is used as a convenient expression for the more awkward term "payment-against-documents contract." For the more accurate and less usual use of the term c.i.f., see Y. P. Barley Producers v. E. C. Robertson Pty., [1927] V. L. R. 194, 200.

[7] "A contract for the sale of goods to be performed by the delivery of documents." Arnhold Karlberg & Co. v. Blythe, Green, Jourdain & Co., [1916] 1 K. B. 495, 510. "The theory of a c.i.f. contract is that it constitutes a sale of goods by delivery not of goods but of documents." Dwane v. Weil, 199 App. Div. 719, 730, 192 N. Y. Supp. 393, 402 (1922), *aff'd* without opinion, 235 N. Y. 527, 139 N. E. 720 (1923). See also Malmberg v. Evans & Co., 41 T. L. R. 38 (1924); National Wholesale Grocery Co. v. Mann, 251 Mass. 238, 146 N. E. 791 (1925); A. Klipstein Co. v. Dilsizian, 273 Fed. 473, 475 (C. C. A. 2d, 1921), *cert. den.*, 257 U. S. 639, 42 Sup. Ct. 51 (1921).

[8] Polenghi Bros. v. Dried Milk Co., 10 Com. Cas. 42, 49 Sol. J. 120 (1904), holds that the buyer must pay on the tender of the documents and has no right to withhold payment until after inspection, even though the goods have arrived; see also: E. Clemens Horst Co. v. Biddell Bros., [1912] A. C. 18, *rev'g*, [1911] 1 K. B. 934. For an American statement of this doctrine, see Brown v. Raritan Chemical Works, 188 App. Div. 578, 584, 177 N. Y. Supp. 309, 312 (1919); California P. & A. Growers v. Jaggers Wholesale Grocery Co., 85 Ind. App. 506, 150 N. E. 317

requirements of the contract, then he need not pay even though the goods have arrived and though he knows that they are the very goods for which the contract calls.[9]

The seeming inequity of these results disappears when one considers the business usages under which c.i.f. contracts are made. Most of the contracts are used in connection with the import and export trade. The importer is very seldom the ultimate consumer. Generally, he does not even sell to the retail merchants. In the majority of instances, the goods go to some wholesale commission merchant. Frequently, the whole amount is disposed of to one party. In any event, the importer has, in most cases, resold the goods before they have arrived, particularly if they are coming from a distant port. In order to dispose of the merchandise in this manner, he must have documents which show what the goods are and which demonstrate the fact that he has control over them. If the documents are in proper form, they do show these facts, and the buyer is properly made to pay against them.

For thereunder, as the bill of lading, with its accompanying documents, comes forward by mail, the purchaser obtains the

---

(1926); Ten Broeck Tyre Co. v. Rubber Trading Co., 186 Ky. 526, 217 S. W. 345 (1919), and authorities cited in the last two cases. See also Strong & Dowler v. Scotia Flour & Feed Co., [1927] 2 D. L. R. 1183 (N. S.), and Smith Co., Ltd., v. Marano, 267 Pa. 107, 110 Atl. 94, 10 A. L. R. 697 (1920) where the buyer was compelled to pay on presentation of documents though the goods had been destroyed. It is submitted, however, that if the buyer knows something is wrong with the goods, or that the documents are fraudulent he can set such facts up as a defense or as a counterclaim to an action by the seller. Hyman-Michaels Co. v. Fox, 298 Fed. 440, 442 (C. C. A. 2d, 1924); see *infra* ch. VI, note 11. That, however, is beside the point—that the buyer cannot refuse payment on the ground that he does not know whether the goods are as represented and so compel the seller to wait until he has inspected them, or require the seller to prove in other ways that the goods comply with the terms of the contract.

[9] Mitsubishi Goshi Kaisha v. J. Aron & Co., 16 F. (2d) 185, 186 (C. C. A. 2d, 1926): "Nothing but such a bill of lading was a performance of the condition upon that promise. . . . There is no room in commercial contracts for the doctrine of substantial performance." Orient Co. v. Brekke & Howlid, [1913] 1 K. B. 531, 536. See also Lundy v. S. Pfeifer & Co., 162 La. 355, 110 So. 556 (1926). Also if goods alone, without any documents, are tendered, he need not accept. Harper v. Hochstim, 278 Fed. 102, 20 A. L. R. 1232 (C. C. A. 2d, 1921); see *infra* note 11.

privilege and absolute power of profitably dealing with the goods days or weeks, or, perhaps in the case of shipments from a distant port, months before the arrival of the goods themselves. This is, indeed, the essential and peculiar advantage which the buyer of imported goods intends to gain under the c.i.f. contract according to the construction which I put upon it.[10]

These considerations show the underlying basis of the rules governing the presentation of documents in c.i.f. contracts. They indicate that it is a just and reasonable rule of law which, in view of the relation between the parties, holds that the buyer is not required to take documents that do not conform, even though the goods themselves conform exactly to the requirements of the contract. This is because the essential advantage of this form of contract is lost to the buyer, unless the documents are in such order that they can easily be resold or delivered under a contract to resell made previously. They cannot easily be so resold or so delivered where the documents themselves raise some doubt as to whether the goods described in the documents are the goods called for by the contract. The question, therefore, as to whether the documents conform to the requirements of the sales contract, is one of the utmost importance, and one which often finds its way into courts for settlement.[11]

---

[10] E. Clemens Horst Co. v. Biddell Bros., *supra* note 8, [1911] 1 K. B. at 958, in dissenting opinion of Kennedy L. J.; see also Hansson v. Hamel & Horley, Ltd. [1922] 2 A. C. 36, 46. "These documents have to be handled by banks, they have to be taken up or rejected promptly and without any opportunity for prolonged inquiry, they have to be such as can be retendered to sub-purchasers, and it is essential that they should so conform to the accustomed shipping documents as to be reasonably and readily fit to pass current in commerce." There are other considerations leading to the same result. The seller has a lien on the goods for the price, as long as the documents are in his possession. On surrendering them he loses the lien and should therefore be paid. Finally, the delivery of the documents is usually made at a central money or goods market, while the shipment may be from one small city to another, e. g., a shipment of sugar from Cuba to Denmark with the contract requiring presentment of documents in London or New York. Normally, when the goods are as represented, the delivery of the documents constitutes for all practical purposes an effective performance of the contract by the seller. The buyer should therefore make payment against such performance.

[11] It is also significant to note that all the conditions of a c.i.f. contract or of a letter of credit may be of importance, and the court cannot, without remaking the agreement, waive any of the provisions, as it is im-

In considering conformity of documents under c. i. f. contracts, three types of problems arise, based upon the following objections of the buyer: (1) that the documents do not represent the state of facts which the buyer thought they would represent; (2) that the particular document presented is not the document described in the contract; and (3) that the goods described in the documents are not the goods for which the contract calls.

As to the first problem, it is generally recognized that, if the document fits the description in the contract, the buyer must pay the purchase price on presentation even though the actual state of facts upon which the document is based is not what the buyer thought it would be or what it normally is. An interesting illustration of this is the case of *Thalmann Frères & Co.* v. *Texas Star Flour Mills.*[12] The contract there called for "clearance not later than May 31." A certificate of clearance authorizing the ship to sail was issued on May 28, but the vessel did not finish loading and sail until June 2. As a result it did not arrive until July 1, a day too late to take advantage of a temporary remission of duty at Havre, the port of destination. Having in the meantime accepted and paid a draft, the buyers sued for breach of contract,

possible to know which are or will become of importance. "Moreover, no court can say that the provisions in the buyer's order requiring signed bills of lading to accompany invoices and to be sent the buyer the day the goods are shipped, were not of financial and business importance to the buyer." Burrows & Kenyon v. Warren, 9 F. (2d) 1, 5 (C. C. A. 1st, 1925); see also Manatee County State Bank v. Weatherly, 144 Ala. 655, 659, 39 So. 988, 989 (1905); Pake v. Wilson, 127 Ala. 240, 28 So. 665 (1899); and dissenting opinion in Talmadge v. Williams, 27 La. Ann. 653, 655 (1875): "Letters of credit are not to be enlarged or varied by the bearers of them, but are to be followed strictly in all material points and conditions. The defendants were willing to bind themselves in a specific manner for the benefit of their correspondents for reasons satisfactory to themselves, and some of which may readily be surmised." Graham v. Farmers & Merchants Bank, 116 Cal. 463, 465, 48 Pac. 384, 385 (1897): "The fact that the numbers of the cars in which the oranges were loaded were given was itself a significant fact. The officers of the bank may well have asked why these particular cars were mentioned, if it was immaterial in what cars the fruit was shipped. It turns out that these cars were about one week on the road and could have been diverted by telegraph so as to reach New York in a day or two—ten days or so earlier than those shipped in the other cars could reach New York. According to the testimony of Graham this was quite material to P. Ruhlman & Co."

[12] 15 T. L. R. 471 (1899), *aff'd,* 16 T. L. R. 460 (1900).

alleging that the vessel sailed too late. The court found for the seller, holding that the latter had performed his part of the contract in obtaining the clearance papers in time, even though the vessel did not sail till later, and even though the obvious purpose of the provision was to procure sailing at a certain time. The buyer had required a document dated before a certain date. This had been obtained. If anything in addition had been desired, it should have been specified.

> If the plaintiffs had chosen to do so, they could have stipulated that the vessel should sail by the date named . . . but such a stipulation is by no means the same as clearing. Clearing and sailing are two quite different things; and clearing and being ready to sail are not necessarily the same thing. The plaintiffs chose their own expression . . . and . . . their own contract must be interpreted according to the meaning which I attribute to the word they have used. In these circumstances it appears to me that the condition in the contract has been performed.[13]

The second type of problem arises in connection with the use of various forms of the same instrument. Is a received for shipment bill of lading sufficient tender under a contract calling for a bill of lading? Is an insurance certificate equivalent to an insurance policy? What are the documents included under the term shipping documents? These are the most serious problems that arise in this connection. Ultimately, their solution will depend upon the custom and usage among merchants. The law must sooner or later be defined in accordance with the practice normally followed in commercial transactions.[14]

---

[13] *Ibid.* 15 T. L. R. 471, 472 (1899); see also Jacob Glass, Inc., v. Banca Marmorosch, Blank & Co., Soc. Anon., 122 Misc. 637, 204 N. Y. Supp. 636 (1924).

[14] See, e. g., A. C. Harper & Co. v. Mackechnie & Co., [1925] 2 K. B. 423, 427. "The certificate was accepted, passed through a bank, and dealt with in the ordinary course, and it is clear from the evidence that the practice of accepting such certificates still survives in spite of the above decisions and the strict rights of the parties." For a discussion of the English cases dealing with these problems, see KENNEDY, C.I.F. CONTRACTS (2d ed. 1928); GOITEIN, C. I. F. CONTRACTS (2d ed. 1926); (1922) 66 SOL. J. 215, 216. This type of problem has arisen mainly as a result of changes in commercial practice. "One of the features of a sale c.i.f. is that, in the absence of special terms, the seller

The third type of problem is usually the result either of carelessness or of the use of ambiguous language in describing the goods in the bill of lading or other documents. When the contract calls for "yellow pine flooring" and the bill of lading uses "yellow pine lumber,"[15] an obvious ambiguity exists and the buyer is entitled to reject the documents, since not only can he not be certain that he is receiving what the contract calls for, but also "the essential advantage of that form of contract is lost to him" as, in view of the discrepancy, he cannot easily resell the documents.[16]

claims payment against presentation of shipping documents. When that form of contract was defined in the law courts, there is no doubt what by mercantile usage were the documents meant; a bill of lading, as a bill of lading was then understood, and a policy of insurance as a policy was then understood." Malmberg v. Evans & Co., *supra* note 7, at 39; See also: Wright, *Opposition of the Law to Business Usages* (1926) 26 Col. L. Rev. 917, 923, 935 *et seq.*; James Finlay & Co., Ltd., v. N. V. Kwik Hoo Tong Handel Maatschappij, 31 Lloyd's List 220, [1928] 2 K. B. 604, *aff'd* without opinion, [1929] W. N. 3; A. C. Harper & Co. v. Mackechnie & Co., *ibid.*; Foreman & Ellams v. Blackburn, [1928] 2 K. B. 60; Kingdom of Italy v. Suzuki & Co., 15 Lloyd's List 219 (1923); Spillers, Ltd. v. J. W. Mitchell, Ltd., 33 Lloyd's List 89 (1929); Loders & Nucoline, Ltd. v. Bank of New Zealand, 33 Lloyd's List 70 (1929); Martin v. Hogan, 24 C. L. R. 234 (Aust. 1917). Some recent American cases are: Johnson & Higgins v. Charles F. Garrigues Co., 22 F. (2d) 454 (S. D. N. Y. 1927); Kunglig Jarnvagsstyrelsen v. Dexter & Carpenter, 299 Fed. 991 (S. D. N. Y. 1924); H. O. Wilbur & Sons v. Lamborn, 276 Pa. 479, 120 Atl. 478, 27 A. L. R. 160 (1923), and cases there cited; Matthew Smith, Tea, Coffee & Grocery Co. v. Lamborn & Co., 276 Fed. 325 (S. D. N. Y. 1921); J. Hungerford Smith Co. v. Lamborn, 200 N. Y. Supp. 292 (1921); Pacific Rice Mills v. Westfeldt, 31 F. (2d) 979 (C. C. A. 5th, 1929); Macondray & Co. v. W. R. Grace & Co., 30 F. (2d) 647 (C. C. A. 9th, 1929). Much of the uncertainty in this connection could be avoided if merchants were more careful to define the terms used. A more general adoption of the "Regulations of 1920" would do much toward settling existing uncertainty. Ward, American Commercial Credits (1922) ch. VII; Edwards, Foreign Commercial Credits, (1922) 216 *et seq.*; 2 Williston, Sales (2d ed. 1924) § 405d; Appendix A, form 20. See also the proposed Warsaw Rules, 1928, discussed in (1929) 29 Col. L. Rev. 652, 813. Both the letter of credit and the c.i.f. contract may contain provisions for the performance of other conditions in addition to the presentation of documents, e. g., that the goods should actually arrive at the port of destination, see Dexters, Ltd., v. Schenker & Co., 14 Lloyd's List 586 (1923). If this provision is in the sales contract, whether it may be deemed a c.i.f. contract is often a nice question, see *infra* note 76.

[15] Brown, Graves & Co. v. Ambler, 66 Md. 391, 7 Atl. 903 (1887).

[16] This distinction should not be confused with the use of technical language, which, as will be seen, involves different considerations. If the plaintiff in Brown v. Ambler could have shown that "yellow pine flooring" was a technical name for "yellow pine lumber" or vice versa, he would have had a very strong case. *Cf.* De Sousa v. Crocker First Nat. Bank, 23 F. (2d) 118 (N. D. Cal. 1927), *rev'd*, 27 F. (2d) 462 (C. C. A. 9th,

Similar problems arise when documents are tendered under a letter of credit. The solution, however, is the same as when they are tendered to the buyer. No new considerations enter because of the fact that the tender is made to a bank.[17] If the buyer is obligated to pay against a properly dated clearance paper, even though the ship sailed later, then it is apparent that the bank is similarly bound to pay. If the court holds that a received for shipment bill of lading is a proper bill of lading when tendered to the buyer, it must hold it to be equally so when tendered to the bank. And, if "yellow pine flooring" and "yellow pine lumber" are or are not interchangeable terms, in popular usage, when the duty of the buyer to pay is under consideration, they are similarly so in the case of the bank.[18] The reason for these results is obvious. The solution of these problems, as has been indicated, depends upon general trade usages among merchants and not upon any particular custom in vogue in any particular trade, concerning which the buyer might have knowlege, but with which the bank would not be in a position to be acquainted. The assumption is reasonable that the bank, being in the business of financing trade, is acquainted with all its general customs and should be held bound by that knowledge.

These questions, therefore, are essentially questions of the law of sales. They arise under letters of credit only because of the relationship between the letter of credit and the sales contract. No new principles are involved. Subject to the instances

1928), discussed *infra* note 21. But, as this was not so and as they really represented two different commodities, or, at least one was a more general term than the other, the buyer was well within his rights in rejecting the documents.

[17] Problems of a different type arise that are peculiar to the situation where the tender is made to a bank. These will be considered later, see *infra* p. 187.

[18] See Decatur Bank v. St. Louis Bank, 21 Wall. 294, 22 L. Ed. 560 (1874). The court held that a bill of lading for hogs was a sufficient compliance with a promise conditioned on a bill of lading for cattle. The court shows that this is a popular, not a technical, interpretation. In other words, the term cattle included hogs in common usage. If a question of the construction of technical terms had been involved, another problem, to be considered presently, would have arisen.

shortly to be considered, the bank here is in exactly the same position as the buyer. A discussion of these principles requires a consideration of elements more appropriate to problems of sales than to the law of letters of credit; hence they require no further detailed consideration here.[19] In the field of sales, however,

[19] The most troublesome problem of this type that has arisen under letters of credit has been to determine which documents must contain the description of the goods as specified in the credit. See Laudisi v. American Exchange Nat. Bank, 239 N. Y. 234, 146 N. E. 347 (1924) holding that a description in the seller's invoice is sufficient where nothing to the contrary is specified. *Cf.* De Sousa v. Crocker First Nat. Bank, *supra* note 16; Camp v. Corn Exch. Nat. Bank, 285 Pa. 337, 132 Atl. 189 (1926); Banco Nacional Ultramarino v. First Nat. Bank, 289 Fed. 169 (D. Mass. 1923); Portuguese American Bank v. Atlantic Nat. Bank, 200 App. Div. 575, 193 N. Y. Supp. 423 (1922); Bank of Montreal v. Recknagel, 109 N. Y. 482, 17 N. E. 217 (1888); Maurice O'Meara Co. v. Nat. Park Bank, 239 N. Y. 386, 146 N. E. 636, 39 A. L. R. 747 (1925). For problems in connection with bills of lading, see: Richard v. Royal Bank of Canada, *supra* note 5; Vietor v. Nat. City Bank, 200 App. Div. 557, 193 N. Y. Supp. 868 (1922), 206 App. Div. 664, 199 N. Y. Supp. 955 (1923), *aff'd* without opinion, 237 N. Y. 538, 143 N. E. 733 (1923); W. A. Havemeyer & Co. v. Exchange Nat. Bank, 293 Fed. 311 (C. C. A. 8th, 1923); Continental Nat. Bank v. Tremont Trust Co., 4 F. (2d) 219 (C. C. A. 1st, 1925); First Nat. Bank v. Bowers, 141 Cal. 253, 74 Pac. 856 (1903); Camp v. Corn Exch. Nat. Bank, *ibid.*; Forman v. Walker, 4 La. Ann. 409 (1849); Westminster Bank v. Banca Nazionale di Credito, 31 Lloyd's List 306 (1928); Nat. Bank of Egypt v. Hannevig's Bank, 1 Lloyd's List 69 (1919); Stein v. Hambro's Bank, 9 Lloyd's List 433, 507 (1921); Brazilian & Portuguese Bank v. British & American Exch. Banking Corp., 18 L. T. N. S. 823 (1868); Cape Asbestos Co. v. Lloyds Bank, [1921] Weekly Notes 274; Nat. Bank of South Africa v. Banca Italiana Disconto, 9 Lloyd's List 501 (1921); Donald H. Scott & Co. v. Barclay's Bank, [1923] 2 K. B. 1; Pioneer Bank v. Canadian Bank of Commerce, 53 Can. S. C. 570, 13 A. L. R. 160 (1916); Standard Bank of South Africa v. Efroiken & Newman, [1923-24] S. A. App. Div. 171; Bank of New York & Trust Co. v. Atterbury Bros., 226 App. Div. 117, 234 N. Y. Supp. 442 (1929).

For cases dealing with insurance policies, see: Brazilian & Portuguese Bank v. British & American Exch. Banking Corp., *ibid.*; Belgian Grain & Produce Co. v. Cox & Co., 1 Lloyd's List 256, 546 (1919); Pan-American Bank & Trust Co. v. Nat. City Bank, 6 F. (2d) 762 (C. C. A. 2d, 1925), *cert. den.*, 269 U. S. 554, 46 Sup. Ct. 18 (1925); (1926) 74 U. of Pa. L. Rev. 308, 310; Borthwick v. Bank of New Zealand, 17 T. L. R. 2 (1900); Donald H. Scott & Co. v. Barclay's Bank, *ibid.*; Kunglig Jarnvagsstyrelsen v. Nat. City Bank, 20 F. (2d) 307 (C. C. A. 2d, 1927); Standard Bank of South Africa v. Efroiken & Newman, *ibid.* On the question of what is sufficient shipment, see: Camp v. Corn Exch. Nat. Bank, *ibid.*; Lamborn v. Nat. Bank of Commerce, 276 U. S. 469, 48 Sup. Ct. 378, 72 L. Ed. 657 (1928), *rev'g*, 15 F. (2d) 473 (C. C. A. 4th, 1926), 2 F. (2d) 23, 36 A. L. R. 509 (C. C. A. 4th, 1924); Bank of Taiwan v. Union Nat. Bank, 1 F. (2d) 65, 67 (C. C. A. 3rd, 1924); Williams Ice Cream Co. v. Chase Nat. Bank, 120 Misc. 301, 199 N. Y. Supp. 314 (1923), *rev'd*, 210 App. Div. 179, 205 N. Y. Supp. 446 (1924); Stein v. Hambro's Bank, *ibid.* On the question of the sufficiency of the description of the goods in the documents, see Lamborn v. Lake Shore Banking & Trust Co., 196 App. Div. 504,

these problems are of great importance and are in need of more attention than has been given them. In so far as the bank occupies the same position as the buyer in regard to the presentation of documents, it is a useful analysis and a helpful simplification, to recognize this fact in stating the law.[20] On the other hand, where the bank occupies a position different from that of the

188 N. Y. Supp. 162 (1921), *aff'd* without opinion, 231 N. Y. 616, 132 N. E. 911 (1921); Brown, Graves & Co. v. Ambler, *supra* note 15; Bank of Montreal v. Recknagel, *ibid.* For a consideration of the problem that the documents do not represent the state of facts intended to be settled by these documents see Stein v. Hambro's Bank, *ibid.* For examples of interpretations of terms of letters of credit raising problems similar to those arising under c. i. f. contacts and being treated in much the same way, see: Richard v. Royal Bank of Canada, *supra* note 5; Wells Fargo Nevada Nat. Bank v. Corn Exchange Nat. Bank, 23 F. (2d) 1 (C. C. A. 7th, 1928); First Wisconsin Nat. Bank v. Forsyth Leather Co., 189 Wis. 9, 206 N. W. 843 (1926); Second Nat. Bank v. Lash Corp., 299 Fed. 371 (C. C. A. 3d, 1924); Citizens Bank v. Perkins Co., 250 Mass. 156, 145 N. E. 280 (1924); Bank of America v. Whitney-Central Nat. Bank, 291 Fed. 929 (C. C. A. 5th, 1923); Banco Nacional Ultramarino v. First Nat. Bank, *ibid.*; Moss v. Old Colony Trust Co., 246 Mass. 139, 140 N. E. 803 (1923); G. Jaris Co. v. Banque D'Athenes, 246 Mass. 546, 141 N. E. 576 (1923); English, Scottish & Australian Bank v. Bank of South Africa, 13 Lloyd's List 21 (1922); Cape Asbestos Co. v. Lloyds Bank, *ibid.*; Lamborn v. Lake Shore Banking & Trust Co., *ibid*; American Steel Co. v. Irving Nat. Bank, 266 Fed. 41 (C. C. A. 2d, 1920), 277 Fed. 1016 (C. C. A. 2d, 1921), *cert. den.*, 258 U. S. 617, 42 Sup. Ct. 271 (1922); Manatee County State Bank v. Weatherly, *supra* note 11; Baeschlin v. Chamberlain Banking House, 67 Neb. 196, 93 N. W. 412 (1903); Allen v. Leavens, 26 Oreg. 164, 37 Pac. 488, 26 L. R. A. 620 (1894); North Atchison Bank v. Garretson, 51 Fed. 168 (C. C. A. 8th, 1892), 47 Fed. 867 (C. C. W. D. Mo. 1891), 39 Fed. 163, 7 L. R. A. 428 (C. C. W. D. Mo. 1889); Germania Nat. Bank v. Taaks, 101 N. Y. 442, 5 N. E. 76 (1886); Craig v. Marx, 65 Tex. 649 (1886); First Nat. Bank v. Bensley, 2 Fed. 609 (C. C. N. D. Ill. 1880); Dexters, Ltd. v. Schenker & Co., *supra* note 14; Brazilian & Portuguese Bank v. British & American Exchange Banking Corp., *ibid.*; Murdock v. Mills, 11 Metc. 5 (Mass. 1846); Bank of New York & Trust Co. v. Atterbury, *ibid.*; Doelger v. Battery Park Nat. Bank, 201 App. Div. 515, 194 N. Y. Supp. 582 (1922). These cases include not only modern letters of credit but also promises to accept made by the buyer himself. In the latter type, it is clear, of course, that all problems must be similar to those under c. i. f. contracts, since the buyer cannot be considered to be in a different position because of the fact that he has made a formal promise. It is only in the case of the issuance of a letter of credit in the modern meaning of the term, that the issuer may be in a different position.

[20] See e. g. Donald H. Scott & Co. v. Barclay's Bank, *supra* note 19, at 11, where the court, after quoting a rule laid down in regard to insurance policies, in a case involving a sales contract remarks: "That statement of principle is just as applicable to a letter of credit as to a contract of sale." The court there cities cases dealing with sales contracts as authorities. See also the cases cited *supra* note 19.

buyer, this distinction should be clearly pointed out and its extent carefully delimited. This occurs chiefly in two instances: where the documents use the technical language of a particular trade,[21] knowledge of which cannot fairly be imputed to the bank; and where the requirements of the credit are different from those of the sales contract on which it is based.[22]

The problem that arises because of the use of technical language is admirably exemplified by a New York decision.[23] The bank sent

---

[21] It should be noted that what is meant by technical language is not merely formulae and other obviously technical terms, but all words that in any way have, or may be thought to have, acquired a special meaning. A good example of this is the distinction between dried grapes and raisins that arose in a recent case. Bank of Italy v. Merchants Nat. Bank, 236 N. Y. 106, 140 N. E. 211 (1923), *cert. den.*, 264 U. S. 581, 44 Sup. Ct. 331 (1924). As may be inferred from the nature of the problem the distinction between technical and non-technical words is not always easy to draw, see Crocker First Nat. Bank v. De Sousa, 27 F. (2d) 462 (C. C. A. 9th, 1928) reversing a decision of the lower court, 23 F. (2d) 118, 122 (N. D. Cal. 1927), which held that "fine sugar" as a matter of common knowledge, meant "fine granulated sugar."

[22] There are other instances also; e. g., where a bank promises to accept a draft accompanied by a bill of lading, the latter instrument should be in such form as to give protection to the bank. Therefore, if the draft is accompanied by a straight bill of lading in favor of the buyer, the bank has no security and need not honor the draft, as the document does not conform to the requirements of the promise. Continental Nat. Bank v. Tremont Trust Co., *supra* note 19; Pioneer Bank v. Canadian Bank of Commerce, *supra* note 19; First Nat. Bank v. Bowers, *supra* note 19; Farmers & Merchants Bank v. Commercial Bank, 221 N. W. 148 (Mich. 1928). It is less certain that the buyer could object if a straight bill of lading in his favor were tendered him under a c.i.f. contract. While the disposal of the documents would not be as convenient as in the case of an order bill of lading, it would not be impossible since he could issue a delivery order on the carrier or assign his interest in the goods. The bank, however, clearly gets no interest in the goods and may therefore properly reject documents which fail to give it the usual lien for reimbursement for its advances. For similar reasons, the buyer should be able to reject a straight bill of lading not issued in his favor. But *cf.* Descalzi Fruit Co. v. Bank of Italy, 73 Pitts. L. J. 954 (1925).

[23] Bank of Italy v. Merchants Nat. Bank, *supra* note 21. The bank in this case wired guaranteeing "payment two cars dried grapes . . . on presentation original bill of lading here." The lower court was evidently of the opinion that the instrument represented a letter of credit transaction, and not a guaranty. 113 Misc. 314, 185 N. Y. Supp. 43 (1920). On appeal, the matter was not considered. It is submitted that the result is the same whether the instrument is a letter of credit or a guaranty. Other cases are, Crocker First Nat. Bank v. De Sousa, *supra* note 21; International Banking Corp. v. Irving Nat. Bank, 274 Fed. 122 (S. D. N. Y. 1921), *aff'd*, 283 Fed. 103 (C. C. A. 2d, 1922); Lamborn v. Lake Shore Banking and Trust Co., *supra* note 19; Nat.

a telegram guaranteeing payment against two carloads of "dried grapes" on presentation of original bills of lading. The plaintiff, relying on the message, bought two bills of lading calling for "raisins" and presented them to the defendant bank which refused to pay on the grounds that the goods described in the bills of lading might not be the same as those called for in the telegram and that they had no practical way of finding out whether or not they were identical. The court denied a recovery and held in part:

> We agree that if the words used in the guaranty and in the bill of lading were as a matter of common knowledge synonomous . . . no question could arise. . . . But where there is a question of fact as to whether the terms used in the guaranty and in the bill of lading are in truth identical, the risk of determining for itself this question is not to be placed upon the guarantor.[24]
> "Raisins" and "dried grapes" may or may not be the same article. We do not know.[25]

The reason for this is clear and has already been suggested. The bank finances trade in many fields. While it can be held to know general customs, to require it to know the language of each particular trade is hardly reasonable.[26] The seller, in order

City Bank v. Seattle Nat. Bank, 121 Wash. 476, 209 Pac. 705, 30 A. L. R. 347 (1922); Old Colony Trust Co. v. Lawyers' Title and Trust Co., 297 Fed. 152 (C. C. A. 2d, 1924), *cert. den.*, 265 U. S. 585, 44 Sup. Ct. 459 (1924); see also: Rozema v. Nat. City Bank, 292 Fed. 913 (C. C. A. 9th, 1923); Moss v. Old Colony Trust Co., *supra* note 19; see also Wallace State Bank v. Corn Exchange Bank 220 Mo. App. 1062, 282 S. W. 86 (1926), where the letter of credit called for pigs and the seller shipped hogs. Plaintiff maintained that the former term included the latter. The defendant showed that there was a technical difference, and the court denied a recovery. *Cf.* this case with Decatur Bank v. St. Louis Bank, 21 Wall. 294, 22 L. Ed. 560 (1874), where on similar facts the court found for the plaintiff after indicating that in *popular* usage the term cattle included hogs, *supra* note 18.

[24] Bank of Italy v. Merchants Nat. Bank, *supra* note 21, at 109, 140 N. E. at 212.

[25] *Ibid.*, at 110, 140 N. E. at 212.

[26] "The business of shipment of wheat or wool from Australian ports is well known in the Commercial Court. I stated it during the hearing and need not repeat it, but I do not think I ought to impute full knowledge of that fact to a South African bank manager." English, Scottish and Australian Bank v. Bank of South Africa, *supra* note 19, at 24; see also Westminster Bank v. Banco Nazionale di Credito, *supra* note 19, at 308.

to be certain that he will get his money on presentation of the documents, should employ the identical language used by the bank in issuing the credit. If he fails to do this and, instead, uses technical language with which only members of his trade are acquainted, it is hardly fair to require the bank to decide at its peril and at a moment's notice whether or not the documents conform. In this type of case, therefore, the bank has the privilege of refusing to honor a draft when accompanied by such documents.[27] The buyer, however, since he is engaged in the particular trade, is presumed to have knowledge of these technical terms. He cannot, therefore, refuse payment on this ground when the documents are presented to him under a c. i. f. contract.

Where the requirements of the credit are different from those of the sales contract, the variation may be of two kinds: the credit may be more precise in its requirements, or it may be more liberal. In the former case, the seller cannot recover against the bank unless he has fulfilled the terms of the credit, which delimit the bank's liability.[28] It is true that the seller may have

[27] See also (1924) 33 YALE L. J. 651. It should be noticed that the bona fide purchaser obtains no greater rights than the seller himself has in this situation. He sees the requirements of the credit and also the language of the documents, and if, notwithstanding, he buys the draft, he assumes the entire risk of the bank's refusal. He has ample notice and there is no reason why he should be in any better position than is the seller. See Banco Nacional Ultramarino v. First Nat. Bank, *supra* note 19, at 175. However, the rule discussed above does not prevent the bank, if it so desires, from taking advantage of trade customs of which the seller has knowledge. Old Colony Trust Co. v. Columbia Trust Co., 210 App. Div. 705, 206 N. Y. Supp. 257 (1924). In this case the issuing bank paid against the invoice weight and found it had overpaid according to the net landed weight. It sued for overpayment, alleging a custom of the import trade to pay against invoice weight subject to adjustment to the net landed weights of the goods. A motion to dismiss the complaint was denied.

[28] "I assume that a buyer, although he has precluded himself from alleging that his seller has broken his contract with him, may instruct his bankers not to honour a letter of credit, the terms of which have not been strictly complied with, and that the banker who acts upon such instructions is not in default; and, indeed, is not in default if under the same circumstances he declines to pay, although he has no instructions to the contrary." English, Scottish & Australian Bank v. Bank of South Africa, *supra* note 19, at 24; see also S. L. Jones & Co. v. Bond, 191 Cal. 551, 217 Pac. 725 (1923). The bank may, however, have the privilege of paying the seller and recovering against the buyer, even

an action against the buyer for not procuring a proper letter of credit,[29] but that is no concern of the bank.[30] On the other hand, where the terms of the credit are more liberal than those of the sales contract, a slightly different problem arises. As far as a bona fide purchaser is concerned, the bank, as has been previously explained, is clearly bound by the terms of its letter of credit. In reference to a seller or beneficiary, a situation may arise in which the bank would not be bound unless the seller has fulfilled the more rigid requirements of the sales contract. An instance of this is to be found in a case where the sales contract specifies a particular document, while the letter of credit speaks of the general class. The position may well be taken that the seller is bound by his knowledge of the sales contract to produce the particular document specified therein rather than any other one of the general class mentioned by the letter of credit. This would not apply to a confirming or a notifying bank, or to a

---

though it is under no duty to do so, see (1924) 12 CAL. L. REV. 500, 508. Practically, this is clearly the desirable result. Since the buyer is obligated to the seller, all the conditions of the sales contract having been performed, there is no reason why the bank, on paying the seller, should not acquire rights against the buyer. Whether it would acquire greater rights than the seller has, e.g., rights to commission for financing the transaction, is more doubtful. The bank has breached its instructions in paying the seller. Its rights against the buyer cannot, therefore, be based on the agreement to reimburse, but must be derived from those of the seller, in which event it is difficult to see how the bank can claim more than the seller is entitled to receive.

[29] For a discussion of this, see Shirai v. Blum, 207 App. Div. 605, 202 N. Y. Supp. 540 (1924), *mod.*, 239 N. Y. 172, 146 N. E. 194, 38 A. L. R. 603 (1924). See also Boer v. Garcia, 240 N. Y. 9, 147 N. E. 231 (1925), where the seller was relieved of his obligation under the sales contract because the conditions of the letter of credit had become impossible of performance without violating the National Prohibition Act. See also Panoutsos v. Raymond Hadley Corp., [1917] 2 K. B. 473; Giddens v. Anglo-African Produce Co., 14 Lloyd's List 230 (1923); S. L. Jones & Co. v. Bond, *supra* note 28; Parker v. Simon, 194 App. Div. 342, 185 N. Y. Supp. 339 (1920), *rev'd*, 231 N. Y. 503, 132 N. E. 404 (1921); Albert De Bary Jr., Inc. v. Agar-Bernson Corp., 208 App. Div. 645, 204 N. Y. Supp. 18 (1924); Isaiou Trading Corp. v. Standard Rice Co., 208 App. Div. 20, 202 N. Y. Supp. 849 (1924).

[30] Unless of course the bank violated its instructions in issuing the credit as it did, in which case, the buyer would have an action against it in the rare situation where damage resulted to the buyer from the act of the bank. This right, however, is based on the agreement to reimburse. *Supra* ch. IV, p. 168.

bona fide purchaser unless he had knowledge similar to that of the seller. Such parties could recover on the presentation of any documents that came within the more general terms of the letter of credit.

The case of *Arctic Ice & Coal Co.* v. *Southgate*[31] presents a situation which is interesting in this connection. The sales contract, in that case, called for payment against a dock receipt or a bill of lading, while the credit issued in connection with the contract called for payment against shipping documents. After the issuance of the letter of credit, the contract between buyer and seller was so altered as to require payment against a delivery order. The seller presented a delivery order to the bank, together with his draft. Payment was refused on the ground that the proper documents had not been presented. The court held that the term "shipping documents" referred to the documents mentioned in the contract at the time the letter of credit was issued. Consequently, a bill of lading or dock receipt should have been tendered.

There may well be a difference of opinion on the question of policy involved in the exclusion of the changes of a sales contract subsequent to the issuance of the letter of credit.[32] It must, nevertheless, be conceded that the court has enunciated a sound proposition in insisting on conformity to the terms of credit as understood between the immediate parties. The real question to be answered is, what was meant by the term, shipping documents, as used in this credit. In the hands of a seller who is familiar with the sales contract, compliance in terms of that

[31] 287 Fed. 48 (C. C. A. 4th, 1923).

[32] Essentially, the bank is interested in the control of the goods so as to have security for the money it has advanced; see discussion, *infra* ch. VI, p. 238. While shipping documents are not necessarily documents of title, yet to a great extent and for most practical purposes, these two classes are identical. The bank, therefore, may very well agree to leave the exact character of the documents unsettled in the letter of credit, to be fixed by arrangement between the buyer and the seller, provided that the documents remain within the necessary category of shipping documents, so that control of the goods is not lost.

contract can be expected. Such a party knows that the term shipping documents is used to mean only those documents mentioned in the contract.[33] In the hands of a bona fide purchaser who is ignorant of the provisions of the sales contract, any documents generally recognized as coming under the head of shipping documents must be held to be sufficient.

To summarize the law as to what will constitute performance of the conditions in a letter of credit transaction upon which the duty of the issuing bank to pay is contingent, we may say that, in general, it is similar to the law on this subject concerning the duty of the buyer under a c.i.f. contract, except in two types of cases: where the bank cannot properly be held to be familiar with the customs of the particular trade involved, as in the use of the technical language of various trades in the documents presented; and where the requirements of the credit are different from those of the sales contract, in which case the result, as indicated above, depends on the kind and amount of variation.

The discussion of the relation between bank and buyer[34] in regard to conformity of documents raises a slightly different problem. In those cases in which the bank is held to be under a duty to pay the seller or bona fide purchaser, clearly, on the analysis already given, it can recover against the buyer.[35] As

---

[33] See also Banco Nacional Ultramarino v. First Nat. Bank, *supra* note 19, at 176.

[34] The inland requesting bank, when it enters the transaction, merely takes the place of the buyer in the conclusions reached here, as was indicated in the analysis given previously, ch. IV, p. 148.

[35] *Supra* pp. 148, 149. See also: Pan-American Bank & Trust Co. v. Nat. City Bank, 6 F. (2d) 762 (C. C. A. 2d, 1925), *cert. den.*, 269 U. S. 554, 46 Sup. Ct. 18 (1925); Laudisi v. American Exchange Nat. Bank, 239 N. Y. 234, 146 N. E. 347 (1924); Farmers Bank v. Stapleton, 118 Kan. 755, 236 Pac. 828 (1925); Phillipine Nat. Bank v. Bowring & Co., 123 Misc. 89, 204 N. Y. Supp. 327 (1924), *aff'd* without opinion, 213 App. Div. 809, 208 N. Y. Supp. 922, 240 N. Y. 658, 148 N. E. 747 (1925); W. A. Havemeyer & Co. v. Exchange Nat. Bank, 293 Fed. 311 (C. C. A. 8th, 1923); Friedlander v. Bank of Australasia, 8 C. L. R. 85 (Aust. 1909); *Ex parte* Agra Bank, *In re* Barber & Co., L. R. 9 Eq. 725 (1870); Camp v. Corn Exchange Nat. Bank, 285 Pa. 337, 132 Atl. 189 (1926). It therefore follows that where the seller has breached the sales contract but not the terms of the letter of credit, the buyer cannot enjoin the seller from presenting or

has been indicated, the conclusion cannot be drawn that where the bank is under no duty to pay, it has not the power to pay and then recover against the buyer. The bank is not bound to pay where the documents are held not to conform to the requirements of the letter of credit,[36] or where, because of the use of technical language, the bank cannot be certain whether or not they do so conform. The problem arises as to what are the rights of the bank in the event that it does pay in either of these cases.[37]

---

negotiating and the bank from paying the draft, particularly where neither bank nor seller is alleged to be in financial difficulties. Frey & Son v. E. R. Sherburne Co. 193 App. Div. 849, 184 N. Y. Supp. 661 (1920). A similar type of case occurs when a buyer gives a bank money to pay against documents or a seller gives it documents to deliver against cash or acceptances. It is clear that unless the bank sees that all the conditions are fulfilled before paying the money or delivering the documents, it is liable to its clients. See: Isler v. Nat. Park Bank, 239 N. Y. 462, 147 N. E. 66 (1925); Kupfer Bros. Co. v. Chemical Nat. Bank, 126 Misc. 13, 211 N. Y. Supp. 852 (1925), *aff'd* without opinion, 216 App. Div. 796, 215 N. Y. Supp. 874 (1926); Kornblum v. Bank of Italy, 64 Cal. App. 170, 222 Pac. 143 (1923); Bank of British North America v. Cooper, 137 U. S. 473, 11 Sup. Ct. 160, 34 L. Ed. 759 (1890). It is also clear that, if the bank refuses to honor the draft when all conditions are performed, the buyer can recover against it for breach of agreement. See Kronman & Co. v. Public Nat. Bank, 218 App. Div. 624, 218 N. Y. Supp. 616 (1926), where the court discusses the method of pleading this type of allegation. Apparently, if the documents against which the draft is to be paid or accepted are in order, the bank violates no duty to the buyer if it pays against these documents, even though additional documents, indicating that the goods are unmerchantable, are presented; see Tocco v. Bank of Italy, 249 Mass. 267, 271, 143 N. E. 905, 906 (1924). An attempt has been made by a number of banks to remove all risk of liability to the buyer as well as any doubt of the duty of the buyer to reimburse the bank, by inserting into the agreement to reimburse a stipulation to the effect that the bank is to be the absolute judge of the conformity of the documents to the requirements of the credit. Even when this provision is used, the bank must act reasonably in dishonoring its credit. "This stipulation that their discretion would alone determine whether the documents were correct or unimpeachable would not warrant the bank in accepting a draft where the documents showed on their face they were not in conformity to the letter, including the contract. . . . To accept a draft under such circumstances would be a manifest abuse of a discretionary power." Camp v. Corn Exch. Nat. Bank, *ibid.*, at 348, 132 Atl. at 193. Within reasonable limits however, this stipulation would apparently be effective. See First Wisconsin Nat. Bank v. Forsyth Leather Co., 189 Wis. 9, 16, 206 N. W. 843, 845 (1926); (1926) 74 U. OF PA. L. REV. 501.

[36] That is, either generally or to the particular holder of the draft and documents because of his knowledge of the facts.

[37] Where the terms of the credit are more liberal than those of the sales contract, clearly the bank, after honoring its credit on presentation

Where payment is made against documents containing technical language, there are two possibilities: either the documents do, or they do not, mean the same thing as the terms of the letter of credit. If the latter, then the bank is paying against documents which do not in fact conform to the requirements of the credit, a problem which will be considered presently. If the former is the case, then the problem that arises is whether the bank has a right against the buyer when it pays against documents, where it is under no duty to pay, because of the use of technical language, and where, in fact, the language of the documents does prove to have the same meaning as the language of the requirements of the letter of credit.

The answer to this question becomes apparent when we consider the basis on which recovery against the bank has been denied. In this situation, it has been argued that since the bank was not engaged in the particular business represented by those documents, it could not fairly be expected to know the technical language of that trade and, therefore, could not be held to decide the question of conformity without adequate preparation and at a moment's notice. No such considerations apply in the case of the presentation to the buyer. He is fully acquainted with the customs of the trade and the meaning of the terms used in it. The bank, here, is at least in as good a position as the seller when the latter tenders the documents to the buyer under a c.i.f. contract, in which case, there can be no objection on the part of the buyer that the documents are couched in such terms that the layman could not tell whether or not they represented the goods described in the contract. The basis for this distinction is that the buyer is not a layman and is held bound to know the technical terms and customs of his trade. The same considerations would

of documents which conform to the requirements of the credit, can recover against the buyer, whether or not it knows of the terms of the sales contract. The bank is obeying the instructions of the buyer and should be fully protected in so doing. It has the power to make the payment though it may not be under a duty to do so, see *supra* p. 149.

seem to apply when the bank tenders the documents to the buyer, and the courts should not, in this case, deny a recovery against the buyer[38] when the problem arises.[39]

When the bank pays against documents that do not conform, it obviously has no right to compel the buyer to take the documents and pay for them.[40] The latter can reject the goods and documents and sue the seller.[41] The question arises, however, as to

[38] It might be suggested that, since the documents are in technical language, the buyer would find difficulty in reselling them and that therefore, since there is a certain loss of control over the goods, he should not have to pay the bank. The suggestion does not seem very forceful. It is doubtful whether there is any particular loss of power to resell, as the buyer would in most cases resell to people who are acquainted with the business customs and the language of the trade in question, and who therefore can be expected to know what the terms signify.

[39] For a somewhat different approach, though arriving at the same conclusion, see (1924) 33 YALE L. J. 651, 655. It is clear that the bank must establish in this case the fact that the two wordings actually mean the same thing. See Rozema v. Nat. City Bank, *supra* note 23. An excellent decision in point is the recent New York case, Bank of New York & Trust Co. v. Atterbury Bros., 226 App. Div. 117, 234 N. Y. Supp. 442 (1929). The letter of credit was in favor of "Arthur James Brown" and required documents showing a shipment of "casein." The bank paid a draft drawn by "A. James Brown" on presentation of documents showing a shipment of "unground casein" and recovered against the buyer, on a motion for summary judgment, the court being satisfied from the record that "A. James Brown" was the identical person intended by bank and buyer, and that "casein" included "unground casein."

[40] Bank of Montreal v. Recknagel, 109 N. Y. 482, 17 N. E. 217 (1888); see also Munroe v. Bonanno, 16 App. Div. 421, 45 N. Y. Supp. 61 (1897); Nat. Bank of South Africa v. Banca Italiana Disconto, 9 Lloyd's List 501 (1921). If the buyer pays the bank before he has knowledge, or reasonable means of acquiring knowledge, of the breach, he can recover the amount paid. Borthwick v. Bank of New Zealand, 17 T. L. R. 2 (1900). See also Williams Ice Cream Co. v. Chase Nat. Bank, 120 Misc. 301, 199 N. Y. Supp. 314 (1923), *rev'd*, 210 App. Div. 179, 205 N. Y. Supp. 446 (1924), discussing the right of a buyer to an injunction preventing the bank from paying the seller directly, where in consequence of the change of conditions by the bank in the letter of credit without the buyer's consent, the original conditions had not been performed.

[41] From the previous discussion of the rule in c. i. f. contracts, *supra* p. 178, it should be clear that the bank cannot recover against the buyer when the latter rejects the documents and goods on the ground that the documents do not conform to the requirements of the letter of credit, even though the goods fulfill the requirements of the sales contract. The bank has undertaken to pay against certain documents; it acquires a right to be reimbursed from the buyer only upon tendering to him the proper documents. The bank's contract is clearly based on documents and not on goods. See Camp v. Corn Exch. Nat. Bank, *supra* note 35, at 344, 132 Atl. at 191; *cf.* however Lamborn v. Lake Shore Banking &

the rights of the bank in the event that the buyer elects to take the documents and goods. There are three possibilities in regard to the rights of the bank against the buyer on the agreement between them: either the bank acquires no rights against the buyer because its payment was against improper documents; or, as the taking of the documents by the buyer might be considered a waiver by him of the breach of the condition, the bank acquires a right to the full amount; or, finally, the view might be taken that the bank can recover the amount paid, less any damage that the buyer might have suffered as a result of the bank's negligence in paying against improper documents.

The first of these is so inadvisable a solution that it may be dismissed without hesitation. As a practical matter, this situation is hardly likely to arise. The bank which has a lien on the goods by reason of its possession of the documents of title,[42] is hardly likely to surrender these documents and so lose its lien unless there is a reasonable certainty that it will receive its money in another way.[43] The rule which would deny the bank all right of recovery against the buyer on these facts has no

Trust Co., 196 App. Div. 504, 507, 188 N. Y. Supp. 162, 164 (1921), *aff'd*, without opinion, 231 N. Y. 616, 132 N. E. 911 (1921); Bank of Montreal v. Recknagel, *supra* note 40, at 488, 494, 17 N. E. at 219, 222; Nat. City Bank v. Seattle Nat. Bank, 121 Wash. 476, 485, 209 Pac. 705, 708, 30 A. L. R. 347, 353 (1922).

[42] 1 WILLISTON, SALES (2d ed. 1924) § 284; 2 *ibid.* § 440; see also *In re* Barned's Banking Co., Coupland's Claim, L. R. 5 Ch. App. 167 (1869). In the absence of special circumstances, the fact that the draft purports to be drawn against a shipment of specific goods, gives the holder of the draft no lien on them. Robey & Co.'s Perserverance Ironworks v. Ollier, L. R. 7 Ch. App. 695 (1872); *cf.* Frith v. Forbes, 4 D. F. & J. 409, 45 Eng. R. 1242 (1862); Muller v. Kling, 149 App. Div. 176, 133 N. Y. Supp. 614 (1912), *aff'd*, 209 N. Y. 239, 103 N. E. 138 (1913).

[43] Even if the bank has an action against the seller or purchaser of the draft and documents for money paid by mistake, an action in a foreign country against the seller, who may be of doubtful financial responsibility, is not a very satisfactory solution as far as the bank is concerned. In the absence of fraud, it is probable, however, that the bank has no such right of action, see cases cited *supra* ch. IV, p. 159, note 36. Where the bank pays against proper documents and later discovers that the goods are of inferior quality, it has been held that the bank cannot recover the amount paid to the seller on the theory of money paid under mistake of fact, *infra* ch. VI, note 27. *A fortiori*, no such action should be allowed in this case as the defects are apparent on the face of the documents.

foundation in justice, business usage, or common sense. It is hardly likely to be followed.[44]

There is little difference in result to be anticipated between the two other suggested alternatives. If the buyer anticipates a loss as a result of accepting the goods, he will in most instances reject both documents and goods and bring an action against the seller, in which case the bank has no rights of any kind against the buyer. If, however, there is likelihood of profit, as in a rising market, he will take the documents and the goods. In that case, he would probably have to pay the same amount under either rule, as generally he could show no damage because of the bank's paying against the wrong documents.[45] Situations, however, may occasionally arise where there might be a different outcome, according to which rule was applied. In cases where the sales contract was more loosely worded than the letter of credit in describing the documents which were required, the documents presented might not be interpreted as fulfilling the conditions of the letter of credit even though they fulfilled the requirements of the sales contract. The buyer would be obligated under the sales contract to accept the documents, while the bank must be regarded as violating its instructions in paying against them. Another illustration may be found in the case where the buyer, though he had suffered some loss, would elect to take the goods and the documents, though inadequate, in order to prevent further damage.

---

[44] Even if this rule were technically adopted, its effect would probably be avoided by granting the bank rights in quasi-contract. If the purchaser is a correspondent of the issuing bank and charges the amount to the latter's balance with the former, it would seem that the issuing bank could recover the amount so charged. Here, unlike the situation discussed in note 43, the issuing bank is charged before it has taken the documents or indicated that they are satisfactory to it. *Cf.* Graham v. Farmers & Merchants Bank, 116 Cal. 463, 48 Pac. 384 (1897).

[45] However, even under these facts the buyer might be able to show some damage, e. g., if the goods called for by the contract sold at a higher price than the goods actually delivered, the difference between these two prices would be his damage, which he could recover from the seller, even though the goods actually delivered were sold above the contract price.

The question is whether or not the acceptance of the defective documents by the buyer indicates a waiver of the conditions breached by the bank in paying against those documents, and so entitles the bank to the full amount of the draft. There seems to be no reason for saying that this is so. In the general law of sales, the weight of authority is that such acts are not interpreted as waivers; and, while at common law there has been some confusion as to the rule, under the Uniform Sales Act it is clearly settled that acceptance by the buyer does not indicate that he intends to give up his rights against the seller, unless he should clearly express that intention.[46] There is no reason why this rule should not by analogy apply to the problem under discussion. The buyer is taking as much as is offered to him and reserves his right against the bank and the seller for such loss as may have occurred to him, as a result of the breach of their obligations. In effect, "it is a partial performance and partial satisfaction, and he takes it as such."[47] The rule that should be adopted, and the one that probably will be followed, is that the bank can, in this case, recover from the buyer the amount of the draft it has paid, less the amount of the damage that the buyer can show he has suffered as a result of the negligent acts of the bank in paying against defective documents.[48]

The law in regard to the performance of the conditions upon which the buyer's duty to indemnify the bank rests may be restated as follows. Acts that are sufficient to obligate the bank to honor its credit will be held sufficient to constitute performance of the

---

[46] See UNIFORM SALES ACT, § 49; 2 WILLISTON, SALES (2d ed. 1924) § 485; *cf.* Royal Card & Paper Co. v. Dresdner Bank, 27 F. (2d) 791, 793 (C. C. A. 2d, 1928). Of course, the buyer loses his right to rescind the contract, but that is not under consideration here. The question is whether he loses his right to damages because of the acceptance of the documents. It seems that he does not.

[47] 2 WILLISTON, SALES (2d ed. 1924) 1263.

[48] It has been suggested that the buyer is obligated to pay the bank only as much as is due the seller in these circumstances. Generally, however, the amount would be the same in both cases, being the purchase price as evidenced by the sales contract or the letter of credit, as the case may be, less the damage to the buyer.

conditions of the buyer's duty to indemnify the bank. In addition, the bank can recover against the buyer where it pays against documents on the presentation of which it is not bound to pay because of the technical language used, if the documents do in fact fulfill the requirements of the credit. Finally, it can recover against the buyer when it honors drafts accompanied by documents that do not in fact conform to the terms of the credit, but only, however, if the buyer accepts these documents. But the amount it should recover in this case is the sum it has paid out, less any damage that might have been caused the buyer because of the non-conformity of the documents.

B. Performance of Conditions Not Requiring Documents

In addition to conditions relating to documents, letters of credit or similar instruments often contain other types of conditions not requiring documents, such as a provision that the draft be drawn either against goods ready for shipment[49] or "as may be necessary for the purchase of lumber."[50] The inclusion of this type of condition in the letter of credit raises the additional problem of the extent to which the issuing bank is obligated to investigate its performance. When the seller presents the draft, there are three possibilities: that the bank is under a duty to accept the seller's representations that the conditions have been performed; that it has the privilege to defer payment until it has investigated the alleged performance, if it should so desire; or, finally, that it is under a duty to the buyer to make such an investigation. A recent case has held that the bank need not rely on the seller's representations in a case where the latter is tendering the draft and documents, but may investigate on its own behalf.

Even if it be thought that the letter of November 4th was enough, taken alone, certainly it did not preclude inquiries by the

[49] Chartered Bank v. Macfayden & Co., 64 L. J. Q. B. 367 (1895).
[50] Merchants' Bank v. Griswold, 72 N. Y. 472 (1878).

defendant. It would be intolerable to submit it to whatever might satisfy the plaintiff, reasonably or not.[51]

Whether the bank is under a duty to make these investigations, has not as yet been passed upon. The view that such is not its duty, particularly where the representations by the seller are reasonable and not likely to arouse suspicion, would seem more in accord with the general spirit of the obligations of the bank. Any other rule would be cumbersome and unworkable. A bank is not equipped to investigate the performance of many varying conditions in different types of trades and it does not contemplate undertaking a responsibility of this nature. To hold otherwise would add but little to the buyer's protection and security for performance by the seller and would also decrease, to an appreciable extent, the value of the letter of credit as an instrument for securing prompt payment to the seller. Probably the courts will not adopt a rule which would greatly hamper the proper functioning of commercial letters of credit.[52]

A similar problem arises when the seller negotiates the draft to a purchaser. The latter may either have a right against the bank based on the seller's representation that the conditions are performed, or his right of recovery may be subject to their actual performance. In respect to conditions not included in the letter of credit and of which he is unaware, the purchaser, as has been indicated, could recover even though they had not been performed.[53]

[51] Commercial Union of America v. Anglo-South American Bank, 16 F. (2d) 979, 981 (C. C. A. 2d, 1927). The credit required "sailing during first half of November 1920." The drafts were presented on Saturday afternoon, November 13th. The bank inquired of the steamship company on Monday, November 15, and was informed that the ship in question would not sail until the 17th. The draft was dishonored on this ground as well as for other reasons. Where the bank is aware that the conditions have not been performed, it is obviously under no duty to honor the draft. See United States Steel Prod. Co. v. Irving Bank-Columbia Trust Co., 9 F. (2d) 230 (C. C. A. 2d, 1925).

[52] If, therefore, a beneficiary's authority to draw is limited to his activities "in making negotiations" and he draws for other purposes, he is not entitled to notice of dishonor as he should have no expectation that the draft will be honored. Dickins v. Beal, 10 Pet. 572, 9 L. Ed. 538 (1836).

[53] *Supra* ch. III, pp. 104, 105.

As regards conditions which are contained in the letter of credit, or of which he has knowledge, and which require that documents be attached to the draft, he is in no better position than the seller as he sees the documents and must be assumed to be content to base his right of recovery on their sufficiency.[54] The problem, therefore, arises only when conditions not requiring documents to be attached to the draft are contained in the letter of credit or are otherwise communicated to the purchaser. Is his right dependent on the actual performance of the conditions, or may he rely on the seller's reasonable representations that they have been performed?[55]

The most important condition involved in this connection is the limitation upon the amount of money for which the credit is available,[56] an item which is specified in almost every letter of

[54] The purchaser is, of course, under no duty to the bank or to the buyer to have the documents conform to the letter of credit. He merely cannot recover from the bank unless they do so conform. See Courteen Seed Co. v. Hong Kong and Shanghai Banking Corp., 245 N. Y. 377, 157 N. E. 272, 56 A. L. R. 1186 (1927), *aff'g*, 216 App. Div. 495, 215 N. Y. Supp. 525 (1926), *supra* ch. IV, note 40.

[55] Where the conditions have actually been performed, the goods shipped, etc., no problem arises since it is clear that the holder of the draft can recover. Dexters, Ltd., v. Schenker & Co., 14 Lloyd's List 586 (1923); Bank of Eclectic v. Sturdivant Bank, 203 Ala. 458, 83 So. 321 (1919); Union Bank v. Shea, 57 Minn. 180, 58 N. W. 985 (1894); Johnson v. Blakemore, 28 La. Ann. 140 (1876); see also Hall v. First Nat. Bank, 133 Ill. 234, 24 N. E. 546 (1890); Farmers and Merchants Nat. Bank v. Illinois Nat. Bank, 146 Ill. App. 136 (1908). As between bank and buyer or requesting bank there is likewise no additional problem. If the bank is under a duty to pay the bona fide purchaser, it can, on payment, recover against the buyer. If it is under no such duty, it is an unauthorized payment and the bank, therefore, acquires by such payment no rights against the buyer.

[56] Of course, there is a date fixed for the expiration of the credit, which also appears in nearly all letters of credit. But this seldom raises a problem, as it is impossible in most cases for a purchaser to take a draft under a letter of credit without knowing whether or not it has expired, unless he is grossly negligent. If no time limit is stated, the credit will be held to expire within a reasonable time, in view of the nature of the transaction. Lamborn v. Nat. Park Bank, 240 N. Y. 520, 148 N. E. 664 (1925); *supra* pp. 88, 89. It has recently been held however that mailing a draft so that in the usual course it would be presented within the life of the letter of credit, is sufficient performance, even though there is a delay in the mails, through no fault of the holder, and the draft does not arrive until after the credit has expired. Second Nat. Bank v. M. Samuel & Sons, 12 F. (2d) 963, 53 A. L. R. 49 (C. C. A. 2d, 1926), *cert. den.*, 273 U. S. 720, 47 Sup. Ct. 110 (1926); *cf.* (1926) 36 YALE L. J. 245, 247. See also section 4 I of the

credit. The problem often arises as a result of fraudulent conduct on the part of the seller. The bank issues a letter of credit for a fixed amount, e. g., $1,000. The seller draws for any amount within that sum, e. g., $800, and discounts the draft with a purchaser, without mentioning the letter of credit. The issuing bank pays this draft, thinking that it was drawn under the credit. The seller then draws another draft, e. g., for $500, so that both drafts together exceed the total amount of the credit, and he sells the latter to another purchaser who relies upon the letter of credit. When the issuing bank as a result dishonors the second draft, the purchaser of it sues on the letter of credit as a bona fide purchaser. We are here in the uncomfortable position of being compelled to throw the burden of the loss on one of two innocent parties. Very few cases have arisen dealing with this problem, and these seem to be in direct conflict with one another. One view is that the issuer of the letter of credit should bear the loss:

> It can make no difference that the defendant may have thought and assumed that the Pineville checks were cashed by that bank on the faith of the letter it gave into Hawk's possession. If Hawk acted irregularly and without authority in dealing with the Pineville bank, such act ought not to be allowed to injure the plaintiff bank, where his act was regular and within authority. If Hawk's act must harm one of two innocent parties, it should fall on the one who put him in position to do the harm.[57]

On the other hand, the Texas courts have taken the view that the purchaser should bear the loss:

> Now, to hold that such a contract has the attributes of negotiability in favor of each person to whom successive orders might be given for portions of the sum deposited, without definite limit of the period in which they should be given, would not only be contrary to the rules of certainty required in bills or notes, but

---

Provisions for Interpretation of Credits, recommended by the American Acceptance Council in coöperation with the New York Bankers' Commercial Credit Conference, providing that an extension of the time of shipment shall also extend the date of presentation or negotiation of the credit for an equal period of time; see Appendix A; *cf.* Doelger v. Battery Park Nat. Bank, 201 App. Div. 515, 194 N. Y. Supp. 582 (1922).

[57] Bank of Seneca v. First Nat. Bank, 105 Mo. App. 722, 727, 78 S. W. 1092, 1093 (1904); see also Omaha Nat. Bank v. First Nat. Bank, 59 Ill. 428, 432 (1871).

also tend to increase the risk of liability of the writer, arising from careless mistakes or even frauds between the holder of the letter and parties acting under it. Such a rule would change the burden of proof necessary to avoid liability, although the writer had honestly paid the full amount of the deposit.[58]

Which of these opinions should prevail, rests in the last analysis upon the business practices and commercial habits that exist among merchants, an analysis of which will be made presently.[59]

---

[58] Roman v. Serna, 40 Tex. 306, 319 (1874). It is worth noting that the certainty running through the law of bills and notes is certainty to the holder and not to the maker or to the acceptor. It is the holder who takes free of most of the defenses that the maker or acceptor may set up. Using this as an analogy, the court should have allowed the purchaser to recover. In any event, not only is the decision unsupported by these considerations but it also impairs the certainty on which the purchaser is entitled to rely. See also Ranger v. Sargent, 36 Tex. 26 (1872).

[59] Other questions may arise which involve the amount for which a draft is drawn, and which do not result from fraudulent activity on the part of the drawer. It has been held for example that a draft drawn for a certain sum with "exchange and collection charges" does not relieve the promisor of his obligation when he promised to pay merely the stated sum, particularly where there were no such charges and the words were mere surplusage. Muentzer v. Los Angeles Trust & Savings Bank, 3 F. (2d) 222, 225 (C. C. A. 7th, 1924); First Nat. Bank v. Muskogee Pipe Line Co., 40 Okla. 603, 139 Pac. 1136 (1914); see also North Atchison Bank v. Garretson, 51 Fed. 168 (C. C. A. 8th, 1892), *aff'g*, 47 Fed. 867 (C. C. W. D. Mo. 1891), 39 Fed. 163, 7 L. R. A. 428 (C. C. W. D. Mo. 1889); Iowa State Savings Bank v. City Nat Bank, 183 Iowa 1347, 168 N. W. 148, L. R. A. 1918F 169 (1918); State Bank of Iowa Falls v. American Hardwood Lumber Co., 121 Mo. App. 324, 98 S. W. 786 (1906); *cf.* Lindley v. First Nat. Bank, 76 Iowa 629, 41 N. W. 381, 2 L. R. A. 709 (1889); State Bank of Fox Lake v. Citizens' Nat. Bank, 114 Mo. App. 663, 90 S. W. 123 (1905). This is somewhat analogous to the problem of whether a draft or note drawn for a certain sum with exchange makes the sum indefinite, thus rendering the instrument non-negotiable. It is generally recognized that the draft remains negotiable. NORTON, BILLS AND NOTES (4th ed. 1914) 77, UNIFORM NEGOTIABLE INSTRUMENTS LAW § 2. On much the same principle the promisor is still bound on his undertaking to accept and pay. The variation is too trivial to have any effect on the rights of the parties. See also First Nat. Bank v. Fiske, 133 Pa. 241, 19 Atl. 554, 7 L. R. A. 209 (1890). Plaintiff bought drafts relying on defendant's letter promising to pay. The drafts were for the full value of the shipment. Defendant dishonored, alleging a custom of that trade of drawing for only three-fourths of the value of the shipment. The drafts in question therefore were in view of the custom, overdrafts, beyond the authority granted or the liability undertaken by the promisor. The court, therefore, found for the defendant on the ground that, since the plaintiff knew of this custom, he was bound by it. "A usage if known to the parties to a transaction to which it relates, is obligatory, and, unless excluded by the terms of the contract, enters into and is regarded as a part of it, as much as though it had been written therein. . . . The usage described in the affidavit is not unreasonable or in conflict with positive law."

As to general conditions not requiring documents, there is the same scarcity of cases, and the same difference of opinion in those that have arisen. In the case of *Chartered Bank* v. *Macfayden,*[60] the credit allowed the seller to draw clean drafts, but required him, before doing so, to buy goods upon which the issuing bank might have a lien in case the buyer failed to indemnify the bank. The seller drew and discounted the draft with the plaintiff without actually buying any goods. The issuing bank discovered this and refused to pay the draft on the ground that the conditions of the credit had not been performed. The court sustained the bank's position:

> But it would not be unreasonable to suppose that the bank manager, on seeing a letter of this kind, would ask Knowles and Co. whether they had bought and paid for the goods upon which their correspondents and the bank would have a lien. It must be assumed that Knowles and Co. would say that they had. If

At 244, 19 Atl. at 555. A purchaser of one draft for an amount greater than that for which the letter of credit is issued, obviously acquires no rights against the issuer, since he is bound by the limit set in the credit. Lititz Nat. Bank v. Siple, 145 Pa. 49, 22 Atl. 208 (1891); Brinkman v. Hunter, 73 Mo. 172 (1880); *cf.* however, Huston v. Newgass, 234 Ill. 285, 84 N. E. 910 (1908), *infra* p. 207, note 66; Texas State Bank v. Press Publishing Co., 250 S. W. 464 (Tex. Civ. App. 1923); see also Seaman v. Tamaqua Nat. Bank, 20 Schuyl. Leg. Rec. 21 (1923), *rev'd*, 280 Pa. 124 (1924); Selma Savings Bank v. Webster County Bank, 182 Ky. 604, 206 S. W. 870 (1918). The analogy is rather to the power of a drawee bank to refuse to pay a check in part when there are not sufficient funds of the drawer on deposit to pay the full amount of the check, 2 MORSE, BANKS AND BANKING (6th ed. 1928) 983, than to the rule that a partial acceptance is binding if assented to by the holder of the draft, UNIFORM NEGOTIABLE INSTRUMENTS LAW, §§ 141 (2), 142.

[60] *Supra* note 49; see Wallace State Bank v. Corn Exch. Bank, 220 Mo. App. 1062, 1066, 282 S. W. 86, 88 (1926), where the suit was on an extrinsic acceptance and the court stated: "It must be held that if plaintiff relied upon Orr's statement to the effect that the shipment was made in accordance with the telegram of acceptance and was thereby misled, defendant may not be held to account." See also Burke v. Utah Nat. Bank, 47 Neb. 247, 66 N. W. 295 (1896); *cf.* Jones v. Crumpler, 119 Va. 143, 89 S. E. 232 (1916), where the addressee was authorized to draw if a certain bill of lading was in the writer's hands. The purchaser took the draft without the condition being fulfilled, and it was held he had no rights against the writer. He took the draft without seeing the letter or knowing of the condition in any way, as the drawer did not inform him of it. He was bound however by the actual terms of the letter, and since he did not even have the representations of the drawer that the conditions had been performed, it is difficult to see how he could, under any theory, be held to have acquired a right against the writer of the letter.

the answer was untrue, the bank, having relied on their good faith, must take the consequences of any breach of good faith on their part. The bank having been misled in discounting these bills, I proceed on the lines of the case of the *Union Bank of Canada* v. *Cole* and give judgment for the defendants.[61]

On the other hand it has been held that a letter authorizing the addressee to draw "in amount necessary for such operations" did not make the purchaser responsible for the proper use of the funds obtained;[62] and that, the plaintiff could recover where the defendant promised to accept a bill subject to the beneficiary's signing and returning a document and where the beneficiary drew and sold to the plaintiff without performing this condition.[63]

Since this is another situation where one of two innocent parties must suffer a loss and since our law consistently negatives the expediency of dividing such a loss, no result satisfactory to all parties can be reached. But what can be done is to adopt the rule that best gives effect to commercial customs. One of the most important purposes of the letter of credit is to finance trade by enabling the seller to discount his drafts on the issuing bank under the letter of credit. If there is thrown upon the purchaser the responsibility for conditions, the performance of which he can verify, if at all, only with great difficulty and trouble, he will be less inclined to purchase the draft than if the other rule were

[61] Chartered Bank v. Macfayden & Co., *supra* note 49, at 372. The court fails to notice that Union Bank of Canada v. Cole, 47 L. J. Q. B. 100 (1877), may be distinguished by the fact that there the plaintiff knew, or should have known if he had not been negligent, that the condition was not performed. No such element enters into this case. *Supra* ch. III, pp. 104, 105.

[62] Bissell v. Lewis, 4 Mich. 450 (1857).

[63] Roberts v. Drovers' Nat. Bank, 199 Ky. 439, 251 S. W. 198 (1923); Adoué v. Fox, 30 Mo. App. 98 (1888); Huston v. Newgass, *supra* note 59; Posey v. Denver Nat. Bank, 24 Col. 199, 49 Pac. 282 (1897); Ulster Bank v. Synnott, I. R. 5 Eq. 595 (1871). These cases bear a strong resemblance to that line of cases in the law of agency which holds that an agent, though he acts without the scope of his authority, may bind his principal, if the latter has put him in a position where he can successfully represent to others that he has such authority. TIFFANY, AGENCY (2d ed. 1924) §§ 17, 18. It may well be argued that the bank in this case has put the seller in a position where he can successfully represent that certain things have been done, and that, therefore, the bank should be bound by the representations of the seller.

adopted.[64] The result is that drafts drawn under credits containing such conditions are either incapable of negotiation or can be negotiated only at a much higher rate of discount, with the additional consequence that the letter of credit fails to fulfill, as efficiently as it otherwise might, the very purpose for which it was instituted.

Another reason for resting the risk of loss upon the bank is that the law should, as far as possible, discourage the issuance of credits containing such conditions, because, in any event, they tend to create confusion and hinder the freedom of negotiation of drafts under the credit. There is no better way of accomplishing this result than by placing the risk of loss on the issuing bank. If it finds that these conditions afford it no real protection, and, in effect, only hinder it in the carrying on of its business, the bank will soon cease to put such conditions into its letters of credit.[65] Since the basis of the rule is the difficulty on

---

[64] Certainly the seller will find much greater difficulty in discounting under a letter of credit such as the one in Chartered Bank v. Macfayden & Co., *supra* note 49, after that decision than he would have found before it.

[65] One interesting effect of the rule that puts the burden on the purchaser has been to lead the courts to interpret words that ordinarily would be held to be conditions, as merely statements of the transactions involved, and so not binding on the purchaser. See Coffman v. D. C. Campbell & Co., 87 Ill. 98 (1877), holding that the words "for stock" were merely a statement of the transaction involved. See also Roberts v. Drovers' Nat. Bank, *supra* note 63; State Bank of Beaver County v. Bradstreet, 89 Neb. 186, 130 N. W. 1038, 38 L. R. A. (N. S.) 747 (1911); Merchants' Bank v. Griswold, *supra* note 50; Whilden v. Merchants' & Planters' Nat. Bank, 64 Ala. 1 (1879); Greele v. Parker, 5 Wend. 414 (N. Y. 1830). Compare the similar results reached in regard to "a statement of the transaction which gives rise to the instrument" found in bills and notes; NEGOTIABLE INSTRUMENTS LAW, § 3 (2); BRANNAN, NEGOTIABLE INSTRUMENTS LAW (4th ed. 1926) 42 *et seq.* Most of the cases cited involved actions on a promise to accept as an acceptance under statutes requiring virtual acceptances to be unconditional; *supra* pp. 62, 66. To allow a recovery the courts held the words used as not equivalent to a condition. There was no necessity for this, however, as the recovery could have been allowed on the promise as such and the words used held to have been a condition with the responsibility for performance on the issuer. See also McPhee & McGinnity v. Fowler, 36 Colo. 202, 85 Pac. 421 (1906), *aff'g*, 13 Colo. App. 185, 56 Pac. 1118 (1899), for another way in which the court avoids the effect of this rule. These devices really achieve the contrary result, and, in effect, reverse the rule and throw the responsibility for the performance of the conditions back upon the bank.

the part of the purchaser in verifying the performance of the conditions, there are instances in which this rule would not apply, where the performance of the conditions, though not requiring documents, is easily ascertainable, and where the purchaser, because of his peculiar relationship or because of information given him, knows, or as a reasonable man ought to know, at the time of purchase, that the conditions have not been performed. In these cases, he should not recover unless the conditions are actually performed.[66]

C. Non-Necessity for Performance of Conditions

Performance of conditions in a commercial credit transaction may be dispensed with on one of several grounds, of which supervening impossibility of performance is one illustration. There are others, as well, such as estoppel, release, and formation of a new contract omitting the unperformed conditions, all of which are generally included under the term waiver, to the great confusion of the law on that subject.[67] In view of the paucity of cases, it is hardly practicable at this time to enter upon a detailed

---

[66] Peoples Savings Bank & Trust Co. v. Landstreet, 80 Fla. 853, 87 So. 227 (1920); Omaha Nat. Bank v. First Nat. Bank, 59 Ill. 428 (1871); First State Bank v. Thuet, 88 Minn. 364, 93 N. W. 1 (1903). See also Union Bank of Canada v. Cole, *supra* note 61; Nevada Bank v. Luce, 139 Mass. 488, 1 N. E. 926 (1885); Stough v. Healy, 75 Kan. 526, 89 Pac. 898, 10 L. R. A. (N. S.) 918 (1907); Hodges v. Iowa Barb Steel Wire Co., 80 Iowa 65, 45 N. W. 541 (1890); Lockwood v. Brownson, 53 Tex. 523 (1880). These cases are explainable on the ground that the conditions had not been performed and that the purchaser was in a position which, at least, should have put him on inquiry. The language of the courts, however, is often broader and might lead to an inference that the purchaser's right to recover was based on the absolute performance of the conditions. *Cf.* Huston v. Newgass, *supra* note 59, for an illustration of the disregard of a condition which the purchaser was aware had not been performed. The letter authorized a draft for $2,300. The drawer drew for $3,300. On refusal to honor, the plaintiff sued for $2,300 and was allowed to recover. But see the strong dissenting opinion.

[67] See Ewart, Waiver Distributed (1917). Mention should also be made of anticipatory breaches by way of express repudiation or otherwise, which also dispense with the necessity for the actual performance of conditions. These have, in this connection, the same legal results as waivers and need not be considered separately. It should be noted that, in the case of anticipatory breaches, the plaintiff would probably be obligated to prove a readiness and willingness to comply with the conditions of the credit, which would scarcely be required of the plaintiff in a suit where a

discussion of all possible grounds which make performance of conditions unnecessary. Nor is this essential. Whether any particular set of facts amounts to an election or an estoppel, is a question which should be determined by the actual situation, as it arises, in each case, and which is subject to the usual rules of law and is not peculiar to the law of letters of credit.[68] We are, however, more interested in the legal effect of a waiver[69] of conditions by the bank, by the buyer, or by both.

---

waiver is alleged. For a consideration of facts sufficient to constitute an anticipatory breach, see *supra*, p. 177, note 5; see also *infra* ch. VII, p. 267.

[68] Moss v. Old Colony Trust Co., 246 Mass. 139, 150, 140 N. E. 803, 807 (1923). It has been held for example that previous acceptance by the bank of documents that are not in order, does not estop the bank from refusing to accept subsequent drafts on this ground. Cape Asbestos Co. v. Lloyds Bank, [1921] Weekly Notes 274; Ulster County Bank v. Mc-Farlan, 3 Denio 553 (N. Y. 1846); also, that payment of drafts after the credit has expired does not estop the bank from refusing subsequent drafts on that ground, Barde Steel Products Corp. v. Franklin Nat. Bank, 281 Fed. 814 (C. C. A. 3d, 1922); and that payment above the amount for which the letter of credit was issued does not estop the issuer from later showing that the credit has been exhausted. Peoples Savings Bank and Trust Co. v. Landstreet, *supra* note 66; see also First State Bank v. Thuet, *supra* note 66. But it has been held that a refusal to pay on one ground will estop a bank from setting up any other ground; Lamborn v. Cleveland Trust Co., 29 F. (2d) 46 (C. C. A. 6th, 1928); Bulliet v. Allegheny Trust Co., 284 Pa. 561, 131 Atl. 471, 42 A. L. R. 1133 (1925); Maurice O'Meara Co. v. Nat. Park Bank, 239 N. Y. 386, 146 N. E. 636, 39 A. L. R. 747 (1925); Bank of Taiwan v. Union Nat. Bank, 1 F. (2d) 65, 66 (C. C. A. 3d, 1924); Second Nat. Bank v. Lash Corp., 299 Fed. 371 (C. C. A. 3d, 1924); International Banking Corp. v. Irving Nat. Bank, 274 Fed. 122 (S. D. N. Y. 1921), *aff'd*, 283 Fed. 103 (C. C. A. 2d, 1922); Sturges v. Fourth Nat. Bank, 75 Ill. 595, 597 (1874). This, however, applies only to grounds for refusal known to the bank at the time of dishonor. Banco Nacional Ultramarino v. First Nat. Bank, 289 Fed. 169 (D. Mass. 1923); Old Colony Trust Co. v. Lawyers' Title & Trust Co., 297 Fed. 152 (C. C. A. 2d, 1924), *cert. den.*, 265 U. S. 585, 44 Sup. Ct. 459 (1924); see also Crocker First Nat. Bank v. De Sousa, 27 F. (2d) 462 (C. C. A. 9th, 1928), *rev'g*, 23 F. (2d) 118 (N. D. Cal. 1927). The same rule applies as between bank and buyer, Camp v. Corn Exchange Nat. Bank, 285 Pa. 337, 132 Atl. 189 (1926); and between buyer and seller, Lamborn v. Allen Kirkpatrick & Co., 288 Pa. 114, 135 Atl. 541 (1927); see also Kunglig Jarnvagsstyrelsen v. Nat. City Bank, 20 F. (2d) 307 (C. C. A. 2d, 1927); *cf.* Western Grocer Co. v. New York Oversea Co., 28 F. (2d) 518 (N. D. Cal. 1928). These are but illustrations of the general rule of contracts that, where a buyer has given one reason for refusing goods, he cannot thereafter reject them on other grounds, particularly where the grounds for rejection are remediable. 2 WILLISTON, SALES (2d ed. 1924) § 494a *et seq.*

[69] As is indicated in EWART, WAIVER DISTRIBUTED (1917), it is doubtful whether the use of the term waiver is anything more than a confused way

As between the seller and the bank, if the acts amounting to the waiver have been performed by both the buyer and the bank, the bank is obligated to pay the seller without the performance of the conditions waived. This would also hold true if the bank alone be considered to have waived the conditions. If, however, the waiver is merely on the part of the buyer, the bank obviously is under no duty to pay the seller without the performance of those conditions waived by the buyer. It is able to insist on the performance of all the conditions originally inserted in the letter of credit, as it has not indicated by any subsequent act that it would excuse the non-performance of any of them.

As between the bank and the buyer, if the waiver arises from the acts of both the bank and the buyer, then it follows that the bank, on paying the seller, acquires a right against the buyer. If, however, the waiver has been on the part of the bank alone, then it also follows that the bank, after paying the seller, acquires no right to be indemnified by the buyer.[70] The bank has performed an unauthorized act for which the buyer is in no way responsible and for which he cannot be held bound to indemnify the bank.[71] If the waiver is by the buyer alone, we apparently have another

---

of saying that there has been an estoppel, release, etc., as the case may be. But since, in this connection, the legal consequences that follow from establishing these different excuses for non-performance are the same, there is no necessity for drawing distinctions at this point. The term is therefore used to include all of them, except supervening impossibility of performance which involves some other considerations and will therefore be considered separately.

[70] Accordingly, some courts are apparently of the opinion that the buyer can enjoin the bank from paying; see Williams Ice Cream Co. v. Chase Nat. Bank, 120 Misc. 301, 199 N. Y. Supp. 314 (1923), *rev'd,* 210 App. Div. 179, 205 N. Y. Supp. 446 (1924). Both courts implied that the buyer in this case could enjoin the bank from paying the seller under a letter of credit where it had changed the conditions without his consent. The reversal was based on the ground that the buyer had waived the breach by accepting the goods; *cf.* however, *supra* ch. IV, p. 171.

[71] In addition, if after such waiver the bank refuses to honor the draft because the conditions waived have not been performed, it apparently is liable to the buyer as well as to the seller, if the former accepts or ratifies the waiver. See Kronman & Co. v. Public Nat. Bank, 218 App. Div. 624, 632, 218 N. Y. Supp. 616, 623 (1926). Whether the buyer has ratified the acts of the bank will depend upon the circumstances of each case. See also Royal Card & Paper Co. v. Dresdner Bank, 27 F. (2d)

illustration of a case in which the bank is privileged to pay the seller, but is not bound to pay him. The buyer, by his conduct, has in effect told the seller that he will, without the performance of certain conditions, accept the goods for which he has contracted. The only reasonable inference that can be drawn from this is that the buyer also consents to the bank's paying the seller without the performance of the conditions. Otherwise, the waiver is a nullity and of no practical consequence. The bank, as has been indicated, is not bound in this situation to pay the seller. The result reached, therefore, is that the bank would have a right to be indemnified by the buyer if it should elect to pay the seller.[72]

Supervening impossibility of the performance of conditions upon which rests the duty of the bank to pay may be caused by external circumstances over which the parties have no control or by the act of one or more of the parties to the transactions. If it is caused by the former, then, generally speaking, the seller acquires no rights against the bank.[73] In the case of *Krakauer* v. *Chapman*,[74] the credit authorized one member of the buyer's firm

---

791 (C. C. A. 2d, 1928); Nat. Bank of Egypt v. Hannevig's Bank, 1 Lloyd's List 69 (1919); *cf.* Westminster Bank v. Banca Nazionale di Credito, 31 Lloyd's List 306 (1928) and discussion, *supra* p. 196, as to whether acceptance of defective documents by the buyer constitutes a ratification of an unauthorized payment by the bank.

[72] It should be noted that where the credit is issued containing terms less liberal than those of the sales contract, the bank has no power to pay against the more liberal terms of the contract, and recover on the agreement to reimburse. *Supra* p. 189. In the case under discussion, however, the subsequent act of the buyer can be taken as directed to both bank and buyer, as otherwise it would be ineffective. Where the credit contains less liberal terms than the sales contract, the terms of the earlier sales contract cannot be taken as a waiver of the terms of the subsequent credit. S. L. Jones & Co. v. Bond, 191 Cal. 551, 217 Pac. 725 (1923). If anything, the letter of credit would be interpreted as narrowing the terms of the sales contract and thus often constituting a breach of the latter. *Supra* p. 190.

[73] 2 Williston, Contracts (1920) § 808. It would depend to a great extent on the nature of the condition. If the credit called for shipment per "X Y Z line" and that company went out of existence, a shipment by an equally responsible line might be interpreted as fulfilling the terms of the contract.

[74] 16 App. Div. 115, 45 N. Y. Supp. 127 (1897), *aff'd* without opinion, 162 N. Y. 623, 57 N. E. 1114 (1900).

to draw on the bank in favor of the seller. After some time, this particular member of the buyer's firm left it, and, after trying vainly to get his money, the seller himself drew on the bank and brought suit when the draft was dishonored. The court, obviously influenced by the general equities of the plaintiff's case, allowed a recovery in spite of the fact that one condition of the bank's duty to pay had not been performed. This was a very unusual case. The buyer had accepted the goods without objection, and the only question at issue was the effect of the supervening impossibility of performance of an apparently inconsequential condition. Certainly this much is clear: if the seller in this case had not delivered the goods and had been presenting documents with the draft, he could not have recovered. No element of forfeiture would have entered, as the seller would still have had his goods, and before he could have acquired a right against the bank, he would have had to perform all the conditions precedent. In commercial contracts of this type, not only is it difficult to know which conditions are essential and which are not; but also any attempt to make such a distinction tends to destroy a great part of that certainty which is so essential in commercial transactions.[75] These considerations hold true even where, as in *Krakauer* v. *Chapman*, the goods have actually been delivered.[76]

[75] *Supra* p. 180, note 11.

[76] *Cf.* Orient Co. v. Brekke & Howlid, [1913] 1 K. B. 531. In that case, the seller was required, under a c.i.f. contract, to present to the buyer, among other documents, an insurance policy. He failed to insure the goods, but the goods had arrived safely and were at the time of the presentation of the other documents at their destination. The court held that the seller could not recover as he had failed to present an insurance policy. The case was even more difficult since the presentation was not made to the bank, but to the buyer, who wanted the goods as much as he wanted the documents. Yet, here, the court recognizes that, as a rule, commercial practices run in certain forms, that these forms have resulted in certain kinds of contracts, which, in turn, are governed by certain rules, and finally that these rules cannot be changed arbitrarily, without affecting the certainty of commercial transactions, even though in particular cases they work hardship. The remedy lies with the parties to the transaction, who should either pick that form of contract that best suits their needs or insert provisions into the contract exempting it from such of the rules as they do not desire to have applied. Where the seller, for example, does not desire to be obligated to present an insurance pol-

In addition, the bank here is not purchasing goods; it is merely financing the transaction. If the buyer has failed, as conceivably might have been the case, there is no reason why the bank, rather than the seller, should bear the loss, especially when the latter has failed to perform one of the conditions precedent to the bank's duty to pay.[77] Above all, this seemingly unimportant condition might actually be of very great consequence.[78] Nor has any method been devised of determining the importance of any one condition. These considerations were recognized by the dissenting opinion in the above case:

> It appears that the defendant was the mere banker or depository of the mining company; not the principal of Jones. He might well be unwilling to assume any liability, the amount of which was not absolutely fixed by a draft drawn by the agent of the company. He is no wise responsible for the failure of the plaintiffs to obtain a draft for the amount of the sale. The plaintiffs could have protected themselves by refusing to deliver the goods until the draft was given them. Had Jones drawn drafts

icy, if he uses that form of contract which, because of the customary usages between merchants, has been held to imply the presentation of an insurance policy, he should insert an express provision to offset that, and not depend upon the courts to make rules to suit each particular case. "In my view, when a seller draws up a document and describes it in large letters as a c.i.f. contract, and says at the beginning that it is to be taken on c.i.f. terms, if he wants to substitute something quite different, he must say so in clear language." *In re* Denbigh Cowan & Co. and R. Atcherley & Co., 90 L. J. K. B. 836, 841 (1921). Compare these cases with the following, where the court held the agreement in question in each instance not to be a c.i.f. contract because of the nature of some of the special terms. Western Grocer Co. v. New York Oversea Co., 28 F. (2d) 518 (N. D. Cal. 1928); Johnson & Higgins v. Charles F. Garrigues Co., 22 F. (2d) 454 (S. D. N. Y. 1927); Nat. Wholesale Grocery Co. v. Mann, 251 Mass. 238, 146 N. E. 791 (1925); Scriven Bros. v. Schmoll Fils & Co., 40 T. L. R. 677 (1924); George Carocopos, Inc., v. James Chieves & Co., 203 App. Div. 104, 196 N. Y. Supp. 425 (1922); A. Klipstein & Co. v. Dilsizian, 273 Fed. 473 (C. C. A. 2d, 1921), *cert. den.*, 257 U. S. 639, 42 Sup. Ct. 51 (1921); Y. P. Barley Producers v. E. C. Robertson Pty., [1927] V. L. R. 194. See also Rule I of the Warsaw Rules, 1928, relating to c.i.f. contracts, (1929) 29 Col. L. Rev. 652, 653.

[77] In Krakauer v. Chapman, *supra* note 74, the bank had funds of the buyer at the time it issued the letter of credit. At the time the seller drew his draft, which was several months later, the money had all been withdrawn by the buyer. It also seems that the buyer was no longer available for the bank to sue. In effect, this was throwing the loss on the bank and for no particularly valid reason. See a discussion of this case in Hershey, *Letters of Credit* (1918) 32 Harv. L. Rev. 1, 35.

[78] *Supra*, p. 180, note 11.

not corresponding with the terms of the letter, the defendant would not have been obliged to pay them. I cannot see that he should be liable when no draft was drawn.[79]

The solution lies with the seller, who must be careful not to permit the insertion into the letter of credit of conditions which might result in making performance of the requirements of the credit impossible, while performance of the sales contract remains possible.[80]

Impossibility of performance when caused by one of the parties may be due to acts of the bank or to those of the buyer. If it is due to the bank,[81] then clearly under the general rule of contracts, the seller would in most cases have an action against the bank on the credit.[82] The bank, however, would probably not have any right against the buyer after it had been made to pay the seller. The reason for this result is that, in effect, there is an unauthorized waiver by the bank, since the act of the bank was without the authority of the buyer and since the law gives to impossibility of performance, when caused by one party, the same effect as it gives to a waiver by that party. A waiver of this type, as has been indicated, gives the seller a right against the bank but does not give the bank any right against the buyer.

When the impossibility of performance is caused by the buyer, the seller would acquire a right against the buyer without the performance of those conditions since the buyer's interference has the effect of a waiver. That the seller would have no right against the bank should also follow. The only question that arises, therefore, is whether the bank is privileged to pay the seller if it decides to do so. In the case of an actual waiver by

[79] Cullen, J., dissenting in Krakauer v. Chapman, *supra* note 74, at 125, 45 N. Y. Supp. at 133.

[80] For an illustration of this type of situation, see S. L. Jones & Co. v. Bond, *supra* note 72.

[81] This situation might conceivably arise when the credit required the presentation of certain documents, blanks of which were procurable only from the correspondent of the issuing bank, and the issuing bank instructed the correspondent not to deliver them to the seller.

[82] 2 Williston, Contracts (1920) § 677.

the buyer, as has been seen, it probably is so privileged. In regard to impossibility of performance caused by the buyer, the situation is not quite so simple. As the problem arises, the seller presents his documents to the bank without certain conditions being fulfilled and shows that performance of these conditions was prevented by the buyer. The buyer may have caused the impossibility in either one of two ways. He may have refused to perform an act required by the sales contract, with the result that the seller was unable to perform all of his obligations under the contract; or the buyer may have voluntarily performed an act that prevented the seller from performing his part of the contract.

If the impossibility of performance is due to the first of these two causes, the bank should not be permitted to pay against the documents and then recover against the buyer. The latter may have had good reasons for not performing his share of the contract, and the bank cannot go into that question. In the case of *Morgan* v. *Larivière*,[83] the buyer refused to supply a certificate of compliance which the seller was supposed to present with his draft. The seller presented the draft without the certificate and sued the bank when it refused to pay. The court denied a recovery and said in part:

> And with respect to the cartridges said to have been supplied and accepted on the 10th of January, and afterwards, but for which no certificates were granted, how can the Appellants be liable for them? Even supposing that Captain Bourdreaux improperly refused to grant certificates, what have the Appellants to do with that? Their engagement is to pay, not upon the mere approval and acceptance of the cartridges, but upon receipt of certificates of reception issued by the French Ambassador or by M. Joulin.[84]

[83] L. R. 7 H. L. 423 (1875); see also Pake v. Wilson, 127 Ala. 240, 28 So. 665 (1899).

[84] *Ibid.*, at 436. *Cf.* Ernesto Foglino & Co. v. Webster, 217 App. Div. 282, 216 N. Y. Supp. 225 (1926), *modified*, 244 N. Y. 516, 155 N. E. 878 (1926). In that case there were anticipatory breaches by the bank and the buyer. One of the requirements of the letter of credit was that the documents be viséd by an official of the buyer, the Italian Government.

If, however, the impossibility of performance is due to a positive act on the part of the buyer, a very difficult situation arises. It may be claimed that the bank is privileged to interpret this act as a waiver, that, in effect, the buyer is authorizing the bank to honor the draft without the performance of those conditions which he has made impossible of performance; or, it may be claimed that the buyer is, in effect, directing the bank not to pay the draft in any event. In the only case that seems to have arisen on this point,[85] the majority took the former view, saying in part:

That change made the carrying out of the contract as originally drawn commercially impossible. And the bank, in arranging as they did for the negotiation of Scott Robson's bills in Buenos Ayres, on presentation of shipping documents, not including pol-

---

The defendant contended that it was impossible to obtain the visé and that therefore the seller had not shown a readiness to perform; see defendant's brief in the Appellate Division and the Court of Appeals. The court stated however: "The respondent thus having thirty days after April 30, 1920, within which to perform its contract with the Ministry, and to become entitled to receive the payments therefor from the irrevocable credits established for it with defendants, appellants, repudiated their contract and became guilty of an anticipatory breach thereof, when they wrote respondent on April 30, 1920, that the credits in its favor had expired. Such act of appellants relieved respondent as well from the idle form of tendering performance to the Ministry, which also had notified respondent that the credits were canceled." 217 App. Div. at 297, 216 N. Y. Supp. at 238. The court is obviously influenced by the fact that the buyer and bank acted together to breach their respective contracts. Their action was doubtless caused by the fall in the market price of the goods involved. The bank, in committing an anticipatory breach of its contract, was acting in concert with the buyer. It could not, therefore, set up as a bar to liability on its part, a condition—that of visé by the buyer's agent—the performance of which was made impossible, partly at least, through its own activities. The court recognizes this and points out that the plaintiff was ready, willing and able to perform all the other terms of its contract. It is submitted that if the bank had not committed an anticipatory breach, but had remained quiescent, it would have been justified in refusing to honor the draft for lack of a visé on the documents. In other words, it is submitted that the rule in Morgan v. Larivière discussed *supra* applies except in cases where the bank, by its conduct, participates in the buyer's wrong. It should also be noticed that in the Foglino case, there was a definite act on the part of the buyer, *i. e.*, advising the seller that the draft would not be honored, which would tend to throw the case into the group to be considered presently, where the buyer, by an overt act, creates the impossibility of performance. On the question of the bank's liability for anticipatory breach, see pp. 267, 268. See also Sears, Roebuck & Co. v. Rouse Banking Co., 191 N. C. 500, 132 S. E. 468 (1926).

[85] Friedlander v. Bank of Australasia, 8 C. L. R. 85 (Aust. 1909).

icies of insurance, carried out the transaction of financing payment of the wheat in the only way in which it could be carried out under the conditions so altered by the appellant's consent and notified to the bank by his agents. Under these circumstances the respondent bank have to my mind clearly established the position that, before the breach complained of, they were exonerated and discharged from the performance of the condition on which the appellant is now relying.[86]

On the other hand, the dissent by one judge took the opposite view:

> If the authority actually given by Friedlander was impossible of performance by reason of Friedlander's act, that would have been a good reason for not performing it at all; but it is no reason whatever for doing on his behalf what he never authorized the bank to do.[87]

To determine which view the courts will generally follow is impossible at present, but the majority opinion in the *Friedlander* case would appear to be the more desirable, since it arrives at a result in harmony with the rights, powers and duties of the bank generally. The seller, in these cases, has a right to the contract price from the buyer, and therefore to permit the bank to pay the seller and to recover from the buyer is only to reach this same result in another way. The minority opinion reaches the rather anomalous conclusion that, while the seller can recover from the buyer, the bank, if it pays the seller, cannot so recover even though the terms of the credit and the sales contract are the same, and the only point in issue is an act of the buyer. This conclusion serves no useful function and tends only to increase the unnecessary technicalities of the law. There is no reason for its adoption.

D. Conditions to Be Inserted in Letters of Credit

This analysis has served to bring out two functions of the commercial letter of credit: that of enabling the seller to obtain

---

[86] *Ibid.* at 101.
[87] *Ibid.* at 113.

payment quickly and easily, and that of protecting the buyer against improper performance by the seller. The problem is to give as much effect to each of these as is consistent with the general purposes of commercial credits. The function of the letter of credit is not to protect the buyer against all improper performance by the seller. The purposes of the conditions in a letter of credit are to give the bank and the buyer the twofold assurance that goods have been shipped and that, in a general way, they are the goods for which the buyer has contracted. The letter of credit is essentially an instrument of finance, and to attempt to use it as an instrument to secure the performance by the seller of all his obligations under the sales contract, is to burden it with more than it can carry. The inevitable result of this would be that not only would this secondary function be inadequately performed but that its original function of financing trade would also be inefficiently carried out. Fortunately, this was recognized soon after the letter of credit came into general use in this country and steps were taken at that time to avert this situation.

At a meeting in New York City held in June, 1921, and attended by representatives of leading mercantile and banking interests, the consensus of opinion reached was that the proper function of a bank in issuing a commercial credit was to afford a means of financing the transaction. The attempt to place responsibility on banks to check the proper execution of the terms of the contract of sale between buyer and seller by incorporating a description of the merchandise or other features of the sales contract in the credit, was felt to be in the long run more harmful than helpful to foreign trade.[88]

[88] Ward, American Commercial Credits (1922) 216; *cf.* however, (1921) 34 Harv. L. Rev. 533, 535. In addition, it is not improbable that courts will substantially limit the effectiveness of such conditions in letters of credit as tend seriously to impair the usefulness of commercial credits. See Hibernia Bank & Trust Co. v. J. Aron & Co., 134 Misc. 18, 19, 233 N. Y. Supp. 486, 488 (1928), where the letter of credit contained the following clause: "This letter of credit is subject to the terms and conditions of contract attached to the guarantee covering this letter." The contract referred to was one between the buyer and a purchaser from him, to which the seller was not a party and of the terms of which he knew nothing.

It follows, therefore, that too many conditions, even though couched in non-technical language, should not be used in letters of credit. The more numerous and complex the conditions are, the greater difficulty will the seller encounter in discounting his draft under the credit, and the more likely will the issuing bank be to reject the documents for unjustifiable or trivial reasons. This will result not only in great annoyance to the seller, but often to the buyer as well, inasmuch as the latter may be in great need of the goods and would be willing to accept the documents in the condition in which they were presented. That letters of credit be clear, concise and definite is to the interest of all parties to the transaction.

Letters of credit in large numbers for vast sums are used in oversea commercial transactions by people whose laws, language, and customs are often different from those of the people where the letter is issued. The safety of the issuing bank, of the buyer for whose account it is issued, and of the seller who often expends much and risks much on the faith of the promise in the letter, require that the terms of the letter shall be sharply defined and strictly complied with in all respects.[89]

Uniformity of language and simplicity of conditions can do much to lessen the hiatus between legal and banking performance of the conditions in a letter of credit.[90]

A copy of the contract was not attached to the letter of credit. The court was of the opinion that the condition was not binding on the seller and that the clause was directed only to the buyer, even though contained in the letter of credit. The case is an extreme one. Normally, in a case of this sort, the letter of credit would contain a reference to the sales contract between buyer and seller. Under the theory of the above decision, a bona fide purchaser of the draft, not being aware of the terms of the sales contract, would not be bound by the clause, even though it might limit the rights of the seller under the credit.

[89] Wells Fargo Nevada Nat. Bank v. Corn Exch. Nat. Bank, 23 F. (2d) 1, 2 (C. C. A. 7th, 1928).

[90] "In this connection it should be noted that there is a distinction to be drawn between the legal effect of the contract with reference to what constitutes performance and banking practice as to the nature of the performance preferred. At the trial evidence was introduced tending to show the practice of certain banks to be to require literal, word for word, compliance with the letter of credit in all of the 'essential' documents. Doubtless such mathematically accurate compliance with the contract is both convenient and desirable. Convenience and desirability from

A series of complex conditions greatly increases the likelihood of a resort to litigation for final adjustment, and no matter what decision is reached, it results in dissatisfaction to all parties.[91] In addition, the buyer is not really protected by minute descriptions in the bill of lading, for the carrier makes no such nice examination as is implied in such a description,[92] and the seller is deprived of prompt payment under the credit.

It is clear that conditions stated in the technical language of any particular trade should, as far as possible, be omitted. Even though the bank is not required to pay against documents in case of any variation in language, the effect of the use of such technical terms is to put the bank in a difficult position. If a bank does not readily and generally pay drafts drawn under its letters of credit, sellers begin to have difficulty in discounting the drafts under the credit, and consequently hesitate to accept letters issued by that bank, with the result that the business of the bank in question tends to decrease. The bank will therefore pay the draft whenever possible,[93] although in doing so, it must assume the

---

the standpoint of the bank are not enough, however, to extend the requirements as to the performance of a contract beyond the scope of its plain terms." De Sousa v. Crocker First Nat. Bank, 23 F. (2d) 118, 120 (N. D. Cal. 1927). See also J. P. Beal, *Utility of Letters of Credit in the Export Trade—A Plea for Standard Forms* (1917) 95 BANKERS MAG. 271.

[91] For an excellent example, see WARD, AMERICAN COMMERCIAL CREDITS (1922) 208.

[92] Laudisi v. American Exch. Nat. Bank, 239 N. Y. 234, 240, 146 N. E. 347, 349 (1924). "A bill of lading in this case, even if it specified the shipment of the particular kind of grapes ordered by the plaintiff would be no guaranty of the fact of such shipment. Of course nobody would expect a railroad company to open and examine the contents of 1,240 boxes of grapes and see that they all complied with the description in the letter of credit." Other methods have been suggested for the protection of the buyer which would not require the insertion of numerous confusing conditions, e. g., documents of various kinds certified by government agencies or experts, and the issuance of the letter of credit for only a partial amount of the price, say ninety per cent. See, e. g., Monark Metal & S. Co. v. Schmidt, 195 Wis. 294, reported *sub nom.*, Monark Metal & Supply Co. v. General Metal & Refining Co., 218 N. W. 179 (1928). This would leave a balance of ten percent. for the adjustment of differences. On this general topic, see WARD, *op. cit. supra* note 91, ch. XIV, "Protection of the Mercantile Risk."

[93] Occasionally, when there is doubt as to the conformity of the documents, the bank will honor its credit, after being furnished by the seller

responsibility for the conformity in the documents. To omit any conditions couched in such language is therefore highly desirable. When this is impossible, care should be taken by the seller to use the identical language of the credit.[94]

On the other hand, the matter of omitting conditions may very well be carried too far. Certain conditions are essential for the proper protection of the buyer and must be inserted in the credit. At this point, the responsibility rests with the bank to interpret these fairly and justly, and without too great an insistence on their purely formal aspects. A bank that refuses to pay against documents because, for example, the custom house permit is not in the same language as the letter of credit,[95] or because the goods were invoiced on two lines instead of one, as in the letter of credit,[96] is not only refusing to perform its legal obligations and ignoring the best interests of trade in general, but is also failing to act with due regard for its own interests.[97]

As to conditions that do not require the attaching of documents to the draft, the conclusion that must be reached, in view of the

with a surety bond indemnifying the bank against loss, see, e. g., Westminster Bank v. Banca Nazionale di Credito, 31 Lloyd's List 306 (1928); Nat. City Bank v. Herbst, 76 N. Y. L. J., Dec. 2, 1926, at 951; Provisions for Interpretation of Credits, § 5, Appendix A, form 20.

[94] One solution might be to have the technical detailed description put in the seller's invoice, while the bill of lading would contain only a general classification. A wilfully false description by the seller would probably bring him into conflict with the criminal law of his jurisdiction and thus act as an additional deterrent. For a similar suggestion see Ward *op. cit. supra* note 91, at 215 *et seq.*

[95] Bank of America v. Whitney-Central Nat. Bank, 291 Fed. 929 (C. C. A. 5th, 1923). See also Pan-American Bank & Trust Co. v. Nat. City Bank, 6 F. (2d) 762 (C. C. A. 2d, 1925), *cert. den.*, 269 U. S. 554, 46 Sup. Ct. 18 (1925); Talmadge v. Williams, 27 La. Ann. 653 (1875); International Banking Corp. v. Irving Nat. Bank, 274 Fed. 122, 125 (S. D. N. Y. 1921), *aff'd*, 283 Fed. 103 (C. C. A. 2d, 1922); Richard v. Royal Bank of Canada, 23 F. (2d) 430 (C. C. A. 2d, 1928).

[96] *Infra* note 97; *cf.* also Forman v. Walker, 4 La. Ann. 409 (1849); Camp v. Corn Exch. Nat. Bank, 285 Pa. 337, 132 Atl. 189 (1926).

[97] A coffee merchant has issued a very interesting list, giving some of the reasons why banks have rejected documents. Some rejections, which seem unreasonable to him, were based upon lack of knowledge of the technical terms of the trade, but others seem to be wholly unjustifiable, e. g., the illustration as given above, where documents were refused because the goods were invoiced on two lines instead of one. The list is reproduced in Ward, American Commercial Credits (1922) 211.

preceding discussion, is that they had better be omitted entirely from letters of credit.[98] When the draft is presented by the seller, the bank will always be in doubt as to whether it should rely upon the seller's representations that the conditions have been performed and, if not, then at least in doubt as to what extent it should investigate the matter itself.[99] In regard to the purchaser of the draft, even if the better rule be followed and the risk of loss be thrown on the issuing bank, a satisfactory result is not reached. Banks feeling that they must pocket the loss or else, as a rule, bring suit against the buyer for reimbursement, will tend to dishonor the drafts wherever possible and so make the purchaser bring suit to obtain the money that is due him. This will in turn, have the unfortunate result of decreasing the factual negotiability of drafts under these letters of credit. Purchasers of drafts are not interested in buying lawsuits. They desire drafts that will pass easily and freely and which will be met promptly and without objection on the part of the issuing bank.

In general, loose use of language and indefiniteness of terms should be avoided. This applies not so much to formal letters of

---

[98] There are only two conditions of this type that must be inserted into practically every letter of credit, the expiration date and the amount for which the credit is issued. As to the former, problems seldom arise. The matter is so simply determined that it may well be assumed that the purchaser knows whether or not the credit has expired. As to the latter, a simple method has been suggested that will practically eliminate any risk of loss to the bank in the great majority of cases. The bank should insert in its letters of credit three requirements in relation to this matter: (1) that all drafts drawn under the credit be so marked on their face; (2) that all purchasers of drafts note the amount of the draft on the back of the letter of credit; and (3) that by sending the draft to the bank the purchaser represents that this has been done. In this way the bank would be assured: (1) that it will not be paying a draft unless drawn under the credit; (2) that every purchaser of a draft knew just how much of the credit had been used at the time he purchased the draft; and, that finally, (3) if this did not appear, because of the negligence of some purchaser, the bank would probably have a right of action against the purchaser for the amount of the credit that it would have to overpay. Since the purchaser from the seller is usually the local bank or some other responsible institution, this right of action is valuable. See the standard forms of modern letters of credit, Appendix A.

[99] See Commercial Union v. Anglo-South American Bank, 16 F. (2d) 979 (C. C. A. 2d, 1927), *supra* p. 200.

credit as to the more informal promises to pay on certain conditions, such as telegrams. Phrases such as "in amounts necessary"[100] or "as per sample"[101] add nothing to the duties of the seller, only confuse the purchaser as to his exact rights under the credit, and so make him less willing to purchase the draft at the usual rate of discount. It should be remembered as a fundamental rule that the clearer, the more concise, and the more definite an instrument of this kind is, the more freely and easily will drafts drawn under it be negotiable, and the less will be the rate of discount. In other words, the better will it fulfill its functions.

While the buyer in each particular case determines the kind of conditions that are to go into the letter of credit, the bank ultimately controls the situation. The bank actually issues the credit and, by continually refusing to insert certain types of conditions into the letter, may gradually cause the elimination of the use of objectionable conditions in letters of credit.[102] Because of its quasi-public functions and activities and because of the multitude of letters of credit which it issues, the bank is best equipped to look beyond the necessities of each individual case to the general tendencies and problems involved. It is to the larger banking institutions that we must turn, therefore, for progress in the non-legal aspect of the simplification and increased efficiency in the use of letters of credit.

---

[100] Bissell v. Lewis, 4 Mich. 450 (1857).

[101] International Banking Corp. v. Irving Nat. Bank, *supra* note 95. The Commercial Credit Committee of the American Acceptance Council has attempted to meet this situation by standardized definitions of the more common nebulous phrases, e. g., "shipment as soon as possible," see Appendix A.

[102] This will require the coöperation of all the larger banking institutions if it is to be expected to work effectively and quickly.

Chapter VI

THE RELATION BETWEEN THE LETTER OF CREDIT AND THE SALES CONTRACT

The sales contract is an agreement between the buyer and the seller. The letter of credit is a contract between the issuing bank and the seller and those holding under him. These two agreements are distinct and independent of each other. Their terms and conditions must be judged by the expressions used in each of them. As a rule the courts have differentiated between these two types of contracts.[1] Our discussion of performance of conditions under a letter of credit has served to emphasize this point of view, as it is in that field of the bank's obligation under letters of credit that

[1] "The letter of credit was not part of the contract between the buyer and the seller, but was an entirely separate and independent contract between the bank and the seller." S. L. Jones & Co. v. Bond, 191 Cal. 551, 555, 217 Pac. 725, 727 (1923). "A bank issuing a letter of credit is in no way concerned with any contract existing between the buyer and seller." Imbrie v. D. Nagase & Co., 196 App. Div. 380, 383, 187 N. Y. Supp. 692, 695 (1921). "The terms of sale as between Kronman and Munoz have nothing to do with the terms of the letter of credit." Kronman and Co. v. Public Nat. Bank, 218 App. Div. 624, 631, 218 N. Y. Supp. 616, 622 (1926); see also: Maurice O'Meara Co. v. Nat. Park Bank, 239 N. Y. 386, 395, 146 N. E. 636, 639, 39 A. L. R. 747, 751 (1925), quoted *infra* note 6; American Steel Co. v. Irving Nat. Bank, 266 Fed. 41 (C. C. A. 2d, 1920), 277 Fed. 1016 (C. C. A. 2d, 1921), *cert. den.*, 258 U. S. 617, 42 Sup. Ct. 271 (1922); Lamborn v. Lake Shore Banking and Trust Co., 196 App. Div. 504, 188 N. Y. Supp. 162 (1921), *aff'd* without opinion, 231 N. Y. 616, 132 N. E. 911 (1921); Frey & Son v. E. R. Sherburne Co., 193 App. Div. 849, 184 N. Y. Supp. 661 (1920); Moss v. Old Colony Trust Co., 246 Mass. 139, 152, 140 N. E. 803, 808 (1923); Nat. Wholesale Grocery Co. v. Mann, 251 Mass. 238, 244, 146 N. E. 791, 792 (1925); Camp v. Corn Exch. Nat. Bank, 285 Pa. 337, 344, 132 Atl. 189, 191 (1926); Kunglig Jarnvagsstyrelsen v. Nat. City Bank, 20 F. (2d) 307, 308 (C. C. A. 2d, 1927). *A fortiori*, the rights of a bona fide purchaser are not limited by the contract between the seller and buyer. Commercial Bank v. First Nat. Bank, 147 La. 925, 928, 86 So. 342, 343, 13 A. L. R. 986, 987 (1920). "Upon these facts, . . . the defendant is liable to the plaintiff for the amount of the check. . . . And this regardless of what may have been the agreement between Pharr and Blumenthal, and of the manner in which it may have been carried out." The action was on a promise to accept as an acceptance.

the distinction is of greatest significance.[2] There is, however, another aspect to the matter. Both the sales contract and the letter of credit arise out of the same commercial transaction. It may be expected, therefore, that this close business relationship will be reflected in some degree in the law of letters of credit and c.i.f. contracts.[3] The precise nature and extent of this relationship can best be determined by considering the effect of the various defenses that may be interposed by the bank and the buyer in actions on letters of credit.

A. Non-Fraudulent Defects in Performance of Sales Contract

The real problem involved in this relationship between the sales contract and the letter of credit is a consideration of the extent to which the bank may go behind the documents presented in order to ascertain that the state of facts represented by them actually exists.

The most important question that has arisen in this connection is whether the issuing bank can refuse to honor its credit on the ground that the goods are of inferior quality, even though it may admit that the documents presented comply with the terms of the credit.

A comparison with the c.i.f. contract will again prove helpful. When a seller presents documents to a buyer under that type of contract, the latter has two courses of conduct open to him. He must either pay or give a valid reason for refusing payment. He cannot, however, refuse payment until such time as he has

---

[2] Practically all of the cases which emphasize this distinction involve the performance of conditions under a letter of credit.

[3] The relationship may become of significance, even when performance of conditions is involved; see *supra* ch. V, p. 190. It was submitted that when the letter of credit uses the term shipping documents and the sales contract specifies the kind of shipping documents, the seller might be held to have his rights under the letter of credit limited to the presentation of the specific documents mentioned in the sales contract. This restriction, however, would not apply to the bona fide purchaser from the seller.

had an opportunity to inspect the goods.[4] On the other hand, if he can demonstrate that the documents are actually forged, there is no doubt that he can refuse payment. Similarly, it is submitted, if the buyer can show that the documents are fraudulent or that the goods are not of the proper quality, he can set up these facts as a defense or counterclaim to any action brought by the seller. In other words, the burden of proof rests on the buyer. The seller has made an apparently valid tender. It is for the buyer to indicate why he need not pay.[5]

It is submitted that the seller's position should not differ under a letter of credit. Because of the nature of a c.i.f. contract, he has certain rights against the buyer. The issuance of a letter of credit would, as a practical matter, destroy an important part of these rights if the bank were given the privilege of investigating before payment. There is no reason for depriving the seller of his right to immediate payment. The issuance of a letter of credit does not alter the nature of a c.i.f. contract. It still remains essentially a contract contemplating payment against documents with subsequent adjustment of all differences that may arise. The bank, by issuing the letter of credit, places itself in the position of the buyer in this respect. Even more than the latter, the bank, by means of the letter of credit, attempts to assure the seller that he will be paid promptly and with a minimum of trouble, according to the terms of the credit.[6] The bank should

[4] *Supra* ch. V, p. 178.

[5] The seller presents his documents and rests his case. In order to put the documents in evidence, he must, of course, introduce prima facie proof that they are genuine. That, however, is the extent of his obligation. The buyer, if he desires to avoid a finding against him, must either offer rebutting evidence to the effect that the documents are forged, that they are fraudulent, or that the goods are of inferior quality. Practically, this means that the buyer must show reasonable grounds for not paying under the terms of the contract. These results follow necessarily from the rule that the buyer, under a c.i.f. contract, has no right to inspect before payment. If the buyer can compel the seller to prove that the documents accurately represent the goods, he is in effect being given the equivalent of a right to inspect, an undesirable result under this form of contract, as has been indicated.

[6] This view is generally recognized in the statements of the courts that the bank is concerned with documents and not with the facts upon which they

not, therefore, acquire greater rights than are given the buyer. Especially should this follow here, where the buyer's interest, as owner of the goods, is much greater than that of the bank. If the former does not have this right, *a fortiori*, the latter should not.[7]

The problem is admirably exemplified in the case of *Maurice O'Meara Co.* v. *National Park Bank*.[8] The bank refused to pay on the ground that:

> There has arisen a reasonable doubt regarding the quality of the newsprint paper. . . . Until such time as we can have a test made by an impartial and unprejudiced expert we shall be obliged to defer payment.[9]

The court there held:

> The defendant had no right to insist that a test of the tensile strength of the paper be made before paying the drafts. Nor did it even have a right to inspect the paper before payment, to determine whether it in fact corresponded to the description contained in the documents. The letter of credit did not so provide. All that the letter of credit provided was that documents be presented which described the paper shipped as of a certain size, weight, and tensile strength. To hold otherwise is to read into the letter of credit something which is not there, and this the court ought not to do, since it would impose upon a bank a duty which in many cases would defeat the primary purpose of such letters of credit. This primary purpose is an assurance to the seller of merchandise of prompt payment against documents.[10]

This is sound law. In view of the business usages under c.i.f. contracts and letters of credit, it is certainly accurate to hold that, in the absence of an express provision to that effect, the bank, on

---

rest. "This contract [the letter of credit] was in no way involved in, or connected with, other than the presentation of the documents, the contract for the purchase and sale of the paper mentioned. . . . The bank was concerned only in the drafts and the documents accompanying them. This was the extent of its interest." Maurice O'Meara Co. v. Nat. Park Bank, *supra* note 1, at 395, 146 N. E. at 639, 39 A. L. R. at 751.

[7] The seller would, of course, as against the buyer, retain his right to payment without inspection, but this is a theoretical, rather than a practical, advantage, as he is looking to the bank and not to the buyer for payment.

[8] Maurice O'Meara Co. v. Nat. Park Bank, *supra* note 1.

[9] *Ibid.* at 397, 146 N. E. at 639, 39 A. L. R. at 752.

[10] *Ibid.* at 396, 146 N. E. at 639, 39 A. L. R. at 752.

a mere suspicion of non-conformity of the goods, cannot refuse payment until it is satisfied by an inspection or other proof that the goods conform to the descriptions in the documents.

The application of the same principles we have been considering leads to a similar result in the case of the alleged non-fraudulent non-performance on the part of the seller of his obligations under the sales contract, e. g., that the goods are not of the quality or quantity indicated or that they are overvalued. There is no allegation of fraud in these cases. They represent a difference of opinion between buyer and seller. Under a c.i.f. contract, where the buyer can prove such non-performance at the time of the tender of the documents, it is submitted that he need not pay.[11] The bank's position under a letter of credit involves considerations leading to a different result. The problem was discussed at length in *Maurice O'Meara Co.* v. *National Park Bank,* though not directly in point.[12] The majority were of the opinion that the bank could not set up this defense.

> The bank's obligation was to pay sight drafts when presented, if accompanied by genuine documents specified in the letter of

[11] See 2 Williston, Sales (2d ed. 1924), §§ 479, 576; 2 Williston, Contracts (1920) ch. XXVI. See also, *supra* ch. V, n. 179; Massey v. Arlitz [1923] V. L. R. 132, 136; Harrower, Welsh & Co. v. John M'William & Sons [1928] S. L. T. 315; Hyman-Michaels Co. v. Fox, 298 Fed. 440 (C. C. A. 2d, 1924). A unique decision is Henry Dean & Sons, Ltd. v. P. O'Day Pty., Ltd., 39 C. L. R. 330 (Aust. 1929). The buyer under a c.i.f. contract refused to accept and pay for the documents. The goods were later found to be defective. In the buyer's action for damages, the seller set up that the buyer was not ready and willing to perform. The court found for the buyer presumably on the ground that the wording of the invoice was such as reasonably to arouse suspicion. A well-reasoned dissent took the position that, the documents being technically correct, the refusal by the buyer to accept was unjustified. It is submitted that the general rule to be laid down is that where the buyer knows or has reasonable grounds for believing the goods to be defective, he may refuse to accept and pay for the documents and nevertheless recover damages for the seller if the goods on arrival actually prove to be defective. Where such refusal is arbitrary, he cannot recover, though goods are defective, and though he cannot be held obligated to perform, as he cannot be deemed to have been ready and willing to perform. See 3 Williston, Contracts (1921) § 1315.

[12] *Supra* note 1. The real defense there was that the bank was not certain that the goods were up to standard and wanted a test made. See *supra* p. 226.

credit. If the paper when delivered did not correspond to what had been purchased, either in weight, kind, or quality, then the purchaser had his remedy against the seller for damages. Whether the paper were what the purchaser contracted to purchase did not concern the bank and in no way affected its liability. . . . The bank was concerned only in the drafts and the documents accompanying them. This was the extent of its interest. If the drafts, when presented, were accompanied by the proper documents then it was absolutely bound to make the payment under the letter of credit, irrespective of whether it knew, or had reason to believe, that the paper was not of the tensile strength contracted for.[13]

---

[13] *Ibid.* at 395, 146 N. E. at 639, 39 A. L. R. at 751. See an excellent discussion of this case in (1925) 34 YALE L. J. 775; see also (1925) 25 COL. L. REV. 829; (1926) 74 U. OF PA. L. REV. 501, 503; and First Wisconsin Nat. Bank v. Forsyth Leather Co., 189 Wis. 9, 17, 206 N. W. 843, 846 (1926): "It is a general rule that the bank issuing an irrevocable letter of credit is not concerned with the quality or kind of goods delivered under the contract. Its sole duty is to see that the invoice and other required documents accompany the draft. If they are fair on their face, as required by the letter of credit, it is the duty of the bank to accept and pay the draft." See also De Sousa v. Crocker First Nat. Bank, 23 F. (2d) 118, 122 (N. D. Cal. 1927), *rev'd* on another point, 27 F. (2d) 462, 464 (C. C. A. 9th, 1928), *cert. den.*, 278 U. S. 650, 49 Sup. Ct. 94 (1928).

See however, Renfrow v. Citizens' State Bank, 158 N. E. 919 (Ind. App. 1927), *supra* ch. II, note 29, where the bank refused to honor a draft drawn by the plaintiff in reliance on a promise to accept made by the bank, on the ground that the goods were of inferior quality. "The contract between the parties resulting from the exchange of telegrams was, in effect, that appellee [the bank] would see that the consideration for the hogs was paid. It was a simple contract between the immediate parties thereto. Appellee knew from the telegram received from appellant [the seller] that a carload of hogs was to be shipped to N. E. Woods & Son, and knew the kind of hogs. Otherwise it might not have agreed to honor drafts for the price. The financial condition of N. E. Woods & Son might have been such that it would not have agreed to honor the draft, had it not been that N. E. Wood's & Son were to get the hogs, and the kind of hogs they were buying." (At 921.) It is submitted that the tenor of the opinion is for the most part contrary to the spirit of the decisions that have formulated the rules governing commercial credits. If anything is clear, it is that the rights between seller and issuing bank are not governed by the usual rules of contract. It is hardly likely that other courts will proceed on the basis indicated above. See also: Merchants Nat. Bank v. Citizens' State Bank, 93 Iowa 650, 61 N. W. 1065 (1895); First Nat. Bank v. Nat. Produce Bank, 239 Ill. App. 376, 390 (1926). The bank, in each of these cases, guaranteed payment of drafts on the buyer. The court in each case took this to mean a draft that the buyer was obligated to pay. Since the goods were defective, the buyer was not obligated to honor the draft; ergo, neither was the bank. "Since Butts never became liable on the draft, the guaranty of the defendant has never become operative, and there can be no recovery on it." Merchants Nat. Bank v. Citizens' State Bank, *ibid.*, at 653, 61 N. W. at 1066. These decisions are obviously influenced by the form of the transaction, and it is to be presumed that the rule will not be extended to the type of promise made

The dissenting opinion by Judge Cardozo took the opposite view:

> I think we lose sight of the true nature of the transaction when we view the bank as acting upon the credit of its customer to the exclusion of all else. It acts not merely upon the credit of its customer, but upon the credit also of the merchandise which is to be tendered as security. The letter of credit is explicit in its provision that documents sufficient to give control of the goods shall be lodged with the bank when drafts are presented. I cannot accept the statement of the majority opinion that the bank was not concerned with any question as to the character of the paper. If that is so, the bales tendered might have been rags instead of paper, and still the bank would have been helpless, though it had knowledge of the truth, if the documents tendered by the seller were sufficient on their face. . . . If the paper was of the quality stated in the defendant's answer, the documents were false.[14]

The dissent, it will be noticed, is based upon two grounds, the need for protection of the bank's security, and the fact that the majority rule would enable the seller fraudulently to ship worthless goods and so get his money even though the bank knew of

---

by banks which the courts class under the category of letters of credit. Certainly the reasoning would not be applicable where the bank promised to honor a draft drawn on itself. Furthermore, it should be noticed that the Merchants' Nat. Bank case was decided in 1895, long before there was any adequate comprehension of the nature of commercial letters of credit and similar instruments. Also in the National Produce Bank Case, decided in 1926, the court expressly refuses to rest its decision on the ground that the goods were defective in quality, though it states that, in its opinion, the views advanced in the former case seemed to have a great deal of force.

[14] Maurice O'Meara Co. v. Nat. Park Bank, *supra* note 1, at 402, 146 N. E. at 641, 39 A. L. R. at 755. It may perhaps be well to indicate that the recent case of Commercial Union of America v. Anglo-South American Bank, 16 F. (2d) 979 (C. C. A. 2d, 1927), does not represent a different point of view from the one indicated. The question involved in that case was the power of the bank to go behind the representations of a seller as to conditions not requiring documents. In the O'Meara case, the power of a bank to investigate certain stated documents is in question. Entirely different principles and considerations are involved there and the results of the two cases have no relation to each other. If, in the Commercial Union case, the letter of credit had called for payment against a *statement of the company* as to when the ship would sail and if the bank had attempted to go behind the statement to make its own investigations, the problem would have been identical with that in the O'Meara case, and it is submitted that a similar result would have been reached.

the fraud.[15] Considering the latter ground, it will presently be seen that where the bank alleges and shows reasonable proof of fraud on the part of the seller a totally different question arises. The bank in that case will be found not only to have the power, but also to be under a duty to the buyer, to refuse payment. Any great discrepancy, e .g., if "the bags tendered were rags instead of paper," would be prima facie evidence of fraud.[16] The law of sales generally recognizes a distinction between differences in kind and differences in quality. The former may well be a case of fraud. The latter seldom is. And despite the language used, it is doubtful if the dissenting opinion meant to imply that differences in quality are always fraudulent.

In regard to the highly technical question that arose in the *O'Meara* case as to whether the paper shipped was of the required tensile or bursting strength, there could very well be an honest difference of opinion. Actually, on the facts as they appear, there was no question of fraud. There was no allegation to that effect, and the whole tenor of the case seemed to represent a mere honest difference of opinion.

The other ground for the dissent, the protection of the bank's security, is valid when there is any possibility of a total loss, or something approaching it. This could occur only in cases where the documents were forged or fraudulent. In the discussion of these problems, it will be indicated that this is an additional reason for granting the bank the power to set these facts up as a basis for refusing to honor its letter of credit. The problem of the protection of the bank's security is however of less importance in this connection. The difference in the value represented is

---

[15] Parts of the dissenting opinion seem to indicate that it was based on the impression that, if the goods were not as represented, it was a case of fraud. If this is so, the difference between the majority and the minority opinions is merely one of interpretation of facts. If the majority had felt that there was fraud in this case, the defense would probably have been allowed.

[16] For a similar suggestion, see (1925) 38 HARV. L. REV. 1117, 1118; see also (1925) 9 MINN. L. REV. 656, 660.

often slight. Since the real reason for the buyer's refusal is usually that the market for the goods has dropped,[17] there is often a loss in the value of the security in any event. In addition, even if the market has remained steady, the bank does not expect, and usually does not actually realize, the entire amount of the sum advanced in a forced sale. Distress sales notoriously bring distress prices.

Finally, sound banking practice requires that the bank's control of the goods be only incidental as security and not the prime factor. The bank is a financial institution and engages in buying and selling goods only as a last resort to protect its advances. Conservative practice therefore requires that the main security for the issue of an irrevocable letter of credit be either collateral deposited by the buyer or his general credit standing.[18] Only if these fail does the bank look to the goods involved. It desires control of the goods not merely to secure its lien on them, but even more to prevent the buyer from obtaining control of them before he has paid the bank, or made some arrangements to that end. To require that the goods fulfill the conditions of the sales contract in every particular is unnecessary for these purposes. It is sufficient if the goods do so in a general way. In the absence of any great discrepancy between the description of the goods and their actual state, the bank can always realize approximately the same amount at a forced sale, whether or not the goods comply in all respects with the terms of the sales contract, and this, as has been pointed out, will in any event rarely be the full amount of the advance. Any glaring discrepancy is usually prima facie evidence of fraud, which raises an entirely different set of problems, to be considered presently.[19]

---

[17] See De Sousa v. Crocker First Nat. Bank, *supra* note 13, for an excellent illustration of the effect of a fall in the market on the buyer's conduct and the extent to which the bank may be influenced to dishonor its letter of credit.

[18] *Cf.* however Renfrow v. Citizens' State Bank, *supra* note 13.

[19] It has been held that if the seller admits that the goods were not of proper value, the bank can refuse to pay. See Lemon Importing Co. v.

This question of the power of the bank to refuse to honor its letter of credit has arisen between buyer and seller, in regard to other differences besides that of quality of the goods. In *Urquhart, Lindsay & Co.* v. *Eastern Bank,*[20] the seller included in his invoice certain increased costs of manufacture, to which he claimed he was entitled under the sales contract. The buyer directed the bank not to pay. The court allowed a recovery by the seller against the bank, holding that this was a matter between seller and buyer with which the bank had no concern.

The buyer having authorized his banker to undertake to pay the amount of the invoice as presented, it follows that any adjustment must be made by way of refund by the seller, and not by way of retention by the buyer.[21]

In *Imbrie* v. *D. Nagase & Co.,*[22] the bank paid the draft and the buyer having refused the goods, the bank brought an action against the seller for the amount of an overpayment due to a shortage in weight. The seller counterclaimed for damages for breach of contract by the buyer. To this counterclaim the bank demurred. The court stated in part:

Garfield Savings Bank Co., 105 Misc. 627, 629, 173 N. Y. Supp. 551, 552 (1919) *aff'd* without opinion, 187 App. Div. 932, 174 N. Y. Supp. 910 (1919). "In the consideration of the case at bar it is well to remember that the original parties to the transaction in question are the only parties now involved. . . . In view of the conceded fact that the lemons in question were not up to standard and failed to conform to the contract and that the United Fruit and Vegetable Company was justified in refusing to accept same in performance thereof, it must be held that plaintiff did not 'receive the bill for value.' This is clearly apparent not alone from the facts stipulated but from the very intent of the parties based thereon. The acceptance and honoring of the draft were dependent on plaintiff's performance of its contract in the terms mentioned and its conceded failure so to do strips the transaction of any consideration moving to defendant by plaintiff which would justify the claim of plaintiff as a holder of the draft for value." This was an action on a promise to accept as an acceptance. The court held that the admittedly inferior quality prevented the transfer from being deemed as made for value under the statute. See discussion, *supra* ch. II, p. 91. It is submitted, however, that this represents a somewhat different point of view from the O'Meara case and to that extent must be deemed overruled by the later decision.

[20] [1922] 1 K. B. 318.

[21] *Ibid.*, at 323.

[22] 196 App. Div. 380, 187 N. Y. Supp. 692 (1921).

> Having in the instant case, however, paid the drafts, and, as it claims, parted with its security, is it or its indemnitor entitled to maintain an action against the seller to recover the proceeds of the drafts? I think not. . . . The bank has been fully repaid by the indemnitor for its advances, and it would seem that if the plaintiff has any remedy it would be against Rothwell & Co. [the buyer], but we are not called upon to decide this question now. We have only to consider the propriety of the order appealed from. If plaintiffs are entitled to maintain the action against defendant, based on the defendant's agreement with Rothwell & Co., defendant's claims against Rothwell & Co. may be properly set up by way of counterclaim.[23]

From these cases, the general proposition may be laid down that the bank has not the power to set up as a defense an honest difference of opinion between buyer and seller as to quality, quantity, price, or any other element of the sales contract, provided the documents are in order, all other terms of the letter of credit fulfilled, and no question of fraud is involved, unless there be a specific provision in the letter of credit giving the bank such a privilege. This, all things considered, is a wise policy. That the goods fulfill in all details the requirements of the sales contract has already been indicated to be no real or necessary pro-

---

[23] *Ibid.* at 383, 187 N. Y. Supp. at 695. Old Colony Trust Co. v. Columbia Trust Co., 210 App. Div. 705, 206 N. Y. Supp. 257 (1924), is not in conflict with this decision. In the latter case, the bank, in suing for overpayment, alleged that payment against net landed weights meant, by the custom of the trade, payment against the weights as invoiced, with subsequent adjustment when the goods were weighed on arrival. On arrival, the goods were found to be short, and the bank sued for the amount of the overpayment. The defendant moved to dismiss the complaint, which raised the question of the sufficiency of the allegations as a cause of action. The court held that the complaint was sufficient and denied the motion. This is clearly sound, because if the custom of adjusting payments as alleged in the complaint was an implied term of the letter of credit, the bank could clearly sue to recover the amount overpaid. This has no bearing on the questions of whether the bank can sue either where there is no such custom; where it pays without knowledge of the custom; or where it refuses to pay because of lack of such knowledge. *Cf.* Old Colony Trust Co. v. Lawyers' Title & Trust Co., 297 Fed. 152, 156 (C. C. A. 2d, 1924), *cert. den.*, 265 U. S. 585, 44 Sup. Ct. 459 (1924), where the bank was held not to be bound by a similar custom and to be required to pay only after the net landed weights had actually been determined. The soundness of this decision is, however, doubtful. It may well be argued that the interpretation of net landed weights as requiring payment against documents with subsequent adjustment for shortages is one well known throughout foreign trade and one by which the bank may well be deemed to be bound, *supra* ch. V, p. 189.

tection of the bank's interest. Furthermore, to allow the bank to set up such a defense is to interfere with the proper workings of the letter of credit. If the bank can introduce matters that are problems primarily between buyer and seller, it is only reasonable and just to allow the seller to do likewise. *Imbrie* v. *D. Nagase & Co.*,[24] furnishes a good example of the confusion which would result from allowing the bank to set up such defenses. Even with the aid of the buyer, the bank is in no position to become involved in a controversy of this kind. In any such situation it must look to the buyer for reimbursement for the credit advanced. This does not mean that the buyer is at the seller's mercy. Practical devices which give him protection have been suggested and are in use.[25] To give the bank this legal weapon, affords it no real protection, and to a large extent merely throws upon it an additional burden which it is in no position to bear. This type of objection is the typical means used by the buyer in a falling market to avoid his contracts.[26] To give the bank the power to refuse payment on this ground is practically to put it under a commercial duty to the buyer to exercise such power, inasmuch as the bank would be compelled for business reasons to accede to the buyer's request and to refuse payment. The result would be to lessen materially the efficiency of the letter of credit as an instrument for the financing of trade.[27]

---

[24] *Supra* note 22.

[25] See discussion, *supra* ch. V, p. 219. Of course, the buyer always has an action against the seller, see e. g., Western Grocer Co. v. New York Oversea Co., 28 F. (2d) 518 (N. D. Cal. 1928).

[26] *Supra* note 17.

[27] Whether the bank can recover after payment to the seller or to the purchaser of the draft on the ground of payment under mistake of fact or for similar reasons, when it is able to show a non-fraudulent defect in the goods, is doubtful. In view of the general opinion that the bank is dealing in documents and not in goods, and because of the hesitancy in permitting questions as to the quality of the goods to be introduced in evidence when the relations between seller and bank are considered, several courts have decided that the bank does not have any such right of action. See Bank of Italy v. Colla, 118 Ohio St. 459, 161 N. E. 330 (1928); Bank of East Asia v. Pang, 140 Wash. 603, 249 Pac. 1060 (1926); Hibernia Bank & Trust Co. v. J. Aron & Co., 134 Misc. 18, 233 N. Y. Supp. 486 (1928). The court, in denying a recovery against the seller in the

Since the seller can recover against the bank irrespective of the question of the performance of the contract, it follows that a subsequent holder, whether for value or not and whether with or without notice, can likewise recover.[28]

Since the bank is under a duty to pay the seller or the purchaser under these circumstances, it follows, in considering the relationship between bank and buyer, that the bank can recover against the buyer after such payment even though it knew of the buyer's claim at the time of payment.

> Before the defendant paid the draft it was notified by the plaintiff that the grapes did not comply with the requirements of the contract but were much inferior thereto and it was notified or requested not to pay the draft. We do not think that it is very earnestly urged by the plaintiff that this fact changed the relations and rights of the parties. It did not. . . . The question between the customer and the vendor is the one whether the goods comply with the contract and if they do not the former has his

---

second case relied on the O'Meara case though noting the distinction between an action by the seller to compel the bank to pay and an action by the bank to recover a payment previously made. See also Imbrie v. D. Nagase & Co., *supra* note 22, discussed *supra* p. 232.

[28] Bank of Plant City v. Canal-Commercial Bank, 270 Fed. 477 (C. C. A. 5th, 1921); Clinch County Bank v. Wyatt-Prock Lumber Co., 82 Pa. Super. Ct. 305 (1923); Roberts v. Drovers' Nat. Bank, 199 Ky. 439, 251 S. W. 198 (1923); Alex Woldert Co. v. Citizens' Bank, 234 S. W. 124 (Tex. Civ. App. 1921). See El Paso Bank & Trust Co. v. First State Bank, 202 S. W. 522 (Tex. Civ. App. 1918) where, in a suit by the bona fide purchaser of a draft against the issuing bank, based on an instrument which the court interpreted as an unconditional guaranty, evidence of poor quality etc. in the goods shipped was held to be no defense. See also the language of the court in Renfrow v. Citizens' State Bank, quoted *supra* note 13. Where the buyer issues his own letter of credit, the same results follow as to bona fide purchasers from the seller; Hall v. First Nat. Bank, 133 Ill. 234, 24 N. E. 546 (1890); Fruit Growers State Bank v. Peters, 181 Ill. App. 432 (1913); American Nat. Bank v. Pillman, 176 Mo. App. 430, 158 S. W. 433 (1913); Whilden v. Merchants' & Planters' Nat. Bank, 64 Ala. 1 (1879). The seller and purchaser with notice are in the same position as the usual seller under a c.i.f. contract. The issuance of a formal statement by the buyer that he will accept drafts cannot be deemed to alter the situation. A similar problem arises when a seller discounts a draft which is drawn on a buyer with documents attached, and the buyer, after paying the draft, discovers that the goods are not up to standard in some way. He sues the purchaser of the draft. The general rule was that the purchaser was not liable. Under the Uniform Bills of Lading Act, some confusion has arisen, owing to conflicting interpretations of its provisions, but the weight of opinion is that the rule still holds. See authorities cited *infra* note 39, where the analogous problem in regard to forgery of documents is considered.

appropriate right of action. The question between the customer and the bank which issues the letter of credit is whether the documents presented with the draft fulfill the specific requirements and if they do, speaking of such facts as exist in this case, the bank has the right to pay the draft no matter what may be the defects in the goods which have been shipped. The bank is not obliged to assume the burdens of a controversy between the vendor and vendee and incur the responsibility of establishing as an excuse for not paying a draft that the vendee's version is the correct one.[29]

Even the other view which holds that the bank has the privilege of refusing payment to the seller on this ground, if it should so desire, would still maintain that the bank is under no such duty.[30]

Correspondingly, it has been held that no injunction will be granted at the request of a buyer against a bank to prevent it from paying a draft to the seller drawn under a letter of credit, on the ground that the goods shipped were of inferior quality[31] or that the facts were not as represented in the bill of lading, where, however, no fraud was alleged.[32]

B. Forged Documents

A bona fide purchaser obviously cannot acquire any rights on a draft where the drawer's signature has been forged or where there has been any unauthorized material change in the draft or letter of credit.[33] Short of this, the matter is not so simple.

---

[29] Laudisi v. American Exch. Nat. Bank, 239 N. Y. 234, 243, 146 N. E. 347, 350 (1924); Benecke v. Haebler, 38 App. Div. 344, 58 N. Y. Supp. 16 (1899), *aff'd* without opinion, 166 N. Y. 631, 60 N. E. 1107 (1901); see also Tocco v. Bank of Italy, 249 Mass. 267, 143 N. E. 905 (1924).

[30] Maurice O'Meara Co. v. Nat. Park Bank, 239 N. Y. 386, 401, 146 N. E. 636, 641, 39 A. L. R. 747, 754 (1925) (dissent) quoted *supra* ch. IV, p. 149.

[31] Williams Ice Cream Co. v. Chase Nat. Bank, 210 App. Div. 179, 180, 181, 205 N. Y. Supp. 446, 447, 448 (1924). The case turned on another point, but these reasons were expressly held not to constitute grounds for an injunction.

[32] Ideal Cocoa & Chocolate Co. v. De Magalhaes, 64 N. Y. L. J., Jan. 18, 1921, at 1324. In connection with the issuance of formal letters of credit, the terms of the agreement to reimburse usually provide that the bank is not to be held responsible for the quality, quantity, etc., of the goods. See Appendix A.

[33] See Orr & Barber v. Union Bank of Scotland, 24 L. T. O. S. 1 (1854); Lewis v. Kramer, 3 Md. 265 (1852). The bank, on payment,

A more difficult question arises when the bank asserts that the documents are forged. In this case, as we have already seen under a c.i.f. contract, the buyer was under no duty to pay if the forgery could be established. In most cases under a letter of credit, the question would arise as a result of information furnished the bank by the buyer. The latter would inform the bank that documents presented or about to be presented were forged and would request the bank not to honor the draft. In considering the question from the point of view of the relationship between the seller and the bank, two views of the situation may be taken: that the bank cannot raise the issue and is obligated to pay the seller if the documents apparently conform; or that the bank has the power either to set this up as a defense or to

---

cannot charge the buyer, and if the latter has paid the bank, he can recover such payments. See British Linen Co. v. Wilson 4 L. T. N. S. 162 (1861). The analogy to forgery of checks, etc., is too obvious to need comment. On the authority of Price v. Neal, 3 Burr. 1355, 97 Eng. R. 871 (1762) and Section 62 of the Negotiable Instruments Law, apparently the bank cannot recover after paying a bona fide purchaser of the forged draft. BRANNAN, NEGOTIABLE INSTRUMENTS LAW (4th ed. 1926) 555 *et seq.* Where a purchaser has been discounting drafts drawn by a partnership under a letter of credit, and discounts a draft drawn in the usual form after the partnership has been dissolved, he has been allowed to recover. See the dissenting opinion, however. Huston v. Newgass, 234 Ill. 285, 84 N. E. 910 (1908). It might be contended that when an advising bank honors a forged draft, the seller, on drawing a proper draft, can recover against the advising bank if it should dishonor his draft, even though normally an advising bank is under no duty to the seller to honor drafts. See Gissing v. Hopper, 6 Up. Can. Q. B. (O. S.) 505 (1843). In the case of checks, there is authority to the effect that a bank is bound to pay the holder, if it has paid the check on a forged endorsement, such payment being treated as an acceptance. Wayne Tank & Pump Co. v. Bank of Eureka Springs, 172 Ark. 775, 290 S. W. 370 (1927); 2 MORSE, BANKS & BANKING (6th ed. 1928) § 474; see also Dawson v. Nat. Bank of Greenville, 144 S. E. 833 (N. C. 1928). The majority view seems to be *contra*, see First Nat. Bank v. Whitman, 94 U. S. 343, 24 L. Ed. 229 (1876); Gordon Fireworks Co. v. Capital Nat. Bank, 236 Mich. 271, 210 N. W. 263 (1926), BRANNAN, NEGOTIABLE INSTRUMENTS LAW (4th ed. 1926) 907 and cases there cited. See also Aigler, *Rights of the Holder of Bill of Exchange against the Drawee* (1925) 38 HARV. L. REV. 857, 878; (1927) 25 MICH. L. REV. 454. It is suggested in Brannan that the only right of the holder is to have the check returned to him. It is only on the refusal of the bank to do this, that an action will lie. The action is not on the check but for the conversion of the instrument, the measure of damages being the amount of the check. The same result, it is submitted, should follow in the case of a forged draft drawn under a letter of credit, if the advising bank should refuse to surrender the latter instrument.

interplead the buyer. To deny this power to the bank would be, as the relations between the parties have been analyzed, to give the bank a right against the buyer and then to compel the latter to sue the seller for redress. Other things being equal, the simpler solution would be to deprive the seller of any rights against the bank, since allowing him rights under these conditions would be to open wide the door to fraud.

It may be argued that, since the bank is only financing the transaction, it is interested merely in the apparent performance of the conditions of the letter of credit. The basic facts on which they rest should, therefore, be left for adjustment between the parties immediately concerned, and the bank should be compelled to stay out of these controversies. The rule laid down in regard to non-fraudulent breaches of the sales contract should, for similar considerations, be carried to its logical conclusion. To consider merely this factor is to have but an imperfect view of the situation. While the bank cannot be regarded as interested in exact detailed performance of the sales contract, e. g., that the "newsprint paper be of certain tensile strength," it is vitally interested in assuring itself that there are some goods represented by the documents and that the shipment is not "rags instead of paper." While the prime factor in the issuance of commercial credits should be the credit standing of the indemnitor, the security afforded by the goods may also be taken into account. The actual existence of these goods is, therefore, a matter of great importance to the issuing bank.[34] It is therefore highly important to give the bank this power to interplead the buyer, that it may properly protect itself. This in effect achieves the same result as is reached under a c.i.f. contract. The buyer would have the burden of proving that the allegation of forgery was true.[35]

---

[34] Maurice O'Meara Co. v. Nat. Park Bank, *supra* note 30, at 402, 146 N. E. at 639, 39 A. L. R. at 755 (dissent) quoted *supra* p. 229.

[35] Even if the bank does not interplead the buyer, no great hardship is thrown upon it. The seller in order to put the documents in evidence at the trial would have to make out at least a prima facie case of their validity.

There is an additional consideration. The buyer authorizes payment against certain documents. Obviously he means genuine documents. A forged document does not fulfill the condition, and the bank in paying against it, knowing it to be forged, is exceeding its authority.

> Obviously, when the issuer of a letter of credit knows that a document, although correct in form, is, in point of fact, false or illegal, he cannot be called upon to recognize such a document as complying with the terms of a letter of credit.[36]

A purchaser with notice of the forgery clearly acquires no greater rights than the seller and therefore cannot recover against the bank.[37] A problem arises only when the purchaser has bought innocently[38] and this may occur at any one of three stages: (1) before acceptance, on the refusal to accept; (2) after acceptance, on the refusal to pay; (3) or after payment, in a suit by the bank to recover back the money paid. Most of the cases have fallen within the last group. The great majority deny a recovery to the bank.[39]

---

[36] Old Colony Trust Co. v. Lawyers' Title & Trust Co., *supra* note 23, at 158. Where the seller is not the drawer of the draft and sues on the credit as a virtual or extrinsic acceptance, certain statutory problems arise because of the provisions of the Negotiable Instruments Law that the holder must have given value for the draft, see *supra* ch. II, page 89 *et seq.*

[37] That the bank can recover against the seller or the purchaser of the draft with notice of the forgery, because of the fraud practiced upon the bank, seems obvious.

[38] Reasonable care must be used in examining the documents. If he be grossly negligent, he cannot recover. There is no case directly in point. The problem has arisen, however, as between bank and buyer, *infra* p. 245, in regard to fraudulent documents, *infra* pp. 246, 247 and in an action by a bona fide purchaser of a draft with forged documents attached against the acceptor; Goetz v. Bank of Kansas City, 119 U. S. 551, 7 Sup. Ct. 318, 30 L. Ed. 515 (1887).

[39] Woodward, Quasi Contracts (1913) § 91; 2 Daniel, Negotiable Instruments (6th ed. 1913) § 1734d. Springs v. Hanover Nat. Bank, 209 N. Y. 224, 103 N. E. 156, 52 L. R. A. (N. S.) 241 (1913); Young & Son v. Lehman, Durr & Co. 63 Ala. 519 (1878); Leather v. Simpson, L. R. 11 Eq. 398 (1871); *cf.* however, First Nat. Bank v. Kempner, 103 Okla. 237, 229 Pac. 840 (1924). It is clear that if the buyer pays the bank and sues the bona fide purchaser, he also cannot recover. Guaranty Trust Co. v. Hannay & Co., [1918] 2 K. B. 623; Guaranty Trust Co. v. Hannay, 210 Fed. 810 (C. C. A. 2d. 1913), distinguishing, Hannay v. Guaranty Trust Co., 187 Fed. 686 (C. C. S. D. N. Y. 1911). A similar problem arises when the buyer, without having made any previous promise, pays the bona fide purchaser of a draft, then discovers that the attached documents are forged, and sues. Here, too, he cannot recover. Hoffman & Co. v. Bank of

This is doubtless sound. Any other view would make the purchaser a guarantor of the validity of the documents, thus tending to hamper and to restrict the natural growth and development of commerce. Purchasers of drafts and documents would incline to buy only from well established and widely reputed firms. The rate of discount to newer and less well established firms would be much greater, and it would often be impossible to negotiate the draft on any terms.

The only legal argument that has been adduced for permitting the bank to recover in this situation is that the money, having been paid under a mistake of fact, should therefore be repaid. Of this the United States Supreme Court has said:

> Money paid under a mistake of facts, it is said, may be recovered back as having been paid without consideration, but the decisive answer to that suggestion, . . . is that money paid, as in this case, by the acceptor of a bill of exchange to the payee of the same or to a subsequent indorsee, in discharge of his legal obligation as such, is not a payment by mistake nor without consideration, unless it be shown that the instrument was fraudulent in its inception, or that the consideration was illegal, or that the facts and circumstances which impeach the transaction, as between

---

Milwaukee, 12 Wall. 181, 20 L. Ed. 366 (1870); First Nat. Bank v. Burkham, 32 Mich. 328 (1875). For a similar ruling denying liability for the validity of the documents, of a bank acting as a collection agency, see Nebraska Hay & Grain Co. v. First Nat. Bank, 78 Neb. 334, 110 N. W. 1019, 9 L. R. A. (N. S.) 251 (1907); Jacobs v. Banque Pour le Commerce, etc., 131 Misc. 162, 225 N. Y. Supp. 410 (1927). There are cases *contra*, Guaranty Trust Co. v. Grotrian, 114 Fed. 433, 57 L. R. A. 689 (C. C. A. 2d, 1902), *cert. den.*, 186 U. S. 483, 22 Sup. Ct. 943 (1902). This case rested mainly on the ground that the acceptance was conditional and that therefore the bona fide purchaser was subject to all the equities against the original drawer. See also the comment on the case in Hannay v. Guaranty Trust Co., *ibid.* See also Allen & Co. v. Hornor, 2 McGloin 177 (La. 1884); (1919) 32 HARV. L. REV. 560. Before the Uniform Bills of Lading Act it was clear that the bona fide purchaser was not responsible. See WILLISTON, SALES (1st ed. 1909) § 435 *et seq.* (1919) 32 HARV. L. REV. 560, 562. Under the Uniform Bills of Lading Act, this is less certain. In spite of some decisions to the contrary, the better opinion still is that he is not liable. See (1926) 26 COL. L. REV. 63, and comment thereon by Professor Williston at p. 330; see also Moses, *Implied Warranties under the Uniform Bills of Lading Act* (1927) 27 COL. L. REV. 251. The bona fide purchaser may guarantee the validity of the documents, but the court is loath to interpret any acts in this connection as a guaranty unless they are very clear. Leather v. Simpson, *ibid.*; Baxter v. Chapman, 29 L. T. N. S. 642 (1873).

the acceptor and the drawer, were known to the payee or subsequent indorsee at the time he became the holder of the instrument.[40]

The Supreme Court, therefore, refused to apply the doctrine of money paid under a mistake of fact in this type of case and laid down what is doubtless the sound rule, that the bank cannot recover against the bona fide purchaser. Where the bank discovers the forgery of the documents attached to the draft before payment and refuses to pay, it has been held that a bona fide purchaser may compel payment. This rule applies not only where the bank refuses payment after acceptance[41] but also, it is submitted, where the bank refuses to accept.[42] The factors leading to this result are similar with, perhaps, an additional element, to those involved in the inability of the bank to recover money paid against forged documents.

It may be argued that since both parties are innocent the loss should lie where it first fell, *i. e.*, on the bona fide purchaser in

---

[40] Hoffman & Co. v. Bank of Milwaukee, *supra* note 39, at 189, 20 L. Ed. at 368. Similarly where the holder of a check obtains payment from a bank, after the drawer has requested the latter not to honor the check, or where the check is drawn against insufficient funds, the bank cannot recover the money if the holder received it without knowledge that the drawer had stopped payment or had drawn against insufficient funds. 2 MORSE, BANKS AND BANKING (6th ed. 1928) 990, 1001; BRADY, BANK CHECKS (2d ed. 1926) 367, 418; (1923) 32 YALE L. J. 733. Citizens' Bank v. Schwarzschild & Sulzberger Co., 109 Va. 539, 64 S. E. 954, 23 L. R. A. (N. S.) 1092 (1909); Riverside Bank v. First Nat. Bank, 74 Fed. 276 (C. C. A. 2d, 1896); Miller v. Chatham and Phoenix Bank, 126 Misc. 559, 214 N. Y. Supp. 76 (1926): "The above cited rule is in accord with commercial practice and is essential to business stability." Contra: Nat. Loan & Exch. Bank v. Lachovitz, 131 S. C. 432, 128 S. E. 10, 39 A. L. R. 1237 (1925). While the drawee bank can probably recover the amount paid to a bona fide holder of a check, if the endorsement has been forged or the amount altered, see Frederic C. Woodward, *Risk of Forgery or Alteration of Negotiable Instruments* (1924) 24 COL. L. REV. 469, 474, 475; this situation can be distinguished from that under discussion because of the different commercial considerations involved.

[41] Goetz v. Bank of Kansas City, *supra* note 38; Craig v. Sibbett, 15 Pa. 238 (1851); Robinson v. Reynolds, 2 Q. B. 196 (1841). Baxter v. Chapman, *supra* note 39, holds that an acceptor cannot sue in equity for a declaration that, because of the forged documents attached, he is not liable on the bill of exchange as acceptor.

[42] No case in point has been found. In connection with fraudulent documents, a similar case has arisen and recovery was allowed. See *infra* p. 246.

this instance.[43] The commercial considerations against this conclusion are overwhelming. Two questions are involved here: whether the purchaser guarantees the validity of the documents; and whether the conditions of the promise have been sufficiently performed when there is apparent conformity. Legal analogies and legal arguments furnish no answer in this case. They can be used to support either conclusion. The problem is to determine what is preferable commercially. From this point of view, the more desirable result is doubtless to free the bona fide purchaser of all such responsibility. The buyer selects his seller, and he should assume the responsibility for his honesty. The purchaser is merely negotiating drafts. He does this mainly on the security of the credit standing of the drawer and drawee. The documents are merely additional collateral security. To say that the bona fide purchaser guarantees their validity is to misstate the facts as they occur. Nothing is further from his mind. To hold that a compliance with the conditions of a letter of credit includes an investigation of the actual state of facts behind those documents, is to create a rule of law and a requirement for conduct which is not only in violation of commercial practices, but is also impracticable and undesirable, in view both of the manner in which these transactions are conducted and of the necessity for prompt action. It is essential, both in the interests of commerce and in order to carry into effect the actual intentions of the parties, that bona fide purchasers be protected in this type of case.

It was not the intention of the appellees, so far as their intention can be collected from the letter, that the bank or banker discounting on its faith the draft of Johnston, should inquire whether Johnston was dealing fairly with them—furnishing them adequate security for their acceptance or payment of the draft. Devolving such a duty on the bank or banker, by the embarrassments which would necessarily follow, would so seriously impair the negotiability of the draft, that the very purposes of the letter of credit would

---

[43] Thiedemann v. Goldschmidt, 1 Giff. 142, 149, 65 Eng. R. 860, 863 (1859). The decision was reversed on appeal, 1 D. F. & J. 4, 45 Eng. R. 260 (1859).

be defeated. All the bank or banker was bound to do, was to see that bills of lading, professing on their face, in the ordinary form, to represent a consignment of cotton to the appellees, accompanied the draft, and that the draft was not in excess of the proper amount. The assurance of the letter of credit was, that such a draft would be paid by the appellees on presentment.[44]

[44] Young & Son v. Lehman, Durr & Co., *supra* note 39, at 525. It should be noted that it is the opinion of Professor Karl N. Llewellyn and other authorities that the bona fide purchaser of a draft with forged documents attached, acquires on dishonor of the draft no rights against the issuing bank, when the draft was purchased before actual acceptance by the bank. This view is based on the following grounds: (1) That the security represented by the goods is of importance to the bank, which should not be compelled to pay where such security does not exist; (2) that an implied condition of the credit is that the documents shall be genuine, the bona fide purchaser being as well aware of this condition as the seller, so that it should likewise operate against him; (3) that the bona fide purchaser is generally closer to the point of the alleged shipment and is, therefore, in a better position to discover the forgery; (4) that the drawer's signature on the draft must be genuine, to enable a purchaser to compel honor after discovery and before acceptance or payment, and that similar considerations operate in respect to the documents; and (5) that to permit the bona fide purchaser of a draft with fraudulent documents attached to recover against the bank, is as far as the rule protecting bona fide purchasers can be extended, the bank, moreover, in the case of fraudulent documents, usually having a right of action against the carrier, and such documents being difficult of detection on the part of a bona fide purchaser. Several considerations should be noted in connection with these factors. The importance of the first two factors—indeed of all of them—should not be minimized. When the seller presents the draft and documents, it is primarily for one of the first two reasons that recovery is denied. When the draft and documents pass into the hands of a bona fide purchaser, it is submitted that considerations of free passage of commercial paper and the methods of transacting this type of business, as indicated above, overbalance all considerations to the contrary. The third reason would not generally apply to through bills of lading or even railroad bills of lading in this country, though it might apply to steamship bills of lading. As to the fourth item, it is submitted that the analogy is poor. In the case of forged documents, the buyer may well be held responsible for the fraud of a seller whom he has selected. In the case of a forged draft, the seller has not acted; the buyer, therefore, cannot be responsible. The last distinction mentioned is sound, but it is difficult to see how it can overbalance the general considerations which have been suggested in this discussion. The solution of this problem must depend upon commercial practice, not upon technical analogies. It is submitted that the commercial considerations suggested here should result in giving the bona fide purchaser adequate protection, even though the documents be forged. The factors we have been considering, however, cannot apply to bona fide purchasers of drafts after acceptance. The documents being usually detached upon acceptance, the purchaser not only cannot examine them but, as he seldom sees the letter of credit, he does not even know of what they consist. In addition, the bank, by accepting the draft, has by implication represented that the documents are sufficient. Finally, the law is well settled that the bona fide purchaser of an accepted draft is not responsible for the validity of the documents, *supra* p. 239.

In considering the relationship between bank and buyer, where the bank has paid the bona fide purchaser, it has a right to be indemnified by the buyer, as indicated by the principles previously discussed, even though the bank knew the documents were forged at the time it paid the draft.[45] When the seller presents the draft, it has been shown that the bank, when it has knowledge of the forgery, has the privilege of refusing payment and the power to interplead the parties. That the bank is under a duty to refuse payment does not, however, follow. A determination of that question involves a slightly different set of considerations. It may well be argued in this type of case that the bank is still under no duty to refuse payment; that it is privileged to pay, but that it should not be compelled to do so. In other words, it may pay the seller and recover from the buyer, even though it has information that the documents are forged. A bank is a financial institution. Its primary function is to finance the enterprise. It may sturdily maintain that it is neither equipped nor inclined to enter into such disputes and that if it is willing to take the risk of a loss of part of its security, the buyer can hardly complain. On the other hand, there is the risk of fraud being practiced on the buyer. To have the immediate parties interplead would be no great inconvenience to the bank. The interference with free commercial activity would be slight. Questions of forgery do not arise every day. Nor is so serious an allegation generally made without some reasonable ground. To put the bank under a duty to refuse payment would be to protect the necessary interests of the buyer. As the burden of proof would be on the buyer, this duty would not seriously affect the seller's position. This rule would not limit his rights to any greater extent than is done under a c.i.f. contract. It cannot affect the bank to any considerable degree nor involve

---

[45] Brown v. C. Rosenstein Co., 120 Misc. 787, 200 N. Y. Supp. 491 (1923), *aff'd* without opinion, 208 App. Div. 799, 203 N. Y. Supp. 922 (1924). It also follows that the buyer may not enjoin the payment of a draft in the hands of a bona fide purchaser. Thiedemann v. Goldschmidt, *supra* note 43.

it in any lawsuit in a serious way, since the bank need merely require the parties to interplead. Since the resulting inconvenience to commercial transactions would be slight, the result reached is certainly desirable.[46] That such must be presumed to have been the intention of the parties cannot be doubted, inasmuch as it is impossible to suppose that the buyer in any event authorized payment against forged bills of lading.

The bank must use reasonable care. If the instruments are so worded or have so unusual an appearance as to put the reasonable and prudent man on inquiry, the bank should be held under a duty to pursue that inquiry or file a bill of interpleader. The test is one of good faith. Where the bank pays in ignorance of any forgery and without any reasonable grounds for suspecting the validity of the documents, it has a right to indemnification agains the buyer.[47] To impose upon the bank a duty to investigate the validity of documents would be as onerous as a similar duty in respect to the quality of the goods. Also, its position is much like that of the bona fide purchaser. In view of commercial usage, the bank cannot be held to have guaranteed the validity of the documents or to have undertaken a duty to go behind the apparent performance of the conditions to verify the facts seemingly represented by them.

Of course, this wire contemplated and could be understood only as meaning true bills of lading for no one would authorize payment on forged, worthless, bills of lading. However, such an

---

[46] Unfortunately, interpleader is not always the simple and certain remedy which it should be, Chafee, *Modernizing Interpleader* (1921) 30 YALE L. J. 814. Special provision is however often made for banks because of the frequency with which rival claims arise as to money on deposit. N. Y. BANKING LAW (1914) §§ 113, 199. It is submitted that this type of protection should be extended to cover the case in which no money is on deposit, the question being whether the bank is obligated to accept a draft. Section 193 (2) of the New York Civil Practice Act represents a step in this direction.

[47] Woods v. Thiedemann, 1 H. & C. 478, 158 Eng. R. 973 (1862); Ulster Bank v. Synnott, I. R. 5 Eq. 595 (1871); W. A. Havemeyer & Co. v. Exch. Nat. Bank, 293 Fed. 311 (C. C. A. 8th, 1923); see also Bank of New York & Trust Co. v. Atterbury Bros., 226 App. Div. 117, 234 N. Y. Supp. 442 (1929).

instruction is far different from one requiring the defendant to ascertain at its peril that such bills were genuine and thus become an absolute insurer thereof. Such an added onerous obligation is unusual in like business dealings and will not legally attach unless it be shown that such added obligation was understood and undertaken by the parties. The rule of law ordinarily applying is that the agent shall use reasonable care in ascertaining that the bills offered are genuine. There is no evidence from which we can infer that the parties intended any such unusual meaning and resultant obligations as contended for by plaintiff.[48]

C. Fraudulent Documents

The problem that arises when the documents attached to the draft were fraudulently procured is very similar to the problem of forged documents. The documents may be fraudulently issued by the seller himself or may be fraudulently procured by the seller from a third party. In either event, when documents are issued or procured through fraud it would be difficult to distinguish the case on principle from a pure forgery. It is true that the problem is not so easily solved. When documents are fraudulently procured, however, as in the issuance of a bill of lading or an insurance policy, the question of fraud involves no great subtleties. All that has been said in connection with forgery also applies here. The seller cannot recover against the bank. The bona fide purchaser, however, not having been negligent in examining the documents, does acquire rights against the bank.

That the date of the bills of lading did not truthfully represent the date of the beginning of actual transportation would be a

[48] Havemeyer & Co. v. Exch. Nat. Bank, *supra* note 47, at 312; see also McCurdy, *Commercial Letters of Credit* (1922) 35 Harv. L. Rev. 715, 734, 735. It should also be noted that the modern form of agreement to reimburse protects the bank in paying against forged documents, see Appendix A. These provisions are doubtless effective, Bank of New York & Trust Co. v. Atterbury Bros., *supra* note 47, at 123, 234 N. Y. Supp. at 449. It is submitted, however, that they apply only where the bank pays in ignorance of the forgery. They do not cover the situation where the bank has knowledge of the forgery, either when the draft is presented by the seller or by a bona fide purchaser.

defense, if it can constitute a defense, if, and only if, the plaintiff knew that fact when it acquired the draft.[49]

Accordingly, the bank recovers against the buyer when it has paid the seller, without notice, or a bona fide purchaser, if it has used reasonable care in examining the documents.[50] When the bank receives notice, however, it is under a duty to refuse to pay the seller, and to protect itself it may interplead the seller and the buyer.[51]

In dealing with documents issued by the seller himself, such as the seller's invoice, the difficulty often is to determine whether he was fraudulent or whether the dispute represents a difference of opinion between seller and buyer. Certain cases are clear. There can be no doubt that the seller is fraudulent when his invoice describes Manilla hemp and he actually ships cotton rags.[52] Other cases are more difficult, e. g., when the dispute is over the question of whether grapes are of a certain quality,[53] or whether paper is of a certain bursting strength.[54] A distinction must be drawn between the fraudulent and non-fraudulent acts of the buyer. The only difficulty is in determining at what point the distinction

---

[49] Bank of Taiwan v. Union Nat. Bank, 1 F. (2d) 65, 66 (C. C. A. 3d, 1924). For a similar result in the case of a buyer's letter of credit, see Vallé v. Cerré, 36 Mo. 575, 591 (1865). If, however, the purchaser knows, or should have known, that the documents are fraudulent he cannot recover. See Old Colony Trust Co. v. Lawyers' Title & Trust Co., 297 Fed. 152 (C. C. A. 2d, 1924), *cert. den.*, 265 U. S. 585, 44 Sup. Ct. 459 (1924).

[50] Basse & Selve v. Bank of Australasia, 90 L. T. R. 618 (1904). Similarly, the bank, on learning of the fraud, cannot recover from the bona fide purchaser after the latter has been paid, *supra* note 39.

[51] It has, accordingly, been held that the buyer can enjoin the bank from paying the seller when the documents were fraudulently obtained. See Higgins v. Steinhardter, 106 Misc. 168, 175 N. Y. Supp. 279 (1919); also discussion of this case, *supra* ch. IV, p. 172. As in the case of forged documents, *supra* pp. 244, 245, the bank can recover after paying the seller or the purchaser who took with notice that the documents were fraudulently obtained.

[52] Bank of Montreal v. Recknagel, 109 N. Y. 482, 17 N. E. 217 (1888).

[53] Laudisi v. American Exch. Nat. Bank, 239 N. Y. 234, 146 N. E. 347 (1924).

[54] Maurice O'Meara Co. v. Nat. Park Bank, 239 N. Y. 386, 146 N. E. 636, 39 A. L. R. 747 (1925).

should be made. Certainly, the mere assertion by the bank or buyer that the seller has fraudulently misrepresented goods should not be sufficient to enable a bank to refuse to pay on this ground. The bank or the buyer should be compelled to show such facts as make an inference of fraud reasonable, such as a great discrepancy between the goods and the description in the documents, or a gross overvaluation.[55] At any rate, the legal principle is clear. Where the bank can show that the seller has acted fraudulently, it is under no duty to pay the seller. The bona fide purchaser, however, is entitled to be paid.

> The bank [the bona fide purchaser] omitted to procure a letter of advice to accompany the drafts, which, if it had done, would have protected it, although the advice was false in fact.[56]

D. Effect of Seller's Fraud in Inducing Buyer to Enter Sales Contract

The considerations raised by this problem are closely analogous to those involved in the effect of a breach of contract by the seller and must be carefully distinguished from the allegation that the documents are fraudulent. In the latter situation, the bank has a right to refuse payment. Here, it is generally assumed there is no such right. The basis for the distinction is clear. The question of the seller's fraud in inducing the buyer to enter the sales contract is not one with which the bank is in any way concerned. The documents are admittedly sufficient. The goods are as represented

---

[55] Bank of East Asia v. Pang, 140 Wash. 603, 612, 249 Pac. 1060, 1063 (1926). "It is alleged in the complaint in the present case that there was failure of consideration and fraud, but these allegations are based upon the fact that the products shipped were not of the kind and quality contracted for by the Sang Lee Company. As already pointed out, this is a question which cannot be inquired into when the action is by the bank against the seller of the product or by the seller of the product against the bank."

[56] Germania Nat. Bank v. Taaks, 101 N. Y. 442, 450, 5 N. E. 76, 80 (1886). The relations between bank and buyer here involve the same principles as in the case of forged documents discussed *supra* p. 244. The bank can recover against the buyer when, without knowledge of the fraud,

in the documents. The bank, therefore, has everything it could have expected to obtain. On the other hand, all the considerations urged against giving the bank this power in the case of non-fraudulent breaches of contract apply here with doubled force. Such power would in effect involve the bank in long and arduous lawsuits in which difficult and subtle points would have to be determined. In addition, if there could ever be a question between buyer and seller with which the bank would have no concern, this is an example of it par excellence. That this is no ground for a refusal to honor drafts is generally recognized in commercial and banking practice and, where the problem has arisen, the cases have reflected this attitude.[57]

---

it pays the seller or when it pays a bona fide purchaser. *Cf.* McCauley v. Georgia Railroad Bank, 245 N. Y. 245, 157 N. E. 125 (1927). When the seller presents the documents and the bank is informed of the fraud, it is under a duty to refuse payment.

[57] This is clearly the rule when the buyer has not rescinded. Even in the case of a guaranty by a party not a bank, the seller's conduct affords no basis for defense to a guarantor, though not a banking institution, unless the buyer rescinds. Reese v. W. T. Rawleigh Medical Co., 115 Ark. 606, 172 S. W. 820, 821 (1914). See also *infra* p. 258. When the buyer has rescinded, the matter is not so clear, though in view of the discussion above, it would seem that the same rule should apply. The question of whether or not the letter of credit requires documents to be presented with the drafts, should not affect the decision. See Bulliet v. Allegheny Trust Co., 284 Pa. 561, 567, 131 Atl. 471, 474, 42 A. L. R. 1133, 1137, (1925). "The third and real defense attempted by the defendant [bank] was to put itself in the position of Mitchell [buyer] and to make the defense against the check that he might have made if he had still been liable on it, and to show as incidental to this defense that the plaintiff [seller] had no record title to the property on account of which the check was given. In being permitted to make the defense which Mitchell might have made, appellant was accorded a greater privilege than it was entitled to. As between it and the plaintiff, no such defense was available. Its undertaking was absolute and unconditional to honor the check and it could not by interposing a defense available to Mitchell repudiate what it had bound itself to do. To hold otherwise it would be necessary to ignore the effect of the certification of a check at the instance of the holder." The action was on a promise to accept a check as amounting to a certification thereof. The drawer had requested the bank not to honor the certification, on the ground that the seller had breached the contract, which was still purely executory. No offer of restitution was therefore necessary on the part of the drawer. Apparently, he had, in effect, rescinded. The general question of the right of an accepting or certifying bank to set up this type of defense is considered, *infra* p. 257.

It therefore follows that the purchaser from the seller, whether in good faith or not, acquires a right against the bank, and that the bank, upon paying the seller or the purchaser, is entitled to indemnification from the buyer. See Midwest Nat. Bank & Trust Co. v. Niles & Watters Savings

E. Effect of Conduct of Buyer

One of the essential purposes of the letter of credit is to substitute the more acceptable credit of the bank for that of the buyer. The seller demands a letter of credit only because he does not think that the buyer is a sufficiently good risk. The bank, therefore, in issuing a credit is in effect assuring the seller that, irrespective of what happens to the buyer, he, the seller, will be paid on the presentation of the required documents. If the letter of credit is to function efficiently, the law must carry this intention into effect. It has therefore been held that the bank cannot refuse to pay its drafts to the seller on the ground that the buyer obtained the letter of credit through fraudulent representations,[58]

Bank, 190 Iowa 752, 180 N. W. 880 (1921). Defendant, after promising to honor at the holder's request, refused payment, alleging that the payee had obtained the check by fraud from the drawer and that the plaintiff was merely the payee's agent. The drawer intervened. In this case also there was a rescission, in effect, as the contract was likewise purely executory. The court found for the plaintiff, mainly on the ground that the promise to pay to the plaintiff had amounted to a new contract between plaintiff and defendant, with which the drawer and payee had no connection. The opinion implied, however, that if the promise had been made at the drawer's request, the defendant's argument would have had more force. The court appeared also to be of the opinion that the plaintiff was a bona fide holder and that the result would be the same, whether or not the promise amounted to a technical acceptance. "It should be remembered, too, that plaintiff is not suing as an indorsee of the land company, but that plaintiff is suing on the acceptance, or the agreement of the defendant to pay; plaintiff claiming that all indorsers are released, and that by the telegrams, there was a new contract between plaintiff and defendant alone, and that neither the land company nor Croke is concerned therein. Much of appellant's argument, or at least some of it, might be applicable were it not for the new contract created by the telegrams." At 759, 180 N. W. at 883. See also Bobrick v. Second Nat. Bank, 175 App. Div. 550, 162 N. Y. Supp. 147 (1916), *aff'd* without opinion, 224 N. Y. 637, 121 N. E. 856 (1918); and Farmers' & Merchants' Nat. Bank v. Elizabethtown Nat. Bank, 30 Pa. Super. Ct. 271 (1906), where the promise to pay a check, made to a purchaser upon his inquiry, was held to amount to a certification and the bank was held bound to pay the purchaser in reliance on the promise though the drawer had stopped payment.

[58] Johannessen v. Munroe, 158 N. Y. 641, 53 N. E. 535 (1899); Sovereign Bank of Canada v. Bellhouse Dillon & Co., 23 Quebec Off. L. R. 413 (1911); See also Moro Supply Co. v. Griffis-Newbern Co., 142 Ark. 231, 218 S. W. 370 (1920); Miltenberger v. Cooke, 18 Wall. 421, 21 L. Ed. 864 (1873).

that the consideration from the buyer has failed,[59] or that he has become insolvent.[60]

The legal theories on which these results have been based vary widely.[61] The courts, however, have seen the desired result and have striven for it in each particular case by the most easily available means. The theory usually adopted has been the one that seemed to the court in question most readily to achieve the desired end, viz., that the relations between the bank and the buyer could furnish no grounds for dishonor of a draft drawn under an irrevocable letter of credit. It has generally been recognized that a letter of credit, if a contract in any sense, is *sui generis,* and that the usual rules of contract do not apply to the extent that they defeat desired results. The very purpose for which the seller desires the letter of credit is to protect him against any vicissitudes of fortune which may occur to the buyer, and to relieve him from assuming the risk of the buyer's integrity. The

[59] "The law is that a bank issuing a letter of credit like the one here involved cannot justify its refusal to honor its obligations by reason of the contract relations existing between the bank and its depositor." American Steel Co. v. Irving Nat. Bank, 266 Fed. 41, 43 (C. C. A. 2d, 1920), 277 Fed. 1016 (C. C. A. 2d, 1921), *cert. den.,* 258 U. S. 617, 42 Sup. Ct. 271 (1922). "The fact that defendant derived no benefit from its promise constitutes no defense to liability on a letter of credit." Bridge v. Welda State Bank, 292 S. W. 1079, 1083 (Mo. App. 1927); Russell Grader Mfg. Co. v. Farmers' Exch. State Bank, 49 N. D. 999, 194 N. W. 387 (1923); Ouachita Valley Bank v. DeMotte, 173 Ark. 52, 291 S. W. 984 (1927); Townsley v. Sumrall, 2 Pet. 170, 183, 7 L. Ed. 386, 390 (1829); see also Bobrick v. Second Nat. Bank, *supra* note 57; De Tastett v. Crousillat, 7 Fed. Cas. No. 3, 828, at p. 542 (C. C. D. Pa. 1807), quoted *infra* Ch. VIII, note 34; Palmer v. Rice, 36 Neb. 844, 55 N. W. 256 (1893); Sears Roebuck Co. v. Rouse Banking Co., 191 N. C. 500, 132 S. E. 468 (1926).

[60] Carnegie v. Morrison, 2 Metc. 381 (Mass. 1841). In the usual buyer and seller relation, the latter knows little of the former's dealings with his bank. The seller is not related in any way to the agreement to reimburse. His position, in this respect, is much like that of the bona fide purchaser who buys from him. It is a test of good faith in regard both to the seller and to the purchaser They are bound by their knowledge. Therefore when the seller is a party to the fraud practiced by the buyer on the bank, or is an agent of the buyer, it is submitted that the misconduct of the buyer or his bankruptcy would be a defense against the beneficiary or the purchaser with notice. See Duncan v. Edgerton, 6 Bosw. 36 (N. Y. 1860).

[61] For a discussion of the various legal theories involved in the right of a seller against the bank under an irrevocable letter of credit, see *infra* ch. VIII, p. 279.

bank, in issuing its letter of credit, takes upon itself these risks. To hold that misconduct or bankruptcy of the buyer is a ground for refusing to honor the seller's draft under the credit would defeat the whole purpose for which letters of credit were instituted and developed.[62]

F. Effect of Mistake in Issuance of a Letter of Credit

Occasionally, the bank, in issuing its letters of credit, may omit by mistake to insert a condition or may change the nature of a condition, e. g., may issue the letter of credit for a greater amount than that requested by the buyer. To what extent the beneficiary obtains rights under the credit against the bank in this situation, is not entirely certain. A similar problem is presented when the bank pays a draft before the error is discovered. Can it recover the money on the theory of money paid under mistake of fact?

The question here is closely analogous to that which arises when the buyer authorizes the bank to pay against documents without the issuance of a letter of credit. If the bank discovers it has paid too much, there will naturally be a determined effort made to recover the overpayment. The case of *National City Bank* v. *Partola Manufacturing Co.*[63] is directly in point. The plaintiff had instructions to pay twenty-six dollars per unit and paid thirty dollars by mistake. It sued for the overpayment, alleging these facts. The defendant, after putting in an answer, moved for judgment on the pleadings. The motion was granted.

> The complaint merely shows that the plaintiff paid more to the defendant for the shipping documents than it was authorized by the Italian company to pay; but does not show that the Italian company was entitled to receive the shipping documents from the defendant on the payment of the amount which it alleges it was authorized to pay or that the defendant would have surrendered them on payment of that amount. It merely alleges a mistake on

[62] Accordingly, it would follow that the purchaser from the seller also recovers without any difficulty.

[63] 191 App. Div. 424, 181 N. Y. Supp. 464 (1920).

the part of the plaintiff in departing from the instructions of the Italian company, but does not allege mistake or fraud on the part of the defendant in receiving the money.[64]

To recover, therefore, the bank must show "mistake or fraud on the part of the defendant in receiving the money." In other words, the seller must receive the money either by mistake or fraudulently, knowing that the bank is overpaying. This principle would also hold true for letters of credit. Where the bank issues a letter of credit by mistake, it can revoke the letter or dishonor drafts drawn under it, when presented by the seller, only by showing that the seller knew that it was a mistake and still acted under it. This would amount to such fraudulent conduct as to entitle the bank to refuse to pay the draft. If, however, the seller is ignorant of the mistake and proceeds to act under the letter of credit as issued, the bank, having made the mistake, is the party that must suffer.[65]

There is no case directly in point.[66] But it is usually fairly simple to distinguish the case in which the seller can be presumed

---

[64] *Ibid.* at 425, 181 N. Y. Supp. at 465.

[65] Thus, what Professor Edwin W. Patterson has termed a "unilateral impalpable mistake" would probably not be sufficient basis for rescinding the letter of credit after the seller had relied thereon, Patterson, *Equitable Relief for Unilateral Mistake* (1928) 28 Col. L. Rev. 859, 884. Compare the rules where the bank by mistake either pays a check drawn against insufficient funds, (1921) 21 Col. L. Rev. 805, or certifies such a check, *infra* note 73.

[66] See Welsh v. Gossler, 89 N. Y. 540 (1882). In this case, the defendant contracted to sell sugar to one Finlay on certain terms, among which were May-June shipments. Finlay procured a letter of credit from the plaintiffs requiring May-June shipments and expiring by its terms on June 30. This was delivered to the seller. At the latter's request, a credit by cable was substituted, the form and language of which was dictated and prepared by him. This cabled dispatch omitted practically all the details, including the date of expiration, June 30, and the requirement for May-June shipments. The seller shipped in July, and the bank paid the draft, accepting the documents. The buyer refused to accept either goods or documents, and the bank, after offering to return the documents, sold them for the seller's account and sued the seller for the difference. The court found for the bank. One explanation is that the defendant, the seller, induced the plaintiff, the bank, to cable the credit without certain terms and then, fraudulently, attempted to take advantage of the omission, which of course the law would not permit. Another and equally valid interpretation, especially in view of the facts, is that the bank cabled the credit and, by mistake, omitted certain conditions, of which the seller had

to have knowledge of the mistake from the case in which it is reasonable to assume that he acted without such knowledge. The distinction would, as a rule, depend on the nature of the sales contract. If the contract provided for sale of a certain amount of goods at a certain price, thus fixing the total sum, the issuance of a letter of credit for a larger sum would indicate to the seller a confusion or error of some kind, and would not entitle him to use the letter for the larger sum without inquiry. On the other hand, the contract may call for the delivery of goods up to a certain amount as ordered from time to time by the buyer, the amount of the orders to be evidenced by the face amounts of the letters of credit to be delivered by the bank to the seller. If the buyer requests the bank to issue a credit for a certain sum and the bank, through some error, issues a credit for a larger sum, the seller, on shipping goods under the credit to the larger amount, would doubtless obtain rights against the bank.[67] The limit of the seller's rights is the limit of his knowledge. It is a test of *bona fides*. If he knows, or has information which leads him to suspect, that a mistake has been made, he cannot take advantage of it; but if, not being in a position to know of the mistake or not suspecting that one has been made, he proceeds to act under the credit as issued, he can recover.[68]

---

been informed from the letter previously issued. Because of this knowledge, the bank could recover a payment made without performance of all the terms and conditions of the credit, since the seller knew the omissions from the cable were due to a mistake.

[67] Unless, of course, the bank notifies the holder and rescinds the letter of credit before the holder has acted in reliance upon the bank's obligation. In this case, it is submitted, the same rule would apply as in the case of a mistake in the issuance of a letter of credit or in certifications. *Infra* p. 257. For a situation involving this type of transaction see E. E. Huber & Co. v. Lalley Light Corp., 242 Mich. 171, 218 N. W. 793 (1928).

[68] Where the seller has rights, it is clear that the purchaser from him acquires similar rights, even though the latter knows of the mistake. Under any other rule, the issuer could make the letter of credit practically valueless to the seller, by notifying the seller's bank and other agencies where the latter might attempt to discount the draft that a mistake had been made in the issuance of the credit. Compare this view with the rule under the Negotiable Instruments Law that when an instrument once gets into the hands of a bona fide purchaser, subsequent purchasers even with notice, take good title. See *supra* ch. II, p. 86. Where the seller

G. Forms of Action

In most of the cases we have been considering, the action was brought for breach of a promise to accept or to pay. An examination of the decided cases and of the principles involved indicates that no different results are to be apprehended if the action is brought on this promise as an acceptance. In other words, the defenses that the acceptor may set up as a ground for refusing to honor the draft do not differ from those which may be set up in an action by the seller against the issuing bank for breach of its promise to accept under its letter of credit. In the first place, where the beneficiary is the drawer of the draft, the results can be no different from those already indicated, whether or not the letter of credit technically amounts to an acceptance. As has been indicated, an acceptor's obligation to the drawer is not based on the draft, but on an agreement between them requiring the acceptor to pay the draft. The failure of the latter to do so is a breach of this agreement for which the acceptor is obligated to pay damages to the drawer.[69] Where the bank issues a letter of credit, the agreement is evidenced by this letter. The bank is obligated to the beneficiary for breach of the undertaking evidenced by the letter. Whether or not the credit technically amounts to an acceptance is immaterial; the agreement is the same. However, when the beneficiary is the payee or endorsee of the draft drawn by the buyer or his agent or when the seller endorses the draft to another or draws in favor of another, the suit may be either on the acceptance or on the promise to accept.

---

has no rights against the bank, the purchaser from him acquires none unless he takes for value and without knowledge of the mistake, as previously indicated, *supra* ch. II, p. 56, ch. III, pp. 104, 105, ch. IV, p. 159. As between bank and buyer, the former acquires no rights against the latter unless payment is made within the terms of the authority as actually given. The mistake being the bank's, it must assume the responsibility and liability.

[69] See the discussion *infra* ch. VII, p. 262. Technically, where the drawer is the payee of a draft, he can also sue on an acceptance. However, as no third parties are involved, the result is the same whether the action is on acceptance or for a breach of a promise to accept, except for a possible shifting of the burden of proof.

and in this case it is possible to anticipate a difference in result if the letter of credit amounts to a virtual or extrinsic acceptance.[70]

Another consideration, previously mentioned, should also be borne in mind. Letters of credit are, with few exceptions, issued before any draft is drawn so that no action on a credit as an extrinsic acceptance is possible. Finally, the credit usually contains requirements regarding documents to be presented with the draft, and therefore the promise evidenced by the letter of credit cannot be deemed to be unconditional, as required by Section 135 of the Uniform Negotiable Instruments Law for an action on a virtual acceptance.[71] In the rare case in which a promise by a bank is actionable as a virtual or extrinsic acceptance, the instrument containing the promise is usually a telegram or similar informal document, often sent by the bank in reply to an inquiry from the seller who refuses to accept the buyer's check or draft on the bank without some assurance from the latter that the instrument will be honored. Attention should be directed primarily to cases of this type in considering defenses which the bank may set up when an action is brought against it on a virtual or extrinsic acceptance.

In regard to defenses based on forged and fraudulent documents, the results reached in an action on an acceptance should be identical with those already indicated in an action against the issuing bank for breach of its promise to accept, since the considerations involved in both actions are the same.

Defenses which are raised by the accepting or certifying bank in an action on an acceptance or certification and which are based on the relations of the bank with the buyer, who, as we have seen, is usually the drawer, should not prevent the holder of the draft from recovering. The factors leading to this result are similar to those we have been considering in the analogous case in which the bank dishonors its letter of credit because the con-

---

[70] See *supra* ch. II, p. 133 *et seq.*

[71] *Supra* ch. II, p. 62 *et seq.*

sideration from the buyer has failed, and in which the seller, as drawer of the draft under the credit, sues for breach of the promise contained in the letter of credit. In addition, the acceptor is generally recognized as assuming the primary liability and as being obligated by his acceptance irrespective of his relations with the drawer.[72]

In the case of a certification by mistake, the bank can rescind, before the holder has negotiated the draft or otherwise acted in reliance on the act of the bank, just as in the case of a letter of credit issued by mistake.[73] In all these various situations, therefore, no difference in result is to be anticipated whether the holder sues on the promise in the letter of credit as a promise or as an acceptance.

The remaining problem is: whether the accepting or certifying bank can set up as a defense to an action on an acceptance or certification the facts that (1) the holder of the draft has breached his contract with the drawer or endorser by delivering goods of inferior value or otherwise, or (2) that he had fraudulently induced the drawer or endorser to enter into the sales contract under the terms of which the draft was delivered. In both of these situations, one of the remedies of the buyer is to rescind the sales contract. We have seen that the bank cannot set up these defenses when the action is not on an acceptance, but for breach of the promise, whether or not the buyer rescinds. In the case of an acceptance or certification the problem, stated generally, is whether the accepting or certifying bank can refuse

---

[72] NORTON, BILLS AND NOTES (4th ed. 1914) §§ 41, 69, 70.

[73] 1 MORSE, BANKS AND BANKING (6th ed. 1928) § 419; 2 DANIEL, NEGOTIABLE INSTRUMENTS, (6th ed. 1913) § 1608; BRADY, BANK CHECKS (2d ed. 1926) § 238; Bank of the Republic v. Baxter, 31 Vt. 101 (1858). It is doubtful whether a bank or any other acceptor can rescind an acceptance made by mistake. The difference in result being explainable by the early conceptions of the two types of obligations, the certification of a check and the acceptance of a draft, see the discussion of Nat. Bank of Commerce v. Baltimore Commercial Bank, 141 Md. 554, 118 Atl. 855, 29 A. L. R. 135 (1922), in (1923) 32 Yale L. J. 733; BRANNAN, NEGOTIABLE INSTRUMENTS LAW (4th ed. 1926) 895, 896 and cases there cited.

payment and set up as a defense facts indicating that the drawer or endorser has grounds for rescinding the transaction as a result of which the draft was drawn or endorsed. Where the endorser or drawer does not rescind, the bank cannot introduce these facts as a defense.[74] Where the drawer intervenes, rescinds, or otherwise indicates that the payee is not entitled to the money, it has been held, in the case of a check certified at the payee's request, that the bank cannot set up as a defense the fact that the drawer has a set-off against the payee.[75] Also, even where the check was certified at the request of the holder acting as agent of the drawer with the latter's knowledge and consent, it has been held that the bank cannot set up as a defense the fact that the plaintiff, an endorsee,

[74] This is the rule in the case of an acceptance by a party other than a bank, and also when the maker of a note attempts to resist an action on it, on the ground that the payee has equitable claims against the holder; *a fortiori*, it would apply in the case of an accepting or a certifying bank. See Brown v. Penfield, 36 N. Y. 473 (1867); Smith v. Adams, 14 La. Ann. 409 (1859); Carrier v. Sears, 86 Mass. 336 (1862); Prouty v. Roberts, 6 Cush. 19 (Mass. 1850); see also Hays v. Hathorn, 74 N. Y. 486, 490 (1878); *cf.* Houghton v. McAuliffe, 26 How. Pr. 270 (N. Y. 1863); Talman v. Gibson, 1 Hall 308 (N. Y. 1828); Bowman v. Wright, 7 Bush. 375 (Ky. 1870). On the grounds of public policy the maker of a note will be allowed to set up the fact that the holder received the note from the payee for an immoral consideration, see Baker v. Sockwell, 80 Colo. 309, 251 Pac. 543 (1926); (1927) 27 Col. L. Rev. 610. If the maker or acceptor has a defense against the payee or drawer as the case may be, he apparently would have the right to set up the fact that the holder's transferor, *i. e.,* the payee or drawer, could rescind the transaction; see note to Berry v. Barton, 12 Okla. 221, 71 Pac. 1074 (1902), in 66 L. R. A. 513. *Cf.* Davidson v. Keyes, 2 Rob. 254, 256 (La. 1842). Likewise where consideration has failed between buyer and bank and buyer and seller, the bank should be permitted to set up these facts as a defense to an action by the seller even though the failure of consideration between only two of the parties cannot be set up by the bank. The acceptor apparently had a defense against the drawer who had drawn the bill for unauthorized purposes. An accommodation acceptor apparently has a defense against the payee when the latter procures the draft from the drawer by fraud, but not for mere breaches of contract; see Marsh v. Low, 55 Ind. 271 (1876), discussed, *infra* note 77.

[75] Carnegie Trust Co. v. First Nat. Bank, 213 N. Y. 301, 107 N. E. 693, L. R. A. 1916C 186 (1915). Similarly, the certifying bank cannot refuse payment on the ground that the payee procured the check from the drawer by misrepresentation and then had it certified. Marie Antoinette Realty Co. v. Yorkville Bank, 123 Misc. 522, 205 N. Y. Supp. 395 (1924). In this case the bank was allowed to counterclaim as assignee of the drawer against the payee. See also Times Square Auto Co. v. Rutherford Nat. Bank, 77 N. J. L. 649, 73 Atl. 479 (1909); *cf.* Wilson v. Mid-West State Bank, 193 Iowa 311, 186 N. W. 891, (1922); Greenberg v. World Exchange Bank, 237 N. Y. Supp. 200 (App. Div. 1929).

obtained the check from the drawer by fraud.[76] Probably, where the bank has accepted a draft, it would likewise be denied the

[76] See Holub-Dusha Co. v. Germania Bank, 164 App. Div. 279, 284, 149 N. Y. Supp. 775, 778 (1914): "Its business and duty was to pay the check to the person to whom the drawer intended, when he made it, that it should be paid. If it did that, as I think it clearly did in the present case, it cannot be held liable for the fraud by which the drawer was led to intend that the amount represented by the check should be paid to a person to whom such drawer owed nothing and from whom it received no consideration." *Cf.* however, Sutter v. Security Trust Co., 96 N. J. Eq. 644, 126 Atl. 435 (1924). Here the court apparently was of the opinion that the bank could, at the request of the drawer, rescind its certification, when the payee obtained the check, previously certified, from the drawer, through "fraud, duress or force and fear, or other unlawful means, or for an illegal consideration," at 648, 126 Atl. at 437. Since the drawer could not prove fraud on the part of the payee in procuring the check, the court held the bank was justified in honoring its certification. This decision, however, resulted in the enactment of a curious statute intended to prevent banks from dishonoring certified checks. N. J. LAWS 1925, c. 115, § 1. "No bank or trust company shall stop payment of any check certified by such bank or trust company at the request of the drawer; and the certification of any check at the request of the drawer shall be of the same effect as if said check had been certified at the request of the holder thereof." See (1925) 23 MICH. L. REV. 531; (1924) 72 U. OF PA. L. REV. 318; *cf.* (1925) 5 BOST. U. L. REV. 119; also, the rule in the analogous situation where promises to accept are held to amount to certifications. See Bulliet v. Allegheny Trust Co., *supra* note 57, at 567, 131 Atl. at 474, 42 A. L. R. at 1137; Midwest Nat. Bank and Trust Co. v. Niles & Watters Savings Bank, *supra* note 57, at 759. 180 N. W. at 883, discussed and quoted, *supra* note 57.

The Midwest Bank case, and to a lesser extent, the Carnegie Trust case, *supra* note 75, place strong emphasis on the fact that the plaintiff obtained the certification from the defendant and that therefore it is an independent agreement with which the other parties have no concern. While this fact may be significant, it is doubtful whether it should be considered the principal factor in determining the right of the bank to set up this type of defense. When the drawer negotiates a check which has been previously certified, he transfers a right against the bank; or, if the bank is in a position to resist payment of the check in his hands, he creates a right in the transferee by the negotiation of the instrument. When the check is negotiated uncertified, the transferor transfers an ability to have a right created in the holder by presentation to and certification by the bank—in Hohfeldian terminology, a "beneficial liability"—as against himself. Legally, the difference is marked. Factually, however, since the drawer generally has sufficient funds on deposit with the bank, which is the assumption upon which this discussion rests, the difference is slight, since the holder can have the check certified as a matter of course. While to a large extent a check certified by the holder is treated by the courts as a promissory note, this is not entirely the case. It still retains traces of its previous character, e. g., the bank is under no duty to honor its certification if an endorsement previously made is forged. BRADY, BANK CHECKS (2d ed. 1926) 395. Factually, no distinction can be made between instruments certified at the holder's request and those certified at the drawer's request. The interest and non-legal responsibility of the latter is slight in either

right to set up as a defense, in an action on its acceptance brought by the payee, facts based on the relation between the drawer and the payee, even though the drawer had rescinded the transaction pursuant to which the draft had been delivered to the payee.[77] Even in these situations, therefore, the same results are to be an-

---

case. The solution to the problem under discussion must depend upon the policy underlying commercial transactions of this nature, and not on purely technical considerations. The factual considerations are identical in the two cases. The rule should therefore be the same.

In this connection, another interesting problem may arise. It is clear that when a check is certified at the request of the holder, the drawer and endorsers are discharged. What is the rule if the bank promises to pay in a writing which is not on the check itself? The reason usually given for the rule discharging the drawer and endorsers, is that the holder, instead of obtaining cash, has elected to take the bank's obligation, as if he had cashed the check, deposited the proceeds, and received a certificate of deposit. It would obviously be unfair to hold the drawer and endorsers under such circumstances. When, however, the promise of the bank is contained in a separate instrument, particularly when the holder is at some distance from the bank and cannot conveniently present the check for certification or payment, and especially when the holder takes in reliance on the promise, these considerations can hardly apply, and the drawer and endorsers may well be held to be secondarily liable. While there is no decision under the statutes on this point, the view is apparently held that they are discharged. See Bulliet v. Allegheny Trust Co., *supra* note 57, at 565, 131 Atl. at 473, 42 A. L. R. at 1135; Midwest Nat. Bank & Trust Co. v. Niles & Watters Savings Bank, *supra* note 57, at 759, 180 N. W. at 883; *cf.* Farmers' & Traders' Bank v. Carter, 88 Tenn. 279, 287, 12 S. W. 545, 547 (1889), decided at common law. This case must be relied upon only with caution, however, as it tends to class certified checks with accepted drafts.

[77] Whether this rule would apply to acceptances by parties other than banking institutions is doubtful. See Marsh v. Low, *supra* note 74, where the defendant was an accommodation acceptor and dishonored the draft because the plaintiff, the payee, had breached a warranty of soundness in a horse sold to the drawer, in payment for which the draft was drawn. The court found for the payee on the ground that the acceptor could not inquire into the failure of consideration between drawer and payee, that the drawer's remedy here was for damages for breach of contract, and that the acceptor had a defense only when the drawer could rescind for fraud. In the case of promissory notes, it is generally assumed that the maker can resist payment in the hands of a purchaser, if the payee rescinds the transaction with the purchaser, see Peaslee v. Robbins, 3 Metc. 164 (Mass. 1841), as interpreted by Carrier v. Sears, *supra* note 74. It would seem that a bank could not rescind in a similar situation where a bank note or certificate of deposit was involved. If this distinction is sound law, it should also apply to acceptances by banks and others. The distinction between bank and trade acceptances, as well as between promissory notes, and bank notes and certificates of deposit, is based on considerations that have often been mentioned and need not be repeated here—the greater negotiability of bank instruments, the larger number issued, etc. See discussion *supra* ch. I, pp. 9, 14 *et seq.*, ch. III, pp. 114, 115.

ticipated whether the action is brought on an acceptance or on a promise to accept.

H. Summary

The foregoing discussion has indicated that the general rule is that the sales contract and letter of credit are mutually independent, though in some situations, the provisions of the sales contract have a direct bearing in determining rights under the letter of credit.

Another consideration which should also be noted is that generally the rights of the parties are determined by their good faith. Not only is the usual rule applied, that a bona fide purchaser of a draft can recover, irrespective of defenses against his transferor, but the same principle is also extended to the immediate parties to the letter of credit. If the bank has a defense against the buyer, the seller can recover against the bank when, and only when, he is not a party to the misconduct or fraud practiced on the bank by the buyer. When the seller practises fraud in performing the conditions of the letter of credit, the bank, on paying him, can recover from the buyer only if it paid without knowledge of the fraud.[78] The test applied to all parties is one of *bona fides*. Have they acted in the usual course of business and without any knowledge of facts which should have altered their course of conduct? This is the rule applied to negotiable instruments. It springs directly from the law merchant and the customs of tradesmen. It is an approach that is foreign to special assumpsit or to any other indigenous common law action.

[78] It has been indicated that if there are non-fraudulent defects in the goods sent by the seller, the bank is under a duty to pay, even though it is aware of this fact. This is not a limitation on the principle suggested above. It is not a situation in which the bank cannot recover, though it paid without knowledge of the breach by the seller. It recovers though it had knowledge, because of other considerations involved. Clearly this is not a limitation of the rules discussed, since it does not affect the general principle as indicated.

Chapter VII

THE MEASURE OF DAMAGES

A. In an Action by the Seller against the Bank

In the analysis first given of the nature of the commercial letter of credit, it was indicated that so far as the seller or beneficiary was concerned, the letter of credit was a promise to pay on stated conditions any amount up to a certain sum. In addition, the credit normally contains an express or implied promise to pay certain sums, to be fixed by the seller, to persons indicated by him in a specified manner, e. g., by drawing and negotiating drafts.[1]

In considering the question of damages, it should further be noted that the promise contained in the letter of credit may occasionally be held to amount to a virtual acceptance. Where this is so, the beneficiary, in the rare case when he is not the drawer of the draft, has in this country two alternatives.[2] He may sue on the letter of credit as constituting a virtual acceptance of a particular draft, or he may bring an action for breach of the promise contained in the letter of credit.[3]

In substance, considering for the present the action for breach of the promise, the letter of credit is a promise by the bank to pay certain amounts on the presentation of documents covering the shipment of certain goods. These amounts are generally the same as those which the buyer is obligated to pay under the sales contract.[4] The seller is merely looking to the bank instead of

---

[1] *Supra* ch. I, p. 11.

[2] If the beneficiary is the drawer of the draft, and not the payee, he can sue only on the promise, so that whether or not the letter of credit amounts to a virtual or extrinsic acceptance is immaterial in this connection, *supra* ch. VI, p. 255.

[3] *Supra* ch. II, p. 42.

[4] This assumes that the terms of payment under the sales contract and the letter of credit are the same, which is usually the case.

to the buyer for payment of that amount. The loss, therefore, arising from the breach by the bank of its obligations under the credit should normally be the same as that which arises from a breach by the buyer of his obligations under the sales contract, and the measure of damages for the breach by the bank, other things being equal, should be the same as the measure of damages for the breach by the buyer.[5]

A consideration of additional factors leads to the same result. The bank has created a general credit in favor of the seller. It has breached its obligations under that credit. The rule as to damages should therefore be similar to the rule applied in the breach of analogous obligations where a general credit is created, e. g., in deposits. The measure of damages in that case includes not only the sum which the bank refused to pay but also all incidental damage that may be directly traced, within the rule of *Hadley* v. *Baxendale*,[6] to the refusal of the bank to perform its obligations.[7] This results in the same amount as is due from the

---

[5] "It seems to us that upon the breach of the contract by the defendant, the plaintiff became entitled to recover from the defendant the damages which it could have established in an action against the buyer." Doelger v. Battery Park Nat. Bank, 201 App. Div. 515, 521, 194 N. Y. Supp. 582, 588 (1922); see also Ernesto Foglino & Co. v. Webster, 217 App. Div. 282, 216 N. Y. Supp. 225 (1926), *modified*, 244 N. Y. 516, 563, 155 N. E. 878, 897 (1926). The assumption is, of course, that the buyer has no counterclaims or bases by which his liability to the seller would be reduced. Any such elements would not aid the bank in any way. It is only when there are no factors of this type present that the measure of damages is the same against both bank and buyer; see Belgian Grain & Produce Co. v. Cox & Co., 1 Lloyd's List 256, 257, 546 (1919).

[6] 9 Exch. 341 (1854); 1 Sedgwick, Damages (9th ed. 1912) ch. VIII, § 144 *et seq.*

[7] 1 Sedgwick, Damages (9th ed. 1912) 282, 283, 326; 2 Morse, Banks and Banking (6th ed. 1928) § 458. There is one difference to be noted. In the case of a refusal to honor checks the measure of damages in a suit by the depositor includes the injury to his general credit. It is in the nature of an action for slander *per se* in a man's trade or profession. This would hardly apply to a draft presented by the seller, since no third party is involved. In addition, there is a difference in the commercial functions of the two instruments. Checks have a much wider use and are regarded as representations that the drawer has a certain amount on deposit. To refuse to honor a check on the ground of lack of sufficient funds is to impugn the drawer's good faith and to impair his credit. The drawer under a letter of credit merely represents that the bank has issued such a document. The third party

buyer since the sum due in both cases is the purchase price of the goods, less certain deductions to be indicated presently, together with all such incidental damage as may be deemed within the rule of *Hadley* v. *Baxendale* to arise from and be directly traceable to the non-performance of the bank's or the buyer's obligation to pay.

Whether the court will use the analogy of the sales contract or whether it will treat the action for breach of the credit as one primarily for the payment of a definite sum of money, depends to a large extent upon the terms and conditions of the letter of credit.

Where the credit calls for a single draft for the whole amount and particularly where no documents are required, the courts are tempted to treat the action for breach of the promise as analogous to the action for breach of an obligation incurred where a general credit is created, and to allow a recovery for the amount due under the credit without any extended consideration.

It seems to me that this is clearly a case of a simple contract to pay money upon the fulfillment of conditions which have been fulfilled. The bank had simply to accept the bill when the proper documents were brought to them.[8]

---

in purchasing the draft usually sees the letter, so that no question of the seller's good faith can arise. A refusal to pay on other grounds, such as the non-performance of conditions, usually represents a difference of opinion or a misunderstanding based on different local trade customs and in no way reflects on the seller's credit. See however Ellis v. Bank of Australasia, 3 N. S. Wales L. R. 96 (1882). The seller therefore could not include in his claim for damages a general loss of credit. Proof of special loss of credit directly traceable, under the rule of Hadley v. Baxendale, to the dishonor of the draft, would be necessary to a recovery for loss of credit. This usual rule of contracts would apply also to a suit against the buyer under a sales contract.

[8] Stein v. Hambro's Bank, 9 Lloyd's List 433, 507 (1921); see also Dexters, Ltd., v. Schenker & Co., 14 Lloyd's List 586, 588 (1923). In using this analogy, the court is theoretically applying a different measure of damages against the bank from that obtaining in an action against the buyer. It is submitted, however, that this type of analogy will be used only when the credit is simple and when it is apparent that a definite sum is due from the bank, no questions of an allowance or set-off being involved. Where this is so, the liability of the buyer is ordinarily equally clear and definite. As a practical matter, therefore, the same amount would be recovered against both bank and buyer even where

Where the credit is more complicated or where the seller either retains the goods and documents or has resold them, the similarity to the liability of the buyer under a c.i.f. contract becomes more apparent, and the courts are likely to approach the problem of the measure of damages from that point of view.[9] In c.i.f. contracts, since normally title passes upon shipment, the general rule appears to be that the purchase price of the goods, often the face amount of the draft, can be recovered from the buyer, less the value of the documents at the time and the place of tender of the documents,[10] together with all incidental damage admissible under the usual rules of damages for breach of contract.[11] The amount the seller

this analogy is followed. Where the situation is more complex, it will be seen that the analogy to the c.i.f. contract is the one customarily followed.

[9] Urquhart, Lindsay & Co. v. Eastern Bank, [1922] 1 K. B. 318, 324. "These damages are not for non-payment of money. It is true that non-payment of money was what the buyer was guilty of, but such non-payment is evidence of a repudiation of the contract to accept and pay for the remainder of the goods; and the damages are in respect of such repudiation." It is interesting to note that this case was decided about the same time as Stein v. Hambro's Bank, *supra* note 8, and by the same judge. The difference between these cases lies in the fact that in Stein v. Hambro's Bank, the draft was for the full amount of the credit, while in the latter case the credit contemplated a series of drafts, one of which having been dishonored, the seller sued for the anticipatory breach of the remainder. The general credit aspect of a commercial letter of credit was more clearly seen in the latter case than in the former. In the former, the court evidently felt that the particular letter of credit was very similar in function to an accepted draft or a virtual acceptance, particularly as all the conditions had apparently been performed. Though an action on a virtual acceptance was no longer possible by statute in England, the language employed by courts in discussing that type of action was also used here. The recovery being the same from either point of view, there was no practical difference. The court, however, failed to notice that since the action was brought by the drawer it was essentially one on the promise to accept and should not have been viewed as analogous to an action on an acceptance.

[10] It should be noted that the place of tender of the documents is not necessarily the place at which the goods are to arrive, a fact which does not seem to have been generally recognized.

[11] Certainly, in view of the essential characteristics of c.i.f. contracts as they have been indicated, *supra* p. 178 *et seq.*, the measure of damages should be determined by the value of the documents at the time and place of delivery of the documents, whether the breach is by the seller or by the buyer. This appears to be the English rule. KENNEDY C. I. F. CONTRACTS (2d ed. 1928) 156, 174; 2 WILLISTON, SALES (2d ed. 1924) § 599. In New York, where the breach is by the buyer, the seller has the alternative right to wait until the goods arrive and then to sue, basing the measure of damages upon the value of the goods at the port of desti-

can recover against the bank is governed by the same rule.[12] Of course, if the seller has resold the documents and the goods, he must deduct the resale price, whether his action is against the bank under the credit[13] or against the buyer under the sales con-

nation. Ruttonjee v. Frame, 237 N. Y. 115, 142 N. E. 437 (1923), *aff'g*, 205 App. Div. 354, 199 N. Y. Supp. 523 (1923); WILLISTON, SALES 1437; *cf.* Kunglig Jarnvagsstyrelsen v. Dexter and Carpenter, 32 F. (2d) 195 (C. C. A. 2d, 1929). Where, however, the breach is by the seller, in an action by the buyer in New York, the time and place of shipment of the goods is the basis of the measure of damages. Perkins v. Minford, 235 N. Y. 301, 139 N. E. 276 (1923); Standard Casing Co. v. California Casing Co., 233 N. Y. 413, 135 N. E. 834 (1922); Seaver v. Lindsay Light Co., 233 N. Y. 273, 135 N. E. 329 (1922); S. B. Penick & Co. v. Helvetia Commercial Co., 212 App. Div. 519, 209 N. Y. Supp. 202 (1925). See also Setton v. Eberle-Albrecht Flour Co., 258 Fed. 905 (C. C. A. 8th, 1919); *cf.* Staackman, Horschitz & Co. v. Cary, 197 Ill. App. 601 (1916).

These New York decisions fail to appreciate that the important element in a c.i.f. contract is the delivery of documents and that normally the buyer will purchase other documents to replace those which the seller has failed to deliver. To some extent this is recognized in Perkins v. Minford, *ibid.*, in the ruling by the court that the date as of which the damages are to be measured is not the date when the goods should have been shipped, but the date when the buyer learns or would normally learn that the goods have not been shipped. While this modification will result in more closely approximating the actual damage to the buyer than the rule as originally stated in New York, it fails to reflect commercial practices as accurately as the English rule. See (1929) 29 COL. L. REV. 652, 813, 824 *et seq.*

The same result as to measure of damages should also be reached even in the case in which the breach by the seller is in relation only to the goods, e. g., where the proper documents have been tendered but the goods are rejected by the buyer because of inferior quality. Under c.i.f. contracts, the buyer is rarely the ultimate consumer and, as a rule, resells the goods purchased, *supra* p. 179. To do so effectively, he must have documents of title and, accordingly, upon learning of the breach, he will ordinarily proceed to purchase such instruments. Of course, the date as of which the damages would be measured would be the date on which the buyer learned, or would normally have learned, of the breach, and not the date of the delivery of the documents. The place used as the basis for the measure of damages, however, would normally be the place of the delivery of the documents. These conclusions would not necessarily follow in the case in which the buyer elects to accept the goods and sue for breach of warranty, as in that situation other considerations come into play. See Brandenstein v. Jackling, 278 Pac. 880, 885 (Cal. App. 1929).

[12] The seller may, of course, turn over the documents and recover the purchase price. Belgian Grain & Produce Co. v. Cox & Co., *supra* note 5. In New York, the courts are apparently inclined to allow the seller the same option as to the measure of damages in an action against the bank as he has in an action against the buyer under a c.i.f. contract. See Ernesto Foglino & Co. v. Webster, *supra* note 5; Doelger v. Battery Park Nat. Bank, *supra* note 5; *cf.* Maurice O'Meara Co. v. Nat. Park Bank, 239 N. Y. 386, 400, 146 N. E. 636, 640, 39 A. L. R. 747, 754 (1925).

[13] Only the net resale price is deducted, *i. e.*, less all charges for custom fees, warehousing, hauling, brokerage, etc. De Sousa v. Crocker First

tract.[14] Irrespective of the analogy adopted by the courts, the results reached are ordinarily the same.

Where the credit calls for a series of drafts, it has been held that dishonor of the first may be treated by the seller as a breach of the entire contract. The analogy to the duties of a buyer under a c.i.f. installment contract is close and obvious.

> In the present case, however, the credit was irrevocable; and the effect of that was that the bank really agreed to buy the contemplated series of bills and documents representing the contemplated shipments, just as the buyer agreed to take, and pay for by this means, the goods themselves. Now, if a buyer, under a contract of this sort, declines to pay for an instalment of the goods, the seller can cancel and claim damages upon the footing of an anticipatory breach of the contract of sale as a whole. . . . I confess I cannot see why the refusal of the bank to take and pay for the bills with the documents representing the goods is not in the same way a repudiation of their contract to take the bills to be presented in future under the letter of credit; nor if that is so, why the damages are not the same.[15]

Nat. Bank, 23 F. (2d) 118, 122 (N. D. Cal. 1927), *rev'd* on another point, 27 F. (2d) 462 (C. C. A. 9th, 1928). See also Maurice O'Meara Co. v. Nat. Park Bank, *supra* note 12, at 400, 146 N. E. at 640, 39 A. L. R. at 754; Second Nat. Bank v. Columbia Trust Co., 288 Fed. 17, 26, 30 A. L. R. 1299, 1309 (C. C. A. 3d, 1923); *In re* Barned's Banking Co., Banner & Young & Johnson, L. R. 5 H. L. 157 (1871); *In re* Barned's Banking Co., Coupland's Claim, L. R. 5 Ch. App. 167 (1869).

[14] UNIFORM SALES ACT, § 60; 2 WILLISTON, SALES (2d ed. 1924) ch. XXI and p. 1437; 2 SEDGWICK, MEASURE OF DAMAGES (9th ed. 1912) § 755. The resale either as against bank or buyer can presumably be either of the documents or the goods as such. The only question that may arise is whether the price obtained on resale has been fair and reasonable in view of the circumstances—principally, a question of fact. The seller can also, of course, rescind the contract. UNIFORM SALES ACT § 61; 2 WILLISTON, SALES § 554 *et seq.* He also has the usual rights of an unpaid seller under the Uniform Sales Act, both against the goods and for breach of contract.

[15] Urquhart, Lindsay & Co. v. Eastern Bank, *supra* note 9, at 323; Doelger v. Battery Park Nat. Bank, 201 App. Div. 515, 194 N. Y. Supp. 582 (1922). The court in the Urquhart Lindsay & Co. case uses the term "anticipatory breach" though the description is not entirely accurate. Dishonor of the first of a series of drafts is a substantial breach by actual non-performance and not wholly anticipatory. An action should, therefore, lie at once. The only possible question is whether the breach can be deemed to go to the essence of the contract. As to that, there can be little doubt since where the credit calls for a series of drafts and the conditions to be performed by the beneficiary are numerous, courts have viewed a refusal to honor one draft as "a breach of the contract as a whole," thus giving rise to an action for breach of the credit. Nichols v.

The rule of damages laid down by the court was that:

The damages to which the plaintiffs are entitled are the difference between, on the one hand, the value of the materials left on their hands and the cost of such as they would have further provided, and on the other hand, what they would have been entitled to receive for the manufactured machinery from the buyers, the whole being limited to the amount they could in fact have tendered before the expiry of the letter of credit.[16]

In addition to the amount of the draft, less certain deductions as have been indicated, the seller would recover, within the limitations laid down by *Hadley* v. *Baxendale,* all incidental damage arising directly from and traceable to the breach by the bank, as in the ordinary breach of contract.[17] Accordingly where the seller has sold the draft to a purchaser who, on the dishonor by the bank, sues the seller as drawer and recovers judgment, the seller has an additional claim against the bank. He can recover, in addition to the amount of the bill, any other items he may have been compelled to pay the purchaser.[18] Similarly if the letter of credit is issued for the accommodation of the beneficiary, it is submitted that, in the event of dishonor, the amount of the recov-

---

Scranton Steel Co., 137 N. Y. 471, 488, 33 N. E. 561, 566 (1893); 3 WILLISTON, CONTRACTS (1924) § 1328 *et seq.* and cases there cited.

If the breach by the bank is purely anticipatory, it is doubtful whether an action would lie. Certainly, if a letter of credit be viewed merely as a promise to pay money upon the presentation of documents before a certain date, it is difficult to see how an action for an anticipatory breach can be allowed. Benecke v. Haebler, 38 App. Div. 344, 348, 58 N. Y. Supp. 16, 18, (1899), *aff'd* without opinion, 166 N. Y. 631, 60 N. E. 1107 (1901); Kelly v. Security Mutual Life Ins. Co., 186 N. Y. 16, 78 N. E. 584 (1906); (1925) 39 HARV. L. REV. 268; (1926) 36 YALE L. J. 263; see also Monark Metal & Supply Co. v. Schmidt, 195 Wis. 294, reported *sub nom.*, Monark Metal & Supply Co. v. General Metal & Refining Co., 218 N. W. 179 (1928); *cf.* Ernesto Foglino & Co. v. Webster, *supra* note 5.

[16] Urquhart, Lindsay & Co. v. Eastern Bank, *supra* note 9, at 324; see also Doelger v. Battery Park Nat. Bank, *supra* note 5, at 522, 194 N. Y. Supp. at 588.

[17] *Supra* p. 265.

[18] See Riggs v. Lindsay, 7 Cranch 500, 3 L. Ed. 419 (1813), where a penalty imposed by statute, as well as a commission, was allowed as part of the damages recoverable by the drawer. In this case the letter was written by the buyer himself, but the rule would apply as well to the usual commercial credit. See also Urquhart v. M'Iver, 4 Johns. 103 (N. Y. 1809).

ery against the issuer by the beneficiary is measured only by the inconvenience caused the latter, within the usual rules of damages for breach of contract.[19]

B. In an Action by the Purchaser

When the draft is discounted, the purchaser has rights on the credit only in respect of that particular draft, the letter of credit being a promise to pay a specific sum as far as he is concerned.[20] His rights are therefore closely analogous to those of the payee or the endorsee of an accepted draft. The measure of damages against the seller as drawer of the draft will be similar to that against the drawer of a draft which has been accepted and then dishonored. Likewise the measure of damages against the bank on the promise contained in the credit will be similar to that against an acceptor of a draft.[21]

---

[19] See Ilsley v. Jones, 78 Mass. 260 (1858); Norton, Bills and Notes (4th ed. 1914) 119, 232, 233. But see Evansville Nat. Bank v. Kaufmann, 93 N. Y. 273, 290 (1883). The sum may of course at times be considerable. The question of the kind of items to be included in assessing the damage is governed by the rules applicable to similar problems in contracts generally. Larios v. Bonany y Gurety, L. R. 5 P. C. A. 346 (1873).

[20] When the draft is bought by a confirming or advising bank, either one may of course sue on the credit in respect of that particular draft. It may also have an action on the agreement between the issuing bank and the advising or confirming bank, if there be one in existence. In the latter case, the measure of damages would follow the usual rule of contracts. Where, however, the draft is drawn on the corresponding bank which accepts and pays, the latter has an action only on the agreement, express or implied, between the issuing bank and itself, the draft being merely evidence of the sum paid. Generally, its relation to the issuing bank is similar to that of the issuing bank to the buyer. See *infra* p. 271.

[21] See Russell v. Wiggin, 21 Fed. Cas. No. 12,165 (C. C. D. Mass. 1842). Justice Story in that case was evidently of the opinion that the measure of damages was the same whether the action was against the acceptor or for breach of the promise to accept. He allowed the amount of re-exchange as an item of damage, however, though acceptors as such were not liable for it. With the general extension of that rule to acceptors as well, there remains hardly any distinction between the two. The rule in regard to re-exchange is generally similar in actions on an acceptance and on a promise to accept. See 2 Sedgwick, Damages (9th ed. 1912) § 700; Norton, Bills and Notes (4th ed. 1914) 229; Brannan, Negotiable Instruments Law (4th ed. 1926) 853.

C. In an Action by the Buyer against the Bank

If the bank refuses to perform, it is not only liable to the seller but to the buyer as well. The rules of damages in actions on drafts do not of course apply as this would be an action on a special agreement and not on the draft.

> But in the case before us the action is not brought on the bill, but on a special contract, the incidents of which differ materially from those which belong to the contract constituted by becoming a party to a negotiable instrument, and which are strictly limited by the law merchant.[22]

The measure of damages is therefore subject to the usual rules of contract.

> We must therefore look at the contract and the circumstances, and see whether the damage in respect of which the plaintiffs sue was, according to the principle of *Hadley* v. *Baxendale*, within the contemplation of the parties.[23]

The buyer was allowed to recover not only the commission paid to the bank but, in addition, the higher rate he had to pay another bank to have the bills accepted, as well as such incidental expenditures as telegraphic charges. However, where the buyer persuaded the bank wrongfully to dishonor its credit for a time, during which period the value of the goods declined, the bank was held not to be liable to the buyer for the resulting damage.[24] In the analogous situation in which the bank is given funds to pay out against shipping documents and, in doing so, violates its instructions, the measure of damages is not the sum paid out but the loss to the depositor, *i. e.*, the buyer. Likewise in measuring the loss, the usual contract rule applies: the buyer can recover only the damages which could not have been avoided or minimized

---

[22] Prehn v. Royal Bank of Liverpool, L. R. 5 Ex. 92, 97 (1870).

[23] *Ibid.*, at 97. See Banque Populaire de Bienne v. Cavé, 1 Com. Cas. 67, 69 (1895), where the court distinguishes the rule in this case from an action against an acceptor for dishonoring the draft.

[24] Camp v. Corn Exch. Nat. Bank, 285 Pa. 337, 132 Atl. 189 (1926).

by him.[25] In all these cases, the approach to the question of damages is that of the usual contract action.

D. In an Action by the Bank against the Buyer

In an action by the bank against the buyer, the basis of the action is the agreement to reimburse. The draft is important merely as evidence of the amount paid by the bank. The measure of damage is the amount of the commission due the bank and either the amount paid or, if the bank sues after the acceptance but before payment, the amount represented by the drafts accepted by it.[26]

E. In an Action on a Virtual or Extrinsic Acceptance

When the promise to accept amounts to a virtual or extrinsic acceptance, the seller, when he is not the drawer of the draft or a bona fide purchaser, may sue as on an acceptance, in which event the usual rules of a suit on an acceptance would apply. The plaintiff would recover the amount of the draft plus interest.[27] From the point of view of the measure of damages, a suit on the promise would seem to be more advantageous than a suit on the acceptance. Where the letter of credit calls for a single draft, the beneficiary would recover at least the amount of the draft and such additional damages as he had incurred and as would be provable under *Hadley* v. *Baxendale*.[28] In an action

[25] Kornblum v. Bank of Italy, 64 Cal. App. 170, 222 Pac. 143 (1923); (1924) 33 Yale L. J. 651, 656, n. 11; *cf.* Second Nat. Bank v. Columbia Trust Co., *supra* note 13, at 26.

[26] This would hold true *mutatis mutandis* in an action by the interior requesting bank against the buyer, and also by the issuing bank against the interior requesting bank.

[27] Norton, Bills and Notes (4th ed. 1914) § 80.

[28] See Larios v. Bonany y Gurety L. R. 5 P. C. A. 346, 357 (1873); Bank of Toronto v. Ansell 7 Revue Legale 262 (1875). The measure of the liability of the promisor in an action for breach of the promise is judged, not by the amount of the draft, but by the loss and inconvenience of the holder of the draft within the rule of Hadley v. Baxendale, *supra* note 6. And this holds true whether the action is by the seller as drawer and therefore necessarily on the promise, or by the seller or purchaser of

on an acceptance, the amount of damages is fixed. In addition, where the promise is for a series of drafts, the seller may, in a suit on the promise after dishonor of one draft, sue for anticipatory breach of the drafts not yet drawn.[29] If, however, he elects to sue on the promise as an acceptance, he can recover only the usual amount for the dishonor of that particular draft. It is unlikely that drafts not yet drawn would be considered as dishonored even in the most liberal jurisdiction.[30]

There are differences, therefore, between the amount recoverable in a suit on an acceptance and in a suit on a promise as such. These distinctions all resolve themselves in favor of the suit for breach of the promise. When the doctrine of virtual and extrinsic acceptance was first considered, the quest was for such a difference as would justify the perpetuation of the doctrine.[31] To do this, it was necessary to indicate a desirable result that could be achieved only, or at least more readily, by the action on the promise to accept as an acceptance than by the action on the promise as such. This discussion indicates that the action on the promise is generally more flexible than the other alternative, that it reaches the same

the draft as payee or endorsee, who has elected to sue for breach of the promise rather than on the acceptance. Where the holder has acquired the draft for value, it is difficult to see how the damage can be less than the amount of the draft. Stein v. Hambro's Bank, *supra* note 8; Belgian Grain & Produce Co. v. Cox & Co., *supra* note 5; Lafargue v. Harrison, 70 Cal. 380, 9 Pac. 259, 11 Pac. 636 (1886). "Whether it shall be held to be an acceptance, or whether he shall be subjected in damages for a breach of his promise to accept, or whether he shall be held to be estopped from impeaching his word, is a matter of form merely. The result in either event is to compel the promisor to pay the amount of the bill with interest." Scudder v. Union Nat. Bank, 91 U. S. 406, 414, 23 L. Ed. 245, 249 (1875). If the holder is not a purchaser for value, then under the Uniform Negotiable Instruments Law, he could not sue on an acceptance and he would therefore be forced to sue on a promise.

[29] If the plaintiff desires not to treat the whole contract as breached, normally there is no reason why he cannot sue for the breach of the one part, *i. e.*, dishonor of one draft. This would have the same result as an action on an acceptance, unless he had suffered additional damage.

[30] In addition, this problem could only arise in liberal jurisdictions like New York and California, where a promise to accept a series of drafts is actionable as an acceptance. In Missouri and under the federal rule, this type of promise would probably be held not to be sufficiently definite to be an acceptance.

[31] *Supra* ch. III, p. 133.

results as an action on the acceptance, and with as little difficulty, and that, in addition, it allows recovery for additional damages where necessary. From this point of view, therefore, no basis for the perpetuation of the doctrine of virtual and extrinsic acceptances can be found.

Chapter VIII

THE LEGAL THEORY

The discussion of the law of commercial letters of credit has served to indicate not only the results reached in the decisions of the cases, but also the manner in which these results have, as a rule, been in harmony with the general practices of merchants and banks in relation to commercial credits. We have seen that the courts, in deciding these cases, have to a large extent recognized these commercial usages and have been quick to give effect to them. It would be futile therefore to expect to find expressed in the decisions any one well recognized common law principle which has guided the various courts of many jurisdictions in deciding the questions that have arisen. And any attempt to do so would seem a priori to be doomed to failure. The genius of the common law has always striven, however, to crystallize results reached in any particular field of the law into recognized legal principles. As to the value of any such formulae in a field of the law where legal rules are essentially merely a recognition of commercial custom, great doubt must always exist. That writers and commentators will, however, from time to time attempt to classify into one or another of the familiar legal categories, the conclusions previously reached, can hardly be surprising. The extent to which these efforts are successful will vary with the extent to which the relationships and conditions encountered in the use of letters of credit are similar to situations previously encountered within the orbit of the common law. On the other hand, to the extent that the commercial credit creates new types of legal problems, it is only to be anticipated that attempts to restate the conclusions reached in terms of familiar principles will necessarily be futile.

In this field, however, courts have been less prone to engage in generalization and have usually been content merely to reach a result in harmony with commercial practice. They have refrained as far as possible from stating general principles and have recognized that:

> Their nature [*i. e.*, that of letters of credit] and use ought to be kept as free as possible from narrowing statements of limitations and from judicial dicta not necessary to a particular decision. They should not be bound by definition so as to become incapable of growth and change in accordance with the development of legitimate business practices.[1]

In view of these considerations, it is submitted that for a complete understanding of the law of commercial letters of credit, it is entirely unnecessary to formulate any one legal principle upon which the rights of a beneficiary under a commercial credit may be rested. Whether essential or not, however, the tendency of commentators and, to some extent, of the courts to generalize and to formulate principles makes it desirable to consider briefly the various technical theories that have been suggested for the purpose of linking up the law of commercial credits with general common law principles. Since any one of these theories is sufficient to support most of the results reached, in discussing each of them, attention will be paid only to those results difficult of explanation.

A. The Virtual or Extrinsic Acceptance

One problem can be dismissed without extended consideration. Where the letter of credit amounts to a virtual or an extrinsic acceptance and the holder of the draft, whether payee or endorsee, elects to sue the issuer as on an acceptance, no question of legal theory arises.[2] A virtual or an extrinsic acceptance

---

[1] Moss v. Old Colony Trust Co., 246 Mass. 139, 151, 140 N. E. 803, 807 (1923).

[2] Where the letter of credit authorizes the seller to draw the draft, he cannot sue as on an acceptance where he draws in favor of another, *supra* ch. VI, p. 255. Actions on modern letters of credit as acceptances are usually, therefore, limited to purchasers.

being an acceptance, the basis of recovery is the same as that of the usual acceptance, *i. e.*, the custom of merchants as incorporated into the common law.[3] Actions on promises to accept as virtual or extrinsic acceptances may therefore be excluded from any further consideration.

B. Types of Letters of Credit

Much of the confusion in the discussion of the action for breach of the promise contained in the letter of credit can be avoided if we recognize that a fundamental distinction exists between the usual banker's letter of credit and that issued by the buyer himself. In regard to the latter type of instrument, there has been no such widespread commercial usage as would make a recognition of a new type of instrument evidencing a novel legal relationship either necessary or desirable. Where the customary promise to accept contained in the buyer's letter of credit is held not to amount to a virtual or extrinsic acceptance, the usual rules of contract or agency are sufficient to explain all the results reached. The promise to accept, if made to an agent, is subject to the usual rules of agency. It binds the writer to all who take the draft relying on the promise contained in the letter and without notice of revocation by the issuer. When addressed to the seller, it is either an offer revocable until accepted by the offeree, or else it constitutes one of the terms of a contract and as such is irrevocable in the same manner as is any other provision of the contract.

A similar distinction should be drawn between the irrevocable commercial credit, on the one hand, and the revocable letter of credit, the authority to pay, and the authority to purchase, on the other hand. Since the last three instruments are all revocable, they may adequately be treated as revocable offers looking to unilateral contracts, which confer no rights on the beneficiary until all the acts specified in the offer as constituting the acceptance have been

---

[3] *Supra* ch. II, pp. 45, 51; ch. III, p. 138.

performed.[4] It is significant to note, however, that even in the case of the buyer's letters of credit and the revocable forms of commercial credits, in which traditional legal formulae satisfactorily explain all results reached, courts have been inclined to regard these instruments in the light of commercial practices and to treat rights as based essentially upon the expectations of tradesmen rather than upon legal precedents.[5]

C. The Purchaser of the Draft

Another distinction should also be borne in mind. In the discussion of the rights of various parties, the difference between the position of the beneficiary and that of the purchaser of the draft has always been found significant. In a discussion of legal principles, the same differentiation should also be made. The rights of a purchaser may be based on one of several theories: (1) that they arise by virtue of an assignment from the beneficiary; (2) that they result from the acceptance of an offer made directly to the purchaser by the issuing bank; (3) that the letter of credit gives rise to an estoppel in favor of the purchaser; or (4) that the rights of the purchaser are based on the custom of merchants, as are the rights of an endorsee of an accepted draft.[6]

The first theory, which has been suggested in some cases, will protect the bona fide purchaser except where the bank has a defense against the beneficiary. In this situation, the purchaser, though bona fide, could not recover, if the usual rule were applied,

---

[4] See *supra* ch. IV, p. 151, for a consideration of the acts sufficient to constitute an acceptance and the extent to which the revocable credits can effectively be revoked.

[5] In reference to the buyer's letter of credit, see Lonsdale & Gray v. Lafayette Bank, 18 Ohio 126 (1849); Oil Well Supply Co. v. MacMurphey, 119 Minn. 500, 138 N. W. 784 (1912); quoted *supra* ch. III, p. 103. See also cases cited, *supra* ch. III, p. 101, note 25. As to revocable credits, see *supra* ch. IV, p. 151 *et seq.* and cases there cited.

[6] See also McCurdy, *Commercial Letters of Credit* (1922) 35 Harv. L. Rev. 539, 717. The suggestion that the bank is bound because the beneficiary acted as its agent in drawing the draft is too obviously untenable to require consideration. Where such is the case, the transaction does not create a letter of credit situation, see *supra* ch. I, p. 20.

as his rights would be subject to those of the beneficiary.[7] It has, however, been held that this rule is sufficiently modified in this type of case so as to cut off equities between the original parties.[8] By doing so, the court has destroyed that essential characteristic of an assignment by which it is distinguished from the negotiation of bills and notes. So altered, it can scarcely be considered as constituting any longer a theory of assignment, but must rather be deemed an entirely new legal principle.[9]

The offer theory is more adequate.[10] The terms of the offer may be held to be only those matters contained in the letter of credit. Only those facts known to the purchaser would be available in determining his rights against the bank. Yet this theory falls short in cases where the bank attempts to cancel an irrevocable credit by giving notice of such revocation to the purchaser. Of course, as to the seller, such notice would be ineffective particularly after the seller has acted in reliance on the credit.[11] It is difficult, however, to see how the purchaser could acquire any rights, if the view be taken that, by discounting the draft, the purchaser is accepting an offer made to him by the bank, since obviously there is, to his knowledge, no such offer in existence at the time

---

[7] See Union Bank of Canada v. Cole, 47 L. J. Q. B. 100 (1877); Carrollton Bank v. Tayleur, 16 La. 490 (1840); Evansville Nat. Bank v. Kaufmann, 93 N. Y. 273 (1883), *rev'g*, 24 Hun 612 (1881); 2 Pomeroy, Equity Jurisprudence (4th ed. 1918) § 703 *et seq.*

[8] *In re* Agra & Masterman's Bank, *Ex parte* Asiatic Banking Corporation, L. R. 2 Ch. App. 391 (1867), discussed *supra* ch. II, p. 53. *Cf.* Roman v. Serna, 40 Tex. 306 (1874), also an action in equity.

[9] In England the objection to the assignability of choses in action was, at one time, one reason for denying the plaintiff who was not the addressee, a right of action on the promise. See Johnson v. Collings, 1 East 98, 103, 102 Eng. R. 40, 42 (1800), quoted *supra* ch. II, p. 52.

[10] "If the letter shows that it was written for the purpose of being shown in order to obtain credit, and the purchaser is within the terms of the letter, it amounts to an offer that, if he purchases the draft, it will be honored. That offer or promise becomes a contract when the draft is negotiated." Banco Nacional Ultramarino v. First Nat. Bank, 289 Fed. 169, 173, 174 (D. Mass. 1923). See also Russell v. Wiggin, 21 Fed. Cas. No. 12,165 (C. C. D. Mass 1842); *In re* Agra & Masterman's Bank, *Ex parte* Asiatic Banking Corp., *supra* note 8.

[11] As to acts sufficient to constitute reliance, see *supra* ch. III, p. 106, ch. VI, pp. 253, 254.

he purchases the draft.[12] To avoid this result, it has been suggested that the acts of the seller in reliance on the credit not only makes the credit irrevocable in regard to such seller, but also in regard to the purchaser. To the considerable extent that this rule alters the usual rules of contract governing the acceptance of offers, the commercial credit cannot be treated, even in regard to the purchaser, as merely an offer to be accepted by the purchaser when he discounts the draft.

In this same situation, no theory of estoppel could be satisfactorily applied, since what the bank is doing when it revokes the credit by giving notice to purchasers is in effect to declare the representation ended before the purchaser has acted or relied upon it in any way.[13]

If the rights of the purchaser are deemed to be based upon the custom of the merchants to which it is desired to give legal effect, all difficulties disappear and the usual rules relating to bona fide purchasers of bills of exchange can be applied without difficulty. This the courts have been inclined to do.[14]

D. The Beneficiary

There remains to be discussed the various theories that have been suggested as a basis upon which the seller's rights under an irrevocable commercial letter of credit can be sustained. These theories may be divided into three groups: (1) the contract theory, (2) the estoppel theory, and (3) the mercantile specialty theory.

(1) There are several variations of the contract theory which may be considered in turn:

---

[12] It is for this reason that the offer theory is adequate in the case of revocable offers both as to the seller and the purchaser. The termination of the offer destroys in fact the power of either party to subject the issuer to any further liability.

[13] The estoppel theory is, in effect, but a variation of a contract theory; see *infra*, p. 285. For a discussion of the nature of the representation necessary to support an estoppel, see *infra* p. 285.

[14] Russell v. Wiggin, 21 Fed. Cas. No. 12, 165 (C. C. D. Mass. 1842 quoted *supra* ch. III, p. 100.

a) The letter of credit as an offer by a bank to the seller looking toward a unilateral contract.

b) The letter of credit as an offer by a bank to the seller looking toward a bilateral contract.

c) The letter of credit as a bilateral contract between the bank and the buyer for the benefit of the seller.

d) The letter of credit as a bilateral contract between the bank and the buyer with a simultaneous assignment thereof to the seller.

e) The letter of credit as a bilateral contract between the bank and the seller as promisee with the consideration moving from the buyer.[15]

If the letter of credit is an offer to the seller looking toward a unilateral contract, the court may consider one of three possible acts as the expected acceptance, *i. e.*, the making of the sales contract, some acts of preparation for the delivery of the goods contracted to be sold, or the presentation to the bank or negotiation of the draft and documents. If the offer factually contemplates any act, probably the last of these three is the one so contemplated. To adopt this view, however, would permit the revocation of the letter of credit during the period of manufacture and preparation

[15] An excellent analysis of these problems can be found in McCurdy, *Commercial Letters of Credit* (1922) 35 HARV. L. REV. 539, 563; *The Right of the Beneficiary under a Commercial Letter of Credit* (1924) 37 *ibid.* 323. The writer is largely in accord with what is said there, particularly in regard to the first four suggested analyses given above. They are therefore stated here rather briefly and reference is made to the articles of Professor William E. McCurdy for a more detailed analysis. See also the discussion of various aspects of these problems in (1924) 12 CAL. L. REV. 500; (1921) 21 COL. L. REV. 176; (1921) 34 HARV. L. REV. 533. It is, at this point, too obvious to need comment that a commercial letter of credit cannot be treated as a guaranty by the issuing bank of the obligations of the buyer under the sales contract, *supra* ch. I, p. 15, ch. II, p. 32; or that the letter of credit creates a trust in favor of the beneficiary or the purchaser. Morgan v. Larivière, L. R. 7 H. L. 423 (1875); Kuehne v. Union Trust Co., 133 Mich. 602, 95 N. W. 715 (1903); Taussig v. Carnegie Trust Co., 156 App. Div. 519, 141 N. Y. Supp. 347 (1913), *aff'd* without opinion, 213 N. Y. 627, 107 N. E. 1086 (1914), see pp. 150, 159; *cf.* Payne Bros. v. Burnett, 151 Tenn. 496, 269 S. W. 27, 39 A. L. R. 1125 (1925); Miltenberger v. Cooke, 18 Wall. 421, 21 L. Ed. 864 (1873).

of the goods, and thus would destroy the distinction between revocable and irrevocable letters of credit. An all-important purpose of the latter instrument, however, is to protect the seller during that period, and in addition it is treated commercially as irrevocable during that period. While this theory may explain most results, in the all-important case where the bank attempts to revoke an irrevocable credit before the draft has been presented or negotiated, no satisfactory explanation can be given of the rules which enable a seller, notwithstanding, to recover against the bank. It has, accordingly, been suggested that the ultimate act, *i. e.*, the presentation or negotiation of the draft, is not the acceptance of the offer, but that only certain acts in reliance on the credit, e. g., purchases made by the seller for the purpose of complying with the requirements of the credit, constitute the acceptance.[16] The objections to this view are twofold: that such is not the intention of the parties, and that the point at which a credit would become irrevocable would always be indefinite and incapable of exact determination, thus to a large extent destroying one of the prime functions of the irrevocable credit.[17]

---

[16] See Urquhart Lindsay & Co. v. Eastern Bank, [1922] 1 K. B. 318, 321. "There can be no doubt that upon the plaintiff's acting upon the undertaking contained in this letter of credit, consideration moved from the plaintiffs, which bound the defendants to the irrevocable character of the arrangement between the defendants and the plaintiffs." *Cf.* Dexters, Ltd., v. Schenker & Co., 14 Lloyd's List 586, 588 (1923); American Steel Co. v. Irving Nat. Bank, 266 Fed. 41, 43 (C. C. A. 2d, 1920), 277 Fed. 1016 (C. C. A. 2d, 1921), *cert. den.*, 258 U. S. 617, 42 Sup. Ct. 271 (1922); see also D. O. McGovney, *Irrevocable Offers,* (1914) 27 HARV. L. REV. 644, 654; *cf.* 1 WILLISTON, CONTRACTS (1920) § 60 *et seq.* Professor McGovney suggests that an offer looking toward a unilateral contract may also be held to contain an implied subordinate offer to keep the primary offer open for a reasonable time and that this secondary offer is accepted and ripens into an agreement by the beginning of performance on the part of the offeree. This suggestion is not only contrary to the facts of the usual situation, as Professor Williston has indicated and as has been stated above, but also tends to alter the entire nature of a unilateral contract. Instead of being an arrangement whereby both parties are free to refuse to enter the contract, which as far as the offeror is concerned is an essential part of an offer looking toward a unilateral contract, Professor McGovney's interpretation would make this type of offer irrevocable as to the offeror, leaving the offeree free to accept or not as he pleased.

[17] See Lafargue v. Harrison, 70 Cal. 380, 9 Pac. 259, 11 Pac. 636 (1886), a case clearly adopting this theory. In New York, this approach has

The letter of credit as an offer looking toward a bilateral contract is obviously too inadequate as a basis for the seller's rights against the bank to require any extended discussion. To find a promise given by the seller in exchange for the promise by the bank is practically impossible from any point of view. If, however, the promise by the seller to enter into a sales contract with the buyer be regarded as the consideration given by the seller for the issuance of the credit, the objection encountered is that the sales contract has usually been entered into by the seller before the credit is issued.[18] If the seller's promise to deliver certain goods to the buyer be regarded as the consideration, the answer is that a promise to do what one is already legally obligated to do is commonly held not to be consideration, and the seller is already obligated under the sales contract to deliver the goods. There is the further factual difficulty that the parties do not have this in mind. If the seller is to furnish any consideration, the act of presenting the documents, rather than the making of a promise, is the act required.[19]

---

been definitely rejected for irrevocable commercial credits. "The appellant argues that a letter of credit is an instrument in the nature of an option, which must be accepted by the performance of certain acts in accordance with its terms before a liability is fastened upon the issuer of the letter. But, assuming that this is a correct statement of the law, as applicable to certain kinds of letters of credit, the fact is that the letter under review was issued upon a valuable consideration and was declared to be irrevocable.

"The letter of credit upon which this action is based was a complete and independent contract between the plaintiff shipper and the defendant bank which issued it based upon a valuable consideration." Doelger v. Battery Park Nat. Bank, 201 App. Div. 515, 521, 194 N. Y. Supp. 582, 587 (1922).

[18] If the seller refuses to enter into a contract with the buyer without the letter of credit, the issuer might issue it in return for the seller's promise to enter a sales contract with the buyer. Ordinarily a bank will not enter into any such agreement with the seller and merely issues, or refuses to issue, a credit at the buyer's request. Occasionally an individual, at the buyer's request, may make such an agreement with the seller. See Mendelson v. Wechsler, 203 N. Y. Supp. 197 (1924); see also Emerson-Brantingham Implement Co. v. Raugstad, 65 Mont. 297, 211 Pac. 305 (1922). This, however, is an unusual situation, and does not come within the field of the present discussion, as it is not a bank credit issued in the usual course of business.

[19] See Moss v. Old Colony Trust Co., *supra* note 1, where the court is, apparently, of the opinion that the seller must give a promise or perform an act in exchange for the promise contained in the credit.

There is an additional difficulty. To complete a bilateral contract, the seller would be required to give notice of acceptance. In practice, there is no such requirement, and sellers customarily give no such notice. While in one case it was intimated that the seller was obligated to give notice of his acceptance of the credit,[20] the weight of authority is *contra* and recognizes the sound commercial practice.

A confirmed irrevocable letter of credit, an irrevocable letter, or a confirmed credit is a contract to pay upon compliance with its terms and needs no formal acknowledgment or acceptance other than is therein stated.[21]

If the letter of credit be regarded as a contract with the buyer for the benefit of the seller, the difficulties are obvious. In some jurisdictions, the beneficiary of a contract cannot sue in his own name,[22] and even in jurisdictions where he may so sue, his rights would be generally subject to the bank's defences against the buyer, such as fraud or failure of consideration.[23] This defeats the very purpose of the irrevocable commercial letter of credit.[24] This same objection could also be raised against the theory of a letter of credit as a bilateral contract between the bank and the buyer with a simultaneous assignment to the seller. A further objection is that this interpretation strains the facts considerably and does not conform to the intention of the parties.[25]

---

[20] See Moss v. Old Colony Trust Co., *supra* note 1.

[21] Lamborn v. Nat. Park Bank, 240 N. Y. 520, 525, 148 N. E. 664, 665 (1925). See also London & San Francisco Bank v. Parrott, 125 Cal. 472, 58 Pac. 164 (1899). Compare the requirement of notice to a guarantor of action taken in reliance on the guaranty, *supra* ch. II, note 209.

[22] See e. g., Dunlop Pneumatic Tyre Co. v. Selfridge & Co., [1915] A. C. 847.

[23] 1 WILLISTON, CONTRACTS (1920) ch. XIII, §§ 394, 395.

[24] See First Wisconsin Nat. Bank v. Forsyth Leather Co., 189 Wis. 9, 16, 206 N. W. 843, 845 (1926); Carnegie v. Morrison, 2 Metc. 381 (Mass. 1841); Hawley v. Exchange State Bank, 97 Iowa 187, 66 N. W. 152 (1896), where the courts view the rights of the seller as similar to those of a beneficiary of a contract.

[25] There seem to be no cases taking this view. See, however, McCurdy, *op. cit. supra* note 6, at p. 583 and cases there cited. As has been indicated, there are suggestions in the books that the right of a bona fide purchaser may be based on an assignment from the beneficiary, but this is a different matter. See *supra* p. 277.

The most acceptable view hitherto advanced has been that the letter of credit is a promise by the bank to the seller with consideration moving from the buyer.[26] This approaches the actual intention of the parties more closely than any of the other theories thus far suggested. Most of the objections encountered do not arise under this view. The contract being complete when the letter is issued, the credit cannot thereafter be revoked, and no necessity exists for notice of acceptance on the part of the seller. The difficulty that arises, however, lies in finding any consideration from the buyer when he becomes insolvent, repudiates the agreement to reimburse, or procures the issuance of the credit by fraud. Even if some ingenious legal analysis be devised to overcome this difficulty, the case of a letter of credit issued by mistake, e. g., where the buyer has not requested the issue of credit, remains as a last stumbling block. In this situation there is no consideration of any kind moving from the buyer, and yet under certain conditions, the seller is permitted to recover against the bank. The suggested answer to this difficulty has been that:

> In order to make the letter irrevocable for all purposes from the moment of issue a better explanation perhaps is that the commission covers the risks of fraud and insolvency of the buyer, and that as a matter of business expediency the risk should be borne legally by the bank. The parties contemplate this result. There is no reason why legal effect should not be given to their intention.[27]

This approach uses the theory of consideration as far as is possible and attempts to have the burden carried the rest of the way

---

[26] For an excellent discussion of this theory, see McCurdy, *op. cit. supra* note 6, at 574. The decisions, however, have not particularly favored this approach. It is a point in only one case. Johannessen v. Munroe, 84 Hun 594, 32 N. Y. Supp. 863 (1895). The final decision rested on another basis, 9 App. Div. 409, 41 N. Y. Supp. 586 (1896), *aff'd*, 158 N. Y. 641, 53 N. E. 535 (1899), see *infra* note 35. See, however, McCurdy, *op. cit. supra* note 6, at 577 et seq., and cases there cited; (1924) 12 CAL. L. REV. 500, 506 n. 26. See also Saylors v. State Bank of Allen, 99 Kan. 515, 163 Pac. 454 (1917).

[27] McCurdy, *Commercial Letters of Credit* (1922) 35 HARV. L. REV. 539, 580. Even this attempted explanation does not, it will be noted, cover the case of a letter of credit issued by mistake.

by a variation of the theory of the letter of credit as some kind of mercantile specialty.[28] Even under this view, therefore, difficulty arises in explaining and justifying the rules that have been laid down governing the rights of the seller under an irrevocable credit.[29]

(2) The theories of estoppel are really varieties of the contract theories, as it is submitted that an estoppel is not, as a rule, the basis of a cause of action.[30] The principle of estoppel might conceivably be applied to each of the various contract theories previously discussed. As a matter of fact, from the nature of the various forms of estoppel that have been suggested, it is apparent that these can apply only to the last contract theory, *i. e.,* that an irrevocable credit is a promise to the seller with the consideration moving from the buyer. The principal difficulty with this view was found in cases where actually, for one reason or another, there was no consideration from the buyer. It has accordingly been suggested that the letter of credit, in addition to evidencing a promise, constitutes a representation:

a) that the bank has received money from the buyer for the issuance of the credit, or

b) that the bank has received a promise from the buyer to put the bank in funds before the date of maturity of the drafts drawn under the credit, or

---

[28] It has also been suggested that this theory be supplemented by an estoppel in order to support the results reached. (1924) 12 CAL. L. REV. 500, 506.

[29] There is an additional objection to this analysis. In England, a promisee cannot sue unless the consideration has moved from him. See McCurdy, *op. cit. supra* note 27, at 581, 582. In the law merchant generally, and particularly in regard to letters of credit, which are so widely used in international trade, it is desirable that all countries proceed on the same theory as far as possible. A theory which cannot be used in one of the principal countries concerned in the use of letters of credit should not readily be adopted, unless the commercial and legal considerations are overwhelming. In this case they are not so compelling.

[30] EWART, ESTOPPEL (1900) ch. XV; *cf.* 3 WILLISTON, CONTRACTS (1924) § 1508.

c) that all questions of consideration have been taken care of by the buyer in some manner satisfactory to the bank.

As to the other elements necessary to work an estoppel, *i. e.*, reliance and damage to the seller, little difficulty arises. The real problem is to determine what is the representation, if any, made by the bank in issuing an irrevocable credit.

The first suggestion would obviously eliminate all questions of consideration, since the bank is estopped to deny that it has received money for the issuance of the credit.[31] The objection is, as has been indicated,[32] that this suggestion is not in accord with the facts inasmuch as in the majority of cases commercial credits are not issued for cash, and no seller acquainted with business usage assumes that such is the case.[33]

The second suggestion, *i. e.*, that the bank represents that it has received satisfactory assurance from the buyer that he will provide necessary funds to meet the drafts which it accepts under the credit, is probably not sufficiently comprehensive. It is a representation that the bank has received a promise. It is no representation that the bank has received performance of that promise. Accordingly, while the bank may be estopped from denying that it has received a promise, apparently it cannot be prevented from showing that the promise was not performed, e. g., that the buyer has failed to put the bank in funds. This type of estoppel, therefore, offers no solution to the difficulties already suggested in

[31] Hershey, *Letters of Credit* (1918) 32 HARV. L. REV. 1.

[32] McCurdy, *op. cit. supra* note 27, at 584 *et seq.*

[33] See Morgan v. Larivière, L. R. 7 H. L. 423 (1875), for a case definitely rejecting this analysis; see also Townsley v. Sumrall, 2 Pet. 170, 183, 7 L. Ed. 386, 390 (1829) stating that a purchaser could recover even though he knew the issuer did not have funds of the buyer in his possession. In isolated instances this may actually be done and the representation may therefore be possible, in which event the bank is bound, though it later permits the buyer to withdraw the funds. Sears, Roebuck & Co. v. Rouse Banking Co., 191 N. C. 500, 132 S. E. 468 (1926). This type of transaction is often more in the nature of a special deposit for the benefit of a third party, than a typical commercial credit transaction, see Seaman v. Tamaqua Nat. Bank, 20 Schuyl. Leg. Rec. 21 (1923), *rev'd*, 280 Pa. 124 (1924); *cf.* cases cited *supra* ch. III, note 67.

connection with problems arising in cases in which there is no consideration from the buyer.

The third suggestion as to the representation made by the bank is clearly more nearly adequate than either of those already considered. A prime purpose of the irrevocable credit is, as has repeatedly been indicated, to add the primary responsibility of the bank to that of the buyer, so that the bank, rather than the seller, carries the risk of the buyer's integrity and solvency. Of necessity, therefore, the bank, in issuing a letter of credit, is, in effect, promising the seller that it will pay him upon the performance of certain conditions and that it will pay him, irrespective of its relations with the buyer—whether the latter becomes insolvent, fails to perform his obligations to the bank, or has fraudulently procured the issuance of the credit. This promise may reasonably be analyzed as containing two elements, a promise to pay on certain conditions and a representation that the bank has made satisfactory arrangements of one sort or another with the buyer as a result of which it is willing to pay drafts irrespective of what happens to the buyer.[34] It is not merely a representation that the buyer has promised to indemnify the bank. It is more than that. It is a representation that the bank considers itself adequately compensated for its promise to the seller and that the question of consideration has ceased to be of any importance. Something substantially like this may reasonably be implied in every irrevocable letter of credit issued. Certainly something of

---

[34] See De Tastett v. Crousillat, 7 Fed. Cas. No. 3,828 (C. C. D. Pa. 1807). The defendant here counterclaimed for damages for the dishonor of a draft drawn under a revocable letter of credit before it had been revoked, and the plaintiff set up as a defense, *inter alia,* the fact that he had no funds of the buyer in his hands at the time the draft was drawn. The court held: "it is of no consequence whether the defendant had or had not funds in the hands of the house of St. Sebastians, unless this had been made a condition of the plaintiffs' engagement to accept; for a man may validly bind himself to accept bills without funds, and if the promise be general, and the transactions fair, he continues bound till a countermand is received." At p. 544. Thus even as early as 1807 we find a recognition of the fact that the bank cannot set up as a defense the fact that it had not received proper consideration from the buyer. See also *supra* ch. VI, p. 250.

the kind is what the parties intend and is the basis for the increased use and popularity of this type of letter of credit.[35]

A comparison with other forms of bank credit should be of value. The certification of a check is usually taken to mean that the drawer has actual funds on deposit or that he has arranged for a loan, which is equivalent to the same thing. The same understanding holds true as to bank acceptances payable at sight. A bank acceptance of a time draft is usually taken to indicate that the depositor has arranged for a loan of credit—an extension of credit—it being understood that he will put the bank in funds before the maturity of the draft, either by making a deposit or by arranging for a loan of cash. This is exactly the situation in the case of a letter of credit, and such is the general understanding in commercial and banking circles.

This type of representation settles practically all the difficulties encountered when the letter of credit is regarded as a promise to the seller with consideration moving from the buyer. The bank, having once represented that the question of consideration has been settled to its satisfaction, is estopped from showing the contrary, and the seller can recover even though the credit has been issued by mistake or the consideration from the buyer has failed.[36]

The amount of reliance by the seller necessary to work the estoppel is of course very small. The exact point at which the estoppel begins to operate cannot be determined beforehand, but must be fixed by the facts of each particular case as it arises. This much is clear, that slight action by the seller in reliance on the letter of credit is sufficient, inasmuch as otherwise the letter

[35] For a case based on this type of estoppel, see Johannessen v. Munroe, *supra* note 26, at 646, 53 N. E. at 536, where the issuer said in response to an inquiry by the beneficiary, "He has made arrangements satisfactory to us." As indicated by McCurdy, *op. cit. supra* note 27, at 590, the representation that gave rise to the estoppel was "*dehors* the letter of credit." The mere issuance of an irrevocable credit may be taken, however, to amount to just such a representation.

[36] The fact that it is innocent is of no consequence. An estoppel can be based on an innocent as well as an intentional misrepresentation. Ewart, Estoppel (1900) ch. VIII, p. 85 *et seq.*

of credit would not, as a practical matter, be irrevocable from the time of issue. This problem is not unique with letters of credit but arises throughout the law of estoppel.[37] It presents no particularly difficult questions in this connection and can readily be solved on the facts of each particular case.[38]

The principal objection to the estoppel theory is that it is unreal and is in the nature of a legal fiction, since commercially the letter of credit is not regarded as a representation but as a promise. In addition, it is based essentially on the contract theory which represents an attempt to take legal principles developed as a result of one aspect of the economic activities of man and apply it to another for which, of necessity, it must be inadequate.

(3) There can be little doubt that in practice the irrevocable credit is regarded as in the nature of a mercantile specialty. The seller in fact regards the bank's promise as irrevocable because of the manner in which it is made. The average business man, though ignorant of legal technicalities, is conscious of the fact that bills, checks, and notes are *sui generis,* that they are contracts peculiar to themselves, and that they have little in common with the usual contract. He would be inclined to classify letters of credit with this group rather than with the usual type of contract. There can also be little doubt that this reaction to the nature and use of letters of credit is sound. Nor can it be denied that this has also been the attitude of the courts in adjudicating rights under irrevocable commercial credits. It has been recognized that they are a definite class of promises to extend credit or to pay money, made under certain conditions and with a certain essential uniformity. If any formal theory be needed as to the rights of

[37] Ewart, Estoppel (1900) 139.

[38] To a great extent this question would solve itself, as in almost all cases the seller would have performed some act in reliance upon the letter of credit before the notice of revocation had arrived. The prudent seller, who had not as yet acted under the credit before the notice of revocation had arrived, would hardly, in normal times, be likely to proceed after he had received the notice.

the seller under this type of instrument, clearly such rights must be regarded as based on the view that the irrevocable credit is a new type of mercantile specialty.

Two principal objections have been urged as invalidating this conclusion: that the problem of consideration would still exist and that there is not sufficient uniformity in the forms used to make it desirable to treat the letter of credit as a mercantile specialty.[39] In support of the first contention, it is argued that the tendency of the law is toward requiring consideration, not away from it, that even in bills and notes the problem of consideration exists as between the immediate parties, and that the effect of the law merchant on the common law is to make bills and notes negotiable but not to make promises binding without consideration.

There is an essential difference between recognizing, in furtherance of commerce, that certain *choses in action* are assignable so as to confer upon the assignee original in distinction to derivative rights, and in recognizing that certain promises need no consideration to be legally enforceable. In the one case the question relates to the transferability of an existing legal right; in the other case the question concerns the creation of that right. To some extent, to be sure, especially in the matter of negotiable instruments, the common law has expanded and modified its strict conception of

[39] McCurdy, *op. cit. supra* note 27, at 563-66. In addition, there is the growing inherent difficulty in the way of the recognition by law of business customs and usages. This problem, however, is not peculiar to the law of letters of credit, see Wright, *Opposition of the Law to Business Usages* (1926) 26 COL. L. REV. 917, 922. Professor Wright considers the manner in which the consensualist theory of contracts raises additional difficulties in the way of legal recognition of these usages. He points out that in order to preserve the theory intact, separate categories must be created for each new type of instrument and goes on to say: "Other forms of obligation may now exist or may come into existence through the activities of business men; and these, because of their inherent qualities—and, incidentally again, to save the day for consensualism—might be at once put into a separate category. But while legislatures may, the courts are unlikely to be willing to take so bold a step. Such obligations, furthermore, are as a matter of fact likely to begin if at all in form as simple contracts and even when deserving of separate treatment outside the domain of the consensual theory, will tend to remain therein. For all these reasons, therefore, and also because this theory is nowadays so universal and so ably expressed, it seems probable that a much stronger obstacle stands in the way of the progress of usage into law than, for example, ever stood in the way of the negotiable instrument in the days of Lord Mansfield."

what constitutes consideration. But the law has never abolished its necessity.[40]

Several factors should be noted in this connection. Even if no such theory has previously been in existence, that alone is no reason why one should not now be adopted if the necessities of commerce so require, particularly if it is the only basis upon which a multitude of actual and wise decisions can be put in order and upon which the point of view underlying the results reached can be adequately expressed. At one point in the development of the common law, the theory of negotiability was also decidedly novel, yet a recognition of the necessities of the times made it imperative that that theory be adopted. An equally intelligent and sympathetic regard for modern commercial needs would result in a repetition of the theorization of the seventeenth century.

Likewise, the recognition of the letter of credit as a mercantile specialty would be no such drastic departure as might at first be assumed. The position of the bank issuing a letter of credit has repeatedly been shown to be closely analogous to that of the acceptor of a bill of exchange. The drawee in accepting a bill is, in effect, promising to pay money. The rights of the payee against him are based upon this promise. But in addition to the promise, the payee must prove either that he purchased the bill for value or that the acceptor received consideration for the acceptance. If neither of these elements appear, the payee cannot recover.[41] If,

---

[40] McCurdy, *op. cit. supra* note 27, at 565. Moreover, the law of negotiability deals with the creation, as well as the transfer, of rights. In cases of instruments fraudulently procured, the bona fide purchaser acquires rights that the original party did not have. It is for the very reason that the Negotiable Instruments Law deals with the creation as well as the transfer of rights, that the bona fide purchaser's rights are deemed to be original and not derivative.

[41] "As two distinct considerations come in question . . . where the payee or indorsee became the holder of the bill before it was overdue and without any knowledge of the facts and circumstances which impeach the title as between the immediate parties to the instrument. Those two considerations are as follows: First, that which the defendant received for his liability, and, secondly, that which the plaintiff gave for his title; and the rule is well settled that the action between the remote parties to the bill will not be defeated unless there be an absence or failure of both

however, he has given consideration then the relations between drawer and acceptor are immaterial. Similarly, the bank under a letter of credit, promises to pay money to, or upon the order of, the seller. If the buyer has given the bank consideration or if the seller has given the buyer consideration, the bank does and should come under a duty to perform its promise.[42] If there is no consideration between any of the parties, the seller acquires no rights against the bank.[43]

The similarity here is marked and definite. The innovation consists merely in the extension of a set of rules relating to certain promises to pay, written upon a draft, to certain other promises to pay or to accept. Part of this extension has already been made in the doctrine of virtual and extrinsic acceptances. From this point of view, that doctrine may be described as the extension of the rules relating to promises to pay written upon a draft, to promises to pay or to accept contained in another instrument made either before or after the draft is drawn. The law would be greatly simplified if this tendency were carried a step further so as to include all promises contained in letters of credit, and not

---

these considerations." Hoffman & Co. v. Bank of Milwaukee, 12 Wall. 181, 191, 20 L. Ed. 366, 369 (1870).

[42] Where the bank has a defense against the buyer, we have seen that the seller can nevertheless recover if he acts before he receives notice of revocation. Since past consideration is sufficient to support an action on a negotiable instrument, the same rule can be applied in this instance, the past consideration being the previous contract of sale entered into by the seller with the buyer. The action by the seller in reliance on the credit can also be viewed as the consideration. This approach is, however, unreal in view of the attitude of the courts toward negotiable instruments. The acceptor of a draft, who, it is submitted, cannot revoke because of mistake, is bound because the payee has received the draft in good faith, in the usual course of business and is in a position similar to that of a bona fide purchaser. The bank certifying a check is bound for similar reasons, and it is submitted that in the issuance of an irrevocable commercial credit the bank should also be held liable upon similar grounds.

[43] He has, however, a power to subject the bank to a liability by selling the draft to a bona fide purchaser. If the issuing bank has received no consideration, the problem arises of the extent to which it may go into the question of the lack of consideration between seller and buyer. This has been considered, see pp. 248, 257 *et seq.* At what point this rule is fixed, is a matter of commercial convenience and does not affect the views here suggested.

merely those which comply with certain arbitrary conditions.[44]

Another objection to the mercantile specialty theory is that the letter of credit is not sufficiently uniform to be classed as a mercantile specialty; hence this extension of the rules applicable to bills of exchange cannot profitably be made. The greater part of these variations is eliminated if the term letter of credit is properly limited to those instruments that perform letter of credit functions. This would exclude all letters issued by buyers themselves. A review of the forms as reported in the cases shows that the widest variations occur in forms issued by buyers. All revocable forms such as the authority to purchase or the revocable letter of credit can also be put to one side as performing an essentially different commercial function from that performed by the irrevocable commercial letter of credit. There remains the irrevocable letter of credit issued by the bank.[45] While forms of this type of letter of credit have varied in the past, the tendency towards uniformity among banks is increasing. Because of their use in different trades and by different nations, letters of credit can never become as nearly uniform as bills or notes. Nor is this necessary. If the general language is similar and if conditions as far as possible are similarly worded, that is all that should be required. The only essential is that commercial letters of credit

---

[44] It is not suggested that letters of credit should be actionable as acceptances, but merely that the principle underlying the acceptor's liability should be extended to letters of credit. The form of the action may well be and should be different. In those jurisdictions where pleading consists merely of stating the facts without specifying the form of action, it would often be difficult, if not impossible, to draw a distinction, see e. g., Midwest Nat. Bank & Trust Co. v. Niles & Watters Savings Bank, 190 Iowa 752, 180 N. W. 880 (1921); see also ch. III, p. 140, and the cases where a judgment creditor attempts to garnishee funds of the drawer in the hands of the drawee-promisor. The question there is, whether the latter is under a duty of any kind to the holder of the draft. The problem therefore of whether the promisor is held to be under an obligation on an acceptance or a promise to accept is immaterial and the cases often fail to specify on which ground the garnishee process is vacated. See e. g., Jones v. Crumpler, 119 Va. 143, 89 S. E. 232 (1916).

[45] Irrevocable letters of credit are seldom issued by others than banks. When they are so issued, however, the special facts of each case usually form a basis for liability on a theory of contract or estoppel. See *supra* note 18.

contain such characteristics that they may be easily recognizable. This degree of uniformity has already been achieved. Cabled and telegraphic communications furnish greater difficulty. Generally, however, they are followed by formal letters of credit. Where such is not the case, there remains a scattering of informal instruments which results from every classification of this kind. Similar doubts arise as to informal documents purporting to be bills or notes. The solution in each instance is to fall back upon the essential commercial functions of these instruments in order to decide whether or not the document in question falls into the specified category. The characteristics and functions of an irrevocable commercial letter of credit are as clearly defined and as easily distinguishable as are those of bills or notes, and have been recognized by the courts with as little difficulty. The doctrine presented here can therefore well be applied to them.

It is possible to explain every case on the basis of its facts. We may develop a number of different theories of the seller's rights under an irrevocable letter of credit explaining as many situations. It is only to be expected that these theories, particularly when they represent an effort to explain, by traditional legal formulae, rights arising under commercial letters of credit, will either overlap or conflict, resulting in decisions unsatisfactory from a commercial point of view. The law relating to letters of credit is largely either made or in the making. The courts have adjudicated the rights of the various parties to these instruments with surprisingly few differences of opinion. The approach in all types of problems has been that of the law merchant. The incidental rules laid down have been those applying to bills and notes.[46] To view the irrevocable commercial letter of credit as a mercantile specialty of a new type, most clearly, simply, and satisfactorily explains the rights of the parties, harmonizes the decisions

[46] See e. g., Second Nat. Bank v. M. Samuel & Sons, 12 F. (2d) 963, 53 A. L. R. 49 (C. C. A. 2d, 1926), *cert. den.*, 273 U. S. 720, 47 Sup. Ct. 110 (1926), discussed *supra* ch. III, p. 116, note 54.

of the past, and makes more dependable the future development of the law, thus enabling both banker and merchant to proceed with their activities with confidence and assurance.[47] The theory that the irrevocable letter of credit is a mercantile specialty has now for some time been acted upon and has been functionally adopted. The ability of the law to develop with the needs of commerce has not yet disappeared, and with the growing consciousness on the part of the courts of the true status of the commercial credit, its formal recognition as a mercantile specialty cannot long be delayed.[48]

---

[47] See McCurdy, *Commercial Letters of Credit* (1922) 35 HARV. L. REV. 539, 564, n. 60; Hershey, *Letters of Credit* (1918) 32 HARV. L. REV. 1, 10, 25, 26.

[48] "Granting that the law is not as yet clearly worked out, it is certain, at least in this circuit, that, when once communicated to the seller, the letter creates a contract which is in fact irrevocable." Pan-American Bank & Trust Co. v. Nat. City Bank, 6 F. (2d) 762, 770 (C. C. A. 2d, 1925), *cert. den.*, 269 U. S. 554, 46 Sup. Ct. 18 (1925) (dissent). "It [a letter of credit] partakes of the nature of a negotiable instrument." Second Nat. Bank v. M. Samuel & Sons, *supra* note 46, at 966, 53 A. L. R. at 54. See also: Maurice O'Meara Co. v. Nat. Park Bank, 239 N. Y. 386, 146 N. E. 636, 39 A. L. R. 747 (1925); American Steel Co. v. Irving Nat. Bank, 266 Fed. 41 (C. C. A. 2d, 1920), 277 Fed. 1016 (C. C. A. 2d, 1921), *cert. den.*, 258 U. S. 617, 42 Sup. Ct. 271 (1922); Sovereign Bank of Canada v. Bellhouse Dillon & Co., 23 Quebec Off. L. R. 413 (1911); Maitland v. Chartered Mercantile Bank of India, London and China, 38 L. J. Ch. 363 (1869); Farmers' & Merchants' Bank v. Davies, 144 La. 531, 540, 80 So. 713, 715 (1919). "The tendency of modern jurisprudence is to get away from the rigid rules of interpretation which seem to have prevailed when the famous expression of Chief Justice Gibson that 'a negotiable bill or note is a courier without luggage' (Overton v. Tiler, 3 Pa. 346) was coined. The law of negotiable instruments, as a part of the law merchant, is based upon the necessities, usages, and customs of business, and must develop with it." (1926) 36 YALE L. J. 245.

Appendix A

MODERN FORMS OF COMMERCIAL LETTERS OF CREDIT[1]

I. Issuing Bank Forms

1. CLEAN LETTER OF CREDIT

LETTER OF CREDIT

X COMPANY

No......................

New York,..

To...

....

Dear Sir:

You are hereby authorized to value on...
of.....................................in drafts at.............................for account
of...for any sums not exceeding in all
....

And we hereby agree with the drawers, endorsers and bona fide holders, respectively, of bills drawn by virtue of this credit, that the same shall be duly honored upon presentation to.........................
....if drawn and negotiated within....................
months from this date, and unless revoked by us.

Please advise..of any bills drawn under this credit and specify in such bills that they are on account of X Co.'s letter of credit No..................dated..................................

Amounts negotiated hereunder are to be noted on the back hereof at the time of negotiation.

Very Respectfully,

Your obedient servants,

[1]For the classification of these forms, see Contents, p. xiii.

2. REVOCABLE LETTER OF CREDIT

THE NATIONAL CITY BANK
OF NEW YORK

New York, May 24th, 1920.

Capital fully paid $25,000,000
Surplus & Undivided
Profits $52,000,000

AH

In replying please quote initials. When referring to this credit, please mention our No. FE;58525.
Cable address Citibank

Messrs. Rockhill & Vietor,
22 Cliff Street, New York City:

Dear Sirs:

We have been requested to open a credit in your favor under the terms and conditions stipulated below: No. 10155.

Opened by National City Bank of New York, Barcelona. Spain.

Account G. Deandreis.

Amount Up to $187,500 (One Hundred Eighty-Seven Thousand Five Hundred Dollars).

Available by draft at sight on us, bearing credit No. FE;58525.

Covering 6,000 cases Tin Plates, 112 plates 270 pounds (weight) per box at $31.25 per box, C. I. F. Barcelona. Shipment within October 15th, 1920.

Drafts drawn under this credit must be presented not later than October 14th, 1920, unless sooner revoked.

Documents required.

Full set ocean bills of lading issued to order of National City Bank of New York, Barcelona, Spain, Invoice in triplicate. Insurance certificate, including mine risk.

Consular Invoice.

Payment will be facilitated if this advice accompanies your documents when presented at our Export Commercial Credit Department. If transfer is requested this advice must be surrendered for cancellation.

This is not to be regarded as a confirmed credit, or an agreement on our part, and is therefore subject to modification or revocation at any time.

Please note that we can only accept Bills of Lading issued by the transportation company carrying the goods.

Respectfully yours,

THE NATIONAL CITY BANK OF NEW YORK,

If impossible to comply with the conditions stated above, communicate with us before making shipment. The conditions embodied in this credit must be adhered to, otherwise payment will not be effected.

Important Notice.

In order to avoid any misunderstanding in regard to the credit outlined in the accompanying communication, we beg to say that this is Not a Confirmed Credit and consequently is subject to revocation at any time, either by the parties granting the credit or by ourselves under certain conditions. In the absence of any statement to the contrary, the National City Bank of New York assumes no obligation whatsoever to make the payment, even if all the conditions of credit have been complied with.

If this is not acceptable to you please communicate with your customer and request him to have his banker amend the instructions.

Please note for your guidance that a Confirmed Credit is absolutely irrevocable provided the conditions of the credit have been complied with.

[Taken from Vietor v. National City Bank, 200 App. Div. 557, 558, 193 N. Y. Supp. 869, 870 (1922).]

3. IRREVOCABLE STRAIGHT LETTER OF CREDIT ADDRESSED TO SELLER

American Steel Company,
Park Building,
Pittsburgh, Pa.

Gentlemen:

You are hereby authorized to draw upon us for account of MacDonnell Chow Corporation at sight to the extent of forty-three thousand two hundred fifty ($43,250.) covering shipment of tin plates.

Documents (complete sets unless otherwise stated) comprising bills of lading issued to order, indorsed in blank.

Invoices.

Insurance policies covering marine and war risk to be delivered to us against payment.

Insurance as above.

Bills of lading issued by forwarding agents will not be accepted, unless specifically authorized herein, and any modifications of the terms of the credit must be in writing, over authorized signatures of this bank.

Drawings must clearly specify the number of this credit.

Yours very truly,

IRVING NATIONAL BANK OF NEW YORK
Vice-president,
Manager, Foreign Department.

[Taken from American Steel Co. v. Irving Nat. Bank, 266 Fed. 41 (C. C. A. 2d. 1920).]

4. IRREVOCABLE STRAIGHT LETTER OF CREDIT ADDRESSED TO CORRESPONDENT BANK

Credit No. C-a........................

................................, ...19.......

....
(correspondent bank)

....
(address)

Dear Sirs:

We request you to advise...
(name)

....
(address) (city) (state)

that we have opened our irrevocable credit in their favor for account of: ....
for a sum or sums not exceeding a total of........................(figures)
..................................(words) available by their drafts on you at
....to be accompanied by
....
evidencing shipment of: ....
From .... To...
....insurance to be effected by
....

We hereby engage with the beneficiary that all drafts drawn under and in compliance with the terms of the advice will be duly honored on delivery of documents as specified, if presented at your office on or before...............................19.........

For your reimbursement you may:

(Put cross in square opposite method desired.)

Debit our account with you.

Draw on us at..

This credit is to be advised to the beneficiary by you on Commercial Credit Conference Form C-a.

Yours very truly,

5. IRREVOCABLE STRAIGHT LETTER OF CREDIT ADDRESSED TO CORRESPONDENT BANK WITH AUTHORITY TO CORRESPONDENT BANK TO CONFIRM THE CREDIT

Credit No. D-a........................

................................, ...19.......
(city)

....
(correspondent bank)

....

Dear Sirs:

We request you to advise..
(name)

....
(address) (city) (state)
that we have opened our irrevocable credit in their favor for account of: ....
for a sum or sums not exceeding a total of........................(figures)
...................................(words) available by their drafts on you at ....to be accompanied by
....
evidencing shipment of: ....
From ....To ....
....insurance to be effected by
....

We hereby engage with the beneficiary that all drafts drawn under and in compliance with the terms of the credit will be duly honored on delivery of documents as specified, if presented at your office on or before...................................19........; we authorize you to confirm the credit and thereby to undertake that drafts drawn and presented as above specified shall be duly honored by you.

For your reimbursement you may:

(Put cross in square opposite method desired.)

Debit our account with you.

Draw on us at...

This credit is to be advised to the beneficiary by you on Commercial Credit Conference Form D-a.

Yours very truly,

6. IRREVOCABLE NEGOTIATION LETTER OF CREDIT ADDRESSED TO SELLER

Credit No. B........................

..............................., ...19........

....

....

Dear Sirs:

We hereby open our irrevocable credit in your favor for account of ....

for a sum or sums not exceeding a total of........................(figures)

....(words) available by your drafts on

....

at ....——.................

to be accompanied by..

....

evidencing shipment of:

....

From ....To ....

....insurance to be effected by

All drafts so drawn must be marked:

"Drawn under..Bank

Credit No. B.................................., dated...........................19........"

(To be used when not all the documents are to accompany draft.)

There must be forwarded by early mail to..................................

............................Bank at.., the follow-

lowing documents...

All remaining documents must accompany the draft.

The amount of any draft drawn under this credit must be endorsed on the reverse hereof, and the presentation of each draft, if negotiated, shall be a warranty by the negotiating bank that such endorsement has been made and that documents have been forwarded as herein required; if the draft is not negotiated this credit and all relative documents must accompany the draft.

This credit must accompany any draft which exhausts the credit and must be surrendered concurrently with the payment of such draft.

Each of the provisions on the back hereof, except so far as otherwise expressly stated, is incorporated as part of this credit.

We hereby engage with the drawers, endorsers and bona fide holders of drafts drawn under and in compliance with the terms of this credit that the same shall be duly honored on due pres-

entation and delivery of documents as specified at..........................

...., if negotiated or presented on or before

.................................., 19......

Yours very truly,

7. IRREVOCABLE NEGOTIATION LETTER OF CREDIT ADDRESSED TO CORRESPONDENT BANK

Credit No. C-b........................

................................, ...19........

....
(correspondent bank)

....
(address)

Dear Sirs:

We request you to advise..
(name)

....
(address) (city) (state)

that we have opened our irrevocable credit in their favor for account of ....

for a sum or sums not exceeding a total of........................(figures)

....(words) available by their drafts on

....
(if on accredited buyer, without recourse)

at ....

to be accompanied by...

evidencing shipment of: ....

From ....To ....

....insurance to be effected by

....

(To be used when not all the documents are to accompany draft.)

There must be forwarded by early mail by the negotiating bank

to ...., at..,

the following documents...

All remaining documents must accompany the draft.

We hereby engage with the drawers, endorsers and bona fide holders of drafts drawn under and in compliance with the terms of this advice that the same shall be duly honored on due pres-

entation and delivery of documents as specified at..........................

...., if negotiated or presented on or before

...., 19.........

If the terms of the advice authorize the beneficiary to draw on you, for your reimbursement, you may:

(Put cross in square opposite method desired.)

☐ Debit our account with you.

☐ Draw on us at..

This credit is to be advised to the beneficiary by you on Commercial Credit Conference Form C-b.

Yours very truly,

8. IRREVOCABLE NEGOTIATION LETTER OF CREDIT ADDRESSED TO CORRESPONDENT BANK WITH AUTHORITY TO CORRESPONDENT BANK TO CONFIRM THE CREDIT

Credit No. D-b......................

..............................., ...19........
(city)

....
(correspondent bank)

....

Dear Sirs:

We request you to advise...

....
(address) (city) (state)

that we have opened our irrevocable credit in their favor for

account of: ....

for a sum or sums not exceeding a total of........................(figures)

....(words) available by their drafts on

....
(if on accredited buyer, without recourse)

at ....

to be accompanied by...

evidencing shipment of: ....

From ....To ....

....insurance to be effected by

....

(To be used when not all the documents are to accompany draft.)

There must be forwarded by early mail by the negotiating bank

to .... at ....

the following documents, ...

All remaining documents must accompany the draft.

We hereby engage with the drawers, endorsers and bona fide holders of drafts drawn under and in compliance with the terms of this credit that the same shall be duly honored on due pres-

entation and delivery of documents as specified at..........................

...., if negotiated or presented on or before

...., 19......... We authorize you to confirm the credit and thereby to undertake that drafts drawn and presented as above specified shall be duly honored.

If the terms of the credit authorize the beneficiary to draw on you, for your reimbursement, you may:

(Put cross in square opposite method desired.)

Debit our account with you.

Draw on us at...

This credit is to be advised to the beneficiary by you on Commercial Credit Conference Form D-b.

Yours very truly,

9. AUTHORITY TO PAY

Authority No. A........................

................................, ...19........

....
(correspondent bank)

....
(address)

Dear Sirs:

We request you to advise..
(name)

....
(address) (city) (state)

that we have authorized you to honor their drafts for account of:

....

for a sum or sums not exceeding a total of........................(figures)
....(words) on you at

....

to be accompanied by...
evidencing shipment of:

....

From ....To ....
....insurance to be effected by

....

This authority is valid for drafts so drawn, with documents as specified, presented at your office not later than................................ ....19........, unless it is previously revoked or modified by receipt by you of notice from us to that effect.

For your reimbursement you may:

(Put cross in square opposite method desired.)

Debit our account with you.

Draw on us at..

This authority is to be advised to the beneficiary by you on Commercial Credit Conference Form A.

Yours very truly,

10. REVOCABLE AUTHORITY TO PURCHASE

INTERNATIONAL BANKING CORPORATION
60 Wall Street, New York

October 3, 1921

American Export Company
New York City

Dear Sirs:

We beg to inform you that we have been authorized by the Manager of our Branch at........Shanghai........ to negotiate your bills on..........The Chinese Import Company to the extent of.......... $1,000 (One Thousand Dollars)........for 100% invoice cost of ....cotton sheetings........shipped to........Shanghai..........................

The bills are to be drawn at........ninety days' sight and must be accompanied by FULL SET OF BILLS OF LADING; INVOICES and MARINE INSURANCE POLICIES, ALL IN DUPLICATE.

Shipping documents must be made out to "ORDER" and blank endorsed.

The above documents must be duly hypothecated to the Bank against payment of the bills.

Please note that this advice is NOT to be considered as being a "BANK CREDIT" and does not relieve you from the ordinary liability attaching to the "DRAWER" of a Bill of Exchange.

All drafts under this Authority to Purchase to be marked "DRAWN UNDER........Shanghai........A. P. No.........0000........"

Kindly hand in this letter with your drafts in order that the amount of same may be endorsed on the back hereof.

This Authority expires on........January 1, 1922,........but is subject to cancellation by our giving you notice to such effect.

Yours faithfully,

....

[Taken from WARD, AMERICAN COMMERCIAL CREDITS (1922) 61.]

11. IRREVOCABLE AUTHORITY TO PURCHASE

CONFIRMED AND IRREVOCABLE CREDIT, DRAFTS DRAWN UNDER THIS CREDIT ARE WITHOUT RECOURSE.

THE DAI-ICHI GINKO, LIMITED

Commercial Letter of Credit

Tokyo, August 9, 1920

L. P. No. 31
Quaker & Co.,
Philadelphia.

Dear Sir:

We hereby authorize you to draw draft or drafts as follows:

Upon Messrs. Masago-Do. Koishikawa, Tokyo.
At usance of Ninety days after sight.
To the extent of Three hundred forty Dollars ($340.00).
For full Invoice cost of
Shipment of Glassware from New York to Tokyo
Not later than October 5th, 1920.

Each draft must be accompanied by an Invoice in duplicate and the full set of Bills of Lading made out to order and blank endorsed. Insurance Policy to accompany the draft.

All drafts against this Credit must bear the clause "Drawn under Letter of Credit L. P. No. 31 dated Tokyo, August 9th, 1920" and the amounts of such draft or drafts negotiated must be written off on the back hereof and this letter is to be returned to us when exhausted or expired.

We hereby guarantee that all drafts drawn in compliance with the terms and conditions of this Credit shall be duly accepted and paid at maturity by the drawee.

We are, Yours faithfully,

For The Dai-Ichi Ginko, Limited,

Sub-Manager.

Drafts against this Credit will be negotiated by The National City Bank of New York, in New York City, without discount.

[Taken from Mead, *Documentary Letters of Credit* (1922) 22 COL. L. REV. 297, 321.]

II. Correspondent Bank Forms

12. ADVICE OF CREDIT OPENED: STRAIGHT LETTER OF CREDIT

Advice No. C-a......................

.............................., ...19.......
(city)

....

....

Dear Sirs:

We are instructed by...Bank to advise you that they have opened their irrevocable credit in your favor for account of..
for a sum or sums not exceeding a total of......................(figures)
..................................(words) available by your drafts on us at
....to be accompanied by
....
evidencing shipment of..
From .... To...
....insurance to be effected by
....

All drafts so drawn must be marked:
"Drawn as per..Bank's
Advice No. C-a..............., dated..................19........"

Each of the provisions on the back hereof, except so far as otherwise expressly stated, is incorporated as part of this advice.

....Bank engages with you that all drafts drawn under and in compliance with the terms of this advice will be duly honored on delivery of documents as specified if presented at this office on or before..................................19.........

This letter is solely an advice of credit opened by........................ Bank and conveys no engagement by us.

Yours very truly,

13. ADVICE OF CREDIT OPENED: NEGOTIATION LETTER OF CREDIT

Advice No. C-b......................

..............................., ...19.......
(city)

....

....

Dear Sirs:

We are instructed by...Bank to advise you that they have opened their irrevocable credit in your favor for account of.. for a sum or sums not exceeding a total of......................(figures) ....(words) available by your drafts on .... at..to be accompanied by .... evidencing shipment of: .... From .... To... ....insurance to be effected by ....

All drafts so drawn must be marked:

"Drawn as per...Bank's
Advice No. C-b..........., dated.......................19........"

(To be used when not all the documents are to accompany draft)

There must be forwarded by early mail by the negotiating bank

to...Bank, at...,

the following documents...

All remaining documents must accompany the draft.

The amount of any draft drawn under this advice must be endorsed on the reverse hereof, and the presentation of each draft, if negotiated, shall be a warranty by the negotiating bank that such endorsement has been made and that documents have been forwarded as herein required. If the draft is not negotiated this advice and all relative documents must accompany the draft.

This advice must accompany any draft which exhausts the credit and must be surrendered concurrently with the payment of such draft.

Each of the provisions on the back hereof, except so far as otherwise expressly stated, is incorporated as part of this advice.

....Bank engages with the drawers, endorsers and bona fide holders of drafts drawn under and in compliance with the terms of this advice that the same shall be duly honored on due presentation and delivery of documents as specified at.., if negotiated or presented on or before.., 19.........

This letter is solely an advice of credit opened by......................... Bank and conveys no engagement by us.

Yours very truly,

14. CONFIRMED IRREVOCABLE STRAIGHT LETTER OF CREDIT

Credit No. D-a......................

..................................., ...19.......
(city)

....

....

Dear Sirs:

We are instructed by..Bank to advise you that they have opened their irrevocable credit in your favor for account of.. for a sum or sums not exceeding a total of.......................(figures) ....(words) available by your drafts on us at ....to be accompanied by .... evidencing shipment of.. From .... To.................................... ....insurance to be effected by ....

All drafts drawn under the credit must be marked:

"Drawn under ....Bank's

Credit No. D-a..........., dated.......................19........."

Each of the provisions on the back hereof, except so far as otherwise expressly stated, is incorporated as part of this credit.

....Bank engages with you that all drafts drawn under and in compliance with the terms of this credit will be duly honored on delivery of documents as specified, if presented at this office on or before...19.......; we confirm the credit and thereby undertake that all drafts drawn and presented as above specified will be duly honored by us.

Yours very truly,

15. CONFIRMED IRREVOCABLE NEGOTIATION LETTER OF CREDIT

Credit No.D-b........................

.................................., ...19........
(city)

....

....

Dear Sirs:

We are instructed by..Bank to advise you that they have opened their irrevocable credit in your

favor for account of...

for a sum or sums not exceeding a total of.........................(figures)

....(words) available by your drafts on

....

at...to be accompanied by

....

evidencing shipment of: ....

From .... To..

....insurance to be effected by

....

All drafts drawn under the credit must be marked:

"Drawn under ....Bank's

Credit No. D-b............, dated........................19........."

(To be used when not all the documents are to accompany draft.)

There must be forwarded by early mail by the negotiating bank to..Bank, at..,
the following documents: ....
All remaining documents must accompany the draft.

The amount of any draft drawn under this credit must be endorsed on the reverse hereof, and the presentation of each draft, if negotiated, shall be a warranty by the negotiating bank that such endorsement has been made and that documents have been forwarded as herein required; if the draft is not negotiated this credit and all relative documents must accompany the draft.

The credit must accompany any draft which exhausts the credit and must be surrendered concurrently with the payment of such draft.

Each of the provisions on the back hereof, except so far as otherwise expressly stated, is incorporated as part of this credit.

....Bank engages with the drawers, endorsers and bona fide holders of drafts drawn under and in compliance with the terms of this credit that the same shall be duly honored on due presentation and delivery of documents as specified at.................................., if negotiated or presented on or before ...., 19......... We confirm the credit and thereby undertake that drafts drawn and presented as above specified shall be duly honored.

Yours very truly,

16. ADVICE OF AUTHORITY TO PURCHASE

HONGKONG & SHANGHAI BANKING CORPORATION
36 Wall Street

New York, July 1, 1921.

Messrs. Black & Co.,
120 Broadway,
New York.

Dear Sirs,

I beg to inform you that I am instructed by the Manager of our Branch at Shanghai to purchase, as offered, your Bills drawn at ninety days on Yamada, Yokohama, to the extent of ten thousand dollars ($10,000) for Invoice cost of mild steel plates shipped to that port.

The Bills must be accompanied by full sets of Bills of Lading, made out to "Order," blank endorsed and marked by the Shipping Company "freight paid," together with Invoices and Policies of Insurance, all duly hypothecated to the Bank against payment of the Bills.

Please note that this is not to be considered as being a Bank Credit and does not relieve you from the liability usually attaching to the Drawer of a Bill of Exchange; also that, although it is considered to be open for five months from July 1, it may be cancelled by us upon giving you notice.

Bills drawn under the above-mentioned instructions must be plainly marked, "Drawn under Hongkong & Shanghai Bkg. Co. letter dated July 1, No. 0" and must be accompanied by this letter in order that the amount of same may be endorsed on the back hereof.

Yours faithfully,

Agent.

[Taken from Mead, *Documentary Letters of Credit* (1922) 22 Col. L. Rev. 297, 331.]

17. ADVICE OF AUTHORITY TO PAY

Advice No. A........................

................................., ...19........
(city)

....

....

Dear Sirs:

We advise you that..Bank have authorized us to honor your drafts for account of................

....

for a sum or sums not exceeding a total of........................(figures)

....(words) on us at..

to be accompanied by..

evidencing shipment of: ....

From .... To ....

....insurance to be effected by

....

All drafts so drawn must be marked:

"Drawn as per..Bank's

Advice No. A..........., dated..............................19........"

Drafts so drawn, with documents as specified must be presented at our office not later than.. 19........

The authority given to us is subject to revocation or modification at any time without notice to you.

Each of the provisions on the back hereof, except so far as otherwise expressly stated, is incorporated as part of this advice.

This advice conveys no engagement on our part or on the part of...Bank and is simply for your guidance in preparing and presenting drafts and documents.

Yours very truly,

III. Buyer's Forms

18. APPLICATION FOR LETTER OF CREDIT

Date...

....
(opening bank)

....
(address)

Dear Sirs:

I/we hereby request you to open and transmit by cable / mail an authority to pay................ / irrevocable letter of credit upon the following terms and conditions:

in favor of..
(beneficiary)

for a sum or sums not exceeding a total of......................................
(amount in words)

available by drafts on..

(if on applicant, without recourse) at...
(tenor of drafts)

if accompanied by the following documents:

Full set of negotiable ocean bills of lading made out to the order of...Bank.
(opening bank)

Commercial invoice
Consular invoice
Marine insurance policy or certificate
War risk insurance policy or certificate

Cross out documents not required. Certificate of ....

Certificate of ....

....

....

evidencing shipment from..

to..of %.......

full invoice cost of ....

(description of property)

C.I.F
F.A.S. ....
F.O.B. (vessel) (name of vessel)

Mine risk / Marine. insurance to be effected by shipper / me/us under blanket policy.

No.............................issued by...

(name of insurance company)

This credit is (not) to be confirmed by a correspondent bank.

Drafts must be drawn and presented, or negotiated, not later than...

(expiration date)

I/we hereby agree to sign, and deliver to you, an agreement for such credit, in the form now used by you, the provisions of which are agreed to as defining your rights and my/our obligations.

Each of the provisions on the back hereof, except so far as otherwise expressly stated, is to be incorporated as part of the credit.

Yours very truly,

19. COMMERCIAL LETTER OF CREDIT AGREEMENT

Dear Sirs:

In consideration of your opening, at our request, your Commercial Letter of Credit No........................., (herein called "The Credit"), the terms of which appear in the copy thereof hereto attached marked Exhibit A and made a part hereof, and are hereby approved by us, we hereby agree as follows:

1. As to drafts or acceptances under or purporting to be under the Credit, which are payable in United States Currency, we agree: (a) in the case of each sight draft, to reimburse you at your ( ) office, on demand, in United States gold coin, the amount paid on such drafts, or, if so demanded by you, to pay to you at your office in advance in such coin the amount required to pay such draft; and (b) in the case of each acceptance, to pay to you, at your ( ) office, in United States gold coin, the amount thereof, on demand but in any event not later than one business day prior to maturity, or, in case the acceptance is not payable at your ( ) office, then on demand but in any event in time to reach the place of payment in the course of the mails not later than one business day prior to maturity.

2. As to drafts or acceptances under or purporting to be under the Credit, which are payable in currency other than United States currency, we agree: (a) in the case of each sight draft, to reimburse you, at your ( ) office, on demand, the equivalent of the amount paid, in United States gold coin at the rate of exchange then current in ( ) for cable transfers to the place of payment in the currency in which such draft is drawn; and (b) in the case of each acceptance, to furnish you, at your ( ) office, on demand, but in any event in time to reach the place of payment in the course of the mails not later than one business day prior to maturity with first class bankers' demand bills of exchange to be approved by you for the amount of acceptance, payable in the currency of the acceptance and bearing our endorsement, or, if you so request, to pay to you, at your ( ) office, on demand, the equivalent of the acceptance in United States gold coin at the rate of exchange current in ( ) for cable transfers at time of transmission to the place of payment in the currency in which the acceptance is payable.

3. We also agree to pay you, on demand, a commission at the rate of................per cent (........%), on such part of the Credit as may be used, and, in any event, a minimum commission of.............. per cent, of the amount of the Credit, and all charges and expenses paid or incurred by you in connection therewith, and interest where chargeable.

4. We hereby recognize and admit your ownership in and unqualified right to the possession and disposal of all property shipped under or pursuant to or in connection with the Credit or in any way relative thereto or to the drafts drawn thereunder, whether or not released to us on trust or bailee receipt, and also in and to all shipping documents, warehouse receipts, policies or certificates of insurance and other documents accompanying or relative to drafts drawn under the credit, and in and to the proceeds of each and all of the foregoing, until such time as all the obligations and liabilities of us or any of us to you at any time existing under or with reference to the Credit or this agreement, or any other credit or any other obligation or liability to you, have been fully paid and discharged, all as security for such obligations and liabilities; and that all or any of such property and documents, and the proceeds of any thereof, coming into the possession of you or any of your correspondents, may be held and disposed of by you as hereinafter provided; and the receipt by you, or any of your correspondents, at any time of other security, of whatsoever nature, including cash, shall not be deemed a waiver of any of your rights or powers herein recognized.

5. Except insofar as instructions have been heretofore given by us in writing expressly to the contrary, we agree that you and any of your correspondents may receive and accept as "Bills of lading" under the Credit, any documents issued or purporting to be issued by or on behalf of any carrier which acknowledge receipt of property for transportation, whatever the specific provisions of such documents, and that the date of each such document shall be deemed the date of shipment of the property mentioned therein; and that you may receive and accept as documents of insurance either insurance policies or insurance certificates.

6. Except insofar as instructions have been heretofore given by us in writing expressly to the contrary, we agree that part shipments may be made under the Credit and you may honor the relative drafts; and that if the Credit specifies shipments in instalments within stated periods, and the shipper fails to ship in any designated period, shipments of subsequent instalments may nevertheless be made in their respective designated periods and you may honor the relative drafts.

7. We agree that in the event of any extension of the maturity or time for presentation of drafts, acceptances or documents, or any other modification of the terms of the Credit, at the request of any of us, with or without notification to the others, or in the event of any increase in the amount of the Credit at our request, this agreement shall be binding upon us with regard to the Credit so increased or otherwise modified, to drafts, documents and prop-

erty covered thereby, and to any action taken by you or any of your correspondents in accordance with such extension, increase or other modification.

8. The users of the Credit shall be deemed our agents and we assume all risks of their acts or omissions. Neither you nor your correspondents shall be responsible: for the existence, character, quality, quantity, condition, packing, value, or delivery of the property purporting to be represented by documents; for any difference in character, quality, quantity, condition, or value of the property from that expressed in documents; for the validity, sufficiency, or genuineness of documents, even if such documents should in fact prove to be in any or all respects invalid, insufficient, fraudulent or forged; for the time, place, manner or order in which shipment is made; for partial or incomplete shipment, or failure or omission to ship any or all of the property referred to in the Credit; for the character, adequacy, validity, or genuineness of any insurance; for the solvency or responsibility of any insurer, or for any other risk connected with insurance; for any deviation from instructions, delay, default or fraud by the shipper or anyone else in connection with the property or the shipping thereof; for the solvency, responsibility or relationship to the property of any party issuing any documents in connection with the property; for delay in arrival or failure to arrive of either the property or any of the documents relating thereto; for delay in giving or failure to give notice of arrival or any other notice; for any breach of contract between the shippers or venders and ourselves or any of us; for failure of any draft to bear any reference or adequate reference to the Credit, or failure of documents to accompany any draft at negotiation, or failure of any person to note the amount of any draft on the reverse of the Credit or to surrender or take up the Credit or to send forward documents apart from drafts as required by the terms of the Credit; each of which provisions, if contained in the Credit itself, it is agreed may be waived by you, or for errors, omissions, interruptions or delays in transmission or delivery of any messages, by mail, cable, telegraph, wireless or otherwise, whether or not they be in cipher; nor shall you be responsible for any error, neglect, or default of any of your correspondents; and none of the above shall affect, impair, or prevent the vesting of any of your rights or powers hereunder. In furtherance and extension and not in limitation of the specific provisions hereinbefore set forth, we agree that any action taken by you or by any correspondent of yours under or in connection with the Credit or the relative drafts, documents or property, if taken in good faith, shall be binding on us and shall not put you or your correspondent under any resulting liability to us; and we make like agreement as to any inaction or omission, unless in breach of good faith.

9. We agree to procure promptly any necessary import and export or other licenses for the import or export or shipping of the property and to comply with all foreign and domestic governmental regulations in regard to the shipment of the property or the financing thereof, and to furnish such certificates in that respect as you may at any time require, and to keep the property adequately covered by insurance satisfactory to you, in companies satisfactory to you, and to assign the policies or certificates of insurance to you, or to make the loss or adjustment, if any, payable to you, at your option; and to furnish you if demanded with evidence of acceptance by the insurers of such assignment.

10. Each of us agrees at any time and from time to time, on demand, to deliver, convey, transfer, or assign to you, as security for any and all of his and/or our obligations and liabilities hereunder, and also for any and all other obligations and liabilities, absolute or contingent, due or to become due, which are now or may at any time hereafter be owing by him or us to you, additional security of a value and character satisfactory to you, or to make such payment as you may require. Each of us agrees that all property belonging to him, or us, or in which he or we may have an interest, of every name and nature whatsoever, now or at any time hereafter delivered, conveyed, transferred, assigned, or paid to you, or coming into your possession or into the possession of anyone for you in any manner whatsoever, whether expressly as security for any of the obligations or liabilities of him or us to you, or for safe-keeping or otherwise, including any items received for collection or transmission and the proceeds thereof whether or not such property is in whole or in part released to us on trust or bailee receipt are hereby made security for each and all such obligations and liabilities. Each of us agrees that upon his or our failure at all times to keep a margin of security with you satisfactory to you, or upon the making by him or us of any assignments for the benefit of creditors, or upon the filing of any voluntary or involuntary petition in bankruptcy by or against him or us, or upon the application for the appointment of a receiver of any of his or our property, or upon any act of bankruptcy or state of insolvency of him or us, all of such obligations and liabilities shall become and be immediately due and payable without demand or notice, notwithstanding any credit or time allowed to him or us, or any instrument evidencing any such obligations or liabilities or otherwise; and each of us, as to property in which he may have any interest, and all of us, as to property in which we may have any interest expressly authorize you in any such event, or upon his or our failure to pay any of such obligations or liabilities when it or they shall become or be made due, to sell immediately, without demand for payment, without advertisement and without notice to us or any of us, all of which

are hereby expressly waived, any and all such property, arrived or to arrive, at private sale or at public auction or at brokers' board or otherwise, at your option, in such parcel or parcels and at such time or times and at such place or places and for such price or prices and upon such terms and conditions as you may deem proper, and to apply the net proceeds of such sale or sales, together with any balance of deposits and any sums credit by or due from you to him or us in general account or otherwise, to the payment of any and all of his and/or our obligations or liabilities to you however arising. If any such sale be at brokers' board or at public auction you may yourself be a purchaser at such sale, free from any right of redemption, which we and each of us hereby expressly waive and release.

11. You shall not be deemed to have waived any of your rights hereunder, unless you or your authorized agent shall have signed such waiver in writing. No such waiver, unless expressly as stated therein, shall be effective as to any transaction which occurs subsequent to the date of such waiver, nor as to any continuance of a breach after such waiver.

12. The word "property" as used in this agreement includes goods, merchandise, securities, funds, choses in action, and any and all other forms of property, whether real, personal or mixed and any right or interest therein.

13. If this agreement is signed by one individual, the terms "we," "our," "us," shall be read throughout as "I," "my," "me," as the case may be. If this agreement is signed by two or more parties, it shall be the joint and several agreement of such parties.

Very truly yours,

IV. Provisions for Interpretation of Credits

20. PROVISIONS ADOPTED BY THE NEW YORK BANKERS' COMMERCIAL CREDIT CONFERENCE[1]

Export Commercial Credits are treated in conformity with the following regulations.

1. No liability or responsibility is assumed for the form, sufficiency, correctness, genuineness or legal effect of any documents or papers, or for the description, quantity, quality, condition, packing, delivery or value of the merchandise represented thereby, or for the good faith or acts of the shipper or any other person whomsoever, or for the solvency, standing, etc., of the carriers or insurers of the merchandise; but documents and papers will be examined with care sufficient to ascertain that on their face they appear to be regular in general form.

2. No responsibility is assumed for consequences arising out of delay or loss in transit of letters and/or documents, or for delay, mutilation or other errors in the transmission of telegrams or cables.

3. The terms "DOCUMENTS," "SHIPPING DOCUMENTS" and words of similar import, will be interpreted as comprehending only full set of ocean bills of lading (sailer bill of lading included) and marine insurance (but not war risk) in negotiable form, with invoices.

4. Instructions shall be interpreted according to our law and customs, but, in any event, in accordance with the following general rules:

A. Forwarders' bills of lading will not be accepted, unless specifically authorized. Railroad through bills of lading will not be accepted, except on exportations to the Far East via Pacific ports, unless expressly stipulated.

B. Bills of lading indicating trans-shipment will be accepted unless direct shipment is specified.

C. Bills of lading shall contain no notations qualifying the acceptance of merchandise in apparent good order and condition.

D. When ocean bills of lading are required, unless otherwise stipulated, we will accept "RECEIVED FOR SHIPMENT" or "ALONGSIDE" or "PORT" or "CUSTODY" bills of lading. The

[1]Adopted in 1920; amended to June 1, 1926.

date of the bill of lading in each case will be taken to be the date of shipment and the insurance, if called for, shall cover from such date of shipment and on whatever vessels carried.

E. When "ON BOARD" shipment is required and such shipment is represented by an "ON BOARD" bill of lading, the bill of lading date will be taken as the date when such shipment was effected; if evidenced by "ON BOARD" endorsement, the endorsement date will be so taken.

F. Documents for partial shipments may be accepted unless expressly prohibited.

G. If shipment in instalments within stated periods is specified, each instalment will be treated as a separate transaction, and if there is a failure to ship in any designated period, shipments of subsequent instalments, made in their respective designated periods, may be drawn against.

H. The use of "TO," "UNTIL," "ON," and words of similar import, in indicating expiration, is interpreted to include the date mentioned.

I. Any extension of the date of shipment shall extend for an equal length of time the date for presentation or negotiation of draft and documents.

J. When the indicated expiration date for presentation or negotiation falls upon a Sunday or legal holiday, the expiration is extended to the next succeeding business day. (This rule, however, does not apply to date of shipment.)

K. The stipulated documents must all be presented not later than 3 P. M. (or twelve o'clock noon, if Saturday) on the indicated expiration date.

We reserve the right to refuse to take up documents if they are not presented within reasonable time after date of shipment.

L. The terms "PROMPT SHIPMENT," "IMMEDIATE SHIPMENT," "SHIPMENT AS SOON AS POSSIBLE," and words of similar import, shall be interpreted as requiring shipment to be effected and (if the credit advice is without expressed duration) the stipulated documents presented for payment within thirty days from the date of our credit advice.

M. Our credit advice if without expressed duration shall not continue in force longer than one year from its date.

N. The terms "APPROXIMATELY," "ABOUT," or words of similar import, shall be construed to permit a variation of not to exceed ten per centum.

When the merchandise, by its nature, does not allow the delivery of the exact quantity indicated, as, for instance, metal bars, oil in barrels, etc., a leeway of 3% more or less will be allowed, even if the terms of the credit call for a fixed weight or measurement.

O. The term "INSURANCE" shall be construed as either policy of insurance or underwriters' certificate of insurance. Brokers' Cover Notes will not be accepted unless specifically stipulated.

P. Definitions of Export Quotations will be those adopted by the National Foreign Trade Council, Chamber of Commerce of the U. S. A., National Association of Manufacturers, American Manufacturers' Export Association, Philadelphia Commercial Museum, American Exporters' and Importers' Association, Chamber of Commerce of the State of New York, N. Y. Produce Exchange, and New York Merchants' Association, at a conference held in India House, N. Y., on December 16, 1919.

5. Correspondents will understand that the above regulations shall govern in all credit transactions in the absence of other specific agreements. If the beneficiary shall make representations, or shall offer security satisfactory to the bank that no loss shall result to its correspondent or client by the waiver of any of such regulations, or any instruction, the bank reserves the right to make such waiver, and shall recognize no claim in the premises unless substantial direct damage shall be shown to have resulted.

Appendix B

EARLY FORMS OF COMMERCIAL LETTERS OF CREDIT

Laus Deo, in London this 29 of February 1654.

Mr. William M.

Sir, My last unto you was of the 12th of January, wherein I wrote you what needful in answer to yours of the seventh of the same month; this serves chiefly to desire you to furnish and pay unto Mr. John G. English Gentleman, to the value of two thousand Crowns at one or more times, according as he shall have occasion, and desire the same of you, taking his Receipt, or Bills of Exchange for the monies which you shall so furnish him with, and put it to my account, and this my letter of credit shall be your sufficient warrant for so doing, Vale.

Yours

Thomas P.

To Mr. William N. Merchant at Paris.

[Taken from Marius, Advice concerning Bills of Exchange (4th ed. 1684) 37.]

Boston, Nov. 4, 1835.

I hereby authorize Mr. William P. Endicott of barque Palinure to value on Messrs. T. Wiggin & Co., London, at six months' sight at any place in India, for account of Ebenezer Breed, Esq., of Charlestown, for any sums, not exceeding in all fifteen thousand pounds sterling. And I hereby engage, as the authorized agent of Messrs. T. Wiggin & Co., that the bills of Mr. Endicott shall be duly honored when presented, if drawn within twelve months from the date of this letter. In case of any accident, by which Mr. Endicott may be prevented from using this credit, I hereby authorize Captain Robert Henderson, Jr., of said barque, to use the same for account of Mr. Breed, for £15,000 sterling.

ROBERT HOOPER, JR.,
Agent, to T. Wiggin & Co.

[Taken from Russell v. Wiggin, 21 Fed. Cas. No. 12,165, at p. 68 (C. C. D. Mass. 1842).]

San Francisco, Sept. 20, 1877.

The Merchants' Banking Company of London (Limited),
112 Cannon Street,
London,

Dear Sirs:

At the request of Messrs. John Mel & Sons of this city, we hereby authorize Messrs. A. Lafargue & Co., of Bordeaux, to draw on you at sixty days' sight for our account to the amount of three thousand pounds sterling (£3,000).

All drafts must be drawn at Bordeaux, and be accompanied by due advice. This credit to be in force for twelve months, from 31st October, 1877, to 31st October, 1878.

We are, dear sir, yours faithfully,

Falkner, Bell & Co.

[Taken from Lafargue v. Harrison, 70 Cal. 380, 382, 9 Pac. 259, 260 (1885).]

Office of John Munroe & Co., Bankers,
No. 32 Nassau Street,

New York, February 26, 1892.

Messrs. Munroe & Co.,
Paris:

Gentlemen:

We hereby open a credit with you in favor of Captain J. A. Johannessen, s/s Raylton Dixon, for fcs. 15,000, available in bills at 90 days date; on acceptance of any bill or bills drawn under this credit you are to draw on Carsten Boe, New York, at seventy-five days date; payable at the current rate of exchange for first-class banker's bills on Paris on day of maturity. Commission is arranged.

Bills under this credit to be drawn at any time prior to May 1, 1892.

Truly yours,

John Munroe & Co.

The bill may be availed of in sterling, if desired; say £600 sterling.

J. M. & Co.

[Taken from Johannessen v. Munroe, 158 N. Y. 641, 644, 53 N. E. 535 (1899).]

TABLE OF CASES

TABLE OF STATUTES

Power of Banks to Issue Commercial Letters of Credit and Accept Time Drafts

Statutes Concerning Virtual and Extrinsic Acceptances

Statutes concerning Letters of Credit Generally

Uniform Negotiable Instruments Law

Uniform Sales Act

INDEX

COLUMBIA LEGAL STUDIES

Edited under the auspices of

THE FACULTY OF LAW OF COLUMBIA UNIVERSITY

EDWIN W. PATTERSON, *Editor*

I. THE HISTORICAL FOUNDATIONS OF THE LAW RELATING TO TRADE-MARKS. By Frank I. Schechter, A.M., J.D., member of the New York Bar, with a foreword by Munroe Smith, J.U.D., LL.D., J.D., Bryce Professor Emeritus of European Legal History in Columbia University. 8vo, cloth, pp. xxviii+211. $6.00.

II. LEGAL ASPECTS OF COMMERCIAL LETTERS OF CREDIT. By Herman N. Finkelstein, LL.B., J.D., member of the New York Bar, with an introduction by Karl N. Llewellyn, LL.B., J.D., Professor of Law in Columbia University. 8vo, cloth, pp. xxviii+390. $7.50.

COLUMBIA UNIVERSITY PRESS
COLUMBIA UNIVERSITY
NEW YORK

FOREIGN AGENT
OXFORD UNIVERSITY PRESS
HUMPHREY MILFORD
AMEN HOUSE, LONDON, E. C.

Bei Fragen zur Produktsicherheit wenden Sie sich bitte an:
If you have any questions regarding product safety,
please contact:

Walter de Gruyter GmbH
Genthiner Straße 13
10785 Berlin
productsafety@degruyterbrill.com